Media Systems and Communication Policies in
Latin America

Palgrave Global Media Policy and Business

Series Editors: **Professor Petros Iosifidis, Professor Jeanette Steemers** and **Professor Gerald Sussman**

Editorial Board: **Sandra Braman, Peter Dahlgren, Terry Flew, Charles Fombad, Manuel Alejandro Guerrero, Alison Harcourt, Robin Mansell, Richard Maxwell, Toby Miller, Zizi Papacharissi, Stylianos Papathanassopoulos, Caroline Pauwels, Robert Picard, Kiran Prasad, Marc Raboy, Chang Yong Son, Miklos Suksod, Kenton T. Wilkinson, Sugmin Youn**

This innovative series examines the wider social, political, economic and technological changes arising from the globalization of the media and communications industries and assesses their impact on matters of business practice, regulation and policy. Considering media convergence, industry concentration, and new communications practices, the series makes reference to the paradigmatic shift from a system based on national decision-making and the traditions of public service in broadcast and telecommunications delivery to one that is demarcated by commercialization, privatization and monopolization. Bearing in mind this shift, and based on a multi-disciplinary approach, the series tackles three key questions: To what extent do new media developments require changes in regulatory philosophy and objectives? To what extent do new technologies and changing media consumption require changes in business practices and models? And to what extent does privatization alter the creative freedom and public accountability of media enterprises?

Abu Bhuiyan
INTERNET GOVERNANCE AND THE GLOBAL SOUTH
Demand for a New Framework

Benedetta Brevini
PUBLIC SERVICE BROADCASTING ONLINE
A Comparative European Policy Study of PSB 2.0

Karen Donders, Caroline Pauwels and Jan Loisen (*editors*)
PRIVATE TELEVISION IN WESTERN EUROPE
Content, Markets, Policies

Tom Evens, Petros Iosifidis and Paul Smith
THE POLITICAL ECONOMY OF TELEVISION SPORTS RIGHTS

Manuel Alejandro Guerrero and Mireya Márquez-Ramírez (*editors*)
MEDIA SYSTEMS AND COMMUNICATION POLICIES IN LATIN AMERICA

Petros Iosifidis
GLOBAL MEDIA AND COMMUNICATION POLICY
An International Perspective

Michael Starks
THE DIGITAL TELEVISION REVOLUTION
Origins to Outcomes

Palgrave Global Media Policy and Business
Series Standing Order ISBN   978-1-137-27329-1   (Hardback)
                                            978-1-137-36718-1   (Paperback)
(*outside North America only*)

You can receive future titles in this series as they are published by placing a standing order. Please contact your bookseller or, in case of difficulty, write to us at the address below with your name and address, the title of the series and one of the ISBNs quoted above.

Customer Services Department, Macmillan Distribution Ltd, Houndmills, Basingstoke, Hampshire RG21 6XS, England

---

Media Systems and Communication Policies in Latin America

Edited by

Manuel Alejandro Guerrero
Universidad Iberoamericana, Mexico City

and

Mireya Márquez-Ramírez
Universidad Iberoamericana, Mexico City

First published 2014 by
PALGRAVE MACMILLAN

Palgrave Macmillan in the UK is an imprint of Macmillan Publishers Limited, registered in England, company number 785998, of Houndmills, Basingstoke, Hampshire RG21 6XS.

Palgrave Macmillan in the US is a division of St Martin's Press LLC, 175 Fifth Avenue, New York, NY 10010.

Palgrave Macmillan is the global academic imprint of the above companies and has companies and representatives throughout the world.

Palgrave® and Macmillan® are registered trademarks in the United States, the United Kingdom, Europe and other countries.

ISBN: 978–1–137–40904–1

This book is printed on paper suitable for recycling and made from fully managed and sustained forest sources. Logging, pulping and manufacturing processes are expected to conform to the environmental regulations of the country of origin.

A catalogue record for this book is available from the British Library.

Library of Congress Cataloging-in-Publication Data

    Media systems and communication policies in Latin America / edited by Manuel Alejandro Guerrero and Mireya Márquez-Ramírez, Universidad Iberoamericana, Mexico City.
       pages cm
    Includes bibliographical references.
    ISBN 978–1–137–40904–1
    1. Mass media – Latin America. 2. Communication policy – Latin America. 3. Journalism – Latin America. I. Guerrero, Manuel Alejandro, 1970– editor. II. Márquez Ramírez, Mireya, 1979– editor.
    P92.L3M435 2014
    302.23'098—dc23   2014022065

Transferred to Digital Printing in 2014

Contents

List of Illustrations

Figures

Tables

Preface and Acknowledgments

This book has come a long way since we originally set ourselves the modest goal of updating the existing literature on Latin American media in the English language. In many ways, that aim was justified as there had not been enough discussion on how Latin American media systems contribute to a better understanding of the relationship between media, power, and democracy on a global scope. As the book shows, the intentional lack of regulation enforcement, the pragmatic exercise of power, the configuration of alliances and the complicity between media barons and political elites all help to explain why private media developed early and why media concentration is so high in the area. Moreover, the fact that media conglomerates in Latin America emerged under the auspices of dictatorships and authoritarian rule clashes with the existing assumptions that private ownership of the media entails distance and autonomy from the state, or that authoritarian states need to employ harsh regulation and secure administration or control of the media to better exert and legitimize power. Hence understanding how media power is intrinsically linked to local forces all of which join together in mutual benefit and gain – and not always and foremost to the global markets – also helps us revitalize our understanding of the key and conflictive relation between media and democracy.

For the past four decades at least, there has been a vast production of media research in the region; a salient leadership from critical and cultural researchers; and a productive, collaborative network of Latin American, Spanish, and Portuguese scholars. However, their lack of sufficient visibility in the English literature may be one of the reasons why there is not enough comparative research between regions that share historical, social, and political contexts such as colonialism and political authoritarianism.

We are aware that, in part, this may be due to insufficient scholarly exchange and global visibility of a doubtless mature line of media research in the region. In comparison to other areas, the number of journal articles in the English language on the realities of media and journalism in Latin American is relatively low and the number of native scholars who publish in English is even less. This absence perhaps reflects the self-perceived sufficiency of knowledge circulation within the vast Spanish-speaking (and Portuguese-speaking) worlds. While there are plenty of reasons for that to happen – after all the Latin American research community is always questioning its linguistic and colonial ethos and the epistemic roots of global knowledge – we are using this book as an opportunity to help strengthen the linguistic bridges and offer common terrain to further explore issues of media policy, pluralism, and concentration across the globe.

Due to the timely context and the changing political landscape, we believe this book needed to be written because of the salient wave of media reforms that have recently sprouted throughout South America. After a wave of progressive leaders came to office – Lula de Silva in Brazil, Néstor Kirchner and Cristina Fernández in Argentina, Evo Morales in Bolivia, Rafael Correa in Ecuador and of course, Hugo Chávez in Venezuela – in most of these countries the private media and their interests have overtly become key and often antagonistic players vis-à-vis the state. Thus, this role once again brings to the discussion table the concepts of the freedom of press, pluralism and political neutrality.

Therefore, this book aims to explore the conflicting roles that global, regional, and local forces are playing in the shaping of media systems, policies and industries in Latin America. In some cases, the way in which specific media markets have reacted to transnational forces is through locally led policy and regulation – often directed towards the protection of already dominant players and not necessarily in favor of expanding pluralism in those markets. While in others, the opposite holds true: the markets react through deregulation or by leaving the sole interaction of economic players and actors unregulated. However, in many cases, where actual regulation and law enforcement do exist, the regulation proves to be ineffective and difficult to enforce or fails to contain concentration and safeguard media pluralism. Therefore, despite the considerable impact of liberalization and deregulation in the region, the relations between the state and the private media actors continue to lie in close-knit personal linkages and agreements often accorded outside (or in spite of) the formal regulatory frameworks. This book aims to offer fresh perspectives on old issues that have long preoccupied the academic community in Latin America.

For that purpose, we have assembled a cohort of established and emerging scholars born in Mexico, Argentina, Brazil, Chile, Colombia, Venezuela, Bolivia, Peru, El Salvador, and Guatemala. Together, we discuss the issues familiar and new to us all and engage, through our arguments and case studies, in a stimulating dialogue about the role that media plays (or fails to do so) in our societies. The book not only attempts to be plural in the number of countries included – or their leading authors – but that such a dialogue benefits from their different theoretical and epistemological backgrounds. Therefore, we are foremost grateful to all of the contributors who participated in this endeavour. Editing a book in which the main arguments and ideas are mostly devised, thought out, and reflected on in our native languages, namely Spanish and Portuguese, has shown us the renewed importance of international dialogue. For that reason, we commend all of the people involved in the translation processes at some stage or another.

We are thankful to the Palgrave Global Media Policy and Business series editors, Petros Iosifidis, Jeanette Steemers and Gerald Sussman, for their most generous invitation to submit this book. We also want to thank the anonymous reviewers who provided much needed advice on the directions to take and the arguments to follow in the very early stages of this book. All the errors, omissions, and shortcomings are, of course, entirely our responsibility. The timely assistance of the editorial team at Palgrave Macmillan especially Felicity Plester with her almost infinite patience and Chris Penfold with his most useful orientations, has been crucial to the successful accomplishment of this work. Back at home, we deeply appreciate the invaluable editorial assistance of Alberto Torres and the support provided by Mariana Anzorena.

Our words of gratitude also go to the Communications Department at Universidad Iberoamericana, Mexico City, for all of the time and facilities provided to conduct this research, as well as to our families and friends for their loving support and patience. Finally, we acknowledge each other in the fulfilment of this work. It could not have been possible without strong and committed teamwork, mutual help, support, feedback and encouragement.

Notes on Contributors

Editors

Manuel Alejandro Guerrero is a professor of communications at the Universidad Iberoamericana in Mexico City. He holds a PhD in Political and Social Sciences from the European University Institute in Florence, Italy, and an MPhil in Latin American Studies from the University of Cambridge in the United Kingdom. He is member of the Executive Board of ORBICOM (UNESCO's International Chair in Communication) and of the National Researchers System in Mexico. His research focuses on the role of the media in new democracies, especially on the framing of political issues, and on the media in relation to political attitudes and electoral behavior. He has published widely about these and other topics, such as audiences, prosumers and media literacy. Recent publications include *Campañas negativas en 2006: ¿Cómo afectaron el voto?* (Negative Campaigns in 2006: How Did They Affect Voting?, 2012); *Medios y Democracia, Perspectivas de México y Canadá* ('Media and Democracy: Perspectives from Mexico and Canada', 2011), and *Empowering Citizenship through Journalism, Information, and Entertainment in Ibero-America* (2009). Email: alejandro.guerrero@ibero.mx

Mireya Márquez-Ramírez is an assistant professor of journalism studies and media theory at the Universidad Iberoamericana in Mexico City. She holds a PhD in Media and Communications from Goldsmiths College, University of London and an MA in Journalism Studies from Cardiff University. She previously worked as a journalist in various print, digital and broadcast outlets and currently chairs the "Press and Democracy" (PRENDE) program of journalism fellowships and training at her university. She is currently in charge of various cross-national studies on comparative journalistic cultures, role performances and journalism education in Mexico. Her research interests include the critical study of journalism's normative values and comparative cultures; and the media's production, comparative systems, digital practices and professional identities in post-authoritarian societies. Email: mireya.marquez@ibero.mx

Contributors

Rodrigo Araya is an assistant professor of journalism and media at the Pontificia Universidad Católica of Valparaíso and a doctoral candidate in American studies at the University of Santiago de Chile. By background a journalist, Araya holds an MA in Communications from the University of Chile. He worked for eight years in local radio stations in South and Central Chile, where he launched and promoted local development projects aimed at strengthening cultural identities. He is currently working on a critique of the predominant concept of journalism in Latin America from the theoretical perspective of peripheral thought. Email: raraya@ucv.cl

Martín Becerra is an associate professor at the National University of Quilmes, Argentina, and at the University of Buenos Aires. He holds a PhD in Communications from the Autonomous University of Barcelona. He is a consultant for public agencies such as UNDP (Argentina's Ministry of Culture) and national and international NGOs. He has written several books on media concentration and communications policy in Latin America. He is the co-author of *Los Dueños de la Palabra y los Monopolios de la Verdad* (The Owners of Words and the Monopolies of Truth, 2009) and *Los Magnates de la Prensa: Estructura y concentración de las industrias culturales en América Latina* (Press Barons: Structure and Concentration of Cultural industries in Latin America, 2006). He regularly contributes with newspaper articles and columns to Argentinean media, such as *La Nación*, *Página 12*, *Caras* and *Caretas*. Email: mbecerra@unq.edu.ar

José Luis Benítez is chair of Communications and Culture Department, Central American University (UCA) in El Salvador. He has published articles in academic journals and edited books. In 2011, the UNDP and UCA published his book *La comunicación transnacional de las e-familias migrantes* ('Trasnational Communication of Migrant E-families'). In 2012, he was an *Internews fellow* at the Annenberg-Oxford Media Policy Summer Institute, University of Oxford. He holds a PhD in Communications from Ohio University, an MA in Communication and Development Studies, and a BA in Philosophy from the Central American University in El Salvador. Email: jbenitez@uca.edu.sv

César Ricardo Bolaño is a professor of media and communications at the Federal University of Sergipe (UFS), Brazil. He was the founder and first chair of the Political Economy of Communications section of the Brazilian Association for Interdisciplinary Communication

Studies (INTERCOM) and of the Latin American Association of Communication Researchers (ALAIC). He was also the first president of the Latin Union of Political Economy of Information, Communication and Culture. He is the current president of ALAIC and editor-in-chief of both the *EPTIC Online Journal* (*International Journal of Political Economy of Information Technologies and Communication*) published by the Observatory of Economy and Communications at the University of Sergipe and the *Journal of Latin American Communication Research* published by ALAIC. He chairs the IPEA/CAPES Institute for Applied Economics Research's professorship entitled 'The Concept of Culture in Celso Furtado's work' and is currently researching the political economy of the Internet and the Brazilian audio-visual sector. Email: bolano@ufs.br

Andrés Cañizález is a professor of communications at the Andrés Bello Catholic University (UCAB), Venezuela, where he researches the relationships between media and democracy, as well as the role of the freedom of the press. He holds a PhD in Political Sciences from Simón Bolívar University, Caracas. He is head of the Venezuelan Association of Communication Researchers and chairs the 'Political Communication and the Media' working group for the Latin American Association of Communication Researchers (ALAIC). He regularly publishes newspaper articles for the Venezuelan press, such as *El Nacional, Tal Cual, El Impulso, El Tiempo* and *La Verdad*, and is the host of a radio program on 94.1 FM. Email: acanizal@ucab.edu.ve

Silvio René Gramajo is a journalist and a senior consultant on media and regulation. He also lectures at the Department of Communication, Rafael Landívar University, Guatemala. He holds a PhD in Social Research and Political Science from the Latin American Faculty of Social Sciences (FLACSO), Mexico City. He holds an MA in Communications from Universidad Iberoamericana in Mexico City. Email: srgramajo@yahoo.com

Jorge Liotti is the director of the School of Journalism at the Catholic University of Argentina (UCA). He is a professor of media and politics and international journalism at both UCA and Universidad del Salvador (Buenos Aires). He holds an MA in International Studies from the University of Birmingham, United Kingdom. He is the co-author of the *UNESCO Model Curricula for Journalism Education* and the editor-in chief of politics at *La Nación* newspaper (Argentina). Email: j_liotti@yahoo.com.ar

Santiago Marino is the academic coordinator of the Postgraduate Programme in Cultural Industries, Policies and Management at Quilmes National University, Argentina (UNQ). He holds an MA in Culture and Communications from the University of Buenos Aires where he is currently a doctoral candidate. He is a lecturer in communications policy and planning at UNQ and lectures on communications at the University of Buenos Aires and at the Universidad del Salvador. He is an advisor for the Latin American branch of the World Association of Community Radios (AMARC). He has co-authored the following books: *Progresismo y Políticas de Comunicación Manos a la obra* (Progressive Rule and Communications Policy: Hands On, 2011); *Making Our Media: Mapping Global Initiatives Toward a Democratic Public Sphere* (2009); *Mordazas Invisibles* (2008); *Fronteras globales: Cultura, políticas y medios de comunicación* (Global Borders: Culture, Policy and Media, 2007); and *Medios, comunicación y Dictadura* (Media, Communications and Dictatorship 2006). Email: smarino@unq.edu.ar

Guillermo Mastrini is an associate professor at National University of Quilmes, Argentina, where he is the director of the MA program in cultural industries. He is also a professor at the University of Buenos Aires. Besides the books co-authored with Martín Becerra (see above), his latest authored and co-authored publications include *Sociedad de la Información en la Argentina: Políticas públicas y participación social* (Information society in Argentina: public policy and social participation, 2006'); *Participación y democracia en la Sociedad de la Información* ('Democracy and Participation in Information Society, with Damian Loreti and Mariana Baranchuk, 2007'), and *Mucho ruido, pocas leyes: Economía y política en la comunicación en la Argentina 1920–2004* ('Lots of Noise but Few Laws: Economy and Politics of Communication in Argentina, 1920–2004') among others. He was the president of the Argentinean Federation of Communication Schools and the chair of the graduate program in Communication Science at the University of Buenos Aires. Email: mastri@mail.fsoc.uba.ar; gmastri@yahoo.com.ar

Carolina Matos is a lecturer in media and communications in the Department of Sociology at City University, London. She was previously a part-time lecturer at the Government Department at Essex University and a former fellow in political communications at the London School of Economics and Political Science (LSE). Matos obtained her PhD in Media and Communications from Goldsmiths College, University of London, and has taught and researched in the UK in political communications, Brazilian media, and politics at the University of East London (UEL),

St. Mary's College, Goldsmiths, and LSE. With 20 years of professional experience both as a journalist and academic, Matos has published many articles in journals and has worked as a full-time journalist in Brazil for Reuters, Unesco, Folha de Sao Paulo, Tribuna da Imprensa and Globo. com. She is the author of *Journalism and Political Democracy in Brazil* (2008) and *Media and Politics in Latin America: Globalization, Democracy and Identity* (2012). Email: Carolina.Matos.1@city.ac.uk

Catalina Montoya is a Postdoctoral Teaching Fellow in the Department of Media and Communication and a member of *The Archbishop Desmond Tutu Centre for War and Peace Studies* at Liverpool Hope University, United Kingdom. She was the editor of *Signo y Pensamiento, Journal of Communication, Information and Languages* at the Pontificia Universidad Javeriana in Bogota, Colombia. She holds a PhD in Politics from the University of Manchester, an MA in Politics from the Universidad de los Andes in Bogota, Colombia and a BA in Communication Studies from Universidad Javeriana, Bogota. Email:catalina.montoya@gmail.com

Javier Protzel is a professor at the Universidad del Pacífico of Lima, Peru. He holds a PhD in Sociology awarded by the Paris School of Higher Studies in Social Sciences (EHESS). His research focuses on media systems, politics, intercultural and urban studies. He is the vice president for Latin America of the World Association of Communication (WCA). Email: javprotzel@gmail.com

Stella Puente directs the postgraduate program in cultural industries at the 'Tres de Febrero' University, in Buenos Aires. She is the author of *Industrias Culturales* (2007). She was formerly the National Director of Cultural Policies and International Cooperation at the Ministry of Culture, Argentina, as well as Deputy Secretary of Cultural Industries in Buenos Aires. Email: stell.puente@gmail.com

Víctor Quintanilla is currently communications coordinator for the Inter-American Association for Environmental Defense (AIDA) in Mexico City. By background a journalist, he holds an MA in Communications from Universidad Iberoamericana, Mexico City and a BA in Communications Science from Universidad Mayor de San Andrés, La Paz, Bolivia. He previously worked in print and broadcast media in Bolivia. Email: vico_qs@hotmail.com

Silvio Waisbord is a professor in the School of Media and Public Affairs at George Washington University. His most recent books are *Media Sociology, A Reappraisal* (2014) and *Reinventing Professionalism: Journalism*

and News in Global Perspective (2013). He was editor-in-chief of the *International Journal of Press/Politics* and in 2014 was appointed the editor of the *Journal of Communication*. He has lectured and worked in more than 30 countries; has written or edited 10 books; and published more than 100 journal articles, book chapters and newspaper columns. He holds a PhD in Sociology from the University of California in San Diego. Email: waisbord@gwu.edu

Introduction: Media Systems in the Age of (Anti) Neoliberal Politics

Mireya Márquez-Ramírez and Manuel Alejandro Guerrero

Media policy is a contentious and highly political issue worldwide. In established democracies, the most heated debates nowadays revolve around the pertinence to more effectively regulate media when their perceived power is abused, the contemporary challenges yet continuing relevance of public broadcasting systems, or the threats that media concentration and marketization pose to press freedom, pluralism and ultimately to democracy (Iosifidis, 2011; Mansell and Raboy, 2011). Advocates of media reform often highlight the negative effects of commercialism and market forces in the weakening of media's societal role and the importance of public broadcasting services in providing a forum of plural expression and debate and thus in the strengthening of democracies (Curran, 2002, 2011; Curran and Seaton, 2003; Gunther and Mughan, 2000; Keane, 1991; Matos, 2012; McChesney and Schiller, 2003; Raboy, 1996; Street, 2011).

In the past three decades, the importance of addressing media policy revitalized with the impact of globalization, which in layman terms has come to signify privatization, deregulation and liberalization of media markets. As a result, there is a recurring clash between the forces that push for unregulated, commercially funded media corporations that deliver content across platforms and cater for demanding global consumers vis-à-vis those who advocate for the provision of content in the spirit of a public service that addresses responsible citizens and fosters deliberative democracy.

Despite the widespread use of globalization as the analytical dimension to either assess or explain media policy, the latest scholarly surveys on media policies across geographies show that at the crossroad between

1

market logics, digitalization and global trends, local politics still play a fundamental role (Freedman, 2006, 2008; Hitchens, 2006; Kitley, 2006; Morris and Waisbord, 2001; Sinclair, 2000). For example, Latin American countries have been historically characterized by uneven and discretional enforcement of media regulation that has barely restricted – and rather enabled – media concentration. Mexico and Brazil alone are the hosts to the biggest media conglomerates of the Spanish and Portuguese languages – Televisa and Globo, respectively – because political elites paved the way for their growth and consolidation. As will become evident in Bolaño's chapter in this volume on development and culture in the Brazilian context, TV industries were key to construct national and hegemonic identities. Private-owned media in Latin America gained enormous economic benefits from local governments and historically played a fundamental role in sustaining the *status quo* for either dictatorial regimes, authoritarian governments or conservative agendas (Fox and Schmucler, 1982; Fox, 1988, 1997; Fox and Waisbord, 2002; Sinclair, 1996, 1999, 2002).

Moreover, most Latin American countries continue to experience wealth disparity, conflictive processes of political democratization, increased polarization across and inside countries and widespread weakness of the rule of law that in turn results in corruption, impunity and political mistrust (Power and Jamison, 2005; Protzel, 2005; Waisbord, 2007). Within that social context, exogenous factors such as commercialism, the globalization of audiences, ownership structures and content fluxes enabled by neoliberal reforms implemented during the 1980s and 1990s may only explain part of the historical development of Latin American media and cultural industries. Certainly, the changing technologies that have deeply modified formats and contents, production channels, delivery platforms or consumption patterns in the digital age have all posed even more challenges for media and cultural policies and industries in Latin America, as Chapter 13 of this volume shows regarding the publishing world (see also Albornoz, 2011; Bolaño, 2013; Bustamante, 2011; García-Canclini and Piedras, 2005; Hernández-Lomelí and Sánchez-Ruiz, 2000; Mastrini, Bizberge and Charras, 2013; Mato, 2002; Sánchez-Ruiz, 2001).

However, one thing remains crucially clear: to speak of media policy – whether in the global or local scope, in the digital or analogue media – still means to discuss the familiar topics that have long preoccupied media scholars across the world in general and in Latin America in particular (Cañizález, 2009; Guerrero, 2013; Mastrini and Bolaño, 2000; Mastrini and Becerra, 2006). Such topics are related to the degree of fairness in the competition game and the specific weight and manoeuvre capability and accountability of the actors at stake. In other words, to speak of media policy still means to speak about pluralism, diversity of voices, freedom of speech, access to information, fair news coverage, the right to communication, media accountability, audiences' rights, and, at the core of all, the construction of an engaged and informed citizenry.

Whether media and cultural industries are left to the (de-) regulation and logics of the (global) markets or devised as public goods in need of protection by State governments on behalf of the national interest, we find that both 'globalization' and 'policy' are not sufficiently interrogated as overarching analytical dimensions. As Silvio Waisbord argues in the opening chapter of this volume, a persistent focus on the impact of globalization in the shaping of media systems and policies has perhaps overlooked the prevailing importance of national actors and politics and, as we argue across the book, the real weight that written laws acquire in the context of post-authoritarian, often pragmatic politics. By adhering to a global perspective alone, we may neglect the middle layers of power struggle that continue to mobilize such power solely amongst local media, economic and political elites and away from citizens.

Likewise, a mere description of the laws and regulations that concern media and cultural industries would be of little help to grasp the context wherein they operate. We hence believe that a purely instrumental focus on 'media policy' as the structural framework that defines media performance may fall in the trap of taking for granted its own operative relevance. In other words, it would assume that policy and regulation, as part of the broader rule of the law, are enabled and enacted in a way that media contents, audiences and actors subjugate and adhere to it. Freedoms and media pluralism are thus guaranteed and protected by law, and are effective by decree. Instead, this book proposes to view media policy in general and in Latin America in particular not only in its legal status or its concordance or not with global media trends, but rather – and most importantly – as a political discourse inserted in specific contexts that, as we shall see across the various countries explored here, mutates and adapts to local circumstances, often in the contentious field of partisan or highly polarized politics.

For example, depending on whom we ask inside Latin American countries, media policy is the flagship of self-proclaimed progressive governments that, on behalf of the people and in open confrontation with certain corporations or individuals, claim to represent the people against powerful and greedy media corporations, as in the case of Argentina, Venezuela, Bolivia or Ecuador. In opposition, media proprietors and international bodies often view media policy – and specifically media policy proposed by left-wing governments – as governmental intervention that threatens press freedom and disguises the return of authoritarian and dictatorial States. Increased levels of censorship, violence and repression against individual journalists in recent years certainly justify that view in part (Hughes and Lawson, 2005; Lugo-Ocando, 2008). On the other hand, however, the role of media power and their alliances, complicities and lack of commitment with the public good are often absent from the debates on press freedom across the region.

Likewise, as shown by various chapters of this book, media policy is not always the source of confrontation between left-wing governments and allegedly conservative media proprietors like in Venezuela, Bolivia, Ecuador or Argentina. In fact some governments with similar progressive credentials, like Brazil's, seem insufficiently motivated to confront politically the privileged status of media conglomerates (see the chapters by Matos and Bolaño in this volume). In many cases, when the traditionally elusive topic of media policy does appear at the forefront of partisan agendas, it does not always stem from a genuine attempt to restrict media power and enable citizens' access to diverse media. Instead, ruling parties and Executives often promote media policy use with hidden agendas: as punitive instruments when political-media disagreements emerge and their alliances begin to crack or when media overtly oppose those in power. As shown throughout the following chapters, when sensitive issues for both political and economic actors are at stake – property regimes, patterns of concentration, political advertisement, electoral regulations – media policy is, in any case, still deeply dependent on local politics, most of which need to be understood in the context of weak institutions and rule of law, as well as pragmatic policymaking. Unlike the liberal tradition of separating the market and the State in established democracies, both need to be viewed in tandem in Latin America. In fact, the book in part challenges the mainstream categorizations of media systems that still view private, liberal media as relatively free from State interference and political instrumentalisation (see Hallin and Mancini, 2004 for an example).

In doing so, this book proposes, tests and analyzes a common theoretical umbrella that helps explain the extent to which globalization in general, marketization and commercialism in particular, regional bodies and the nation State all play contesting roles in redefining the media's role in Latin American societies: the captured liberal model. In a nutshell, it is a technically – and in many ways formally – liberal commercial model that has been captured both by economic and political interests and thus shows that political instrumentalisation and State intervention in private media need not to happen necessarily at the formal or legal level. This collection addresses the diverse shades, nuances and extents of 'capture' by either the State or the market in a variety of issues. The book explores the configuration of national media systems and their challenges, the competing forces shaping communication policies, the reporting cultures stemming from authoritarian political regimes, the journalistic ethos shaped by global discourses per se, and to a lesser extent, the degree to which certain cultural markets –be it 'national cultures' or the publishing industries – are either overlooked and left entirely to the forces of market or protected by political interest and national agendas. Below we explain how the term 'capture' must be understood in this context, though a larger discussion is found in Chapter 2.

Media systems, policy and pluralism

After World War II, and as a consequence of (mostly US) political science developments and modernization theories, the media systems were originally conceived as press theories and philosophies that resembled Cold War categories. They distinguished contrasting degrees of freedom of speech and categories of governmental property and state intervention, hence establishing totalitarian, authoritarian, social democratic and liberal models of the press (Siebert, Peterson and Schramm, 1956). These models were also the basis for establishing a normative linkage between 'free media' and democracy, mostly – though not exclusively – understood as a private commercial media system (Meiklejohn, 1960; Michnik and Rosen, 1997).

So far, in a market-led economy with minimal State intervention, control, regulation or interference, the liberal model of the media – often called libertarian – assumed private property is essential to oversee governmental wrongdoing, uphold journalistic independence and guarantee press freedom (Siebert et al., 1956; Ungar, 1990; Hallin and Giles, 2005; Hallin and Mancini, 2004; Christians, Glasser, McQuail, Nordenstreng and White, 2009). According to this view, the media is required to operate within the market logics and thus necessitates minimal intervention and regulation by the government or the state. It is, therefore, 'simply assumed that the market will provide appropriate institutions and processes of public communication to support a democratic polity' (Garnham, 1992: 363).

The more socially-committed versions of the liberal model are the post-War debates on social responsibility, that nowadays underpin the core philosophical tenets of public broadcasting services in European countries. In this approach, freedom implies a duty towards accountability and social responsibility, which might call for some degree of external limitation or intervention in order to control media markets and to oversee the public good; hence a balance between freedom and regulation prevails. Such a view has thus become the ideal contemporary press template that resembles the model of the public sphere developed by Jürgen Habermas (1989). In any case, media's role in society is to serve the public interest, to provide objective information, to offer a forum for the contemplation of a diverse spectrum of political opinions, and to monitor existing power structures. In many aspects, this paradigm of the press resembles the Anglo-Saxon tradition of journalism (Allan, 1997; Bennett and Serrin, 2005; Christians et al., 2009; Hackett and Zhao, 1998; Hallin, 2000; Schudson, 2005; Schudson and Anderson, 2008).

On the other hand – and leaving out the extreme cases of totalitarian models – authoritarian political regimes in their various degrees, have been perhaps the most common forms of political organization in the 20th century. In authoritarian regimes, as defined by Linz (1975), a crucial feature is their limited political pluralism that makes competition for power a relatively closed process that remains within the control of a leader or a small political elite.[1] Political participation in authoritarian regimes is also restricted because the individual's political and civil rights, though not necessarily revoked, are usually not respected. For Linz, under an authoritarian regime, the different types of media may vary greatly in autonomy, even under the same regime, since the limited pluralism that exists readily generates some 'islands of exemption' on which certain kinds of publications (like church publications in Franco's Spain, or academic material in Mexico during the 1960s) remain free from government censorship. Nevertheless, authoritarian regimes tend to exercise a certain control – through various means from generating conditions for self-censorship to open censorship – over broadcast, print and other sorts of mainstream media. Siebert and colleagues (1956) in any case consider that under authoritarian regimes the media system becomes functional and propagandistic and thus it is very difficult for the media to keep or develop a truly informational or watchdog role.

The past decade saw the emergence of a seminal work for a comparative assessment of media systems that expressly deals with the way in which nation States intervene – or fail to do so – through regulation, policy, political parallelism or instrumentalisation of the media. Political scientists Daniel Hallin and Paolo Mancini (2004) observe a much broader and nuanced set of differences and similarities between geographically or culturally close countries. They are able to devise three models that share particular variables. According to both authors, four dimensions define media systems: the first is the level of development of media markets and mass circulation press. The second is the degree of political parallelism between the media and political parties, as well as how major political divisions and echelons in society are represented in the media. The third is the development of journalistic professionalism that reflects the degree of autonomy of journalists, their patterns of training, as well as the professional norms they embrace and the presence of a 'public service orientation,' as opposed to the 'instrumentalisation' of news media as vehicles for political intervention. Finally, their fourth dimension analyzes the degree of state intervention in the media system through ownership, regulation, subsidies, or public service broadcasting orientation.

From these four dimensions Hallin and Mancini put forward three ideal types of media systems that encompass only Western consolidated democracies. While media systems of developing countries are absent in their typology, there are connections to be made. In their 'North Atlantic or Liberal Model' – which comprises the Unites States, Canada, Ireland, and Britain – newspaper circulation is of medium scope, mass circulation press developed early, and journalistic 'professionalism' is rooted in an ideology of public service and fact-oriented, impartial reporting. In these North Atlantic countries, commercial media tend to dominate, mirroring the wider economic system in its relatively small role for the state, alongside a relatively large private sector. Political parallelism and instrumentalization of the media are hence low in liberal media systems, and internal pluralism exists as individual media report on all contesting actors, unlike in the external pluralism of Southern Europe, where each media adheres to a specific ideological stance. Similarly, commercial broadcasting is regulated by independent agencies with substantial political autonomy, even though there is considerable heterogeneity and contradictions among the country members, with the United States particularly distinct from the three others.

Their second 'Democratic Corporatist' model includes countries from Northern and Central Europe. It combines private and government efforts for the sake of social responsibility, through a 'pillarised' system that seeks to represent the voices of all the competing actors in society.

A third model, the 'Polarized Pluralist' comprising Mediterranean countries, includes Italy, Greece, France, Portugal, and Spain – the latter three sharing colonial, historical, or cultural ties with most Latin American countries. According to Hallin and Mancini, this model is characterized by low newspaper circulation and the predominance of an elite-oriented, politicized press. Its political parallelism is high, because the government or political parties are represented ideologically in the press. Likewise, the media perform some form of state or governmental intervention via content and editorial policy. Journalism relies heavily on commentary and partisan opinion, and practitioners have a low level of professionalization. There is a parliamentary or governmental model of broadcast governance, and a good degree of censorship and press subsidies.

While Latin American countries may easily be coupled with their Mediterranean counterparts (See Hallin and Papathanassopoulos, 2002), throughout this book we shall see examples of media systems that are both commercially funded but politically instrumentalized. So far, Hallin and Mancini's categories have proved extremely useful as ideal models of press-State relations and news media performance in established democracies. Yet even when their work does not attempt to account for broader differences in the world or countries outside the West, they still assume market and State are opposite forces that counterbalance each other. While they acknowledge – as many studies have – that neoliberal politics have resulted in the spreading of the liberal model of the media across the world (Schiller, 1976; Comor, 2002; Fitzgerald, 2012; Mirrlees, 2013), the narrative appears to assume that State-intervened and highly instrumentalized media show lower journalistic professionalism and independence, while liberal media are better capable of ensuring independence and professional performance. This view, however, not only leaves the economic power relatively unscrutinized (Curran, 2002), but also fails to fit the contemporary world order (Gunaratne, 2001, 2009) and as a result, overlooks the alternative and hybrid pathways that some countries have followed in Latin America.

In fact, the liberal model – anchored as it is in the private ownership of the media – has garnered considerable criticism in the developing world (see, for instance, ICSCP, 1980) due to the failure of the commercial media-models to deliver democratic expectancies and ideals. The critical tradition of media political economy has repeatedly highlighted the flaws of the liberal conception of the press by debunking the assumptions that commercial media intrinsically enable journalistic autonomy, public service, pluralism or equitable access to the media content, production of content, or media property. Instead, the argument goes, private-oriented media have transformed media content into commodity to be traded, media publics into consumers, and has submitted editorial policy to conservative economic powers and corporate interests, therefore resulting in market-driven journalism (Herman and McChesney, 1997; MacManus, 1994; McChesney, 1999; Schiller, 1981; Thussu, 2007). As Curran observes: 'the market can give rise not to independent watchdogs serving the public interest but to corporate mercenaries which adjust their critical scrutiny to suit their private purpose' (2002: 221).

The captured liberal model of media in Latin America

Unlike the classical liberal philosophy that envisioned the media as a marketplace for diverse ideas that required operation outside the reach and control of the State, a pervasive element has historically shaped the development of media systems in most Latin American countries. During authoritarian rules, governments used a double standard with the media: pestering – or even repressing – the critical press on the one hand, while forging close-knit relations with the most established owners of the media whom political elites favored – and not infrequently so – with protections, subsidies, and contract awards on the other (Fox, 1988; Fox and Waisbord, 2002; Sinclair, 1996).

In fact, as early as the 1960s, Latin American media research began to address the negative effects of commercial models of communications supported by authoritarian states in local cultures and societies. A historical line of critical scholarship emerged to denounce the unequal flows of information between the so-called core and periphery and thus Latin American scholars were instrumental in the talks leading to the drafting of the so-called McBride report (Fuentes-Navarro, 1988; Mansell and Nordenstreng, 2006; Pasquali, 2005).

In the context of dictatorships and authoritarianism, critics denounced how through their contents, news and formats, the local private media helped to legitimize repressive regimes. Media and dictatorships became allies and reporting in the region was conducted in local and foreign news from the perspective of US values and interests (Beltrán, 1970; Furtado, 1984; Marques de Melo, 1989; Mattelart, Piccini and Mattelart, 1976; Schiller, 1976; Reyes-Matta, 1979). As scholars claimed that news agencies and information discourses distributed information to the local population in ways that supported US' geopolitical interests and perspectives, news media either ignored, invisibilized, and most frequently demonized, opposed or discouraged social change or revolution in the area (Fox and Schmucler, 1982). In Chile alone, for instance, commercial media legitimized military dictatorship, suppressed news about the government's systematic repression of opponents, and helped the regime to maintain a liberal façade despite a self-imposed censorship and silence (Muzinaga, 1982).

After sharing contexts of authoritarian political rule, some 30 years ago the majority of the countries in the region began to move away from different forms and degrees of authoritarian rule and turned toward more democratic and politically pluralistic models (Malloy and Seligson, 1987). By recognizing – at least *de jure* – the existence of fundamental guarantees – which include freedom of speech, freedom of the press, and freedom to own property – the political groups that gave shape to the post-authoritarian regimes that came to power in the 1980s and 1990s took legitimacy away from the direct exercise of violence or from open censorship as recurring and explicit mechanisms of power. Latin America approached the 21st century with a strengthened (neo-) liberal discourse that in theory would reinforce media competition and plurality, as well as more financial and editorial autonomy, but in practice, greatly benefited the largest media corporations. In fact, as we shall see throughout the chapters, it had ambiguous and sometimes fatal consequences for media systems, communications policies and cultural industries and their regulatory frameworks, but also for the practices of journalism and business models of news media.

As Márquez-Ramírez (Chapter 15) argues in this collection, a dominant tradition of thought asserts that commercialism, privatization and political and neoliberal reforms were said to have a positive impact in both media and regime democratization across Latin America (Lawson, 2002; Hughes, 2006; Tironi and Sunkel, 2000). In contrast, an important segment of scholars are reluctant to connect neoliberal reforms with citizen empowerment: they argue that the structural conditions of the post-colonial past in Latin America mean that the communicative nature of democracy is not in the service of the citizens, but of the elites, even through global discourses of freedom or professionalism, as Rodrigo Araya argues in Chapter 14 of this collection. Instead, the focus is on making sure that formal democratic organizations are efficient, so that the proper performance of the market can be guaranteed (Alfaro-Moreno, 2006: 302; see also Bresnahan, 2003; Poblete, 2006).

In fact, what we see across Latin America – becoming evident in every chapter – is that the ascent to power of new political groups has presupposed the establishment of close relations to varying degrees – formal and informal – with a 'media class' that already existed in various countries. This has translated into the acceptance of favorable conditions to a media *establishment* that has not necessarily served the interests of media pluralism and democracy, but to the legitimation of political elites and the consolidation of media conglomerates in the region. However, these approaches do not imply that the relations between media and politics are free from tensions (Santos-Calderón, 1989; De Lima and Lopes, 2007). In fact, as will become clear in the chapters on Argentina, Venezuela and Bolivia in this collection, there is a sharply clear antagonism and animosity between executive powers and some private media.

Furthermore, returning to the historical ties between the media and political elites in the region, some authors have long documented the way in which the shaping of the states in Latin America has taken place in history when forging clientelist relations with various sectors and social groups (Strickon and Greenfield, 1972). One of the most significant consequences of clientelism is that, being a privileged space for negotiation and exchange, it may affect the efficacy of the implementation of legal frameworks – both normative and regulatory (Eisenstadt and Roniger, 1984; Corzo Fernández, 2002). In the case of the media, this type of relations brings them directly into the political process both by enabling their owners to build alliances with certain political groups – in particular by using their own corporations to intervene in politics, and by pulling their strings to reduce or circumvent the effects of regulations that may affect their interests. For Hallin and Papathanassopoulos (2002), clientelism is in fact the main defining feature of the relationship between the media and the political system in Latin America. Clientelism reduces the effectiveness and efficacy of the regulation, creates conditions that allow for undue interference of the media groups in politics and, as we will see later on, also plays a part in undermining the development of professional reporting practices.

As a result of a trend that has been favorable to relationships based on clientelism and a clear orientation towards de-regulation and liberal market reforms in the 1990s, the new ruling elites of the transition crafted spaces for exchange and mutual support with a relatively conservative media elite. Far from having changed, these media elites found better conditions for accumulation and concentration in the face of some rules that were either disappearing or ended up being ineffectively applied. The arrival of neoliberal politics in the region – and the consequent deregulation and privatization of the few state-funded channels across the region – initially increased the already established strategic and advantaged position of key media conglomerates. Examples are Globo in Brazil, Grupo Televisa in Mexico, Grupo Cisneros-Venevisión in Venezuela, or Grupo Clarín in Argentina.

Many industrialized countries have witnessed the emergence of creative economies along the deregulation of media markets that result from a healthier competition between several players and actors, and effective policies that regulate and limit concentration. However, the opposite has happened in Latin America, wherein media elites strongly linked to the State – and often within the State itself – have enjoyed unlimited privileges and historically opposed any attempt to regulate and limit such privileges. In an environment shaped by media conglomerates formally modeled after the commercial media corporations of the United States, the lack of open competition, pluralism and a true representation of social groups is a continuing concern. However, at the very same time, in some countries there has emerged an opposing trend that seeks to reposition the State vis-à-vis the power of those large corporations, as in the case of Argentina (Chapters 5 and 10) or Venezuela (Chapter 8).

Thus, one can find that while some industries and markets are entirely shaped by market logics (Chapter 13), the past decade has witnessed the revival of a 'neo-interventionist' type of State that has sought to counter – to varying degrees of success – Latin American powerful media corporations through either a stronger governmental control or through tighter media policy and regulation (See the Bolivian case in Chapter 9). The aim is not to substitute the commercial media model, but to counterbalance it with strong regulatory frameworks or with other forms of state-funded media.

Nevertheless, in its actual forms State intervention is not necessarily stimulating widespread pluralism and diversity either, but instead, retorting to the very authoritarian-type of political control and propaganda. In many cases, like Venezuela, Bolivia or Argentina, as we shall see, local government's main objectives has been, at least in theory, to implement more efficient mechanisms of control vis-à-vis the power of the strongest media corporations and their alleged bias in reporting. The process has been a very challenging one, though, often deepening social polarization and prompting intense debate over press freedom, freedom of speech and access to information.

In any case, what must be noted is that both trends: Neoliberal privatization and the re-emergence of state intervention – move in Latin America within the same context of clientelism and of discretional and uneven application of regulation and the law. At the end, the context in which both trends unfold contribute to the distortion of a private commercial model that does not foster pluralism and where conditions are kept for preventing the development of watchdog roles (See Guerrero's Chapter 2). Thus, as we argue thoughout the book, the formally liberal model consisting of private media remain constantly – and complicitly – captured either by corporate or political interests: the cases analyzed in this volume in Colombia (Chapter 3), Perú (Chapter 4), El Salvador (Chapter 6), Guatemala (Chapter 7) and Mexico (Chapter 15) attest to this.

Though a wider discussion is found in Chapter 2 on the way we use the term 'capture' in this work, some words are necessary here. The term has been linked to what is referred to as 'state capture' along different studies that have analyzed the ways in which certain powerful groups in society – mostly, but not only big corporations and firms – affect the outcomes of the policy-making process or the shaping of rules and regulations in their own benefit and at the expense of a wider social or general interest (Laffont and Tirole, 1991; Hellman, 1998; World Bank, 2000). A large number of studies, mostly focused on Eastern European countries, have used the concept of 'state capture' to asses the forms in which diverse interests take over – often weak – spaces of law and policy-making (Begovic, 2005; Omelyanchuk, 2001; Pesic, 2007; Zhuravskaya, 2000). In Latin America, Guerrero (2010) has used the concept to analyze three cases where big media corporations shaped broadcasting policy-making in Mexico at the expense of the social interest.

In this work we use the term in a slightly different manner. Whereas 'state capture' refers to a condition where some aspects of the policy-making process and of the design of the rules of the game are twisted in favor of certain specific private interests – a phenomenon that we fully acknowledge that continues to happen in media and communication policy, though – the term 'capture' goes even further in some of the chapters: it stresses also a condition where extra-journalistic criteria shape, determine and limit the watchdog role of the media. These external criteria may be coming either from global discourses of professionalism, from market logics, from politicians and state agencies, or from the political or economic interests of media proprietors (and sometimes also editors). Thus, what we rescue from the term is the negative – and undue – impact of two aspects that will be discussed along many chapters: the regulatory inefficiency of the State and the constantly challenged watchdog role of journalism. In the case of the few cultural industries addressed in this collection – Spanish-language publishing industry in Chapter 13 and Brazilian cultural production in chapter 12 – the capture may result from the inefficiency of state agencies and national policies to keep up with technological change and digitalization to properly regulate certain industreis, or else, from challenges posed by ineffective policy that fails to address the role of class and ethnicity in legitimizing an hegemonic national culture.

Whether addressing the configuration of media systems, communication policies, journalistic practices and discourses or cultural industries, various aspects favor conditions of capturing the devising and application of policies, laws and regulations, as well as media pluralism, citizen's access to, handling of and engagement with the media, and the professional journalistic performance. We may thus claim that all of the aforementioned aspects are captured either by corporate interests whose loyalties also change depending on the actors in power, or by political groups in a context dominated by private commercial media organizations.

Of course, as discussed in Chapter 2, when we talk here about a 'captured liberal' media system model in Latin America, we are talking neither of a normative model, nor of an homogeneous all-encompassing and static picture. There are varying degrees and different ways in which journalism's watchdog role – and by watchdog role we do not only mean to hold the government to account, but also economic and corporate powers – and communications policies aiming (or not) at media pluralism and equitable access have been captured in Latin American countries. For example, as said before the authoritarian episodes marked the dominance of the political regime over different aspects of the social life, including the ways in which the media reported and informed about public issues. However, the transtions from authoritarianism in Latin America have generated different settings and terms of capture. Though in general we find contexts of regulatory inefficiency in a media landscape dominated by commercial corporations, the capturers may vary: in some cases, like Central America, Brazil, Mexico or Colombia, the weigth of the corporations or of certain political groups acting in their own interest may be strong to favor certain regulatory or policy outcomes at certain times or to shape the topics of the public agenda in certain ways, whereas in Argentina, Venezuela or Bolivia it is the state – not necessarily acting in favor of a wider social interest, but against specific private groups – the one that hinders the media watchdog role and favors a discretional application of the regulation and norms.

In proposing the 'captured liberal' model of media systems, we also analyze how the narratives of media transition, journalistic processes of professionalization and even the paradigm of journalism in itself are trapped in contesting forces of global vis-à-vis local discourses. The chapters of this book discuss the realities that journalism business models, practices, performances, and conditions of autonomy are facing, and the consequences for plurality and diversity in Brazil, Chile, Argentina, Venezuela, Bolivia, Colombia, Peru, El Salvador, Guatemala and Mexico. Many chapters partly examine the democratic deficit of news organizations working between the growing pressures of the market, the confrontation or complicity with local governments and elites, the economic interests of media proprietors, the growing political polarisation and drug violence in many countries, and the difficulties to adopt and adapt the norms of the profession, besides the lack of press accountability, regulation, collegiality or protection for journalists.

In general, this collection examines the ways in which the nation state, especially through regulatory frameworks and media policies, has developed an ambiguous relation to media conglomerates, in some cases, by restraining their power and influences, while in others, maintaining a favorable environment for concentration. One chapter in particular (Matos in Chapter 12) even deals with the necessity of Latin American media systems, and Brazil in particular, to shift towards public service broadcasting, showing the great contribution that they would bring to the democratic processes in Latin America despite the challenges and shortcomings of PBS in the European context.

As we argue that local and regional politics still have an important effect on the modeling of the media systems and on media regulatory policies, ultimately, the book surveys the relationship between the changing stake – and in cases such as Argentina, Venezuela or Bolivia, a straightforward revival – of the State and local political actors in media regulation vis-à-vis the continuity of unregulated media that dominate local markets.

In debunking the importance of globalization as conceptual framework, leading scholar Silvio Waisbord opens the book with a chapter in which he reminds us how governmental policies, civic mobilization, coalitions and alliances, and political opportunities are important dimensions of media policies. He proposes to assess the significance of global, national, state, and local forces in the reconfiguration of media systems, but also reminds us that not all media and information policies fall squarely within the purview and interests of transnational, national, and municipal actors. In surveying Latin American media systems, in Chapter 2, Manuel Alejandro Guerrero examines the impact of continuing clientelism, political transitions and the liberalization in devising the 'captured liberal' model of the media, that is used as the theoretical umbrella that ties the volume chapters together. After these two opening chapters, we assess the nation-states in which private-oriented media have hold a predominant stake. Chapters explore how media markets in Peru, Colombia, El Salvador, Guatemala and Argentina have all evolved in contexts of low readerships and close alliances with political elites. For her part, Catalina Montoya shows how different sorts of exchanges between media and politics have characterized the Colombian media landscape, having a combination of economic deregulation, low levels of regulatory efficiency and high instrumentalization. Javier Protzel focuses on the importance of the local context in shaping media development in Peru: the rise and fall of political parties and a lack of solid institutions, as well as dictatorships, terrorism, hyperinflation and State censorship facilitate pragmatic partisanship. Media take positions following pressure-group interests or selected candidates, according to a broad ideological spectrum, eagerly attacking or defending allies or foes. In discussing pluralism in El Salvador, José Luis Benítez shows us the face of rampant commercialism in Central America, wherein market liberalization and de-regulation in media and telecommunications have curtailed media pluralism, audiences rights, press freedom and strengthened the privileges for private commercial corporations. Similarly, Silvio René Gramajo argues that in Guatemala, poor regulatory efficiency, on top of obsolete normativity, both generate a relational framework within which media and political power maintain a relationship of mutual convenience. Jorge Liotti analyzes – the first essay on Argentina – the development of media through authoritarian and democratic periods, paying considerable attention to the impact for print markets and to the exercise and practices of journalism. Then, the book explores the most emblematic cases of media policies aimed at constraining powerful and established media gropus existing in those countries – with the exception of Bolivia – or to retain the centrality of the government in media control. We start with Venezuela, a country which had had traditionally powerful media. Here Andrés Cañizález describes the late president Hugo Chavez's model of central communication. This included the construction of a legal framework which endowed the state with wide capabilities, significantly increased the mass-media machine controlled by the government, and launched a strategy of regional influence. Likewise, the media landscape in Bolivia has changed with the arrival of Evo Morales to power in 2006. Víctor Quintanilla observes how a new constitution has been enacted that limits media property concentration while establishing public supports for community media, although as he argues, the strategy seems more oriented towards strengthening a pro-governmental media structure, than to contributing to pluralism. Argentinian scholars Guillermo Mastrini, Martín Becerra and Santiago Marino analyze more in detail one of the most controversial – yet arguably innovative – media policies in the region. They compare media policy throughout Kirchnerism, and determine how far and how deep have true structural changes come into effect after the passing of the 2009 broadcasting Law, emphasizing the changes in the audiovisual sector.

In a context that had traditionally been characterized by the effects of rampant commercialism and concentration, and more recently, by a return of the State and excutive branches in the shaping of media policies, much of the discussion of the region has once more turned into the option of public broadcasting service. That is why Carolina Matos makes a case for the necessity of public broadcasting in the region and Brazil in particular in a context where European nations debate its future: while the challenges are aplenty, public service may be the alternative to commercial media conglomerates or to populist leaders taking over communication systems.

Chapters 12 and 13 are more orientated towards cultural policy and thus go further away from the media system: they also consider consequences for cultural markets and constructions of national identities. For the case of Brazil, César Bolaño examines, through the work of well-known scholar Celso Furtado, how the configuration of cultural production and the media structure in Brazil have responded to impacts from external and globalized processes throughout history, but also from local factors, where class and ethcicity have had a key role. His chapter reviews the development of Brazilian media and cultural industries, briefly drawing from the helpful – and contrasting – example of India, a country in similar economic development than Brazil. The contrast illustrate the particularities that helped the TV Brazilian industry to consolidate. Communication policies, have therefore, followed complex patterns wherein multiple social layers are at stake. For her part, Stella Puente analyzes how the market has dramatically changed with the digitalization of the production chain in the publishing world, and both regional/local agencies and publishers themselves in Ibero-America still struggle to devise strategies to face technological change. Her chapter therefore briefly introduces the discussion wherein States are rarely preoccupied for policies that best guarantee pluralism and competition and thus leave the industry of Spanish-speaking publishers to the forces of market, which are traditionally lead by Spain, and in much lower degree, by the most advantaged countries in Latin America.

Finally, the last two chapters deal with journalistic practices and professional discourses in relation to the global discourses of freedom, professionalism and democracy. In Chapter 14, Rodrigo Araya reminds us how even normative concepts such as professionalism are deeply engrained in a European vision of modernity that, packaged as globalization, clash with local understandings of news and information. Similarly, in Chapter 15 Mireya Márquez Ramírez reviews the narratives of professionalism and news media democratization in Mexico, by arguing that post-authoritarian journalistic cultures may be explained through the observation of change within continuity, via the structural, organizational, and environmental conditions that have historically shaped media development and press-State relations.

We finally close the book with a summary of the multiple findings across ten countries, which show the ways in which the captured liberal model materializes in media systems, communication policies and cultural industries in Latin America. By briefly referring to the most recent media reform in Mexico – that once again protects the interest of predominant actors such as Televisa – we highlight the tensions, areas of ambiguity and conflicting forces curtailing media pluralism and ultimately democratic life.

Note

1. According to Linz, 'authoritarian regimes are political systems with limited, not responsible, political pluralism, without elaborate and guiding ideology, but with distinctive mentalities, without extensive nor intensive political mobilization, except at some points in their development, and in which a leader or occasionally a small group exercises power within formally ill-defined limits but actually quite predictable ones' (Linz, 1975: 264).

References

Albornoz, L. A. (2011) *Poder, Medios, Cultura: Una Mirada Crítica desde la Economía Política de la Comunicación* (Buenos Aires: Paidós).

Alfaro-Moreno, R. M. (2006) 'Citizens and media cultures: hidden behind democratic formality,' *Global Media and Communication*, 20(3): 299–313.

Allan, S. (1997) 'News and the Public Sphere: towards a history of objectivity and impartiality,' pp. 296–329 in M. Bromley and T. O'Malley (eds) *A Journalism Reader* (London: Routledge).

Begovic, B. (2005) 'Corruption, lobbying and state capture,' Center for Liberal-Democratic Studies (CLDS) and School of Law, University of Belgrade, March 2005. Available at http://danica.popovic.ekof.bg.ac.yu/106.pdf (accessed March 2014).

Beltrán, L. R (1970, November) *Apuntes para un diagnóstico de la incomunicación social en América Latina: la persuasión a favor del status quo*. Paper presented for the Seminar on Communication and Development, CIESPAL/Fundación Friedrich Ebert/CEDAL, La Catalina, Costa Rica.

Bennett, W. L. and Serrin, W. (2005) 'The watchdog role,' pp. 169–188 in G. Overholser and K. Hall Jamieson (eds) *The Press* (New York: Oxford University Press).

Bolaño, C. (2013) *Industria Cultural, información y capitalismo* (Barcelona: Gedisa).

Bresnahan, R. (2003) 'The Media and the Neoliberal transition in Chile: democratic promise unfulfilled,' *Latin American Perspectives*, 30(6): 39–68.

Bustamante, E. (ed.) (2011) *Industrias creativas: amenazas sobre la cultura digital* (Barcelona: Gedisa).

Cañizález, A. (ed.) (2009) *Tiempos de cambio: Política y Comunicación en América Latina* (Caracas: Universidad Católica Andrés Bello).

Christians, C. G., Glasser, T. L., McQuail, D., Nordenstreng, K. and White, R. A. (2009) *Normative Theories of the Media: Journalism in Democratic Societies* (Urbana: University of Illinois Press).

Comor, E. (2002) 'Media corporations in the age of globalization,' pp. 309–323 in W. B. Gudykunst and B. Mody (eds) *Handbook of International and Intercultural Communication* (Thousand Oaks, CA: Sage).

Corzo Fernández, S. (2002) *El clientelismo político como intercambio* (Barcelona: Universidad de Granada, Edición ICPS).

Curran, J. (2002) *Media and Power* (London: Routledge).

Curran, J. (2011) *Media and Democracy* (London: Routledge).

Curran, J. and Seaton, J. (2003) *Power without Responsibility* (London: Routledge).

De Lima, V. A. and Lopes, C. (2007) *Rádios Comunitárias – Coronelismo eletrônico de novo tipo (1999–2004)* (Brazil: Instituto para o Desenvolvimento do Jornalismo, Projor).

Eisenstadt, S. N. and Roniger, L. (1984) *Patrons, Clients and Friends: Impersonal Relations and the Structure of Trust in Society* (Cambridge: Cambridge University Press).

Fitzgerald, S. W. (2012) *Corporations and Cultural Industries* (Maryland: Lexington Books).

Fox, E. (1997) *Latin American Broadcasting: From Tango to Telenovela* (Luton: University of Luton Press).

Fox, E. (ed.) (1988) *Media and Politics in Latin America: The Struggle for Democracy* (London: Sage).

Fox, E. and Schmucler, H. (eds) (1982) *Comunicación y Democracia en América Latina* (Lima: Desco/CLACSO).

Fox, E. and Waisbord, S. (eds) (2002) *Latin Politics, Global Media* (Austin: University of Texas Press).

Freedman, D. (2006) 'Dynamics of power in contemporary media policy-making,' *Media Culture and Society*, 28(6): 907–923.

Freedman, D. (2008) *The politics of media policy* (Cambridge: Polity).

Fuentes-Navarro, R. (1988) 'La investigación mexicana en comunicación: sistematización documental 1956–1986,' pp. 61–84 in E. Sánchez-Ruiz (ed.)

La investigación de la comunicación en México. Logros, retos y perspectivas (Guadalajara: Ediciones Comunicación/Universidad de Guadalajara).

Furtado, C. (1984) *Cultura e desenvolvimento em época de crise* (São Paulo: Paz e Terra).

García-Canclini, N. and Piedras, E. (2005) *Las industrias culturales y el desarrollo de México* (México: Siglo XXI Editores).

Garnham, N. (1992) 'The media and the public sphere,' pp. 359–376 in C. Calhoun (ed.) *Habermas and the public sphere* (Cambridge: MIT Press).

Guerrero, M. A. (2013) 'La reforma electoral y los medios,' pp. 233–295 in A. Alvarado (ed.) *México: Democracia y Sociedad. Más allá de la Reforma Electoral* (Mexico: Tribunal Electoral del Poder Judicial de la Federación/El Colegio de México.

Guerrero, M. A. (2010) 'Broadcasting and democracy in Mexico: from corporatist subordination to State capture,' *Policy and Society*, 29(1): 23–35.

Gunaratne, S. A. (2001) 'Prospects and limitations of World System Theory for media analysis: the case of the Middle East and North Africa,' *Gazette: The International Journal for Communication Studies*, 63(2–3): 121–148.

Gunther, R. and Mughan, A. (eds) (2000) *Democracy and the Media: A Comparative Perspective* (New York: Cambridge University Press).

Habermas, J. (1989) *The Structural Transformation of the Public Sphere* (Cambridge: Polity Press).

Hackett, R. A. and Zhao, Y. (1998) *Sustaining Democracy? Journalism and the Politics of Objectivity* (Toronto: Garamond Press).

Hallin, D. (2000) 'Commercialism and professionalism in the American news media,' pp. 218–237 in J. Curran and M. Gurevitch (eds) *Mass Media and Society* (London: Arnold).

Hallin, D. and Giles, R. (2005) 'Presses and democracies,' pp. 4–16 in G. Overholser and K. Hall Jamieson (eds) *The Press* (New York: Oxford University Press).

Hallin, D. and Mancini, P. (2004) *Comparing Media Systems: Three Models of Media and Politics* (New York: Cambridge University Press).

Hallin, D. and Papathanassopoulos, S. (2002) 'Political clientelism and the media: Southern Europe and Latin America in comparative perspective,' *Media, Culture and Society*, 24(2): 175–195.

Hellman, J. (1998) 'Winners take all: the politics of partial reform in post-communist transitions,' *World Politics*, 50(2): 203–234.

Herman, E. and McChesney, R. (1997) *Global Media: The New Missionaries of Corporate Capitalism* (New York: Continnum).

Hernández-Lomelí, F. and Sánchez-Ruiz, E. (2000) *Televisión y mercados: Una perspectiva mexicana* (Guadalajara: CUCSH).

Hitchens, L. (2006) *Broadcasting Pluralism and Diversity: A Comparative Study of Policy and Regulation* (Oxford/Portland, OR: Hart Publishing).

Hughes, S. and Lawson, C. (2005) 'The barriers to media opening in Latin America,' *Political Communication*, 22(1): 9–25.

ICSCP (International Commission for the Study of Communication Problems) (1980) *Many Voices, One World: Towards a New, More Just and More Efficient World Information and Communication Order* (Paris: UNESCO).

Iosifidis, P. (2011) *Global Media and Communications Policy* (Basingstoke, UK: Palgrave).

Keane, J. (1991) *The Media and Democracy* (Cambridge: Polity Press).

Kitley, P. (2006) *Television, Regulation and Civil Society in Asia* (London: Routledge/ Courzon).

Laffont, J. and Tirole, J. (1991) 'The politics of government decision-making: a theory of regulatory capture,' *Quarterly Journal of Economics*, 106: 1089–1127.

Linz, J. (1975) 'Totalitarian and authoritarian regimes,' pp.187–350 in F. I. Greenstein and N. W. Polsby (ed) *Handbook of Political Science: Macropolitical Theory*. Vol. III (Reading, MA: Addison-Wesley Publishing Co.).

Lugo-Ocando, J. (ed.) (2008) *The Media in Latin America* (Maidenhead: Open University Press).

Malloy, J. and Seligson, M. (1987) *Authoritarians and Democrats: Regime Transitions in Latin America* (Pittsburgh: University of Pittsburgh Press).

Mansell, R. and Nordenstreng, K. (2006) 'Great media and communication debates: WSIS and the MacBride report,' *MIT Information Technologies and International Development*, 3(4): 15–36.

Mansell, R. and Raboy, M. (2011) *The Handbook of Global Media and Communication Policy* (Oxford: Blackwell).

Marques de Melo, J. (ed.) (1989) *Comunicaçao na America Latina: Desenvolvimento e Crise* (Sao Paulo: Papirus).

Márquez-Ramírez, M. (2012) 'Valores normativos y prácticas de reporteo en tensión: percepciones profesionales de periodistas en México,' *Cuadernos de Información*, (30): 97–110.

Mastrini, G. and Becerra, M. (2006) *Periodistas y magnates. Estructura y concentración de las industrias culturales* (Buenos Aires: Prometeo).

Mastrini, G. and Bolaño, C. (2000) *Globalización y monopolios en la comunicación en América Latina* (Buenos Aires: Biblos).

Mastrini, G., Bizberge, A. and De Charras, D. (eds) (2013) *Las políticas de comunicación en el Siglo XXI* (Buenos Aires: La Crujía).

Mato, D. (2002) 'Miami in the transnationalization of the Telenovela industry: on territoriality and globalization,' *Journal of Latin American Cultural Studies*, 11(2): 195–212.

Matos, C. (2012) *Media and Politics in Latin America* (London: I.B. Tauris).

Mattelart, A., Piccini, M. and Mattelart, M. (1976) *Los medios de comunicación de masas: La ideología de la prensa liberal* (Buenos Aires: Schapire/El Cid).

McChesney, R. (1999) *Rich Media, Poor Democracy: Communication Politics in Dubious Times* (Urbana: University of Illinois Press).

McChesney, R. and Schiller, D. (2003) *The Political Economy of International Communications: Foundations for the Emerging Global Debate about Media Ownership and Regulation* (Technology, Business and Society, Programme Paper No. 11). United Nations Research Institute for Social Development.

McManus, J. (1994) *Market-driven Journalism: Let the Citizen Beware?* (Thousand Oaks, CA: Sage).

Meiklejohn, A. (1960) *Political Freedom: The Constitutional Powers of the People* (New York: Harper).

Michnik, A. and Rosen, J. (1997) 'The media and democracy: a dialogue,' *Journal of Democracy*, 8(4): 85–93.

Mirrlees, T. (2013) *Global Entertainment Media. Between Cultural Imperialism and Cultural Globalization* (New York: Routledge).

Morris, N. and Waisbord, S. (2001) *Media and Globalization: Why the State Matters* (Oxford: Rowman and Littlefield).

Muzinaga, G. (1982) 'Políticas de comunicación bajo regímenes autoritarios: el caso de Chile' pp. 41–68 in E. Fox and H. Schmucler (eds) *Comunicación y Democracia en América Latina* (Lima: Desco/CLASCO).

Omelyanchuk, O. (2001) 'Explaining state capture and state capture modes: the cases of Russia and Ukraine,' Department of International Relations and European Studies, Central European University, Budapest.

Pasquali, A. (2005) 'The South and the imbalance in communication,' *Global Media and Communication*, 1(3): 289–300.

Pesic, V. (2007) 'State capture and widespread corruption in Serbia,' *CEPS Working Documents*, Number 262 http://papers.ssrn.com/sol3/papers.cfm?abstract_id=1338021 (accessed March 2014).

Poblete, J. (2006) 'Culture, neo-liberalism and citizen communication: the case of Radio Tierra in Chile,' *Global Media and Communication*, 2(3): 315–334.

Power, T. and Jamison, G. D. (2005) 'Political mistrust in Latin America,' *Comparative Sociology*, 4(1–2): 55–80.

Protzel, J. (2005) 'Changing political cultures and media under globalism in Latin America,' pp. 101–120 in R. A. Hackett and Y. Zhao (eds) *Democratizing Global Media: One World, Many Struggles* (Oxford: Rowman & Littlefield).

Raboy, M. (ed.) (1996) *Public Broadcasting for the 21st Century* (Luton: University of Luton Press).

Reyes-Matta, F. (1979) 'El concepto latinoamericano de las noticias,' *Cuadernos de Comunicación*, 54: 24–31.

Sánchez-Ruiz, E. (2001) 'Globalization, cultural industries and free trade: the Mexican Audiovisual sector in the NAFTA age,' pp. 86–119 in V. Mosco and D. Schiller (eds) *Continental Order? Integrating North America for Cybercapitalism* (Oxford: Rowman and Littlefield).

Santos-Calderón, E. (1989) 'El periodismo en Colombia. 1886–1986,' *Nueva Historia de Colombia* (Bogota: Planeta Colombiana Editorial S.A., Vol.VI).

Schiller, H. I. (1976) *Communication and Cultural Domination* (New York: International Art and Sciences Press).

Schudson, M. (2005) 'The US model of journalism: exception or exemplar?,' pp. 94–106 in H. De Burgh (ed.) *Making Journalists: Diverse Models, Global Issues* (London: Routledge).

Schudson, M. and Anderson, C. (2008) 'Objectivity, professionalism, and truth seeking in journalism,' pp. 88–101 in K. Wahl-Jörgensen and T. Hanitzsch (eds) *The Handbook of Journalism Studies* (London: Routledge).

Siebert, F., Peterson, T. and Schramm, W. (1956) *Four Theories of the Press* (Urbana: University of Illinois Press).

Sinclair, J. (1996) 'Mexico, Brazil and the Latin World,' pp. 33–66 in J. Sinclair, E. Jacka and S. Cunningham (eds) *New Patterns in Global Television: Peripheral Vision* (Oxford: Oxford University Press).

Sinclair, J. (1999) *Latin American Television: A Global View* (New York: Oxford University Press).

Sinclair, J. (2000) *Televisión: comunicación global y regionalización* (Barcelona: Gedisa).

Sinclair, J. (2002) 'Mexico and Brazil: the aging dynasties,' pp. 123–136 in E. Fox and S. Waisbord (eds) *Latin politics, global media* (Austin: University of Texas Press).

Street, J. (2011) *Mass Media, Politics and Democracy* (London: Palgrave Macmillan).

Strickon, A. and Greenfield, S. (eds) (1972) *Structure and Process in Latin America: Patronage, Clientage and Power Systems* (Albuquerque: University of New Mexico Press).

Thussu, D. K. (2007) *News as Entertainment. The Rise of Global Infotainment* (Thousand Oaks, CA: Sage).

Tironi, E. and Sunkel, G. (2000) 'The modernization of communication: the media in the transition democracy in Chile,' pp. 165–194 in R. Gunther and A. Mughan (eds) *Democracy and the Media: A Comparative Perspective* (Cambridge: Cambridge University Press).

Ungar, S. (1990) 'The role of a free press in strengthening democracy,' pp. 368–398 in J. Lichtenberg (ed.) *Democracy and the Mass Media* (Cambridge: Cambridge University Press).

Waisbord, S. (2000) *Watchdog Journalism in South America: News, Accountability, and Democracy* (New York: Columbia University Press).

Waisbord, S. (2007) 'Democratic journalism and statelessness,' *Political Communication*, 24(2): 115–119.

World Bank (2000) 'Measuring governance, corruption and state capture: how firms and Bureaucrats shape the business environment in transition economies,' *Working Paper* 2312, WB Institute.

Zhuravskaya, E. (2000) 'Incentives to provide public goods: Fiscal federalism, Russian style,' *Journal of Public Economics*, 76(3): 337–368.

1
Latin America Media and the Limitations of the Media 'Globalization' Paradigm

Silvio Waisbord

Latin America and media globalization

The study of media globalization has often tripped over muddled definitions. As an analytical concept, media globalization has proven to be frustratingly flexible and porous. Although it is one of the fundamental ideas of the current age, it remains too ambiguous (Caselli, 2012). The mini-industry of research produced in the past decades has not settled these matters. More than a clear set of questions and theories, media globalization is an appealing buzzword to be praised or criticized that is the inevitable backdrop for all media-related processes in contemporary societies; the *über*-trend that defines our times. Globalization is used to refer to different developments such as the interconnectivity among media platforms, the planetary expansion of media corporations, the international spread of commercialism and consumerism, the communication infrastructure that nurtures and facilitates cosmopolitanism and global solidarity, the cross-border traffic of content, and so on. Applied to media policy making, globalization refers to 'a shift from the nation state to the global' (Mansell and Raboy, 2011: 4; also see Iosifidis, 2011).

Before media globalization became a central matter of analysis in media studies in the West, it was already a key issue in Latin American communication scholarship. No matter how globalization is understood – either as a process by which media policies, economies, institutions, and actors are increasingly connected across borders, or as another name for 'neoliberalism' – it has been a constant scholarly preoccupation in the region. Understanding media systems, policies, and content within the context of globalization has been a singular characteristic in the way communication studies in the region approached the media. In fact, the genealogy of the field is grounded in the conviction that virtually any question about the media needs to consider the context of international flows of media capital, production, content, and reception (Fox and Waisbord, 2002).

This past is why Latin American scholars justifiably reacted with a shrug when globalization became a central preoccupation for media scholarship elsewhere. No doubt, the privatization policies in the United States and Europe, the formation of regional blocs, the end of the Cold War in the 1980s, and the consolidation of a global digital network has profoundly refashioned and deepened media globalization. Yet as a phenomenon that challenges information sovereignty and state autonomy, globalization was already at the center of the research agenda in Latin America.

This focus was the result of the theoretical premises that characterized the field and the empirical realities of media systems from Mexico to Uruguay. The notion that globalization is central to the analysis of the media is found in the critique of media dependency and imperialism that laid out the foundations of communication studies in the 1960s and 1970s. They shaped the conceptual frameworks and research agenda of media studies. Indeed, some scholars of the region trailblazed the tradition of media dependency and imperialism writings that reflected both the political and academic realities of the time (McAnany, 2012).

The focus on globalization was also the result of the historical evolution of the region's media. The development of Latin American media cannot be analyzed without addressing the multiple dimensions of globalization – the flows of capital and content, the linkages between internal and external actors, the connection between media industries and political and social forces, and the relations between national and global political actors. These processes confirmed that *fin-de-siècle* globalization was, in fact, the prolongation of historical processes rather than a completely new development. Indeed, the evolution of the media was inseparable from earlier globalizing dynamics – colonialism, U.S. influence in the region, and the influence of European models of journalism.

Globalization was a defining characteristic of the Latin American media before market policies transformed the media landscape in the West and elsewhere during the 1980s and 1990s. The media in the region has historically been open to international flows. Media systems have historically developed according to the basic tenets of market-led globalization: privatization, commercialization, and deregulation (Fox and Waisbord, 2002). Consequently, they were never autonomous media systems sheltered from global trends, but instead, they have been historically located at the crossroads of international flows of capital, migration, technology, and ideas.

Latin America's newspaper industry developed in close contact with trends in US and European newsrooms. Journalistic practice also evolved in close contact with the trends and debates on both sides of the North Atlantic. Likewise, the development of the radio, music, and film industries were inseparable from global developments, particularly the influence of the United States. One cannot understand the historical evolution and central features of any media industry without foregrounding how they were connected to global developments. Before Immanuel Wallerstein's (1976) notion of a 'world system' became an influential concept to comprehend historical development, Latin American researchers had already insisted that the media in the region can only be properly analyzed within the historical development of global power dynamics.

This form of analysis shows that if globalization is narrowly understood as another name for 'Americanization,' then Latin America has long been Americanized. It was the first, prime market for the expansion of US capital, technology, and content. Foundational texts in the 'media imperialism' tradition viewed Latin America as the perfect illustration of a Hollywood-dominated global media order (Beltran, 1976). The region's media history during the 'American century' is incomprehensible aside from the extensive presence of US interests. It came as no surprise, then, that the work of emblematic scholars of the critical political economy tradition such as Herb Schiller (1969) and Noam Chomsky found a receptive audience in the region. Their views dovetailed with positions that dominated communication and media scholarship and infused the revolutionary euphoria of the time.

Whereas the orthodoxy of globalization theories, including Marxist theories of media dependency and imperialism, assumed the invincible power of American culture and global capital, some strands of Latin American scholarship remained skeptical about such an argument. The latter argued that the media and other forms of globalization have always underpinned the media cultures in the region. They found those positions simplistic and wrongheaded to understand the long-standing dynamics between indigenous and global forces. Despite commercialism and the inevitable presence of global forces, the media as a whole never became a solid, homogeneous cultural cloth that replicated the U.S.

order. Instead, it suggested, media industries managed to reflect, albeit incompletely, the richness of cultural expressions and contributed to the combination of local and global forces that defined the syncretism of the media and cultural landscapes in the region.

The work of Nestor García-Canclini (2005) and Jesus Martín Barbero (1993) represent this tradition that largely reacted against the structural-functionalism and economicism of media dependency. García-Canclini pioneered the notion that 'hybridization' is the essential feature of contemporary cultures in late capitalism. Hybrid cultures were the outcomes of the particular ways in which Latin America became modern and interacted with Western modernity. The forces of multiculturalism, colonialism, and conflict shaped media cultures. Martín-Barbero (1993) shone a light on another blindspot of the idea of 'globalization as homogenization': the failure to consider the 'mediations,' that is, the sense-making processes that incorporate and consume media content in multiple and unexpected ways. His concern was with the process of cultural production that assimilated media forms and meanings. Both authors set the foundations for an ambitious research agenda interested in understanding the various ways in which global and local cultures interact in the media's reception and production.

It is not exaggerated to state that the works of García-Canclini and Martín-Barbero single-handedly shifted the paradigm of Latin American media and communication scholarship. They steered it away from the view of globalization as simply flows of capital, technology, and content and moved it closer to a historical-culturalist perspective interested in understanding cultural innovation and collective creativity amidst an interconnected world. Their work relocated globalization within the emergent tradition of cultural studies in the region that combined the nuanced study of the political economy of the media with processes of reception/recreation and notions of citizenship and rights. They warned about understanding globalization simply as a *deux ex machina* process, disconnected from local processes of cultural (re)formation and the media's production and use.

One significant insight coming out of this argument is that globalization tells only part of the story about the media in Latin America. Media policies and content do not merely reflect global trends. International economics and geo-politics should be considered, but they offer partial snapshots of the configuration and dynamics of media systems. From conditions for broadcasting production to the characteristics of journalistic cultures, several issues fall through the analytical cracks of globalization theories (Fox and Waisbord, 2002). Consequently, the question needs to be inverted – rather than asking what globalization does to media and cultures, what needs to be interrogated is how local media and cultural processes engage with globalization. Rather than asking about the impact of media globalization, it is necessary to studying media systems and cultures *within* globalization.

In line with this position, my interest in this chapter is to review recent research on Latin American media that disputes key arguments of the media globalization paradigm. My intention is to question the primacy of the global over the local and the national, and demonstrate the need to foreground domestic politics in the study of media policy. Specifically, I review ongoing policy reforms and debates in the region that reflect the centrality of domestic politics and the state.

Is 'methodological nationalism' irrelevant?

The adherents of the media globalization paradigm subscribe to Ulrich Beck's (2005) indictment of 'methodological nationalism.' Beck asserts that the latter erroneously assumes that the arbitrary boundaries of nation-states remain analytically significant in a time of global challenges. As unit of analysis, the nation-state narrows the perspective by imposing artificial geo-cultural and political limits and ignoring global processes that affect planetary civilization. The critical, transforming processes and challenges of our age exceed the analytical boundaries and capacity of nation-states. Furthermore, methodological nationalism uncritically assumes the existence of the hyphenated entity known as the nation-state. This assumption leads to focusing on its presumed unity where, if nonexistent, it is exceedingly complex in ways that challenge the notion of a single hyphenated entity. It misdirects our attention by elevating arbitrary political boundaries into real categories and ignoring planetary issues and actors. It incorrectly assumes that the nation-state is the dominant site of power while downplaying the power of global actors and the centrality of planetary processes. The fundamental mistake of methodological nationalism is that it remains moored in a conception that loses sight of the fact that the global has displaced the nation-state as the prime site of academic inquiry.

Beck's provocation is not only aligned with the conviction about the distinctive nature of global problems that exceed state power. It also endorses academic cosmopolitanism, the notion that scholarly pursuits should engage with the global phenomenon of our times and need to be wary about the parochialism of state-centered studies and the resurgence of nationalism. It feeds on aspirations to nurture a global public sphere where planetary problems can be discussed and acted upon. It rejects the modernist vision of nations and states as both benign actors and all-powerful containers of social, political, and cultural experiences. Applied to media studies, Beck's argument underpins the approaches that believe that global mediated processes should be the central unit of analysis. The multiple dimensions of media globalization such as industries, technologies, and use have turned the nation-state into analytically limiting and hopelessly passé. For example, today's global media policy refers to the planetary ambitions of industrial corporations; the ascendancy of Internet powerhouses such as Google, Twitter, and Facebook; new challenges for copyright and fair use; and unfettered access to digital content. The consolidation of global networks has catalyzed novel forms of transnational media activism. Global networks have also changed the conditions and routines of media work, making interconnectivity central to the way content is produced, distributed, and marketed. None of these issues can be properly understood as long as the nation-state remains the subject of attention. Because it is no longer the main container of mediated processes and experiences, scholarly attention needs to zoom out and take a global perspective.

The point is not whether these developments are relevant that doubtlessly they are or demand a different analytical perspective that they do. Rather, the issue is whether attention to the global should displace the focus on the nation-state, which, admittedly, is a complex and equivocal concept. The fact that certain media developments demand a post-state, post-national approach does not exclude the relevance of states and nations as subjects of study or containers of media experiences. The study of regulation on Internet content, the relations between governments and digital behemoths, and global citizenship anchored in digital platforms certainly requires a different analytical approach. Yet, one can study global media phenomena without discarding or minimizing the nation-states as a unit of analysis. The reason is rather obvious: they remain preeminent sites of action and debate over media matters, as countless non-global studies continue to show.

Eager to call attention to the particular analytical challenges posed by global problems, the critique of methodological nationalism sets up a false choice about the relevant units of analysis. This critique rushes to conclude that important questions irrevocably escape the nation-state, dismissing it as an analytical cadaver of the social sciences and humanities. It tidily separates what belongs to the global from the national and the state as if these dimensions and actors are completely disconnected.

It dissolves nations and states because it identifies huge problems that they are incapable of addressing. So, just as Beck believes that global risks such as nuclear arms and environmental challenges demand a trans-state, transnational perspective, media globalists are convinced that global media, networks, activism, citizens, and technologies surpass the conventional analytical boundaries of nations and states.

This position paints itself into a corner by positing the global as the master explanation and the analytical prism to analyze the media. One can scarcely doubt that global dimensions are critical to understanding the media in relation to a host of questions – policy, activism, politics, practice, identity, and social experience. But the twin argument about the global as the dominant unit of analysis and the irrelevance of the nation-state is, if not strategically unwise, completely wrong. It assumes ex ante that everything is connected to seemingly unstoppable, ubiquitous global forces.

What if globalization explains little about the vast world of media policy making? Are media cosmopolitans the only mobilized actors around policy reform? Are national media policies necessarily a reflection of global forces? Is media activism only or mainly transnational? Is media work strongly influenced by global forces and trends?

The debate between methodological nationalism and globalism can be summarized in the following question: What approach best explains the fundamental characteristics and development of contemporary media systems in Latin America? The answer proposed here is as follows: Methodological globalism actually explains little about the central features at the national or regional levels, from patterns of ownership and funding to the relations between media and organized politics. Instead, it is necessary to address domestic politics and the role of the state to capture the defining elements of media ecologies in the region.

To discuss the limitations of the media globalization paradigm, I review three themes in contemporary Latin America scholarship: the role of the state in media policies, media activism/reform, and media work.

The return or the persistence of the state?

The past decade has been a laboratory of media reforms throughout Latin America. Debates and legislation have dealt with a range of issues, such as freedom of information legislation, content and speech regulation, media ownership rules, the legal status of community media, and the management of public funding and advertising. These developments need to be understood by considering the state and traditional aspects of policy making – stakeholders, coalitions, influence, and results. State institutions, namely the presidency, congress, and the judiciary, have played critical roles in policy making: introducing bills, leading legislative debates, holding public audiences, bringing lawsuits, issuing decisions, enacting policies, and so on. Changes in government have affected policy agendas by steering debates and legislation in different directions. Of all of the recent examples of media policy changes, the case of populism nicely represents the persistent importance of the state and domestic politics.

Undoubtedly, the return of populism in several countries (Argentina, Bolivia, Ecuador, Nicaragua, and Venezuela) during the past decade has been one of the most significant political developments in the Latin America. A complex and ambiguous concept, Latin American populism refers to political movements that traditionally drew support largely from the working class and the poor, a leadership style characterized by charisma and personalism, economic statism and distributionism, and rhetorical appeals to the people against its enemies (e.g., the oligarchy, imperialism, and anti-patriotic forces). The coming to power of populism significantly changed the political landscape in specific countries and regionally too. It brought distinctive economic and social policies, political dynamics, and public debates and drove the formation of regional alliances built against the neoconservative order identified with market-driven globalization.

Just as it aims to cause a rupture in the fundamental social, economic, and political structures, as envisioned by Ernesto Laclau (2005) in his influential work, populism is similarly inclined to spearhead important changes in media systems. Populism's distinctive characteristic is its intention to reform media systems by strengthening the role of the state, particularly the prowess of the executive (Waisbord, 2011, 2013). Governments have frequently clashed with dominant media companies identified with conservative economic and political interests. Presidents have regularly criticized leading media companies for representing unpopular interests and conspiring to overthrow them.

Under the justification that they need to battle media enemies, governments have strengthened media apparatuses under the control of the executive. They have done so through several strategies: pouring resources into state-owned media, rewarding sympathetic private owners with government advertising and contracts, and expropriating media companies (as happened in Venezuela and Ecuador in the past). They also tried to muzzle press criticism by passing 'gag' laws and, with the help of judges, imposing hefty fines on libelous content.

Also, populism has supported the legalization of community media that have historically existed in legal limbo and survived on shoestring budgets. In Argentina, the Fernandez de Kirchner administration successfully pushed for the 2009 broadcasting law that assigns a third of broadcasting frequencies to 'social' (noncommercial, nongovernment) licenses. The Chávez government has provided funding for dozens of community media in Venezuela, and it has also supported a network of radio stations sympathetic to President Evo Morales in Bolivia. However, whether these stations effectively function as community voices or extensions of government designs is debatable, and it is unquestionable that official initiatives bolstered the status of those stations.

Expectedly, populist media policies have generated a great deal of controversy. Whereas they have garnered the support of selected community media, unions, and intellectuals, they have been vigorously opposed by traditional media trade associations, professional organizations, and freedom of expression groups. The debate cannot be succinctly summarized because it is a task that falls outside the goals of this chapter. In line with increased polarization, assessments about the impact of those policies widely vary. Supporters believe that they have effectively curbed the power of media corporations and strengthened popular voices; instead, critics believe that they have ultimately benefited governments, particularly their interest in keeping the media on a short leash and buttressing their own communication prowess.

Populism has not tried to curb international flows of capital and content like their predecessors did in the region in the late 1960s and early 1970s. Instead, recent policies represent the return of a statist conception of media system according to which the executive should play a critical role in media ownership, funding, and production. Certainly, the state never went away even when governments favored privatization, liberalization, and deregulation in the 1990s. The main difference is that populism has beefed up the state's presence in the media and aggressively set out to reconfigure the private sector by aiming to limit the power of oppositional media.

More than a counter-tendency to globalization, populism represents the return of the conception of a powerful presidency as the embodiment of the state, particularly on media matters. The presidency uses state levers to reshape media systems in its own image. If populism is symptomatic of a political crisis that opens new opportunities for citizens' mobilization and the reformulation of the political order, as Laclau (2005) writes, then it is not obvious that media globalization is at the center of that crisis. Populism and its media policies reflect the perpetual crisis of political systems beset by weak democratic institutions (Congress, political parties, and media laws) and prone to charismatic, personalistic leaderships. Populism has successfully ridden an unprecedented economic bonanza in Latin America driven by strong global demand for agricultural products, sources of energy, and minerals. Populism's electoral success and social policies financed by revenues from oil, gas, soybean, and other exports are inseparable from global economics.

Aside from the experience of populism, recent policy-making changes in other countries also suggests the persistent importance of the state and domestic politics. In Uruguay, landmark legislation on community media and public advertising was passed in the past under the government of the Frente Amplio, a center-left coalition with a congressional majority. At the time of this writing, the congress is discussing an ambitious bill aimed at reforming key aspects of the country's media including setting up an autonomous regulatory body, limits on media ownerships, and regulation of child content. Likewise, various congressional bills that deal with media ownership and content are currently considered in Brazil, Chile, Honduras, and Mexico.

The vibrancy of media policy reforms in the region confirms the persistent importance of the state and domestic politics (Morris and Waisbord, 2001; Sparks, 2007). The forementioned cases can hardly be understood in terms of the ascendancy of transnational forms of policy making or the consolidation of global policy actors superseding the state. These experiences need to be analyzed by examining the traditional stuff of media policy making: national politics, actors, and institutions. Globalization does not explain why and how administrations effectively transform important aspects of media legislation or why current media systems in countries, particularly those governed by populism, are different than a decade ago. Paradoxically, as globalists are busy dismissing the state into the dustbin of history, Latin America has experienced a wave of policy activism centered on the state. The state remains the central arena to discuss and implement changes, the target of a wide range of demands for reform, and the actor with unmatched power to spearhead transformations.

These developments should not be interpreted as the resurgence of the state after its apparent moribund condition a decade ago in the hands of neoliberalism. Instead, they need to reflect the persistent power of the state to affect key aspects of media systems. Government officials – administrations, legislators, and judges – have always retained significant ability to make decisions that affect media actors (companies, workers, advertisers, and audiences), content, and consumption.

More than the sudden resuscitation of the state, what has been different is the coming to power of administrations headed by populist and center-left coalitions that decided to use various state mechanisms to drive changes. Assessing whether these are positive or negative changes for media democracy goes beyond this article (see Waisbord, 2013). What is important is to understand policy reforms in the context of ongoing political shifts. Producing fine-grained analysis about who and what drives reforms as well as the political labyrinth of media policy making is necessary to unpack 'how states work' and move beyond what at this point are sterile assertions about the analytical significance of the state.

The localism of media movements

It is also important to revisit the focus of the media globalization paradigm on cosmopolitan policy activism. Global activists and organizations have been hailed for ushering new forms of political engagement and supporting transnational media policies. No doubt, the consolidation of the global public sphere of policy networks and institutions merits close attention. It signals novel forms of participation and influence beyond the traditional state-bounded frameworks. Its significance, however, does not weaken the persistent importance of local and national mobilized publics in policy making. Although they maintain various linkages with regional and global movements, they are essentially interested in affecting media policies across municipalities and countries. Therefore, it is unwise to discard methodological nationalism because it is still necessary to analyze the causes, organization, objectives, and impact of media movements (Waisbord, 2010).

Latin America offers plenty of examples in support of this view. Civic participation played critical roles during the policy debates and legislative processes previously discussed. They promoted public debates, conducted advocacy with legislators, drafted congressional bills and technical reports, and gave public testimonies. It is hard to imagine that any of these legislative reforms would have happened without civic participation, particularly given the limited interest in media reform among political parties.

Consider, for example, the significant legislative advances in community broadcasting in the region. Community media has a tradition that goes back over half a century. The number of community media, particularly radio stations, mushroomed in the past decades due to two main causes: lower technological costs and myriad forms of social activism. This phenomenon shows the continual significance of local media amidst globalization (Coyer, 2011). However, legislation never caught up with this reality, and it continued to ignore the presence of hundreds of stations. Because they existed in a legal limbo, community media has been frequent targets of political persecution. The situation has changed in important ways in the past decade (Asociación Mundial de Radios Comunitarias, 2009; Hintz, 2011). Community media is now recognized by law in various countries, including Argentina, Chile, Colombia, Mexico, Paraguay, and Uruguay (Klinger, 2011). Expectedly, legislation did not suddenly change day-to-day operations for most stations, as they continue to face chronic funding shortages. Yet recent transformations have driven important changes in the community media movement. It is hardly a unified political actor, as it was during much of its history, that is opposed to the state and the private sector. Although the movement has been ideologically and institutionally eclectic, it brought together stations identified with myriad causes – from catholic to leftist ideas, from neighborhood to university media. Yet it rallied behind the common goal of achieving legal status. Recent developments, however, show fissures largely based on the positions of various actors vis-à-vis governments. In Argentina and Bolivia, for example, community stations took different positions about legislative and funding decisions made, respectively, by the Fernandez de Kirchner and Morales administrations (Aguirre-Alvis, 2012).

What is important to underscore for the purpose of this chapter is the central role of domestic politics and actors in recent legal changes. Without exceptions, indigenous organizations and local chapters of the World Association of Community Radio led the process by building policy coalitions and advocating with legislators.

Similar citizen mobilization took place regarding legislation allowing public access to government records in over a dozen of countries. Whereas less than a handful of countries had such legislation over a decade ago, 19 countries in the hemisphere have national laws (in addition to dozens of states and municipalities). Although plenty of challenges persist for the effective implementation of the law, the existence of legislation represents a landmark development. A similar pattern in the process of policy making has been observed across countries. Typically, initial demands were raised by civic coalitions integrated by nongovernment organizations, professional associations (lawyers, journalists), academics, and news companies who basically led the process to its conclusion. Examples include Mas Información, Mas Derechos in Colombia, C Libre in Honduras, and Grupo Oaxaca in Mexico. Among other activities, these coalitions held information sessions, produced position papers, advocated with legislators, and contributed to the drafting of bills (Mendel, 2009). Global organizations such as International Transparency, foundations, and aid agencies provided critical support by funding activities and acting as conveners of meetings and policy debates.

Similar developments have taken place regarding initiatives to promote ambitious reforms in broadcasting legislation. Whereas in some cases these initiatives are still ongoing in some countries at the time of this writing such as Honduras, Mexico, and Uruguay, they culminated with the passing of new laws in Argentina and Ecuador. The Argentine case was particularly innovative given that the bill introduced to congress by the Kirchner administration was drafted after a participatory process led by the Coalición para una Radiodifusión Democrática. The Coalición brought together more than 300 civic associations, including professional, media, and neighborhood organizations (Busso and Jaimes, 2011; Córdoba, 2011).

A common theme across these three examples is that the local actors, namely governments and civic coalitions, lead the policy transformations while the global agencies and organizations play a supporting role. Although media movements have been linked to regional and global initiatives, they have been essentially grounded in domestic politics. The particular features of domestic politics explain the different states of various policy issues – the evolution of policy questions; the existence (or absence) of mobilization, debates, and legislation around specific media issues; and the application of laws. These issues are important to understand, for example, because the question of why some countries have national legislation on public access to information, community media, and specific content regulations, but others do not.

This issue deserves an in-depth, comparative treatment to understand specific circumstances that lead or discourage policy changes in support of media pluralism and accountability. It is important to underscore that the available country studies foreground the importance of domestic politics, rather than global forces, to explain the evolution of specific policies. Domestic politics includes the agenda of governments, the strength of civic coalitions, political opportunities, the balance of congressional forces and the relations between media movements with political parties, media companies and other stakeholders. Different outcomes across the region reflect the persistent significance of local mobilization and politics in policy making. Civic coalitions are able to promote media reforms in some countries because domestic politics offers suitable conditions: the parties in the government favor specific laws, astute advocacy strategies, broad agreements among mobilized constituencies (from legislators to unions); and divided positions among media companies vis-à-vis proposed reforms.

All media work is local?

Another idea that needs to be critically revisited is the idea that the global media policy increasingly shapes the basic conditions for media work. This is based on the process of policy harmonization and convergence in recent years linked to the consolidation of global forms of policy making and participation. New forms of global governance, we are told, provide a new framework that sets up transnational conditions that affect media workers worldwide regarding issues such as access to information and communication technologies, intellectual property, Internet freedom, and content regulation. The government leadership and the participation of global civil society in forums such as the World Summit on the Information Society have produced important advances towards the definition and implementation of the global legal framework.

The focus on the question of global governance is, certainly, warranted given a great deal of activism and developments that have reshaped old conceptions of media policy. The unbridled enthusiasm about these issues, however, ignores the fact that the media work fundamentally remains grounded in local conditions and policies. Global governance does not have an immediate impact on everyday media work.

The recent debates in Latin America regarding the press and journalism, specifically content regulation, censorship, and reporters' safety, patently demonstrate the persistent importance of domestic legal frameworks on the media's performance. An example is the annual reports of the Rapporteur for Freedom of Expression of the Inter-American Commission on Human Rights Organization of American States (2013). These detailed reports not only painstakingly document the continuous heavy burden of libel laws and the verbal and physical violence to journalists. They also implicitly show the relatively limited impact of global governance in successfully addressing chronic problems that limit the freedom of expression as a central principle of journalistic practice.

Verbal intimidation and physical violence have long been features in the region, particularly in countries and regions with long-standing problems of statelessness and the strong presence of parastatal forces. Despite modest advances in terms of investigations and trials, impunity remains high. Needless to say, there are better mechanisms for monitoring reporting attacks that are in place thanks to the work of local and regional organizations. Although their work makes it possible to assess the situation and produce denunciations, it is insufficient to redress the long-standing problems related to the quality of governance.

The main challenge remains producing sustainable reforms to curb attacks and strengthen the ability of states to investigate and hold perpetrators accountable. States are directly responsible either when officials perpetrate physical attacks or launch verbal criticisms of reporters, or when they are unable to prevent attacks and provide justice. In these situations, global governance is too remote to address deep-seated problems of weak rule of law, to tame the intentions of government officials to ride roughshod over the press, or to provide safety to reporters who put their lives on the line. Local lawlessness results from the power of violent actors and the complicity or inaction of public officials. Global frameworks for the freedom of expression and mobilization are toothless in areas with rampant violence.

Another critical problem is the persistence of laws that criminalize expression (such as contempt legislation) and establish hefty liabilities for reporters and publishers found guilty of offending public officials. In many countries, criminal codes on freedom of expression are not adjusted to regional standards, thereby giving officials the upper hand vis-à-vis journalists. The consequences are predictable, namely, chilling effects on reporting and self-censorship in newsrooms (García de Madariaga and Solís-Domínguez, 2006). Here the problem is, again, that states retain considerable autonomy to dictate and enforce laws that affect journalistic work even if they contravene international frameworks. Governments not only have disregarded demands by local and transnational organizations to derogate gag laws, but they have also stepped up efforts to criminalize speech as demonstrated by recent laws in Bolivia, Ecuador, and Venezuela (Montúfar, 2013; Waisbord, 2013).

The point is not to minimize the impact of global legal frameworks on media work, an issue that cannot be assessed in general given that global media governance includes a wide range of issues. Rather, my intention is to call attention to the complex dynamics between local/regional/global dimensions in which states do not ensure adequate conditions for journalistic practice, and headstrong governments maintain significant autonomy to limit speech. Governments' reluctance to follow international legislation on the freedom of expression and ample discretion to enforce laws continues to influence, if not determine, working conditions.

Putting domestic politics into global media studies

Des Freedman (2008: 1) has correctly observed that 'media policy [...] is a deeply political phenomenon.' Recent experiences in Latin America confirm this affirmation and suggest that understanding media policies needs approaches that are sensitive to domestic politics. The vitality of media policy making in the past decade makes it necessary to develop nuanced approaches about the formation and impact of policy coalitions that bring together governments and private and civic actors.

These developments confirm that local politics is essential to understanding current media policies. This conclusion hardly breaks new ground, but it is worth reiterating it in light of the global turn in media studies. Globalization has bolstered a proto-libertarian enthusiasm that fulminates against the state and minimizes old-fashioned domestic politics. It assumes that globalization invariably overshadows local and national politics (for better or worse), and it views the state as a recalcitrant, conservative institution invariably opposed to democratic change or market freedom.

The globalization paradigm is problematic for several reasons. It offers an incomplete, distorted analysis of policy making. It flatly rejects the possibility that state policies contribute to media pluralism. It is too imprecise to capture the significance of the state and domestic politics in policy making. It condemns the state as if it were a single, monolithic unity.

The main limitation is that although states may not be completely autonomous and sovereign as scholars have demonstrated (Volkmer, 2007), they retain substantial capacity to determine policies that regulate media systems within a certain political-geographical space. Media policies may further strengthen the hand of powerful actors or introduce reforms towards improving conditions for democratic speech.

Latin American cases illustrate the limitations of the global turn in media studies. Indeed, fundamentals policies regarding issues such as ownership, funding, and regulation can be grasped with minimal references to global trends or actors. The recent reforms suggest that not all contemporary policy debates and transformations are neatly inscribed in the logic of global developments. The levels of state autonomy cannot be explained by visions of global logics at work that weaken and ultimately render states ineffective. The conclusions that are applicable to media policy making in the European Union do not necessarily apply to Latin America where similarly ambitious regional initiatives are missing. Also, what may be valid in some areas of global policy making, such as audiovisual trade, copyright, or Internet neutrality, do not necessarily translate to other issues, such as media ownership, funding, and media practice. Global governance neither displaces states and domestic politics nor does it bring immediate, tangible changes to the organization and the functioning of media systems.

What are needed are approaches that are sensitive to the interaction between global and local power dynamics, institutions, and actors (see Price, Verhulst and Morgan, 2013). These questions redirect our attention to questions about the autonomy of state politics and the nature of collective action in a globalized world. These issues remain important for examining the power of transnational actors and globally connected citizens in media policies. Nuanced perspectives that are sensitive to local and national politics are needed to reassess assertions, fill analytical gaps, and revisit the global turn in media studies. Rediscovering the importance of local politics in global media studies is overdue. The stuff that makes the politics of policy making, issue identification, participation, proposed solutions, and mobilized resources (see Braman, 2004), remains solidly grounded in domestic dynamics and calculations.

Latin American scholarship needs to address theoretical questions in media policy and avoid narrow descriptive analysis. The studies about the region should not only aim to be relevant to fellow Latin Americanists interested in empirical developments in the hemisphere. They should also engage with critical contemporary debates in media policy research (see Puppis and Just, 2012). The recent experiences in the region offer a treasure trove of cases to probe, challenge, and/or refine conventional theories and arguments in the field of media policy making.

Just to suggest a few questions for further examination: Are we moving away from the historically dominant pattern of state capture by powerful elites towards a pluralist model in policy making? Have media movements transitioned from a model of opposition and resistance to states and corporations to policy advocacy and dialogue? Do examples of civic participation represent the affirmation of democratic, multi-stakeholder forms of policy making? What do recent policy reforms suggest about the distribution of power and resources? How does the growing Internet penetration and patterns of usage help us rethink traditional arguments about media pluralism? Under what conditions can truly independent regulatory agencies exist in ways that they support a range of public interests? What virtuous policies strengthen public broadcasting systems in the region? Does Latin America offer examples of success policies that curb media concentration? What political conditions make those policies possible?

The current dynamic policy scenario in the region offers plenty of cases to address these questions and parse out their empirical and theoretical implications. Just as the region produced groundbreaking studies forty years ago, it is poised to produce a new wave of important research about the linkages between politics and media and information policy.

References

Aguirre-Alvis, J. L. (2012) 'Estado y oportunidades para una normatividad de medios de comunicación más inclusiva en Bolivia,' *Punto Cero*. Available at: http://bit.ly/1cEDGPC (accessed June 2013).

Asociación Mundial de Radios Comunitarias (2009) *Las mordazas invisibles: Nuevas y viejas barreras a la diversidad en la radiodifusión*. Buenos Aires: AMARC.

Beck, U. (2005) *Power in the Global Age: A New Global Political Economy* (Malden, MA: Polity).

Beltran, L. R. (1976) 'Alien Premises, Objects, and Methods in Latin American Communication Research,' pp. 15–42 in E. Rogers (ed.) *Communication and Development: Critical Perspectives* (Beverly Hills: Sage).

Braman, S. (2004) 'Where has media policy gone? Defining the field in the twenty-first century,' *Communication Policy and Law*, 9(2): 153–82.

Busso, N. and Jaimes, D. (2011). *La Cocina de la Ley: El proceso de incidencia en la elaboración de la Ley de Servicios de Comunicación Audiovisual en Argentina* (Buenos Aires: Farco).

Caselli, M. (2012) *Trying to Measure Globalization: Experiences, critical issues and perspectives* (New York: Springer).

Córdoba, L. (2011) 'La Coalición por una radiodifusión democrática: regeneración del espacio público y ejercicio de ciudadanía,' *Argumentos. Revista de crítica social*, (13): 133–157.

Coyer, K. (2011) 'Community media in a globalized world: The relevance and resilience of local radio,' pp. 166–179 in R. Mansell and M. Raboy (eds) *The Handbook of Global Media and Communication Policy* (United Kingdom: Wiley).

Fox, E. and Waisbord, S. (eds) (2002) *Latin Politics, Global Media* (Austin: University of Texas Press).

Freedman, D. (2008) *The Politics of Media Policy* (Cambridge: Polity Press).

García-Canclini, N. (2005) *Hybrid Cultures: Strategies for Entering and Leaving Modernity* (Minneapolis: University of Minnesota Press).

García de Madariaga, J. M. and Solís Domínguez, C. (2006) 'La construcción de la realidad desde los medios venezolanos: Censura, autocensura y militancia política de los profesionales de la información,' *Redes.com*, (3): 319–333.

Hintz, A. (2011) 'From media Niche to policy spotlight: Mapping community-media policy change in Latin America,' *Canadian Journal of Communication*, 36(1): 147–59.

Inter-American Commission on Human Rights (2013) *Annual Report of the Office of the Special Rapporteur for Freedom of Expression 2012* (Washington, DC: Organization of American States/Inter-American Commission on Human Rights).

Iosifidis, P. (2011) *Global Media and Communication Policy* (Basingstoke: Palgrave).

Klinger, U. (2011) 'Democratizing media policy: community radios in Mexico and Latin America,' *Journal of Latin American Communication Research*, 1(2): 1–19.

Laclau, E. (2005) *On Populist Reason* (London: Verso).

Mansell, R. and Raboy, M. (2011) 'Introduction: Foundations of the theory and practice of global media and communication policy,' pp. 1–20, in R. Mansell and M. Raboy (eds) *The Handbook of Global Media and Communication Policy* (United Kingdom: Wiley).

Martín-Barbero, Jesús (1993) *Communication, Culture and Hegemony: From media to Mediations* (London: Sage).

McAnany, E. (2012) *Saving the World: A Brief History of Communication for Development and Social Change* (Urbana: University of Illinois Press).

Mendel, T. (2009) *The Right to Information in Latin America: A Comparative Legal Survey* (Paris: UNESCO).

Montúfar, C. (2013) 'La conversión del derecho a la libertad de expresión en servicio público,' *Newsweek* (Ecuador), August 4: 16–17.

Morris, N. and Waisbord, S. (eds) (2001) *Media and Globalization: Why the State Matters* (Lanham: Rowman and Littlefield).

Price, M. E., Verhulst, S. and Morgan, L. (eds) (2013) *Routledge Handbook of Media Law* (New York: Routledge).

Puppis, M. and Just, N. (eds) (2012) *Trends in Communication Policy Research: New Theories, Methods and Subjects* (Chicago: Intellect, The University of Chicago Press).

Schiller, H. (1969) *Mass Communication and American Empire* (Boston: Beacon Press).

Sparks, C. (2007) *Globalization, Development and the Mass Media* (Los Angeles: Sage).

Volkmer, I. (2007) 'Governing the 'spatial reach'? Spheres of influence and challenges to global media policy,' *International Journal Of Communication*, 1(1): 56–73. Available at: http://bit.ly/18YfpD6 (accessed June 2013).

Waisbord, S. (2010) 'The pragmatic politics of media reform: Media movements and coalition-building in Latin America,' *Global Media and Communication*, 6(2): 133–153.

Waisbord, S. (2011) 'Between support and confrontation: Civil society, media reform, and populism in Latin America,' *Communication, Culture, and Critique*, 4(1): 97–117.

Waisbord, S. (2013) *Vox Populista* (Buenos Aires: Gedisa).

Wallerstein, Immanuel (1976) *The Modern World-System: Capitalist Agriculture and the Origins of the European World-Economy in the Sixteenth Century* (New York: Academic Press).

2
The 'Captured Liberal' Model of Media Systems in Latin America

Manuel Alejandro Guerrero

Introduction

In their seminal *Comparing Media Systems* (2004), Dan Hallin and Paolo Mancini put forth three ideal models of media systems predominant in Western democracies: the 'polarized pluralist,' the 'democratic corporatist,' and the 'liberal.' In some respects, Latin American media systems share certain features of the polarized pluralist model, especially regarding clientelism. However, this chapter proposes a series of compared criteria toward the definition of a general model of the actual Latin American media system. The model is anchored in the *Weberian* ideal types and lacks normative aspirations about the roles media must play in Latin American public and political life. The model is called 'captured liberal' due to the predominance of private commercial media organizations and to the conditions that hurdle states' regulatory capacities and that afflict the watchdog role of journalism by economic and political interests. Of course, as is the case with all ideal types, there are varying degrees of similarities among the different countries and the model.

Post-transitory politics and the media systems

Following Hallin and Mancini (2004), this chapter departs from two key assumptions. First, in broad terms, the political system delineates the contours of the media systems. In this sense, for the authors it is possible to define some aspects of the political systems as 'independent variables' given the fact that many of them are 'made up of aspects deeply rooted in social and cultural structures' (2004: 47). Second, in spite of such a relation, there are no direct univocal influences between 'variables' of the political system and those of the media system (Hallin and Mancini,

2004). In this chapter I use the term 'aspect' instead of 'variable' since the latter may imply quantitative notions of correlations. Additionally, as with all theoretical pretenses of generalization, it is possible to find particular cases and situations that may not fit the model. Yet, as examined below, the model helps explain cases of apparent deviation. The following section re-states what I have said elsewhere (Guerrero, 2014): in Latin America, three aspects of the political system have shaped the outlines of the post-transitory media systems.

Post-transitory politics: relations between new ruling elites and traditional media elites

During authoritarian rule, governments use a double standard with the media: chasing after the critical press while forging close relations with the most established media elites whom they favor – and not infrequently so – with protections, subsidies, and contracts (Waisbord, 2000a). However, by the late 1970s, Latin America began to shift away from different forms of authoritarian rule and turned toward more pluralistic regimes (Malloy and Seligson, 1987). By recognizing – at least *de jure* – the existence of fundamental guarantees (freedom of speech, freedom of the press, and so on), the post-authoritarian regimes delegitimized any direct use of violence and open censorship as explicit mechanisms of control. However, the arrival of new political groups in a context of competition, elections, and marketing implied both the creation of close relations, formal and informal, with already well-established media groups and the recognition of their interests at the expense of pluralism. In this way, a renewed arrangement developed in post-transitory Latin America between the new political groups and the established media: politicians needed the media for conveying their message and competing for power whereas traditional media needed politicians to maintain their privileges (Mastrini and Becerra, 2006; Corrales and Sandoval, 2005; Matos, 2012).

Historical clientelism and informality

Some authors have long documented the way in which the shaping of the states in Latin America has – to varying degrees – bred clientelist relations with diverse sectors and social groups (Strickon and Greenfield, 1972). Being a privileged space for negotiation and exchange, clientelism affects the efficacy of the legal frameworks – both normative and regulatory (Eisenstadt and Roniger, 1984). In the case of the media, clientelism brings them directly into the political process both by enabling their owners to forge alliances with certain political groups and by pulling their strings to reduce the consequences of regulations contrary to their interests. For Hallin and Papathanassopoulos (2002), clientelism defines the relationship between the media and the political system in Latin America. Moreover, clientelism ends up reducing the effectiveness and efficacy of the regulation, creating conditions that allow for undue interference of the media groups in politics and that play a part in undermining the development of professional informative practices.

Economic reforms and market deregulation

Upon analyzing media markets' economic liberalization in the Mediterranean countries, Hallin and Mancini (2004) find that across different fields these policies suggest the withdrawal of the state in such a sloppy and abrupt manner that they call the process 'savage deregulation.'[1] Beginning in the late 1980s, Latin America joined a global trend of liberal-ridden market reforms (Gwynne and Kay, 2004). In the case of the media, well-organized corporations with clear-cut interests occupied the spaces left by the state's retreat (Mastrini and Bolaño, 2000). The already prevailing commercial media structures in Latin America – both in the press and in broadcasting – were given a boost by these new liberal reforms, which eventually favored not those market conditions necessary to promote pluralism but a broader expansion of predominant corporate groups. In certain cases, exclusively local conglomerates consolidated, like Globo in Brazil, Televisa and TV Azteca in Mexico, Grupo Clarín in Argentina, Grupo El Comercio in Peru, and Grupo Santo Domingo in Colombia. In other cases, foreign capital allied with local corporations, like in Chile's Megavisión and Colombia's Casa Editorial El Tiempo; and yet in another, foreign capital directly entered to own local corporations, like Albavisión in most of Central America, Peru, Ecuador, Chile, and Bolivia. At the end, stronger corporations emerged from the process, but not more pluralistic and open markets. Thus, in a context that combined new conditions for political power competition, historical trends toward clientelism, and neo-liberal reforms that reduced state's regulatory capacities, the new ruling groups of post-trasitory Latin America ended up exchanging benefits and support with traditional media groups that, far from having changed with the transitions, found better conditions for accumulation and concentration at the expense of pluralism.

The media model in Latin America

This chapter suggests that the three above mentioned political aspects combine to negatively affect two interrelated core fields that shape the media systems across the region: media regulation and the watchdog role of journalism. In general terms, the economic reforms and deregulation of the 1990s dramatically reduced the state's capacity to enforce the law or, worse, left diverse unregulated spaces profited on by strong actors in the markets – including here the large media corporations to increase their benefits. Also, the new ruling elites preferred to find accommodation with traditional media groups rather than reforming the media landscapes for the sake of wider pluralism. And finally, the prevalence of clientelism favored a context where notwithstanding the diminished capacities of the state, the political groups maintained a wide array of resources – from the allocation of public funds and direct benefits, like tax exemptions, to the selective enforcement of the law – to exchange with different social and economic actors, including here not only the media corporations, but also media employees and journalists. These aspects then combine to create conditions for regulatory inefficiency and, partly derived from that, they then contribute to engendering a context where extra-journalistic interests constantly inhibit the watchdog role of the media; a role that from the point of view of democratic politics is crucial for keeping an open and pluralistic society.

Regulatory inefficiency

In Latin America, all countries grant individual freedoms and rights to speech, press, and expression in their constitutions and, in the case of the media, many have even created administrative authorities to regulate broadcasting and telecommunications. However, in spite of complex, and sometimes even comprehensive, legal frameworks, regulatory inefficiency prevails. Media regulatory inefficiency is connected with both the inconsistent application of legal frameworks and the lack of adequate and updated regulations. In most cases, freedoms and rights are actually protected by the legal frameworks, however they do not apply just by decree. The law, regulation, and policy enforcement are discursive practices inserted into specific contexts that are contingent upon local circumstances. The political aspects mentioned above negatively affect mostly four aspects where regulation should be expected to work, since they favour or fail to prevent: market concentration; discretional public spending on advertising, the colonization of media structures by political actors and of political spaces by media corporations, and the capture of regulatory spaces by large media groups.

Trend toward the concentration of media markets

With their arrival to power, the post-transitory ruling elites did not alter the property system in the media, so the traditional groups that grew under authoritarianism not only survived transitions, but also became key actors in the new scenarios. The economic reforms of the 1990s helped the companies consolidate their position. The move gave rise to certain kinds of oligopolies in domestic media markets (Sunkel and Geoffroy, 2001). Major media groups cashed in on both the reduction of the role of the state and on the absence or weakness of antitrust regulation (Fox and Waisbord, 2002). It is estimated that the largest media corporations own the production, storage, commercialization, and distribution processes and units of over 80 percent of the contents that citizens receive. In fact, the dominance of oligopolies in the region rose from an index of 0.77 in 2000 to 0.82 in 2004 (Mastrini and Becerra, 2006).

Even though greater variety of channels and services spread out since the 1990s, the same corporations offered most of them. In most countries, the beneficiaries of liberalization and deregulation were normally the same local elites, most of whom already participated in the media prior to the political transitions.[2] In Chile, for example, deregulation brought about the consolidation and growth of media companies in the printed press that were intimately linked to the dictatorship (El Mercurio and COPESA), to the detriment of oppositional publications linked to the left (such as La Época newspaper or Hoy magazine). As for the Chilean TV market, three channels, Televisión Nacional (TVN), Universidad Católica TV (UC TV), and Megavisión, take over 80 percent of the publicity market (Ruiz-Tagle, 2011). In Brazil, media concentration is one of the weakest aspects of its democracy, as barely eight groups – seven of which are family owned– dominate the TV industry (Lima, 2003). In Guatemala, the Albavisión TV network, owner of Channels 3, 7, 11, and 13, controls the TV market and only three corporations hold the licenses of more than 90 percent of the radio frequencies (Lucas, 2009). In Colombia, though the TV Law of 1995 does contain restrictions on property holding, the Santo Domingo and Ardila Groups control over 70 percent of the different types of media. In Argentina, after the passing of the Reform of State in the early 1990s that modified the so-called Broadcasting Law 22,285 (which dated back from the military dictatorship), the barriers to cross-ownership and control disappeared and the consolidation of the Clarín Media Group began. At this point one must note that President Néstor Kirchner contributed to this growth when he authorized the fusion of the cable networks, Multicanal and Cablevisión, giving Clarín a virtual monopoly in cable TV, in spite of regulations to the contrary (Sirven, 2011). Curiously, his widow and successor, Cristina Fernández de Kirchner has been defying this privileged position of Clarín in the last years with arguments against monopolies and in favor of pluralism (See Chapters 5 and 10). Whatever the good intentions, those arguments have begun to lose credence when the government focuses its actions solely against the Clarín Group and approves the trespassing of channels directly between other less antagonistic private corporations disregarding the law and the percentage of market share. More examples come from Peru, where not only the levels of media concentration appear higher than in Brazil or Argentina (Mastrini and Becerra, 2006), but also according to some researchers, the Ministry of Transportation and Communications in that country has been inclined to side with the larger radio broadcasting groups to the detriment of communitarian radio stations (Rivadeneyra Olcese, 2007). Finally, one of the flagship cases of media concentration in the world is found in Mexico where despite a more fragmented printed press market exists (although not necessarily with oppositional agendas), the broadcasting sector shows worrisome figures of concentration: two TV networks Televisa and TV Azteca control over 90 percent of the market (Guerrero, 2010; Trejo, 2010). Televisa per se is the largest Hispanic media conglomerate in the world with unrivaled predominance in several segments: from cable and satellite television to the publishing market.

Discretional governmental public spending in the media

Perhaps one of the clearest manifestations of the clientelistic exchanges is the discretional use of governmental public spending in Latin America, as underlined by O'Donnell (2007). On the subject, Silvio Waisbord notes that,

> Despite the development of the media under market and commercial designs, the governmental propaganda continues to be a substantial source of revenue, particularly in countries with small economies and reduced advertising markets. Thus, government officials and politicians woo the media as they look for favorable coverage, whereas those media closest to power obtain economic benefits, including major public advertising investment, tax breaks, import permits, and broadcasting licenses. The media, instead of identifying themselves with the parties and serving as their organic speakers, offer only occasional support to the sitting governments and administrations. (2008: 4)

For the most part, the domestic media in Latin America depend, at different levels, on official advertising for their survival. However, one must note that post-transition ruling groups came into power at a time where communication, public relations, and political marketing began to boom in tandem to the fall of the Soviet Union and the so-called 'real socialism.' In this new scenario, the media became key instruments in the search and preservation of power. The funds stemming from governmental propaganda campaigns have been used both to benefit and punish different types of media. According to a comprehensive study, Latin American governments allocate public resources to the media for official advertising mostly at their complete discretion (ADC/Open Society, 2008). In the 1990s, public resources were intensively – and not so transparently – used for campaigning in Peru (Fujimori), Argentina (Menem), Ecuador (Abdalá Bucaram), and Brazil (Collor de Mello). Although the laws in many countries now impose restrictions on advertising spending during electoral campaigns and on public funds with propagandistic aims, widespread practices are still found. In Mexico, besides the lack of regulation in public spending (Trejo, 2010) a growing practice is the insertion of 'infomercials,' propagandistic ads in the format of news items placed just between the cut of a news-broadcast and one of its commercial blocks. In Latin America, most of such funds are allocated to private corporations, preserving the predominance of the commercial media over public or community media.

Colonization of media structures by the political class and of political spaces by the media

The growing importance of the media in vying for power has thus implied the search for approaches and string-pulling with the traditional media class or, even more, the transformation of politicians into media entrepreneurs (Mastrini and Becerra, 2006; Guerrero, 2009; Lima, 2003; Sánchez Ruiz, 1987; Sunkel and Geoffroy, 2001). In Brazil, members of the military have obtained licenses to operate radio stations in several areas of the country (Christofoletti, 2003). Moreover, according to the journalists Bachtold and Freire, 'local stations of the private main TV channels [...] as well as small radios are owned by 61 politicians who were elected during the 2010 elections' (cited in Matos, 2012: 52). In Chile, the current president, Sebastián Piñera, was for a long time the major stockholder of Chilevisión until it was sold to Time Warner in August of 2010. In Colombia, the most representative case is the Santos family, owners of El Tiempo, the country's main newspaper with strong political influence. The former vice president (Francisco

Santos), currently serving as the managing director of the radio broad-caster RCN Radio, and the current president of Colombia, Juan Manuel Santos, illustrate the case. In Mexico, though the relation between politicians and media entrepreneurs has become more complex in the last years, for decades the mainstream media sided undoubtedly with the dominant ruling party, the Revolutionary Institutional Party (PRI). Just as an example, during the presidential electoral process of 1988, Emilio Azcárraga, president of Televisa, declared that as a private firm, the company had the right to present what it considered to be informa-tion, and that regarding politics there should be no doubt: 'We are with the PRI; we are members of the PRI; and we have always been with the PRI. We do not believe in any other formula. And as members of that party we will do everything possible for making our candidate win.'[3] It is difficult to find a clearer political commitment from the media entre-preneurs to a candidate.

Capture of regulatory spaces by large media groups
One consequence of the state's reduced regulatory capacities, of the strengthening and growth of media corporations, and of the prevailing clientelism is both the media's capturing of regulatory spaces and the state's lower efficacy in applying media regulation. This is framed into what Matos (2012) calls a 'culture of promiscuous relationships' between governmental officials and the media. In Argentina and Brazil during the late 1990s, media corporations were able to subdue the state in a way that it could neither regulate nor generate alterna-tive contents (Mastrini and Bolaño, 2000). In Brazil, Costa and Brener (1997) point out the configuration of what they describe as 'electronic colonelism' to define the persistence of clientelistic exchanges. Cited in Matos (2012: 52), Azevedo says, 'Although the current legislation limits to five the number of television channels per group, the national TV stations explore loopholes of the law. They associate themselves with stations owned by others which merely repeat the channels or the national program.' And this same pattern can be seen in Mexico, where the 2006 Media Law, the so-called 'Ley Televisa,' spawned loud criticism owing to its perceived bias in favor of the largest media conglomerates (Guerrero, 2010; Trejo, 2010). As for Colombia, the National Television Commission (NTC) was considered to be 'held hostage by a sector of the corporations,' particularly from the time the third private channel was put out for bidding during President Uribe's administration in 2010 (Bonilla Sebá and González, 2010). Apparently due to its inefficiency, by 2012, the NTC was replaced by a new National TV Authority. However,

it still lacks proper funding and may resort to clientelistic practices (Rey, 2012). But, perhaps one of the clearest cases of blatant capture of both regulatory and political spaces by the media could be exemplified in Central America by the Mexican tycoon Ángel González, owner of Albavisión, who has frequently been pointed out by journalists to induce the tailoring of regulation to suit his personal interests and, in the case of Guatemala, to 'even help appoint presidents' (Reséndiz, 2007, my translation).[4]

Interference in the media's watchdog role

The three political aspects discussed at the beginning of this chapter hinder the development of the media's informative duty, one which is typically defined as the media's watchdog role and that implies the timely supply of information in order to prevent the abuse of power (Marder, 1998). Acknowledging that there is a growing debate about what should be considered as professional journalistic performance (Márquez-Ramírez, 2012), from the perspective of democratic politics, the watchdog role is crucial to check the abuses of power and to provide relevant information for keeping an open and pluralistic society. In most Latin American countries, the watchdog role of journalism lacks the necessary distance from the established powers and the adequate conditions to challenge them. Instead, journalistic performance is constantly 'captured,' as will be discussed below, by the illegitimate and undue influence of corporate and political interests not only in terms of topics, tones, and frames, but also in the most basic issues regarding journalists' freedom of speech and personal security. Such interferences can be assessed in two critical fields: the lack of adequate mechanisms to protect journalistic performance and the difficulties for research and investigative journalism as current practice in the region. In the best of cases, watchdog journalism in Latin America has revealed exposés that have prompted political accountability and fostered a greater debate about corruption and wrongdoing, but this type of journalism has not been either consistent or has resulted from active investigation or quality reporting techniques. Silvio Waisbord (2000) has widely documented how most watchdog journalism has heavily relied on leaks, fragmentary and unverified information, and on the crossfire of mutual denunciations on the part of elite actors. Hence, while selected cases of high-profile watchdog journalism across the region have fueled democratic aims, many have only advanced political agendas and gains for certain actors, yielding political cynicism rather than accountability (Márquez-Ramírez, 2012).

Inadequate mechanisms to protect journalistic performance and practice

Regardless of the political shade of the sitting ruler, critical journalists have for the most part been considered inconvenient figures by the governments in the region, and such a state of affairs has outlived military dictatorships. The law and court rulings have been the tools used by politicians and businessmen to prevent journalists from doing their work free from constraints, especially regarding investigative reporting. In fact, according to the Committee for the Protection of Journalists, in 2010, censorship in Latin America reached one of its highest levels since the regional democratization process took place 30 years ago (CPJ, 2010). In spite of legal and constitutional safeguards in almost every country in Latin America regarding freedom of speech and the press, organizations like Freedom House report setbacks in the region. For instance, between 2002 and 2012, the status of four countries changed from 'free' to 'partly free' (Panama, Bolivia, Chile, and Peru), and three other from 'partly free' to 'not free' (Mexico, Honduras, and Venezuela). The rest remained the same with only Uruguay and Costa Rica enjoying a 'free' press (Freedom House, 2002, 2012).

However, for the most part, the challenges to the freedom of the press do not result from post-transitory elected governments' policies to resume persecutions on critical journalism as happened under authoritarian rule. Instead, they result either from a lack of guarantees for the exercising of journalism, or worse, from the incapacity of public authorities to carry out effective investigation processes in cases of violence against journalists.[5]

Thus, neither such violence nor the lack of guarantees for their professional performance ended with the transitions. In most cases, the sources of the violence just multiplied or shifted: in the past the main perpetrator and threat to press freedom was the state – through the security and administration apparatuses. Now, the sources are fragmented and come from multiple origins ranging from organized crime and paramilitary groups (like in Mexico or Colombia) to corrupt politicians who no longer act – as they once did – in the name of the state, but in the defense of particular interests.[6] Unscrupulous businessmen also profit from the fact that few countries have amended their legislations regarding defamation and slander, which are pre-transitory, that imposes severe penalties on journalists. Chile, Uruguay, and more recently Argentina and Mexico are notable exceptions.

Conditions adverse to the development of research and investigative journalism

For Hallin and Mancini (2004), journalistic professionalization relates to the educational levels of journalists, the 'neutrality' used in reporting notes and information, and to the journalists' degree of autonomy from owners and editors in handling their production process. Important advances regarding the hiring of professionals trained in the areas of journalism, communication, and related disciplines are already common practice in the most modern media organizations in the region. Some examples are Argentina's Grupo Clarín, Brazil's Globo or Folha de Sao Paulo, Colombia's El Tiempo, Mexico's Reforma and El Universal, and Chile's El Mercurio. In this sense, Latin America does not quite differ from what occurs in other modern regions. Yet the higher educational levels of journalists do not necessarily translate into deep coverage and journalistic debate over the most pressing issues. And the reason is usually not a lack of commitment.

At first glance, the front pages of printed media and the news broadcasts in Latin America are overloaded with political issues and debates. It cannot be denied that the media have uncovered scandalous cases of corruption, documented situations of human rights abuse, and even publicized crucial stories on drug trafficking or paramilitary groups, thus jeopardizing the very lives of journalists and reporters. Nor can it be denied that day in and day out, the media produce a broad picture about the ups and downs of local politics. But, what stories are actually covered, and how? In a thorough and fully documented work on watchdog journalism in Latin America, Waisbord discovers that the media's unveiling of corruption cases and other improper conducts responds more to the re-alignments of media groups with specific political groups and to the use of the media by politicians as an arena to settle their power struggles, than to decisions made by the media to create investigative journalism to promote and keep a watch over the public interest (Waisbord, 2000b).

In Mexico, some works suggest that the coverage of corruption responds to a combination of the media's commercial interests and to the closeness of media and political groups rather than to the media's compromise with accountability (Hallin, 2000; Hughes, 2006; Guerrero, 2009). In more extreme cases, Rick Rockwell and Noreene Janus (2003) document how investigative journalism in Central America has been cornered by media structures dominated by oligarchic groups with broad economic and political interests as well as by governments that – although formal democracies – have not hesitated to resort to tactics that oscillate between censorship and the tolerance of violence against critical journalists.

As said before, the pressures to prevent political investigative and research journalism do not only come from politicians. In the region, there is little media coverage of topics dealing with corporate corruption. Once again, Waisbord notes:

> It is hard to imagine a *watchdog journalism* exposing corporate corruption given that many of the big media in countries like Colombia, Ecuador, and the Dominican Republic, belong to a handful of corporate groups with broad interests in key industries (like banking, agribusinesses, tourism, mining, food, and telecommunications). Although it does not exclude watchdog journalism, the absence of media diversity does limit the scope of their potential research topics.
> (2008: 9)

To top it off, as part of an international trend toward competitiveness and larger corporate revenues, bigger budget cuts are dramatically reducing spaces in the media for investigative journalism. This means not only a lower capacity to carry out broad research projects on specific topics and follow up on them, but also a larger dependence on information and statements provided by official and governmental authorities (Márquez-Ramírez, 2012). McChesney (1997) has noted a global trend in this regard where corporate property of the media ends up influencing how topics are chosen and covered.

The 'captured liberal' media system model

This part presents a model that in general terms and to varying degrees can be considered to define the media systems in Latin America. The model is labeled 'captured liberal,' and though an apparent oxymoron, the term clearly reflects the contradictions inherent to public life in Latin America – the 'magic realism' as some say. Why captured? And why liberal?

Though the research area regarding rent seeking, competition, and politics is, of course, older, the term 'capture' dates back to the 1980s when some scholars were already analyzing the forms in which certain groups affected policy decision-making processes (Laffont and Tirole, 1991; Bardhan and Mookherjee, 1999). Then the term popularized by the end of the 20th Century due to the research projects originated at the World

Bank (Hellman, 1998; Hellman, Jones and Kaufmann, 2000; Hellman, Jones, Kaufmann and Shankerman, 2000; World Bank, 2000) that focused on the outcomes of the political and economic transitions especially in Eastern Europe. Hellman, Jones and Kaufmann say that:

> In designing reform strategies in the initial stages of the transitions in Eastern Europe and the former Soviet Union, the dominant challenge was to reduce and reorient the state's role in the economy. In particular, the strategies of liberalization and privatization were intended to change the way in which the state interacts with firms, shifting from command methods to market mechanisms. Throughout the transition, little attention has been paid to the flipside of this relationship, namely the ways in which firms exert influence on the state. Yet in the context of weak states and underdeveloped civil societies, such forms of influence have had a powerful impact on the pace and direction of reforms, on the design of economic and political institutions and, ultimately, on the general quality of governance in the transition countries. After only a decade of transition, the fear of the *leviathan state* has been replaced by a new concern about powerful *oligarchs* who manipulate politicians, shape institutions, and control the media to advance and protect their own empires at the expense of the social interest. (2000: 5)

What is of interest then to these authors is the role that new actors (powerful firms) are playing in determining specific outcomes in the economy – at least some key sectors – by capturing certain functions and decision-making mechanisms of the state in order to extract rents in their own benefits at the expense of a wider general or social well-being. In a further work, Hellman and Kaufmann clearly identify 'state capture' with corruption and define it as 'the efforts of firms to shape the laws, policies and regulation of the state to their own advantage by providing illicit private gains to public officials' (2001: 1). However, they also recognize that the advance of powerful firms' interests may also be due to 'influence' that is then defined as 'the firm's capacity to have an impact on the formation of the basic rules of the game (regulations, decrees, laws) *without* necessary recourse to *private* payments to public officials (as a result of such factors as firm size, ownership ties to the state, and frequent interactions with state officials)' (Hellman, Jones and Kaufmann, 2000: 6). There are many academic works that have been studying the different forms of state capture by different economic interests, mostly in Eastern Europe (Begovic, 2005; Omelyanchuk,

2001; Pesic, 2007; World Bank, 2000; Yakovlev and Zhuravskaya, 2006; Zhuravskaya, 2000). In the case of the media in Latin America, Guerrero (2010) has used the term to refer to the forms in which some big media corporations imposed their interests on the shaping of broadcasting policy and regulation in three specific cases in Mexico.

Having said that, this chapter stresses two complementary meanings for the term 'capture'. Most of the authors cited above associate the term to 'state capture' and refer to a condition where some aspects of the policy-making process and of the design of the rules of the game are twisted in favor of certain specific private interests. Here we use the term 'capture' to underline both the capacity of groups to twist the rules in their favor or make their application selective and ineffective, and the condition where extra-journalistic criteria shape, determine, and limit the watchdog role of the media. These capture pressures may be coming either from politicians and state agencies, or from the political or economic interests of the owners (and sometimes also editors) of the media corporations. Thus, here the term 'capture' is not linked only to the specificities defining state capture, but to the condition where it depicts two aspects that have been discussed in this chapter: the regulatory inefficiency of the state and the constantly challenged watchdog role of journalism in a context dominated by private commercial media organizations.

In this regard, the undue interference of political actors in media coverage and journalistic professionalism might seem contrary to liberalism, but it is precisely the result of the dissolution, the weak application, or the absence of well-defined norms and regulations. It might also suggest that the regulatory inefficiency prevents an adequate defense for the guarantees of journalists and communicators. Going back to the definitions of Hallin and Mancini, it is a 'savage liberalization' (dating back to the market-driven reforms) that paradoxically opens up areas of influence and irregular pressures to politicians and corporate actors. The model is summarized in Table 2.1.

As with every theoretical model, this cannot be considered homogeneously for all Latin American countries. Along the project research, particularities and exceptions have been discovered. However, Figure 2.1 shows the 'degree of proximity' of selected countries in the region considering the two defining aspects of the model: the regulatory efficiency and the degree of interference on the media's (and journalists') watchdog role.

It should be noted that over the last decade the ruling groups in some countries have been harshly questioning the retreat of the state and the blatant predominance of private commercial media organizations.

Table 2.1 The 'captured liberal' model

Aspect	Definition	Fields or criteria
Low regulatory efficiency	Inconsistent application of legal frameworks and/or lack of adequate and updated regulations.	Trends toward the concentration of media markets. Good judgment regarding public spending on advertising Colonization of media structures by the political class and of political spaces by the media class. Capture of regulatory spaces by large media groups.
High degree of interference on the media's watchdog role	Unfavorable conditions for professionalism and weak guarantees for journalistic practice.	Absence of adequate mechanisms of protection for journalistic performance (poor research and spaces of tolerance in the event of violence). Lack of conditions favorable to the emergence of professional journalism (influence of extra-journalistic interests, notably political and corporate).

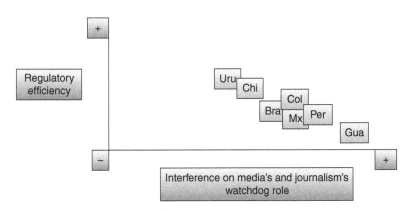

Figure 2.1 Location of cases in relation with the 'captured liberal' model

Such are the cases of Venezuela, Ecuador, Bolivia, and more recently Argentina. The common argument for passing new reforms and regulations regarding the media is, in general terms, to provide wider access to diverse and plural voices and groups in society. Conversely, traditional media groups and elites claim that these regulations severely restrict the freedoms of speech and of the press. It must be accepted that the new regulations have decreased the powerful influence of traditional media groups, have brought back the state as a direct player in the media and communication policies, and all these without seeking to destroy the commercial media model in those countries, but attempting to reduce its scope and space within a wider media landscape. However, in spite of containing legal precepts regarding media pluralism, access to diverse voices and the recognition of communication rights, these new regulations, laws and policies have been selectively applied. Such partiality has created the impression that far from seeking a true reconfiguration of the media system based on pluralism, diversity, and autonomy the new legal frameworks seek to reinstate forms of political control on the media through direct and indirect mechanisms. The chapters on Venezuela, Bolivia, and Argentina in this book explore this trend in detail. How to explain these developments within the captured liberal model?

This chapter contends that the answer is found in the kind of political groups that have made their way to power either outside the traditional political channels (Venezuela and Bolivia) or posing as reformers of systems that they label as oligarchic or conservative (Ecuador and Argentina).[7] In her work on Latin America's populism, Susanne Gratius explains that it is possible in these four countries to identify a 'third wave' of populism in the region that is characterized this time by its leftist leanings (unlike other populist episodes in Latin America) and that when responding to the challenge of a growing crisis both of democracy and of the state, they tend to 'weaken the former and strengthen the latter' (2007: 1). One must not forget that the key to the post-transitory arrangement has consisted on the agreements, supports, and exchanges between traditional media and new political groups in a context of inefficient regulation and market conditions. In Venezuela and Bolivia, the rupture of the agreements can be attributed to the entry of outsiders, and in Ecuador and Argentina (the second Kirchner administration) of reformers that seek to reestablish some degree of control in the media system. In any case, the effort made by the ruling politicians in these countries to reshape the alliances and/or links between the political system and the social and economic groups is obvious. Their unending calls to build radical, participative, or direct democracies provide clear examples (Gratius, 2007: 5). Apparently, they do not want to destroy the private commercial model in the media, but only want to reestablish control mechanisms (directly through granting licenses and passing new laws and indirectly by withdrawing government advertising and exhaustive fiscal review on critical media companies) and even support the emergence of new loyal commercial media organizations. In this way, the system is kept formally liberal, but the capture of the media strengthens, though the capture here plainly comes from the political camp –not from the corporations.

Final remarks

The captured liberal model of the media proposed for Latin America has no normative aspirations. Instead, it brings together some of the most obvious coincidences of the political context that affects the operation of the traditional media systems. As it happens with every ideal type, one might expect to find differences from the model within each country by type of media.

The three most important core aspects of the political system affecting the media are:

• The degree of closeness between new ruling politicians and traditional media groups.
• The historical trend toward clientelism.
• The kind of deregulation and market reforms.

The two core fields of the media system affected by the political system are:

• (Low) Quality of regulatory efficiency.
• (High) Degree of interference on the media's (and journalism's) watchdog role.

The captured liberal media model is defined as liberal because in general it keeps the formalities of a predominant commercial media system; but due to its late development under historical circumstances that made them dependent on governments and public funding, it subordinated the media system from the start. The chapters on Peru, Brazil, Bolivia, Guatemala, and Liotti's Argentina clearly depict this situation. The post-transition changes that brought the economic reforms that diminished the state's capacities also brought new ruling elites that rapidly found accommodation with traditional media elites in a context where clientelism predominated as a form of relation and exchange between public, social, and economic actors. If the state's capacities to properly regulate and apply the law were diminished, clientelism gave power to particular political groups to press on the media and to particular media to colonize the political spaces. The formalities of a liberal media system maintained but also the conditions for capturing it through the capacity of groups to twist the rules in their favor or make their application selective and ineffective, and to prevent the development of the watchdog role of the media.

Recently, some countries, like Venezuela, Bolivia, Ecuador, Argentina, and surprisingly and recently Mexico, have all issued new policies and even constitutional reforms to bring the state back into media and communication policy. In the first four cases, if it is true that the new regulations contain precepts regarding the right to information and that they promote other voices and social groups different than the pure commercial groups into broadcasting, then many recent examples show that these laws may be – again in the best tradition – selectively applied and used mostly as instruments to regain control on behalf of the state but not to promote pluralism. In the case of Mexico, the most recent media reform – called the Telecommunications Law, apparently responding to convergence – opens the gate to content pluralism, to different voices in the media, and to market competition. However, this law requires secondary regulatory ordainments that should have been (but were not) approved by early December 2013. Further, many of the corporations that saw their interests limited and restricted still have lots of spaces and opportunities to modify the terms of its application. One must here recall that some of the representatives of the highly controversial Mexican Green Party in the Chamber of Deputies' Broadcasting Commission are relatives and former employees of TV Azteca and Televisa. Thus, even in this apparent trend of re-regulating the media, opportunities for keeping capturing conditions both from politics and from corporations remain still.

Finally, the Captured Liberal Model is intended to define traditional types of media in relation to the political system. The model does not encompass the new digital media landscape, which is increasingly developing, more varied, and pluralistic. What can be seen in today's Latin America are two opposing trends: one –on the traditional media track – defined by the Captured Liberal Model; and another –on the digital media track – characterized by fragmentation, pluralism, and notably individuals who are using actively the new platforms to consume, interact, inform and disseminate diverse kind of contents. If it is true that digital media are mostly used for entertainment, in many respects, they are also becoming alternative spaces for public debate, but this topic requires another space for discussion.

Notes

A preliminary version of this work appeared as 'Latin American media: the challenges to pluralism,' in Peggy Valcke, Miklos Sükösd and Robert Picard (2014) *Media Pluralism: Concepts, Risks and Global Trends* (London: Palgrave). However, whereas that work deals with the concept of pluralism, the present one proposes a model for defining the Latin American media systems. I want to thank Mónica Luengas, Pablo Aburto and Martha Palacios for their invaluable collaboration in collecting and revising data and notes.

1. The author takes the expression from Nelson Traquina (1995).
2. An exception here is Albavisión that besides Central America, acquired stations in Argentina, Chile, Peru, Paraguay and recently in Uruguay.
3. In 1988, the president of Televisa declared his sympathies for the PRI. This was not the first – nor the last – time that Emilio Azcárraga Milmo declared himself as 'a soldier of the PRI,' just before the general elections (Monsiváis, 1997: 58).
4. The Mexican entrepreneur Ángel Remigio González has been able to build a media empire across different Latin American countries as can be seen in many of the other chapters of this book.
5. To illustrate, simply by taking any ten days from July 30 to August 2, 2010, one is likely to notice the different pressures to which journalists in the region are subject. For example, different Mexican media reported the kidnapping of four reporters by drug traffickers near the border between the Mexican states of Durango and Coahuila, a region known as La Laguna. Peru's El Comercio newpaper reported the aggression against a journalist by a political candidate; in Brazil, Folha de Rondonia presented information on the persecution and aggression suffered by the editor of the newspaper Correio de Noticias by individuals close to the former mayor of Cerejeiras, a city in the Eastern part of the country; also in Brazil, La Folha de Sao Paulo denounced the persecution of one journalist that was investigating a probable case of corruption and embezzlement of government funds in the city of Sinop; in Argentina, both La Nación and El Clarín reported public threats against the main supplier of paper in that country through the posting of papers on neighboring buildings; in Paraguay, the Sindicato de Periodistas y Reporteros sin Fronteras pointed out that radio broadcasters as well as newspapers correspondent, Gabriel Bustamante, have been the target of three assassination attempts in one week by one of the directors of the electric power company Yacyretá by the brothers of the latter; in Colombia, the Fundación para La Libertad de Prensa denounced the disappearance of a graphic reporter in the port of Buenaventura. These are some examples of frequent stories challenging professional journalism in Latin America. All the cases cited above were taken from 'Periodismo de las Américas,' a blog sponsored by the Knight Center for Journalism in the Americas (http://bit.ly/1cXHI9o) between July 30 and August 3, 2010.
6. For example, the cases reported by the media in Brazil, Paraguay, and Peru cited above. It is no coincidence that the International Press Institute (IPI) (2010) points out in its first semi-annual report for 2010 that when it comes to journalism, Latin America has surpassed the Middle East and Africa to become the world's most dangerous region.

7. The case of Ecuador is briefly explained here, since other chapters in this book deal extensively with those of Venezuela, Bolivia, and Argentina. In September of 2009, Ecuador's President, Mr. Rafael Correa, send the bill for the Organic Law of Communication to the National Assembly. The bill was debated first in January and then again in July 2010 before a public referendum was held on May 7, 2011, where 44.9 percent was in favor and 42 percent opposed it (Notimex, 2011).

Among the bill's most salient points was the creation of The National Council for Communication and Information, a public entity that according to Articles 65 and 66, shall maintain a registry of the media that should contain data on their editorial and information policies, their corporate structure, the composition of their social capital or property, and their code of ethics. Also, all media are required to maintain such registry and to inform the Council of any changes. In addition, Article 102 authorizes the Council to sanction the media for noncompliance with their own code of ethics. José Miguel Vivanco, Human Rights Watch (HRW) director for the Americas remarked in a letter written to the President of the Assembly that, given that the codes of ethics are norms intended for the internal use of the media, the interference by the Council would constitute an 'arbitrary and disproportionate' measure (Vivanco, 2010). Although in principle the law forbids anticipated censorship, the language is ambiguous. Article 9 states that the freedom of speech comprises the 'search, reception, exchange, production, and dissemination of information that is truthful, factual, opportune, contextualized, pluralistic,' all of which goes against the Declaration of Principles for the Freedom of Expression, which states that 'prior conditioning – such as the veracity, opportunity, or impartiality by the states – is incompatible with the right to freedom of speech as recognized in international instruments' (Inter-American Commission on Human Rights, undated).

References

ADC/Open Society (2008) *El precio del silencio: Abuso de publicidad oficial y otras formas de censura indirecta en América Latina* (Buenos Aires: Asociación por los Derechos Civiles/New York: Open Society Institute).

Bardhan, P. and Mookherjee, D. (1999) 'Relative capture of local and central governments. An essay in the political economy of decentralization,' *CIDER Working Paper*, 99–109.

Begovic, B. (2005) 'Corruption, Lobbying and State capture,' Center for Liberal-Democratic Studies (CLDS) and School of Law, University of Belgrade, March 2005. http://danica.popovic.ekof.bg.ac.yu/106.pdf (accessed March 2014).

Bonilla Sebá, E. and González, J. I. (2010) 'La decisión de la CNTV no garantiza el derecho a la información,' *Eje 21*, April 12. Available at http://bit.ly/1cXGXNv (accessed October 2013).

Christofoletti, R. (2003) 'Dez impasses para uma efetiva critica de midia no Brasil,' work presented at the INTERCOM meeting, Belo Horizonte, September.

Corrales, O. and Sandoval, J. (2005) 'Concentración del mercado de los medios, pluralismo y libertad de expresión,' Working Paper (Santiago: Universidad de Chile). Available at http://bit.ly/JlZsR3 (accessed December 2013).

Costa, S. and Brener, J. (1997) 'Coronelismo eletronico: o governó Fernando Henrique e o novo capitulo de uma velha historia,' *Comunicacao e Politica*, 4(2): 29–53.

CPJ-Committee to Protect Journalists (2010) 'Attacks on the press 2010: Americas analysis. In Latin America a return of censorship,' Committee to Protect Journalists. Available at http://bit.ly/1cXHoaD (accessed November 2013).

Eisenstadt, S. and Roniger, L. (1984) *Patrons, Clients and Friends: Impersonal Relations and the Structure of Trust in Society* (Cambridge: Cambridge University Press).

Fox, E. and Waisbord, S. (eds) (2002) *Latin Politics, Global Media* (Austin: University of Texas Press).

Freedom House (2002) *Map of Press Freedom*. Available at http://bit.ly/QGJl2f (accessed October 2013).

Freedom House (2012) *Map of Press Freedom*. Available at http://bit.ly/1cXHD5H (accessed November 2013).

Gratius, S. (2007) 'The "Third Wave of Populism" in Latin America.' *Working Paper 45* (Madrid: Fundación para las Relaciones Internacionales y el Diálogo Exterior).

Guerrero, M. A. (2009) *The Emergence of Political Pluralism in Mexican Broadcasting* (Germany: VDM Verlag).

Guerrero, M. A. (2010) 'Broadcasting and democracy in Mexico: from corporatist subordination to state capture,' *Policy and Society*, 29(1): 23–35.

Guerrero, M. A. (2014) 'Latin American media: the challenges to pluralism,' in Peggy Valcke, Miklos Sükösd and Robert Picard (eds) *Media Pluralism: Concepts, Risks and Global Trends* (London: Palgrave).

Gwynne, R. and Kay, C. (eds) (2004) *Latin America Transformed: Globalization and Modernity* (London: Arnold).

Hallin, D. (2000) 'Media, political power and democratization in Mexico,' pp. 97–110 in James Curran and Myung-Jin Park (eds) *De-Westernizing Media Studies* (London: Routledge).

Hallin, D. and Mancini, P. (2004) *Comparing Media Systems. Three Models of Media and Politics* (Cambridge: Cambridge University Press).

Hallin, D. and Papathanassopoulos, S. (2002) 'Political clientelism and the media: southern Europe and Latin America in comparative perspective,' *Media, Culture & Society*, 24(2): 175–195.

Hellman, J. and Kaufmann, D. (2001), 'Confronting the challenge of state capture in transition economies,' *Finance & Development*, 38(3), http://www.imf.org/external/pubs/ft/fandd/2001/09/hellman.htm (accessed January 2014).

Hellman, J. (1998) 'Winners take all: the politics of partial reform in post-communist transitions,' *World Politics*, 50(2): 203–234.

Hellman, J., Jones, G. and Kaufmann, D. (2000) 'Seize the state, seize the day: state capture, corruption and influence in transition,' *World Bank Policy Research Working Paper* No. 2444.

Hellman, J., Jones, G., Kaufmann, D. and Schankerman, M. (2000) 'Measuring governance, corruption, and state capture: how firms and Bureaucrats shape the business environment in transition economies,' *World Bank Policy Research Working Paper* No.2312.

Hughes, S. (2006) *Newsrooms in conflict Journalism and the Democratization of Mexico* (Pittsburgh: University of Pittsburgh Press).

International Press Institute (IPI) (2010) *Investigative Reporting of Corrupt Public Officials a Vital Aspect of Journalism*. Available at http://bit.ly/1cXHGOI (accessed September 2013).

Knigth Center for Journalism in the Americas (n.d.) *Blog Periodismo de las Américas*, University of Austin, Texas. Available at http://bit.ly/1cXHI9o (accessed July 30 and August 3, 2010).

Laffont, J. and Tirole, J. (1991) 'The politics of government decision-making: a theory of regulatory capture,' *Quarterly Journal of Economics*, 106: 1089–1127.

Lima, V. (2003) *Existe concentração na mídia brasileira? Sim. Observatório da Imprensa*. Available at http://bit.ly/1cXHYFs (accessed September 2013).

Lucas, M. C. (2009) *La estructura de la Televisión en Guatemala: La incidencia político social y el análisis de los contenidos informativos*, PhD Thesis (Madrid: Universidad Complutense). Available at http://bit.ly/1cXIgMC (accessed September 2013).

Malloy, J. and Seligson, M. (1987) *Authoritarians and Democrats: Regime Transitions in Latin America* (Pittsburgh: University of Pittsburgh Press).

Marder, M. (1998) 'This Is Watchdog Journalism,' *Nieman Reports*, 53(4) (Nieman Foundation for Journalism at Harvard University).

Márquez-Ramírez, M. (2012) 'Valores normativos y prácticas de reporteo en tensión: percepciones profesionales de periodistas en México,' *Cuadernos de Información*, (30): 97–11.

Mastrini, G. and Becerra, M. (2006) *Periodistas y Magnates: Estructura y concentración de las industrias culturales en América Latina*. Buenos Aires: Prometeo Ediciones.

Mastrini, G. and Bolaño, C. (2000) *Globalización y monopolios en la comunicación en América Latina* (Buenos Aires: Biblos).

Matos, C. (2012) *Media and Politics in Latin America* (London: I.B. Tauris).

McChesney, R. (1997) *Corporate Media and the Threat to Democracy* (New York: Seven Stories).

Monsiváis, C. (1997) 'Entretenimiento sin concesiones; fracaso en la incursión cultural,' *Proceso*, (1068): 58.

Notimex (2011) 'Vuelve a debate ley sobre medios tras referendo en Ecuador,' *Hispavista*, May 22. Available at http://bit.ly/1cXIq6F (accessed October 2013).

O'Donnell, M. (2007) *Propaganda K: Una maquinaria de promoción con dinero del Estado* (Buenos Aires: Planeta).

Omelyanchuk, O. (2001) 'Explaining state capture and state capture modes: The cases of Russia and Ukraine,' Department of International Relations and European Studies, Central European University, Budapest.

Pesic, V. (2007) 'State capture and widespread corruption in Serbia,' *CEPS Working Documents*, Number 262. http://papers.ssrn.com/sol3/papers.cfm?abstract_id=1338021 (accessed March 2014).

Reséndiz, F. (2007) 'El fantasma detrás del poder en América Latina,' *El Universal*, January 28. Available at http://bit.ly/1cXIx1Y (accessed October 2013).

Rey, G. (2012) 'La nueva ley de televisión o el síndrome del comunero,' *razónpública.com*, January 16. Available at http://bit.ly/Jm04WU (accessed September 2013).

Rivadeneyra Olcese, C. (2007) 'Las otras radios: El complejo escenario de la radio en el Perú,' *Contratexto Digital*, 6(7). Available at http://bit.ly/1cXICCW (accessed September 2013).

Rockwell, R. and Janus, N. (2003) *Media Power in Central America* (Champaign, IL: University of Illinois Press).

Ruiz-Tagle, P. (2011) 'Propiedad de los medios y principios de intervención del Estado para garantizar la libertad de expresión en Chile,' *Revista de Derecho*, 18(2): 347–359.

Sánchez Ruiz, E. (1987) *Centralización, poder y comunicación en México* (Guadalajara: Universidad de Guadalajara).

Sirven, P. (2011) *Perón y los medios de comunicación, la conflictiva relación de los gobiernos justicialistas con la prensa. 1943–2011* (Sudamericana).

Strickon, A. and Greenfield, S. (eds) (1972) *Structure and Process in Latin America: Patronage, Clientage and Power Systems* (Albuquerque: University of New Mexico Press).

Sunkel, G. and Geoffroy, E. (eds) (2001) *Concentración Económica de los Medios de Comunicación* (Santiago: Lom).

Traquina, N. (1995) 'Portuguese Television: the Politics of Savage Deregulation,' *Media, Culture & Society*, 17(2): 223–238.

Trejo, R. (2010) *Simpatía por el Rating. La Política Deslumbrada por los Medios* (Mexico: Cal y Arena).

Vivanco, J. M. (2010) 'Carta al Presidente de la Asamblea Nacional, Fernando Cordero Cueva,' Human Rights Watch. Available at http://bit.ly/1cXIHq5 (accessed September 2013).

Waisbord, S. (2000a) 'Media in South America: Between the rock of the state and the hard place of the market,' pp. 50–62 in James Curran and Myung-Jin Park (eds) *De-Westernizing Media Studies* (London: Routledge).

Waisbord, S. (2000b) *Watchdog Journalism in South America* (New York: Columbia University Press).

Waisbord, S. (2008) 'The myth of media globalization – By K. Hafez,' *The British Journal of Sociology*, 59(3): 592–594.

World Bank (2000) 'Measuring governance, corruption and state capture: how firms and Bureaucrats shape the business environment in transition economies,' *Working Paper* 2312, WB Institute.

Yakovlev, E. and E. Zhuravskaya (2006), 'State capture in a federation,' *CEFIR-NES Working Paper Series, Working Paper 93*, http://www.cefir.ru/download. php?id=715 (accessed March 2014).

Zhuravskaya, E. (2000) 'Incentives to provide public goods: fiscal federalism, Russian style,' *Journal of Public Economics*, 76(3): 337–368.

3
In Search of a Model for the Colombian Media System Today

Catalina Montoya-Londoño

Introduction

In the past decade, there has been an increased interest in the scholarly study of media systems as intrinsically and structurally linked to their political contexts. For example, Hallin and Mancini (2004) propose three models to categorize media systems in relation to political variables in 18 countries around Europe and in the United States and Canada that serve as ideal types and share systemic relations and patterns common to countries with similar historical, economic, and sociopolitical contexts. In another work, Hallin and Papathanassopoulos (2002) identify Portugal, Brazil, Colombia, and Mexico with the *Mediterranean* or *polarized pluralist* systems. In particular, the authors argue that until the 1990s these countries shared a low level of development of the mass press, a partisan tradition in journalism, high instrumentalization of the press and public broadcasting systems, and weak regulation of the private sector, which facilitated the consolidation of monopolies (2002: 176–182). Political clientelism not only meant that information could be traded for deference but also that the journalistic autonomy, public service ethos, and the horizontal solidarity among media professionals were broken. Nevertheless, the authors identify urbanization and industrialization, the growth of the middle class and civil society since the 1960s, and the globalization of journalistic cultures as forces of transformation for media systems in the region.

This chapter presents an analysis that, on the basis of the models introduced above, accounts for the transformation of Colombia's media systems after the 1990s. Drawing on a literature review of media history and current reports on media and democracy in the country, I propose that although some features of the *polarized pluralist* model are still in place, more recent developments in the Colombian media system also suggest that it is approaching the *liberal* model. Consequently, the current model is closer to what Guerrero has called the *captured liberal* model (see Chapter 2) or a system in which, despite their commercial orientation, media outlets have not consolidated yet as truly competitive, which is to of detriment true pluralism and diversity. In addition, in the *captured liberal* model journalistic professionalism has been hijacked by the interests of media proprietors, political groups, and other social actors, which is a situation that is reinforced by a lack of effectiveness in state regulation.

Accordingly, this work describes the development of the Colombian media market in relation to the effectiveness of regulation in guaranteeing the democratization of media property in the context of growing concentration and privatization. Subsequently, it explores the levels of political parallelism and freedom of the press and their effects on journalistic professionalism in the context of ongoing clientelism, polarization, and internal armed conflict.

The development of media markets and the role of the state

Colombia's press developed in an elitist fashion until the first decades of the 21st century when the Internet introduced it to a wider number of readers that also allowed the emergence of a great quantity of media outlets in a relatively short space of time. Even so, television still holds the largest audiences. Moreover, the country developed a media market under corporate leadership in a context of deregulation and low regulatory efficiency to protect the constitutional anti-concentration spirit.

In a seminal work on the history of the press in Colombia, Vallejo-Mejía (2006: 23, 337–340) refers to the weak development of the mass press between the end of the 19th century and the beginning of the 20th. Accordingly, despite the boom in new titles (about 800 between 1911 and 1915), press circulation levels and their sustainability were generally low.[1] Although many newspapers were produced with the latest technology, low levels of literacy among the population reduced the potential readership to an educated urban minority. Furthermore, sociopolitical conflicts in Colombia, along with censorship imposed by the government and the Catholic church, undermined the development of an autonomous industry.

Newspapers were family businesses supported by political alliances. Their aim was to defend partisan ideologies rather than to be a source of profit (Melo, 2012: 47; Rey, 1998: 169; Vallejo-Mejía, 2006: 346–348). Nevertheless, and as Vallejo-Mejía observes in a later work (Vallejo-Mejía, 2012: 25), this condition guaranteed the newspapers' economic survival in the midst of the precarious sociopolitical conditions in the country. As the country went through the process of urbanization and modernization in the second half of the 20th century the press maintained a high degree of technological investment, moved toward commercial and multimedia management strategies, and sought out new markets and social sectors. Moreover, the regional press formed networks in which one regional newspaper also owned newspapers in other cities. In addition, newspapers widened their range of topics and introduced entertainment and lighter sections for readers increasingly viewed as consumers (Melo, 2012: 47–50; Rey, 1998: 169–170).

Nevertheless, more recent data from UNESCO (n.d.) suggests that development of the Colombian press was still slow by 2004, with 23 daily newspaper titles compared with 532 in Brazil and 1,486 in the United States. The average circulation of daily newspapers per 1,000 inhabitants was 22.65 in Colombia, 35.55 in Brazil, and 193.19 in the United States.

Broadcasting

Television and radio have enjoyed greater audience levels than newspapers. Radio started in Colombia during the 1930s; privately owned radio stations were first consolidated locally and then, from the 1960s onwards, owned by private economic groups at a national level (Caracol, RCN, and Todelar). The fast-growing technological development of these radio stations allowed a wide range of content and a quick news response to national and international events. By the 1990s, economic groups not only included new investors but also the owners of the main radio stations; Caracol (Group Santo Domingo) and RCN (Group Ardila Lulle) expanded their control over the main television channels. In order to counteract the dynamics of concentration within media outlets, the Government Decree 1447 of 1995 opened the way for community radio stations (Melo, 2012: 47–50; Rey, 1998: 169–170).

Television was introduced in 1954 during the dictatorship of Gustavo Rojas Pinilla and remained under state control until 1963, a period known as the National Front,[2] when a mixed system was introduced (Decree 3267). Accordingly, the governing party retained control over the property, administration, regulation, and concession (via call for tenders) of commercial television while private bodies were in charge of TV production and programming (Vizcaíno, 2005: 131–140).

In 1984, there was a democratizing impulse reflected in the granting of concessions for TV news programs to different political sectors (Decree 222). In addition, its controlling body INRAVISION became an associative and public organization, and the government created the Commission for Surveillance of Television with the participation of sectors within the civil society such as the Catholic church, universities, and trade unions. The state also opened the way for the creation of regional (Decree 3100, 3101 de 1984) and subscription TV channels.

Nevertheless, some economic and political sectors lobbied successfully for a regulatory framework based on free market competition, inspired by neoliberal ideology and the so called 'Washington consensus' (Mastrini and Becerra, 2007: 20; Vizcaíno, 2005: 140–144). The government of César Gaviria Trujillo and the 1991 Constitution brought with them the privatization of television and telecommunications and their consequent co-opting by Colombia's most powerful economic groups. Although, under Law 14 of 1991, the state was still in charge of the direction and control of television, it allowed the private sector to develop their own initiatives in alliance with foreign companies. Despite technological and content renovation, privatization fostered market concentration and commercially driven programing dependent on the interests of these companies, their affiliates and political bodies (Rey, 1998: 121–124).

Alternative measures by the government to counteract the trend toward concentration included, first, the creation of profit-oriented local channels and then regional and community channels (Rey, 1998: 156–157; Vizcaíno, 2005: 140–141). Second, the Law of Television of 1995 included some ineffective antitrust measures, such as setting limits for shareholding, forbidding one group's presence in more than one channel, and measures to facilitate auditing (Rey, 1998: 104). Third, the National Television Commission (CNTV) was created to take charge of general policy on television and to replace the previous National Television Council (Vizcaíno, 2005: 140–141). However, the inefficiency of the CNTV led to its dissolution in 2012 and its replacement by the National Television Authority (ANTV) (Law 1507, January 10, 2012). Nevertheless, according to Alfredo Sabbagh, a representative of the organization,[3] the ANTV is still sorting out processes inherited from the dissolved CNTV. In addition, private television funds public television, Colombian Public Radio, and TV (RTVC), as well as the regional channels, which is an indication of the precariousness of the public sector in relation to the private television sector.

The most recent data from UNESCO (n.d.) confirm the dominance of the industry by the private sector in 2006: 888 radio and television outlets, 460 citizen media, 181 radio stations, and part-ownership of 15 television channels. In Colombia, 78.2 percent of radio stations are privately owned compared to 21.8 percent owned by the state, and 73.6 percent of television outlets are in private hands compared to 26.4 percent that are public or state owned.

Moreover, trends of media convergence and concentration, businesses diversification, and the internationalization of media property have deepened through the first two decades of the 21st century. For instance, the Santo Domingo group sold Caracol radio to the Spanish conglomerate Prisa (Melo, 2012: 50) that in turn owns some of the most important Colombian radio stations (Réniz-Caballero, 2011). Meanwhile, Santo Domingo has been the majority shareholder of Colombia's second national daily newspaper, El Espectador, since 1997. In addition, the group also owns Caracol TV, Shock, Cromos, and Vea magazines, as well as online media; and it leases the radio frequency of Melodía FM, which operates along with Blu Radio. The Santo Domingo group participates through Cine Colombia in an alliance with Virgin Mobile Latin America. In terms of business diversification, the group's interests include the ownership of an estate agency and hotels, a presence in the finance and banking sectors, retail (Lozano-Garzón, 2012), the oil sector (Portafolio, 2012), and the mobile phone business (Castro-Cervantes, 2012).

Telecommunications and Internet

In the global context of economic deregulation during the 1990s, the state also created the Commission for the Regulation of Telecommunications and restructured the Ministry of Communications. As a result, and as Tamayo, Delgado and Penagos (2009) argue, the Internet-integrated telecommunications industry played a part in the process of media convergence in the country. For the authors, between 1994 and 2000 the state granted concessions to private providers of aggregated services such as mobile phones, long-distance calling, etc. In addition, some 220 licenses were granted to provide infrastructure and domestic Internet services. At the same time, state programs such as 'Compartel' and 'agenda de Contectividad' drove Internet demand up by improving access across the country. By 1998, the private sector led the Internet service provision; and, from 2001 to 2007, private companies moved toward becoming oligopolies and continued the convergence of services and capital: out of 14 providers in 1998, there were only 8 by 2006.

By 2012, according to the latest quarterly report by the Ministry of TIC (MinTIC, 2012), there were five fixed Internet providers left who represented 91.8 percent of the market (19). In addition, six providers were in charge of mobile Internet services (24), and the market had five providers of mobile phone services (13).

Despite market concentration, information services have increased as well as the supply of journalism. In 2010, Colombia had 391 digital news media outlets, 88 of which were web based, while the rest were versions of existing radio or newspapers services. This media was either public (state owned), private, nonprofit (funded mainly by international cooperation agencies), or versions of existing mainstream media outlets (Rey and Huertas, 2010). By 2013, according to Miriam Forero, Coordinator of Research in Consejo de Redacción,[4] there were 745 news websites on the Internet, 306 of which do not depend on traditional media outlets.

With regards to audiences, the most recent General Report on Media (ACIM, 2011) shows the dominance of television (94 percent), followed by radio (67 percent), independent magazines (44 percent), Internet (39 percent), and newspapers (35 percent). According to the Ministry of TIC, by September 2012, Colombia reached 7,037,241 subscriptions to the Internet: 61.2 percent were fixed Internet subscriptions and 38.7 percent were to mobile Internet services. In addition, there were 48,699,217 mobile phone users, which represented a market penetration of 104.5 percent (MinTIC, 2012).

Arguably then, there has been an important development in the media led by the private sector, and it is the market that to a great extent dictates the rules by which the media operates in the country. Although it is not possible to argue that there is a mass-circulation press in Colombia, the Internet has increased the number of readers in recent years.[5] Nevertheless, a development of the industry that guarantees its competitiveness, autonomy, and future sustainability in the face of global competition is still missing. The greatest move forward seems to be represented by digital and mobile technologies, which are redefining the dynamics of production and consumption and also increasing access to traditional media.

Parallelism, state guarantees and instrumentalization of journalism

Journalism has traditionally been in the hands of political sectors and media owners in a context of clientelism and low regulatory efficiency. In addition, internal armed conflict has made it very hard to guarantee journalistic independence, so Colombia is still one of the most dangerous places to practice the profession. Although partisan parallelism has weakened, the news media still reflects the prevailing political forces in the country. In addition, media regulation remains generally inefficient and more concerned about content than the concentration of ownership.

Vallejo-Mejía (2006: 288–325) observes that in the transition from the 19th to 20th centuries, legislation and economic sanctions in Europe against the press were in decline, while in Colombia the opposite process was taking place. It was spelled out in the Constitution of 1886 that the press was free in times of peace, but legally accountable for attacks on the honor of individuals, social order, or public peace. Such a regulatory framework fostered censorship during the 20th century. Newspapers, up to the National Front, belonged to political families who used them to express their political opinions against other parties. In addition, there was a revolving door between journalism and political office (Posada-Carbó, 2012: 15; Vallejo-Mejía, 2006: 68).

The National Front (1958–1974) meant a transition toward a controlled (pacted) democracy that 'civilized' the struggle among political parties, taming sectarianism in the mainstream press. Nevertheless, a new wave of anti-communist ideology followed by which left-wing press and political groups were stigmatized, marginalized, or excluded altogether (Vallejo-Mejía, 2006: 79–80, 327–332). Meanwhile, the armed conflict developed with the emergence of left-wing guerrilla groups, right-wing paramilitaries, and drug traffickers. The mandate of a responsible press in times of conflict written into the 1886 Constitution perpetuated itself by legitimizing the censorship of information about the armed conflict. For example, in 1992, the government forbidded interviews with illegal armed activists or the broadcasting of subversive or terrorist actions (Melo, 2012; Rey, 1998: 107; Vallejo-Mejía, 2006: 332–336).

Corrupt politicians used the legal obligation of the media to respect an individual's honor to protect themselves against accusations by the press (article 15). Consequently, Melo (2012: 45) argues that the first sentences handed down by the constitutional court did not distinguish between judicial and political impunity. Journalists were prevented from reporting accusations of crimes that had not been tried in court in a climate of exorbitant impunity. Although in recent years the court has given greater weight to the freedom of the press, the resolution of conflict over principles has depended more on casuistry than on fixed principles and norms.

In addition, political clientelism has also prevailed in broadcasting. Scandals around exchanges of concessions for political support are nor infrequent while economic groups consolidate their political power (Rey, 1998: 129) and control over media and telecommunications. Economic groups not only have funded political campaigns but also show a high degree of interference in editorial policies by actively avoiding overly critical views against the government or their own companies (Melo, 2012: 50–51). Cases such as that of the Casa Editorial El Tiempo (CEET) illustrate this trend. León (2010) reports that when most of the shares in CEET were purchased by the Spanish group Planeta, the real interest behind the acquisition was the concession of the third TV channel in Colombia. President Alvaro Uribe's government (2002–2010) was over-represented in CNTV, and this had several consequences for CEET, including: progovernment treatment of the news, the inclusion in the El Tiempo newspaper of columnists such as Jose Obdulio Gaviria who was at the time Uribe's advisor, the exclusion of columnists Claudia López and María Jimena Duzan who were critical of the government's policies, and the closure of Cambio magazine. Cambio had played an important role in uncovering scandals such as one involving governmental subsidies to powerful families in exchange for their support for the re-election of Alvaro Uribe. León concluded that the new government of Juan Manuel Santos would keep the decision over the third channel on hold since the Santos family has a small interest in CEET, as has indeed happened.

Even today, political forces control and create media outlets. For instance, in February 2013, the launch of the digital newspaper www.periodico-debate.com was formally announced. It was to be based in Medellin and to be supported by the ex-President Alvaro Uribe and his right-wing movement, 'Pure Democratic Center', in order to 'disseminate the thesis of Alvaro Uribe and his followers' (El Espectador, 2013).

The editorial direction of newspapers has been kept under the control of political families or prominent politicians who have also developed connections with big businesses. Examples of this include La Opinion newspaper from Cucuta (Laguado-Nieto, 2009), El País newspaper from Cali (LaRazón.com., 2012), and Vanguardia newspaper from Bucaramanga (Vanguardia Redacción, 2009). Family and political clans have ensured their survival well into the 21st century 'with the sons and grandsons of the founders of the influential press who also inherited governmental posts' (Vallejo-Mejía, 2006: 75, translated by Montoya).

The state still lacks regulatory efficiency, then, to control the high degree of concentration in media ownership and its instrumentalization by political and corporate sectors. Such instrumentalization is reflected not only in the dynamics by which concessions are granted by the state but also in the allocation of official advertisements, as the survey of 600 journalists published by the firm Cifras y Conceptos – the biggest one to date – shows (Cifras&Conceptos, 2012; León, 2012). According to the survey, journalistic independence is significantly affected by the allocation or withdrawal of advertisements by local governments (13 percent), censorship by the private sector (11 percent) or the state (11 percent) through allocation or withdrawal of advertising in news media, and journalists' self-censorship out of fear of retaliation by government officials (10 percent). In addition, a telling 67 percent of those polled across the country think that official advertising is not allocated in a transparent fashion. On the other hand, 29 percent of journalists polled know other journalists who have changed their opinions in exchange for advertising or political favors, and 31 percent confirm that they know journalists who have contracts with government or private institutions.

In addition, the safety of journalists is not guaranteed. According to a recent survey (Cifras&Conceptos, 2012), 59 percent of journalists in Colombia hold the lack of security as an obstacle to carrying out their profession. The main aggressions include authorities´ restrictions on mobility (18 percent), attacks by state security forces (17 percent) and subversive groups (16 percent), web and electronic attacks (14 percent), and illegal surveillance by state bodies (12 percent).

The armed conflict and drug trafficking foster the pressure on the press. Gómez and Hernández (2008) carried out a survey of 235 journalists in 27 cities around the country in 2007. Accordingly, the main bodies responsible for violations to the freedom of the press were left-wing FARC guerrillas (5.06 percent), right-wing paramilitaries (4.95 percent), left-wing ELN guerrillas (4.55 percent), drug traffickers (4.44 percent), and politicians (4.03 percent).[6]

More recently, the latest report from Reporters Without Borders places Colombia 129th out of 170 countries for freedom of the press (Reporteros Sin Fronteras, 2013). In addition, the Foundation for the Freedom of the Press (FLIP, 2013; Redacción Política, 2013) reports 158 aggressions against journalists in 2012, 31 cases of violence against journalists by the state security forces, and high levels of impunity: from 140 cases of assassination of journalists between 1977 and 2012, forty of them remain unsolved, 59 expired, and another 6 could expire in 2013. Besides state impunity and self-censorship, the report also highlights an increase in the prosecutions of journalists as a method of censorship.

An example of the co-opting of journalists by illegal state bodies is reflected on the links between right-wing paramilitaries and directors and founders of the regional newspapers. A notorious example is Ulilio Acevedo Silva, director of Hoy Diario del Magdalena, who received a warrant for his arrest in February 2009 on charges of aggravated conspiracy to commit a crime and suspected links with the paramilitary bloc 'Resistencia Tayrona' from the United Self-Defense Forces of Colombia (AUC). The allegations were supported by statements from Hernán Giraldo Serna, former leader of the paramilitary group, who confirmed the economic support that paramilitaries gave to Acevedo's political aspirations. The director of the newspaper was also the director of the Conservative party in the Department of Magdalena and a representative and a candidate to the House of Representatives (Morales and Vallejo, 2012: 11–13). This case is indicative of a wider phenomenon: the co-opting of political sectors of the establishment by drug traffickers and paramilitaries over the last few decades (López, 2010; Romero, 2007). In so far as directors and founders of newspapers have been part of or related to the political establishment, these illegal armed groups have permeated the ownership and direction of the news media.

Journalistic professionalism

The context described has had consequences for the professionalization of journalism. Vallejo-Mejía (2006: 30–43) describes how, during the first half of the 20th century, journalists not only carried out various roles within the newspapers but also needed other jobs to survive financially. Although the trade of journalism was learned within newspapers, many internationally recognized writers such as the Nobel Prize winner Gabriel García Márquez started as journalists. Trade unions were social and partisan rather than pressure groups seeking to improve working conditions until the mid-20th century. The Association of Journalists of Antioquia (1946), the Circle of Journalists of Bogota (1947), and the National School of Journalists (1957) discussed ethical norms, wages, and recognition, creating Journalists' Day on the 9th of February along with prizes for the best news stories.

By the end of the 1990s, Rey (1998: 129–130) observes that media organizations such as Asomedios, Andiarios, Anda, and Ucep were very active in defending media, advertisers, and advertising agencies' interests. Nevertheless, their activities encompassed a 'focus on their own members rather than on their social role with regards to the problems the country was facing' (translation by Montoya).

Nevertheless, during the 1990s, journalists' nongovernmental organizations (NGOs) were also created to promote the freedom of the press, journalists' contribution to peace and democracy, and investigative reporting. Fundación Nuevo Periodismo Iberoamericano (1994), Corporación Medios Para La Paz (1998), Fundación para la Libertad de Prensa (2000), Proyecto Antonio Nariño (2001), and Consejo de Redacción (2006) have generated an important number of initiatives both individually and in alliance with the media and other sectors. In addition, Vallejo-Mejía (2012) points out that despite the slow development of a professional consciousness and great pressures arising from the armed conflict and political corruption, investigative journalism has survived.

The professionalization of the field has indeed had a slow academic development in Colombia. The first school of journalism was created in 1949 in the Faculty of Philosophy at Javeriana University, but it was not until 1971 that it became an independent faculty offering a BA in social communication (Facultad de Comunicación y Lenguaje, 2006). The first PhD program in communication was opened in the Universidad del Norte and, by 2012, there were 68 professional programs active (Roveda-Hoyos, 2012). In contrast, 'By 1960, more than a dozen U.S. universities, including Minnesota, Wisconsin, and Michigan State, had institutionalized mass communication research institutes or centers and were awarding doctorates in communication' (Rogers, 2004: 8). Furthermore, the professional card or certificate accrediting journalists was eliminated by the mid-1990s on the basis of the constitutional principle of the universal right to communicate.

Today, most information comes from official sources through brief news items rather than investigative journalism. A recent report by Proyecto Antonio Nariño describes relationships between sources and journalists as shaped by hierarchies established by official sources. Such hierarchies are reflected in concealment and leaks that are used as punishments or rewards for journalists. In turn, there is a superficial, commercial, biased, and ill-informed treatment of the news by journalists, as well as mutual accusations between journalists and sources of working with illegal armed actors (PAN, 2004).

Moreover, the move toward a neoliberal business model has brought with it precarious working conditions for journalists, particularly in outlying regions, even today. Low incomes not only force journalists to have several jobs but also prevent media outlets from having their own staff in conflict areas (PAN, 2004: 2).

In summary, in the last two decades there has been a high degree of commitment to journalistic professionalism in the country and a significant defense of independence and freedom of expression by journalists' organizations and the third sector. Nevertheless, the professionalization of journalism has been slow to develop. Pressures on journalists from state, corporate, and illegal bodies in the context of the armed conflict are high, and the state has done little to guarantee the safety and independence of journalists across the country.

Conclusions

The comparison of media systems and the models proposed (Hallin and Mancini, 2004; Hallin and Papathanassopoulos, 2002) are useful in identifying the features of and the implications for the media system in Colombian democracy. It has been argued that Colombia today is experiencing important market developments, a high level of political parallelism, high professional consciousness – despite the problems associated with practicing the profession – and low regulatory efficiency.

In addition, this work argues that, although Hallin and Papathanassopoulos placed Colombia in a *polarized pluralist* model at the beginning of the 21st century, further developments suggest that it is now closer to the *captured liberal* model that Guerrero proposes on Chapter 2 in this book. *Liberal* in so far as Colombia has medium levels of press circulation, external pluralism, and market dominance and low state intervention in the context of a weaker welfare state. Nevertheless, it has been *captured* by state, corporate, and illegal interests.

First, the media market and public broadcasting have been led by the private sector, and although levels of circulation and readership of the press are still low in comparison with the consumption of radio and television, they have improved enormously thanks to mobile technology and the Internet. Second, there is a high degree of political parallelism, reflected in the management of news media, which is still co-opted by political families; a high degree of political participation by economic groups through the funding of political campaigns and representatives in office; and, in some cases, the co-opting of journalists or media by illegal armed forces involved in armed conflict, and particularly paramilitaries. Consequently, the degree of instrumentalization of journalism is high given the dynamics of funding through advertising, censorship, self-censorship, and precarious working conditions. Third, regulatory efficiency has failed to protect the anti-concentration spirit of the Constitution or provide safety for journalists or measures against impunity for violence against them. Moreover, in many cases public information is still managed as a private good by public officials and civil servants.

Nevertheless, from the 1990s onwards, journalists' NGOs have been created in alliance with other organizations and sectors to protect their social role, autonomy, and freedom. At the same time, communication at the local and community levels has generated opportunities for including other voices and local agendas outside of commercial and government circles. In addition, the Internet has brought with it the possibility of creating alternative media projects, as well as generating increased circulation and consumption of mainstream media that widens the journalistic supply nationally.

Going back to Hallin and Mancini's models, it is important to analyze not only the levels of development of the press but also to include digital, mobile, and electronic media. In addition, and given the number of bodies (besides the state) intervening in politics in a time of armed conflict, the variables that must be considered increase in correspondence with such a complex media and political landscape.

Accordingly, it is important to take into account recent developments in the production and consumption of media in Colombia, centered on mobile technology and the Internet, as well as the influence of the third sector in strengthening journalistic professional ideology. The variables included in the models of the compared media systems are a useful starting point to evaluate some features of the reality of the situation in Colombia and the region, and update it in the light of democratic and economic developments, as has been attempted in this work.

Notes

1. El Espectador produced around 500 copies and El Tiempo around 3,000 at the beginning of the 20th century while newspapers in Buenos Aires, Argentina, published around 130,000 copies during the same period.
2. The National Front (1958–1974) was the result of an agreement between the main political parties, the Liberal and the Conservative, in which they took turns in office every four years (Presidential term).
3. Official's remarks during an event organized by the Faculty of Communication and Languages: *Where is Our Television Going? From CNTV to ANTV*, March 18, 2013, Atico Auditorium, Pontificia Universidad Javeriana, Bogotá, Colombia.
4. Interview with Miriam Forero, Coordinator of the Research Area of Consejo de Redacción, March 15, 2013, in light of the latest report on digital media that was launched in April.

5. El Tiempo registered 101,453,000 unique Internet users by December 2012 according to its web page (El Tiempo, 2012).
6. FARC stands for Revolutionary Armed Forces of Colombia; and ELN for National Freedom Army.

References

ACIM (Asociación Colombiana de Investigación de Medios) (2011) 'Estudio General de Medios EGM. Estructura de Medios 1–2011 Estratos 1 al 6'. Available at http://bit.ly/1bw6toy (accessed June 2013).

Castro-Cervantes, F. (2012, February 3) 'El Grupo Santodomingo regresa a las comunicaciones móviles' (Bogotá: Portafolio.co). Available at http://bit. ly/1bw6rgw (accessed June 2013).

Cifras&Conceptos (2012) *¿Qué dicen 600 periodistas obre su oficio y la libertad de expresión? Resultados de la encuesta nacional a periodistas sobre la libertad de expresión y acceso a la información pública* (Bogotá: Andiarios, FLIP, FNPI, FESCOL, UNDEF, MPP, PAN).

El Espectador (2013, February 7) 'Uribistas lanzan su periódico', *El Espectador*: 6.

El Tiempo (2012) 'ElTiempo.com supera los 100 millones de usuarios únicos en el 2012', *El Tiempo*. Available at http://bit.ly/Jnn2Nl (accessed January 28, 2013).

Facultad de Comunicación y Lenguaje (2006) 'Reseña histórica', Pontífica Universidad Javeriana. Available at http://bit.ly/JnmTcL (accessed March 11, 2013).

FLIP (Fundación para la Libertad de Prensa) (2013) *De las balas a los expedientes. Informe sobre el estado de la prensa en Colombia, 2012* (Bogotá: Fundación para la Libertad de Prensa).

Gómez, J. C. and Hernández, J. C. (2008) 'Libertad de Prensa en Colombia: la contradicción en la búsqueda de la verdad', *Palabra Clave*, 11(1). Available at http://bit.ly/Jns9gw (accessed August 2013).

Hallin, D. and Mancini, P. (2004) *Comparing Media Systems. Three Models of Media and Politics* (Cambridge: Cambridge University Press).

Hallin, D. and Papathanassopoulos, S. (2002) 'Political clientelism and the media: southern Europe and Latin America in comparative perspective', *Media Culture Society*, 24(2): 175–95, doi: 10.1177/016344370202400202

Laguado-Nieto, O. (2009, May 29) 'Senado Exaltó la labor de Eustorgio Colmenares Baptista', *AsíEsCúcuta.com*. Available at http://bit.ly/1bw6ysC (accessed June 2013).

LaRazón.com. (2012, February 14) 'Álvaro José Lloreda: De exitoso empresario a prófugo de la justicia', *LaRazónDeCali.com*. Available at http://bit.ly/Jnjril (accessed July 2013).

León, J. (2010, October 18) 'La transformación de *El Tiempo*', *Lasillavacia.com*. Available at http://bit.ly/JnjwCK (accessed September 2013).

León, J. (2012, May 3) 'Rayos X al periodismo nacional', *Lasillavacia.com*. Available at http://bit.ly/JnsVKh (accessed August 2013).

López, C. (ed.) (2010) *Y refundaron la patria ... De cómo mafiosos y políticos reconfiguraron el Estado Colombiano* (Colombia: Random House Mondadori).

Lozano-Garzón, R. (2012, September 24) 'Grupo Santodomingo se creció con nuevo timonel', *Portafolio.co*. Available at http://bit.ly/JnjIBT (accessed June 2013).

80   *Catalina Montoya-Londoño*

Mastrini, G. and Becerra, M. (2007) 'Presente y tendencias de la concentración de medios en América Latina', *Zer*, (22): 15–40.

Melo, J. O. (2012) 'La libertad de prensa en Colombia: su pasado y sus perspectivas actuales', pp. 36–55 in J. I. Arboleda (ed.) *Un papel a toda prueba. 223 años de prensa diaria en Colombia* (Bogotá: Andiarios y Biblioteca Luis Ángel Arango).

MinTIC (Ministerio de Tecnologías de la Información y las Comunicaciones) (2012) *Boletín trimestral de las TIC. Cifras tercer trimestre de 2012* (Bogotá: Ministerio de Tecnologías de la Información y las Comunicaciones).

Morales, M. and Vallejo, M. (2012) *Informe final del observatorio de medios de comunicación en elecciones locales (Octubre de 2011). Sucre, Magdalena y Norte de Santander* Bogotá: Pontificia Universidad Javeriana.

PAN (Proyecto Antonio Nariño) (2004) *El papel de las fuentes oficiales en el periodismo colombiano* (Bogotá: Fundación Friedrich Ebert Stiftung, Centro de Competencia en Comunicación para América Latina).

Portafolio (2012, May 9) 'Grupo Santodomingo entre al negocio de servicios petroleros', *Portafolio.co*. Available at http://bit.ly/1bw70qB (accessed October 2013).

Posada-Carbó, E. (2012) 'Prensa y democracia en la historia de Colombia', pp. 4–17 in J. I. Arboleda (ed.) *Un papel a toda prueba. 223 años de prensa diaria en Colombia* (Bogotá: Andiarios y Biblioteca Luis Ángel Arango).

Redacción Política (2013, February 7) 'Acoso judicial como forma de censura', Informe anual, *El Espectador*: 6. Available at http://bit.ly/1bwhWo7 (accessed August 2013).

Réniz-Caballero, D. (2011) 'Democracia, información, medios de comunicación y poder político en Colombia', *Working Paper* (Bogotá: Plataforma Democrática, Konrad Adenauer Stiftung).

Reporteros Sin Fronteras (2013) *Clasificación Mundial de la libertad de la prensa 2012–2013*. Available at http://bit.ly/1bw73CT (accessed July 2013).

Rey, G. (1998) *Balsas y medusas. Visibilidad comunicativa y narrativas políticas* (Bogotá: Cerec, Fesol y Fundación Social).

Rey, G. and Huertas, C. E. (2010) *El quién y el cómo de los nuevos medios* (Bogotá: Consejo de redacción, Centro Ático, Pontificia Universidad Javeriana).

Rogers, E. (2004) 'Theoretical diversity in political communication', pp. 3–16 in L. Lee-Kaid (ed.) *Handbook of Political Communication Research* (New Jersey and London: Lawrence Erlbaun Associates, Publishers).

Romero, M. (ed.) (2007) *Parapolítica. La ruta de la expansión paramilitar y los acuerdos políticos* (Bogotá: Intermedio).

Roveda-Hoyos, A. (2012) '¿Es posible la formación de un Pensamiento Estratégico en Comunicación?', *Signo y Pensamiento*, 26(51): 99–107. Available at http://bit.ly/1bwj0bP (accessed September 2013).

Tamayo, C. A., Delgado, J. D. and Penagos, J. E. (2009) 'Génesis del campo de Internet en Colombia: elaboración estatal de las relaciones informacionales', *Signo y Pensamiento*, 28(54): 238–264.

UNESCO (n.d.) *Build your Own Table* [Database], Institute for Statistics. Available at http://bit.ly/JnmYgw (accessed February 22, 2013).

Vallejo-Mejía, M. (2006) *A plomo herido. Una crónica del periodismo en Colombia (1880–1980)* (Bogotá: Planeta).

Vallejo-Mejía, M. (2012) 'Los genes de la prensa nonagenaria y centenaria', pp. 18–35 in J. I. Arboleda (ed.) *Un papel a toda prueba*. *223 años de prensa diaria en Colombia* (Bogotá: Andiarios y Biblioteca Luis Ángel Arango).

Vanguardia Redacción (2009, September 11) 'Alejandro Galvis Blanco: Sin independencia económica no hay independencia periodística', Bucaramanga: vanguardia.com. Available at http://bit.ly/JnjZEZ (accessed August 2013).

Vizcaíno, M. (2005) 'La legislación de televisión en Colombia: entre el Estado y el mercado', *Historia Crítica*, (28): 127–144.

4
Media Systems and Political Action in Peru

Javier Protzel

Introduction

In Latin America, where media-politics relations have historically been highly controversial, it is not easy for the local observer to free her analysis from personal preferences conditioned by context and experience. Exposed daily to infotainment, this observer – academic or otherwise – might easily generalize his or her interpretations, as the observer takes for granted personal preferences, regardless of any particular cultural framing. This is because it is difficult to watch the daily programing as if we were ethnographers in the field. However, if anything significant must be said about how the main Peruvian mass media articulates into political practice, then we must transcend common knowledge.

We depart from assuming that the political system represents some sort of 'independent variable,' since it has the capabilities to influence and even control the media system as blatantly happened during authoritarian periods. Here we also seek to identify within the media system those traits that derive from politics, which then are our 'dependent variables.' To complete this chapter some regional comparisons are called for.

Our first reference is Hallin and Mancini's solid *Comparing Media Systems: Three Models of Media and Politics* (2004) where they present a suggestive taxonomy of media systems in most industrialized Western countries on both sides of the Atlantic. The value of this book lies on establishing very broad patterns of classification and comparability that allow for a variety of specific national cases that were conceived upon the 'ideal types' of Weberian methodology. We must recall that the term 'system' brings to mind the organicist metaphor beneath functionalist sociology and anthropology, and suitable for studying politics at the level of the nation-state, that is, a unity with territorial sovereignty free to build its legitimacy, enforce laws, and yet has an existing diversity of actors. Under this conception power can be perceived as operating within a national 'political system.' Since 1953, David Easton generically formalized a theory of the political system portraying it as the successful accomplishment of two functions: assigning values for a society and having its members accept them as obligatory (Easton, 2007: 225). Likewise, an equivalent formal pattern could be called a 'media system,' thus enclosing the media companies and all other stakeholders in the political communication field within a national range.

The three media models proposed by Hallin and Mancini refer each to the most thriving areas of the Western world: the *liberal* or North Atlantic (USA, UK, Canada, Ireland), the *democratic corporatist* in North/Central Europe, and the *polarized pluralist* or Mediterranean. They remark how the main features of the two latter models got blurred toward the end of the 20th century, while the dominance of the North Atlantic patterns intensified. This must obviously be related to the neoliberal economic orientation that has prevailed after the downfall of the Soviet Union. In politics, the model matches with electoral democracy. Today we have around 117 nation-states whose governments are elected through universal suffrage (Freedom House, 2013). This surge (there were 80 before the fall of the Berlin Wall and less than 50 in the 1970s) triggered a wave of electoral marketing activities.

Is this alleged world-spread 'Americanization' to be interpreted as a consequence of successful commercial liberal media systems well matched with fairly stable democratic political systems? Is this North Atlantic liberal model the actual materialization of functionalist sociology guidelines and, consequently, indicative of superior efficiency? Are we facing a hegemonic scenario, devoid of functionalist approaches? Certainly neither Hallin nor Mancini suggest the 'superiority' of this or any other model. They only ascertain its expansion and pinpoint the comparative variables to be analyzed, thus demonstrating the tensions between capitalism, democracy, and political cultures.

Hallin and Mancini (2004) narrow down the incidence of political systems variables upon the mass media to four factors: (i) the structure of journalism markets, (ii) political parallelism, (iii) the professionalization of journalists, and (iv) state intervention. Notwithstanding the differences when compared with Latin America, some similarities may be drawn. Hallin and Papathanassopoulos's (2002: 175–205) comparison of the political life and journalism of four countries in southern

Europe with those of Brazil, Colombia, and Mexico shed some light on the survival of some forms of mass media power, for example, family ownership of newspapers, and the social relations of dependency, clientelism, as well as the time lags in the creation of a mass press. It is in this setting where we can locate the case of Peru.

The markets of print journalism and the nascent radio broadcast

In Peru, despite a study by global consultancy firm KPMG (2012) that indicated a 50 percent increase in daily newspaper sales from 2007 through 2011, the national rate of penetration is hardly over 60 copies per 1,000 inhabitants. This modest figure represents a significant increase from the figures of 1998 of about 22 copies per 1,000 according to UNESCO. Contrary to what an external observer might assume, the makeup of the newspaper readership in Peru is undoubtedly complex by reason of its nonlinear development. In the early 20th century, a popular press readership existed in coastal Peru – El Comercio newspaper was favored among the conservative elites. Conversely, the more densely populated Andean region was kept in backwardness. The backdrop is a matter of cultural history: the absence of readership among the illiterate indigenous peasant population who for centuries has lived subordinated to pre-capitalist organizations.

It is true that illiteracy has receded over time. The nationwide illiteracy rate of 81 percent in 1876 fell to 60 percent in 1940, and to 13 percent in 1993. This long, unfinished path toward full literacy has coexisted with the mass migrations from the Andean *sierra* – the Highlands – to the coastal areas – particularly Lima – with the consequent acquisition of full citizenship rights. Part of this decelerating mobility has seen years of terrorism, cycles of inflation and stagnation, and long periods of either authoritarian or military rule, or both. Although the formation of the political system occurred in the late 19th century – as with many other Latin American countries – it remained closed to popular participation until 1931.[1] This came about with the emergence of APRA (Spanish acronym for Popular Revolutionary American Alliance) that is a radical left-wing party whose base was composed of a very small number of militants from the poor Andean peasantry (Stein, 1980; Cotler, 1978).[2] The growth of Peruvian exports during the 1950s triggered the concentration of income in Lima, which subsequently led to an uninterrupted flow of Andean Quechua-speaking people for the next 50 years. Lima's population soared from 1 million in 1955 to more than 9 million in

2011. All these features have marked the development of the Peruvian media and press markets, but there is more to say.

When the term 'co-evolution' is employed to describe the parallel enlargement of mass media and political systems, there is usually an underlying hypothesis of mutual linkage as well as one of institutional continuity. This has not been Peru's case. The extreme contrasting example is the history of both the press and politics in Great Britain, where parties began to form in the 18th century, clear government-opposition divisions were being drawn, and the daily press was expanding. The acceleration of Peruvian history is abrupt, disruptive, and discontinued. The formation of a Peruvian market for the press came relatively late owing to the few literates who actually enjoyed full citizenship.

The literary and political discussion circles at the bourgeois European halls could also be found in Latin American history. In Peru it was limited to small elite groups. Likewise, the physical integration of the territory – something essential if one speaks of a national press market with a somewhat common agenda of issues – was not possible until the 1930s. Following the wars of Independence (1821–1825), El Comercio was the only newspaper among many that lasted to date. Founded in 1839, it was a literary, political, and commercial daily newspaper. Having survived wars, dictatorships, and economic recessions, it is now at the top of the most important Peruvian media group. During the 'Aristocratic Republic' (1895–1919), El Comercio was considered the leading newspaper among the small upper- and middle-class sectors in Lima. It maintained its rightist orientation, a distinctive trait of Partido Civil (Civilian Party).

Although rotary press technology became available in 1903, it was not until the 1950s that a real press market emerged. At this time, El Comercio and its liberal competitor La Prensa – founded in 1903 – benefited from the after II World War economic boom. At the same time, migration and urbanization created the conditions for a particular type of yellow journalism. Última Hora, founded in 1950, became the first sensationalist tabloid ever and over time gained enormous success with its big and hilarious jargon headlines replete with lavish women, crime, and cartoons. Its owner, Pedro Beltrán – also the owner of La Prensa – was a right-wing liberal (Gargurevich-Regal, 2005). Yellow journalism developed within a highly fragmented, partly literate media market, albeit more inclined to listening to music from their provinces than to discussing public issues. This factor unleashed a boom of low-cost popular radio stations, which became the most important communication media in terms of audience and reach in Peru until the 1980s.

Nevertheless, the growing number of broadcast stations and printed outlets did not match the ideological diversification of the population – especially to the left. In 1956, after the end of General Odría's military dictatorship, a system of political parties emerged to participate in the presidential election. The bulk of the press, though, remained aligned with the subsistent 'oligarchy.' The newborn political system was small, albeit able to fit into Giovanni Sartori's polarized plural model (1980), where negotiations among political actors are replaced by political zero-sum games, since it replicated the post-war ideological cleavages. Meanwhile, the media remained unchanged as it clung to old creole (criollo) patrimonialist values: politics and social life were depicted and analyzed from a traditional conservative point of view.

Unlike Odría's dictatorship (1948–1956), General Juan Velasco Alvarado's leftist military coup in October 1968 enraged the *oligarquía* – the traditional, extremely conservative upper classes. Both press and broadcasters discharged all their artillery against the government's radical reforms. In July 1974, the government reacted against the constant criticisms of the media by taking over the national newspapers' headquarters and, in an extremely populist move, entrusting them to the so-called organized sectors of the population: El Comercio was handed over to the National Agrarian Confederation and La Prensa to 'communities' of industrial workers (Peirano Bartet, Ballón and Váldez, 1978). And although the military took over the two largest broadcasting networks, the business model was not altered: stations and outlets continued to operate on the basis of advertising. The governmental measures cannot, therefore, be construed as strict expropriation. Quite limited market liberalism was mixed with strong state interventionism. In the end, however, not even those 'organized sectors' were able to bring new topics or debates into the public agenda since, in real terms, the military tightened the controls over most journalistic content. Explicit censorship became the rule. Upon being seized, newspapers, radio stations, and national TV networks were transformed into misleading instruments of pompous military propaganda.

The end of the Velasco Alvarado dictatorship in 1980 brought about the restitution of the political *status quo ante* as well as a newly elected civilian government whose first political decision was to restore the mass media to their owners. Shortly thereafter, the old polarized pluralist political system was restored, but society had changed and new actors – from entrepreneurial organizations to the lethal anti-establishment terrorist group Sendero Luminoso (Shining Path) – wanted to secure their place in the aftermath of the dictatorship. Under such circumstances, journalism became excessively instrumentalized and public opinion reflected such belligerence. The accumulation of economic demands soon led to a political overflow during most of the two five-year presidential terms of the 1980s. The economic results were disastrous: a hyperinflation exceeding 2,000 percent and 2,170,000 percent,[3] respectively, for the Fernando Belaunde and Alan García consecutive administrations, and a reduction of real salaries to pre-1960 levels. Concurrently, a situation of warfare caused by the emergence of terrorist and violent organizations brought one-third of the national territory under military control. The struggle against terrorism resulted in more than 70,000 victims (Comisión de la Verdad y la Reconciliación, 2003).

Those difficulties notwithstanding, media markets continued to operate through publicity and advertising. However, this operation was always adapting to the uncertain conditions induced by the crisis, as manifested by the sudden investment cutbacks and the close scrutiny of the government. The election of Alberto Fujimori – an outsider – in 1990, brought to light the general discredit of the political parties and the distrust of the popular sectors toward the mass media. Twenty months after taking office, Fujimori staged a self-coup that was pushed through and backed as much by the military as by the intelligence services. The national media was quick to throw its support behind this civilian-military regime, and both the entrepreneurial community and the majority of the public opinion promptly followed suit. The bitter memories of the failures of Alan García's administration – in particular the decomposition of the social tissue – coupled with Fujimori's successful neoliberal recipes to stop inflation and his defeat of Sendero Luminoso legitimized Fujimori's actions and transformed him into the guardian of the social order and monetary stability. This indulgent acceptance of authoritarianism did not prevent either the most serious print media – the center-left La República (founded in 1981) and El Comercio – or some radio stations from criticizing the regime, even though the influence of their observations did not reach beyond the middle classes and a few trade unions. It must be recalled that the economic breakdown led to a decrease in newspaper circulation – 20 copies per 1,000 inhabitants – whereas television audiences rose higher. A 1991 study reported that 87.5 percent of households in Lima – and 56 percent nationwide – were equipped with at least one TV set (Saavedra, 1992).

The increasing popularity of television among a public that has largely lacked a tradition of readership sealed the fortunes of the printed media at a time of economic upheaval. Readership only slightly increased again before the end of the century. In opposition, the profits for the yellow press boomed. The growing figures reported by these tabloids, known as *prensa chicha*[4] in Peru, hid a series of state subsidies from 1999 to 2000. The subsidizer was no more and no less than the intelligence services, the real political brain of the Fujimori regime. Specific orders were constantly given to publicly slander opposition leaders. However, even after Fujimori's downfall the readership of this kind of press continued to increase as it proved to be a successful business model – the cheapest newspapers cost US$0.20. The clever use of popular jargon, the humor, the attractive layout, and the flashy colors express the feeling of a new market, which in the words of Marcel Velásquez is composed of '[...] a plebeian culture where the oral and the visual trump written reasoning, where parody and making fun of politicians abound' (2007: 187). In this century, *chicha* press is the print media's main resource for survival. Both the inclusion of political information in their pages as well as the adoption of the *chicha* style by other publications have brought about its transformation. In 2001, El Comercio decided to launch a *chicha*-like tabloid called Trome, Peruvian slang for 'smart guy.' Its share of newspaper readership rapidly reached 40 percent, twice that of El Comercio. The profile of a 'serious' press has been modified by other contents, oriented to a more casual readership. The extreme contrast between the sensationalist and the 'serious' press has somewhat faded and been replaced by a variety of hybrids (Velásquez, 2007: 184). From 2007 to 2011, newspaper circulation – especially that of *chicha*-like tabloids – rose nationwide. In 2012, Trome ranked among the top-selling tabloids in South America, with more than half a million copies in Lima alone.[5]

Television

Unlike print media, television channels defined their commercial and non-political vocation from the outset by transposing the U.S. liberal model based on the sale of advertising time (Vivas-Sabroso, 2008; Gargurevich-Regal, 1987). Owing to the exiguity of markets, TV came late to Peru. The booming economy of the 1950s, though, allowed for the consolidation of radio broadcasting companies. In 1958 and 1959, Radio América and Radio Panamericana began to broadcast TV commercial programs[6] – the latter in cooperation with NBC, the former with CBS – as was the case elsewhere in Latin America (Sinclair, 1999). Ferocious competition for audiences ensued among these radio stations. Just over a half of the stations founded in the 1950s survived until 1970: Channel 9 (owned by El Comercio); and three networks, Panamericana, América, and the state-owned TV Peru. In Lima, the TV market slowly – albeit steadily – expanded from less than 8 percent of households in 1960 (only 55,000 TV sets) to 80 percent from 1975 and 1985 (Protzel, 1994: 208), before reaching 90 percent in this century. In 2008, 93 percent of urban Peruvian households had at least one TV set; 97 percent for Lima (CPI, 2009). By that time, cable and satellite broadcast subscriptions reached 25 percent of households. In 2012, approximately 1,259 TV stations and 3,273 radio stations were registered in Peru (ConcorTV, 2012). During the 1990s, the TV market witnessed a growing property concentration process. By the beginning of 2013, five large media groups could be identified. The group ECO (acronym for El Comercio) – which owns both Trome and the successful political tabloid Peru 21 – as well as Gestión, a daily specializing in corporate business. Moreover, in 1999, ECO launched Channel N, which is a cable news broadcast service tailored along CNN format and style. Later, ECO bought América Televisión, the most watched TV network closely connected to Mexico's Televisa. A minor shareholder of América is La República Group, founded in 1981 by a social-democrat entrepreneur. Despite a rather low readership, La República is influential and well respected for the quality of its editorials. This group decided to publish two popular *chicha*-like daily papers: El Popular and Líbero.

In September 2013, ECO took over the Epensa Group, formerly the third Peruvian conglomerate. With the acquisition of Epensa, ECO concentrates more than 80 percent of the newspaper market's sales: more than three times the concentration of the TV and printed press markets in Brazil (Mastrini and Becerra, 2006: 31). The publications of Epensa include the ultra-rightist Correo and three other sensationalist tabloids, as their names suggest: Ojo, Ajá and El Bocón. The fourth media group is mainly involved in radio. It owns the six leading stations, of which the first RPP – or Radio Programas del Perú – broadcasts the most listened newscasts nationwide: RPP reaches 30 percent of the audiences in Lima; 32 percent in the provinces. In 2011, RPP's new TV broadcasting and an Internet news service put them in direct competition with El Comercio's Canal N (Cisneros-Hamann, 2009: 68–77).

The fifth and most recent media group belongs to Mexican entrepreneur Ángel González, who also owns various other Latin American TV networks through his Albavisión Communications Group. In Peru, he owns ATV (Andina de Televisión), a national network, along with Red Global (Global Network) and ATV Plus, among other local stations in smaller towns. Besides these five networks, there is Plus TV, a transnational broadcast corporation based in Lima that belongs to Media Networks, itself controlled by Spain's Telefónica.

According to Mastrini and Becerra (2006: 33), the first four TV corporations concentrate 87 percent of the market and 82 percent of the audiences in Peru where the degree of concentration, in their estimate, surpasses those of Argentina and Brazil. In Argentina, Artear (channel 13), Telefé (channel 11), and Canal 9 Argentina concentrate 46 percent of the market, whereas the colossus Globo network from Brazil owns 49 percent of the TV market (Mastrini and Becerra, 2006: 126–134).

'Captured liberalism' and polarization: political parallelism and media alignment

Since the 1950s, practically all of the significant Peruvian mass media have operated under the liberal commercial model. However, the Peruvian media system was explicitly captured by the state during the military intervention (1974–1980) and – more subtly – during the Fujimori government (1992–2000). Despite those moments of open state intervention, the media in Peru has been organized under a pluralist and frequently polarized pattern. This pattern is clearer in the press than in broadcast.

The increasing relevance of the media in Peru has coincided with the decreasing prestige of political parties. The decay of parties relates to diverse critical factors upon which the parties were unable to offer viable solutions: the emergence of the guerrilla, hyperinflation, and rampant political corruption. There was, as Tanaka argues (1998: 201–203), a breakup of the tacit pact made among the parties at the end of the military government in 1980. Fujimori's economic stability restored confidence to recently urbanized popular sectors whose brief experience of post-military constitutional governments was disappointing. Despite the suppression of civic rights – a common practice among dictators – Fujimori's plebiscitary authoritarianism was the rule, and it became so successful among the broad majority that 'traditional parties' lost their meaning as legitimate vehicles of political interests. As corporate business recovered and foreign investment returned to benefit from the privatization of public companies, the political spectrum was moving to the right. The disastrous political and economic failures of the 1980s were identified by Fujimori's administration with an excess of rhetoric and ideology. Simultaneously, the short-term positive results – most notably the economic recovery – increased the civilian-military regime's legitimacy and prestige, despite its self-coup's origins. Opposition was dramatically cornered, and it garnered little popular sympathy.

In such a media setting, it was no surprise that the media – TV in particular – became a natural ally of Fujimori's regime. Support for the government was not only the consequence of corporate success and financial stability, but mainly of a deliberate attempt by the state to instrumentalize the media's information tasks. The pressure coming from the intelligence services directed by Vladimiro Montesinos, the so-called presidential advisor, hung like the sword of Damocles over the highest rated networks. Journalists and media entrepreneurs were bribed, while the 'serious press' – like El Comercio and La República – lost readership and the *chicha* press, which was subsidized by the intelligence services, mushroomed. Both the defeat of Sendero Luminoso and the subduing of inflation consolidated the image of an efficient yet silent leader (*caudillo*) to whom absolute, unfettered trust and loyalty was due. O'Donnell (1995) defines a *delegative democracy* as characterized by the unlimited control of the executive in all decisions, and a subsequent overshadow of intermediation mechanisms and political accountability. This meant a crisis of representative democracy.

Hence the notion of political parallelism used by Hallin and Mancini is somehow unfit to describe Peru from the 1990s on. Inspired by geometry, this metaphor of two trajectories running together without touching each other implicitly assigns a certain continuity to parties and – more broadly – to the institutional system, as it could be the case of other Latin American countries like Mexico. Parallelism, understood as media support (or criticism) to party orientations through instrumentalized discourses, is a valid notion *if parties really serve as intermediaries between the institutional system and the civil society*. But, as we previously said, the Peruvian party system had collapsed by the end of the 20th century. For instance, the only 'historic' Peruvian party, APRA, went into decay (while new parties and coalitions were created) just for supporting *ad hoc* candidacies in specific elections. Strong figures led these catch-all political organizations '[...] with an inclination to present a diversified political offer, with lax ideological proposals, and a tendency to the political center that feebly differentiated them from other political forces' (Grompone, 1999: 260). However, an exception to this new political landscape was Ollanta Humala's Nationalist Party, which enjoyed strong support in the Andean region.[7] The deep demobilization that extended during the Fujimori years – a corollary of the sort of delegative democracy that Peru was experiencing – gave the government an unchecked capacity for imposing its policies and actions.

Most media outlets kept their brand and some of their previous style, although the owners decided to instrumentalize the editorial lines.

Expreso, a former pro-Communist Party tabloid of the military years, suddenly became center-right. The wealthy Miró Quesada family, the main shareholders of El Comercio, witnessed the changes that took place in the outlets' political orientation in function of who was in control of the board of directors. Nevertheless, the instrumentalization of the media never reached the extremes of Venezuela, where the executive hosted programs like Aló Presidente, and where a powerful broadcast network (RCTV) was shut down by decree (Cañizález, 2012; see also Chapter 8 in this book).

After Fujimori's departure and the scandalous disclosure of corruption, the media – particularly TV networks – shifted back to their traditional criticisms.[8] For instance, América Televisión – the then-powerful governmental propaganda agency – briefly turned into a highly critical and pro-democratic network, before reverting to a conservative position. In Peru, a truly liberal media model did not come with the restoration of the private commercial model. The decline of parties – which coincided with the emergence of new media contents, channels, and outlets – suggests that political parallelism – as described by Hallin and Mancini (2004) – has not occurred in Peru. However, this situation has not prevented the instrumentalization of the media and journalism; and although instrumentalization may, under specific circumstances, be accompanied by polarization instead of following ideological or party affiliations, it now moves along the political cleavages left by Fujimori.

Two features define today's media landscape in Peru. First, the predominance of political sensationalism – both in broadcast and print media – over political debate: It is not that such topics were absent before, but have become the only kind of 'politics' being reflected and reported in the media. The corruption of political actors feeds this sort of 'journalism' and contributes to the continued discredit of politics in Peru. Second, the growing economic power of the strongest media organizations that use their capacity to show images and give (or deny) voice to politicians become themselves inevitable actors in politics. In this regard, the relevance of visual media contributes to what Bernard Manin (1997) calls an *audience democracy,* turning these media into *de facto* powers.

These two aspects were reinforced after the Fujimori regime during the catch-all political orientation of the Toledo, García, and Humala administrations. The only recognizable – but sometimes blurry – political cleavage in today's Peru is the confronting authoritarianism associated to Fujimori and his legacy to a 'civic' democracy impersonated by public opinion leaders, civil society organizations, and even well-known journalists. It is evident that actors – not parties – represent such cleavage. Consequently, in a setting where the parties are weak, the media coverage ends up focusing on the actors while contributing to the personalization of politics in Peru. Nevertheless, such personalization cannot be blamed solely on the media – especially not the broadcast media. They have just fit – due both to semiotics and formats – with a new style of politicians who obviate the support of a solid party apparatus that is almost nonexistent anyway – which is very different to what happened in Peru in the 1980s (Grompone, 1999: 289–292).

How to evaluate, then, the predominance of Peruvian media within its political system? After Fujimori's authoritarian regime, Peru's political system has not fully regained its legitimacy and now, three administrations later, Peruvian transition to democracy is still unfinished. The governments of Toledo, Garcia, and the current Humala's are comparable in their use of center-right – in Alberto Adrianzén's words – 'welfare populist projects' (2009: 171–176). The media, defined by sensationalism and the consolidation of corporations, have become the perfect battlefield where the crossfire of scandals, denunciations, and insults has brought some journalists to the forefront where their opinions and investigative reports confer them tremendous symbolic power. They are the spokespeople of a *cultura de guerra* – culture of war – a continuum throughout the history of the republic (Dargent-Bocanegra, 2009: 111–112). Political 'operators' – some of them retired members of the armed forces – may frequently be found therein, as they accomplish important tasks of hidden intermediation with the media and other organizations. They know how to record telephone conversations and copy e-mail messages of facts and issues of public interest to maybe sell selectively to either sensationalist media or even to investigative reporters.

Another circumstance that favors a journalistic practice without political parallelism is the limited interest of the established parties toward emergent social movements, particularly those active in rural marginal zones (Grompone, 2005: 77–115). The demands of these groups are usually located on the extreme left – outside the formal political spectrum – or, less commonly, criticized by most established parties and the majority of the largest media. Only small local print media and community radio stations cover these kinds of movements – journalists do not normally report on these matters – thus setting the stage for ideological debate. It is only in the state – only outside the market, that is – where pure political parallelism can be found. Both the government-funded media outlets, the Institute for Radio and Television in Peru (IRTP, by its Spanish acronym) and El Peruano (the official daily) have strictly followed the line given by every government.

Journalistic professionalism and its margins of autonomy

The predominance of liberal market conditions does not bring the Peruvian media closer to the journalistic practices of 'neutrality' that some U.S. newspapers pride themselves on having. After the Fujimori regime, though, a renewed purpose of journalism for research and investigation – coupled with some degree of journalistic autonomy from the mass media – has brought hope.

The Peruvian republican 'culture of war' mentioned above is part of an old élite-oriented journalistic tradition which somehow predated political parties (McEvoy, 1999). For over a century, most political journalism was the work of nonconformist intellectuals. Except for strictly manual tasks and internal management, very low salaries were the rule as journalism – unlike law or medicine – was not considered a profession. Journalists were rarely paid. Non-remunerated symbolic power was a countervailing factor to professionalization, with most content-related decisions being left in the hands of the editor-owner.

The consolidation of the reporter's tasks and the establishment of distinct norms of exercise – two of the three elements required for professionalization according to Hallin and Mancini (2004: 33–34) – were achieved with the emergence of El Comercio and La Prensa around 1930 (Gargurevich-Regal, 1991: 112–115). But the third element, namely commitment to public service on the part of the professional journalist, was barely understood because of the persistent patrimonialism and family ownership of the newspaper companies that gave enormous power particularly to the editor's position.

As advertising incomes grew and media business became sustainable during the 1990s, the absence of a truly 'neutral' press did not prevent the recognition of a true professionalism based on respect to common principles. This entailed a minimum of internal pluralism. Unlike the best years of the Mirror in Great Britain, L'Humanité in France, or L'Unità in Italy, no print media in Peru has survived on ideological popular readership. Moreover, without state protections or subsidies, good critical journalism had to be built upon a difficult balance between immediate profit and readership and time-consuming quality investigative journalism. Since state intervention in Peruvian media has not been oriented to helping citizens receive information, supports like postal distribution or subsidies are absent and so is the idea of building a public broadcast service, like those in Spain, France, and Germany. Actually, the debate on such a proposal is closed given the bitter experience of the 1974 confiscation. The well-intentioned journalists and intellectuals who originally believed that change was necessary were soon deceived by the 1974 experience. The memory of the confiscation makes today's academics and professionals reluctant to accept any sort of state intervention in the media.

Coupled with the expansion of the markets and the technological revolution, the recovery of media spaces 'captured' during the Fujimori regime has consolidated a media system characterized by re-segmented audiences, the predominance of *chicha*-like outlets, and politically non-aligned media organizations. The outcome is a clear stratification of readership and audiences matching the socioeconomic differences of the population and regions.[9] Internal pluralism predominates in these new mostly tabloid outlets, but the decision-making power from both editors and owners remains strong. Young, poorly paid graduate students make up most of the task force in the country's media organizations. Some trainees do not even get paid. These semi-informal labor conditions allow editors to bypass the standards of internal pluralism, save money, and maintain old patrimonialistic habits.

Conclusion: some words on politics and communication in the digital environment

In Peru, the media operates in a context where political parties are weak. In this context politicians have established different sorts of relations with the media that, on the one hand, enable them to directly address audiences, and on the other grant the media constant sensationalist contents to sell. It may be difficult to classify such a system under the polarized pluralist model of Mediterranean countries described in Hallin and Mancini's (2004) seminal work. Rather, it approaches the liberal model to the extent that dependency on sales and advertising increases the current configuration of media conglomerates. However, the resemblance with a truly liberal model stops there, since it is not only the commercial and market-driven orientation that define the Peruvian media landscape. If it is acknowledged that the relatively recent territorial expansion of information and political bids reaches very diverse audiences and readersthat forces the media to practice pluralism, then such pluralism has led to a kind of coverage that favors political sensationalism instead of public interest debatesthat has sacrificed the development of professional journalism.

If it is true that this trend has been present since the emergence of growing mass audiences and readers, then the expansion of TV audiences during the 1980s was a milestone in the history of the Peruvian public sphere, as public leaders were made visible for the vast majority. And politics began to be turned into a spectacle. Television enabled politicians to directly address citizens, thus giving rise to common discourses nationwide. It also brought to daylight the hidden sides of power, thereby making some organizational, logistic, and ideological functions of the parties irrelevant.

This chapter has discussed the general configuration of the traditional media landscape in Peru and its linkages with politics, but here a few words need to be said regarding the emergence of digital technologies and their irruption into politics, since the growing penetration of the Internet and mobile telecommunications make a more radical difference.

Between 2005 and 2010, Internet access grew from 3.7 percent to 14 percent of the total population, while the penetration of mobile telephones went from 20.5 percent to 95.5 percent (Freundt-Thurne, Pita and Ampuero 2012: 15).[10] This almost sudden increase has deprived the Peruvian map of collective actors – let alone parties – who are losing their already weakened centrality. Political interaction is no longer exclusive of parties; access to it is possible for a broad variety of people and institutions, the beneficiaries of this revolution. New communication platforms emerge both as sources of information and opinion and as forums to hurl insults and engage in blackmail. Political maps redefine themselves in terms of access to ICTs. For example, some 80 percent of Internet users in Lima are affiliated to either Facebook or Twitter, or both (Ipsos Perú, 2012).

Hence, political actors – including the president – are obliged to cope with these changes and move beyond television to websites and Twitter to communicate more directly and personally. The 2011 presidential campaign, which saw the intense use of Internet and social networks for the first time, launched Pedro Pablo Kuczynski's rightist candidacy to a surprising third place. This outsider gained support among the upper and middle classes, regular users of Facebook, with a very well designed campaign; conversely, Ollanta Humala appealed to the poorest. The weight of the greater media was diminished, contrary to what happened in the 1995 election, when private mass media operated within – in Manuel Alejandro Guerrero's labels – a captured liberal model (See Chapter 2 in this collection) as well as with the 2006 election of Alan García, when most media took a pro-García stance with the aim to prevent Ollanta Humala's allegedly anti-system victory.

Though traditional media are still preferred by largest audiences, they are using digital tools to obtain feedback from readers and viewers, which might either generate or confirm opinion flows. Traditional media fill their digital sites with multimedia contents, whose sources are also in the Web. In this sense, these media are not blind to what Manuel Castells calls 'self-mass communication' (2009: 99–108), that is, the capacity for individual media users to become advocates (or detractors) of public issues with the aim to attract followers or team up with peers.

At the same time, a new sort of journalism is developing in the digital media that does not submit to the market or to the tactical requirements of either candidates or parties struggling for power. This journalism, '[...] has become an alternative for the dissemination of issues which corporations find uncomfortable and which may be politically incorrect' (Freundt-Thurne et al., 2012: 43). Likewise, investigative reporting practiced with digital tools and without market pressures is frequently a source for journalistic TV programs, especially in matters of corruption. These unusual margins of autonomy are also redefining journalism with better standards of proficiency.

Notes

1. The Argentinian Unión Cívica Radical (Radical Civic Union) appeared in 1891 and after a 21-year struggle it achieved the introduction of secret voting, expanding democratic participation. The Chilean Communist Party originated as early as 1912, and the foundation of the Chilean Socialist Party goes back to 1933, almost the same as the APRA.
2. Since its beginnings the APRA party was a sizable collectivity not only of militants, many of them rural workers from the sugar plantations of northern Peru and its Andean *hinterland*, but also of Lima's working-class movement and the educated middle-class sectors.
3. From 1975 to 1994, the Peruvian annual inflation rate was consistently above 20 percent.
4. The word '*chicha*' is the name of an Andean alcoholic beverage, which has served to name a hybrid popular music gender in the urban context, but has been generally applied to the whole popular urban culture, derogatively or otherwise.
5. *Source*: KPMG (2012).
6. The first signal on the air was not really private but public. The Peruvian Ministry of Education, backed by UNESCO sponsorship, inaugurated its transmissions in January of 1958 when the historian Jorge Basadre was at the helm of the ministry (Gargurevich-Regal, 1976: 152).
7. The party enjoyed support from the Andean highland towns. Before transforming into a party, it was an anti-system organization with strong affinities with Venezuelan *Chavismo*. Once in the presidency, Ollanta Humala moved to a center-right orientation.

8. Perhaps one of the worst scandals relates to what is known as 'Vladivideos,' hidden-camera video tape recordings of Vladimiro Montesinos – Peru's Chief Security Officer – handing bundles of cash to corrupt broadcasters, politicians, and judges.
9. A complete list of daily Peruvian newspapers published in print or digitally may be consulted at www.diariosdeperu.com.pe.
10. An index calculated upon the number of active SIM cards as a percentage of the total population.

References

Adrianzén, A. (2009) *La transición inconclusa. De la década autoritaria al nacimiento del pueblo* (Lima: Otra Mirada).
Cañizález, A. (2012) *Hugo Chávez: la presidencia mediática* (Caracas: Alfa).
Castells, M. (2009) *Comunicación y poder* (Madrid: Alianza).
Cisneros-Hamann, L. J. (2009 December) 'El poder de los grupos (mediáticos),' *Poder 360º*, 15. Available at http://bit.ly/1doGsZF (accessed December 2013).
Comisión de la Verdad y la Reconciliación (2003) *Informe final*. Available at http://bit.ly/1lvNUqh (accessed March 24, 2013).
ConcorTv (2012) 'Informes anuales.' Available at: http//bit.ly/1dQngpi (accessed March 25, 2013).
Cotler, J. (1978) *Clases, Estado y Nación en el Perú* (Lima: IEP).
CPI (2009–2013) 'Boletines,' Compañía Peruana de Estudios de Mercado y Opinión Pública SAC. Available at http://bit.ly/1kXwncY (accessed March 8, 2013).
Dargent-Bocanegra, E. (2009) *Demócratas precarios. Élites y debilidad democrática en el Perú y América Latina* (Lima: IEP).
Easton, D. (2007) 'Categorías para el análisis sistémico de la política,' pp. 221–230 in A. Batlle (ed.) *Diez textos básicos de ciencia política* (Barcelona: Ariel).
Freedom House (2013) *Freedom in the World 2013*. Available at http://bit.ly/1enF37V (accessed March 10, 2013).
Freundt-Thurne, Ú., Pita, C. and Ampuero, M. J. (2012) *Mapping Digital Media: Peru*. Open Society Foundations. Available at http://osf.to/1lvOrbL (accessed April 11, 2013).
Gargurevich-Regal, J. (1976) *Introducción a la historia de los medios de comunicación en el Perú* (Lima: Horizonte).
Gargurevich-Regal, J. (1987) *Prensa, radio y televisión: una historia crítica* (Lima: Horizonte).
Gargurevich-Regal, J. (1991) *Historia de la prensa peruana 1594–1990* (Lima: La Voz).
Gargurevich-Regal, J. (2005) *Última Hora. La fundación de un diario popular* (Lima: La Voz).
Grompone, R. (1999) *Las nuevas reglas del juego. Transformaciones sociales, culturales y políticas en Lima* (Lima: IEP).
Grompone, R. (2005) *La escisión inevitable. Partidos y movimientos en el Perú actual* (Lima: IEP).
Hallin, D. and Mancini, P. (2004) *Comparing Media Systems. Three Models of Media and Politics* (Cambridge: Cambridge University Press).

Hallin, D. and Papathanassopoulos, S. (2002) 'Political clientelism and the media: Southern Europe and Latin America in comparative perspective,' *Media, Culture & Society*, 24(2): 175–195.

Ipsos Perú (2012) *Perfil del internauta limeño* (Lima: Ipsos Perú).

KPMG (2012) *Circulación de diarios en el Perú*. Available at http://bit.ly/1lvOzbf (accessed March 22, 2013).

Manin, B. (1997) *The Principles of Representative Government* (Cambridge: Cambridge University Press).

Mastrini, G. and Becerra, M. (2006) *Periodistas y magnates. Estructura y concentración de las industrias culturales en América Latina*. Buenos Aires: Prometeo.

McEvoy, C. (1999) *Forjando la Nación. Ensayos de historia republicana* (Lima: PUCP/ The University of the South, Sewanee).

O'Donnell, G. (1995) '¿Democracia delegativa?,' pp. 7–23 in R. Grompone (comp.) *Instituciones políticas y democracia* (Lima: Instituto de Estudios Peruanos).

Peirano, L., Bartet, L., Ballón, E. and Váldez, G. (1978) *Prensa: apertura y límites* (Lima: Desco).

Protzel, J. (1994) 'El paradigma del Príncipe: el líder, la Razón de Estado y los medios electrónicos,' *Contratexto*, 7: 21–29.

Saavedra, M. (1992) *El rating* (Lima: Mercadeo Latino).

Sartori, G. (1980) *Partidos y sistemas de partidos Marco para un análisis* (Madrid: Alianza).

Sinclair, J. (1999) *Latin American Television. A Global View* (Oxford: Oxford University Press).

Stein, S. (1980) *Populism in Peru. The Emergence of the Masses and the Politics of Social Control* (Madison: University of Wisconsin Press).

Tanaka, M. (1998) *Los espejismos de la democracia. El colapso del sistema de partidos en el Perú* (Lima: IEP).

Velásquez, M. (2007) 'El mal/estar en la cultura chicha: la prensa sensacionalista,' pp. 181–198 in Santiago López et al. *Industrias culturales. Máquina de deseos en el mundo contemporáneo* (Lima: Red para el Desarrollo de las Ciencias Sociales en el Perú).

Vivas-Sabroso, F. (2008) *En vivo y en directo. Una historia de la televisión peruana* (Lima: Universidad de Lima).

5
The Complex Relationship Between the Media and the Political System in Argentina: From Co-option to Polarization

Jorge Liotti

Introduction

Recent Argentinian history has been marked by constant political, economic, and social alterations. The drastic changes, including periodic and deep crises, experimented and redefined the logics in the exercise of power, the role of the state, and the economic system, and even altered some aspects of national identity. Moreover, the population became used to an ineffective rule of law and to political discourses and actions that easily fell into extremes.

It is necessary to situate the development of media and journalism and their linkages to the political and economic systems within this fluctuating and unstable context (Ruiz, 2010). In these aspects, Argentina has faced similar processes to other Latin American countries, especially during democratic transitions. In this period, it is undeniable that freedom of speech and important technological developments regarding communication were achieved and these allowed the multiplication of broadcasting possibilities. The simultaneity of both processes gave way to the transformation of the media scenario according to the new ruling political coordinates in the continent. Nevertheless, Argentina has had variations of its own that have turned the country into a special case inside this context.

Taking into account the central consideration of Hallin and Mancini (2004) that the political system and the institutional tradition of a country find a direct relation in the media ecosystem (Hallin and

Mancini, 2004), this chapter assesses the case of Argentina in order to identify how both matrixes have influenced each other since the end of the dictatorship, and its effects on the development of journalism. In this evaluation, it is possible to identify at least three stages in the past four decades, when the current media map was developed. Each of them presents very different characteristics and shows the depth of the contrast generated by political, economic, and technological transformations. Then some considerations on journalism are analyzed.

Under the control of the military dictatorship

During the first stage, under the military dictatorship between 1976 and 1983, politics dominated the relationship with the media. A whole submission occurred in the case of radio and television through direct management. In the case of the print media – where property was kept private thanks to basic agreements with the military – control was exercised through absolute surveillance of contents and the harrying of dissidents. The state co-optation of the media sought to shape its editorial policy and contents and to regulate their functions almost absolutely. In order to achieve that, a structure of control and organization was created that was composed of several public agencies and offices all governed by the three armed forces (Navy, Air Force and Defense). Broadcasting Law Decree No. 22,285 was passed: it gave the authority ample capacities for the regulation of contents, although at the same time, it allowed the private holders of licenses to make good profits.

The Decree excluded the participation of nonprofit organizations, but it fostered a mutually beneficial coexistence model with the private sector. The most important example was the creation of Papel Prensa, the only supplier of newsprint that was a joint venture between the state and the newspapers Clarín, La Nación and La Razón. These distortions produced by the military dictatorship had a lasting existence even after democratic restoration, since they gave shape to a concentrated media structure connected to the variations in political power and unconcerned with the construction of pluralistic regulatory frameworks. Moreover, the proximity of media owners with political elites and their close role in the changes that took place within the system were set as guaranteed principles of continuity and progress. In some way, this period promoted an indulgent way of thinking about the relation between media and politics defined by their reciprocal utility.

The second stage started with the democratic restoration in 1983 with President Raúl Alfonsín. The recovery of public liberties undermined the censorship model established by the dictatorship, giving rise to a 'democratic spring' that could also be seen in arts and culture in general (Ulanovsky, 1997). In spite of the revival of a variety of opinions unheard in the previous years, the Alfonsín administration had a tortuous relationship with the media. His administration was prey to its own hesitancy and lack of determination to transform the media system. This was a result of the pressures still exerted by the military, together with invigorated trade unions and the Peronist party, that despite losing the elections, was still ruling many provinces. As part of the discussions held by the Consejo de Consolidación para la Democracia – COCODE, a council aiming at consolidating democracy, the government elicited debate on reforming the dictatorship's Law Decree No. 22,285. Nevertheless, this debate was unsuccessful due to the government's failure to offer proper support to any of the multiple initiatives, even inside the ruling party.

Despite this failure, debates on media reform did give rise to two clear concepts. The first was the proposal to consolidate a commercial media model with low regulatory levels and high participation of the private sector. The second concept was close to a decentralized European regime with higher participation of the state and intermediate organizations. As Sergio Com points out, 'the Radical ruling party was dubious and ambiguous, and these aspects also reached broadcasting. These doubts by the Executive Branch and the lack of coordination by the opposition party brought about broadcasting bills introduced mainly by individual party members that were not the result of consensual projects' (Com, 2009).

Consequently, while a new legal framework could not be outlined during the Alfonsín administration, two antagonistic models were on the table. However, due to the political impasse in practical terms the influence of the private sector grew, taking good advantage of the opportunities created by the new discourse on freedom and the new business opportunities in the horizon. The possibility to create large media holding companies was an unavoidable attraction and a trend all over the world.

At this stage, the electronic media were still under the control of the state (the most relevant exception was Channel 9 owned by businessman Alejandro Romay), strongly influenced by the political power, but the airs were moving toward content pluralism. It was in this changing atmosphere where the Clarín Group was granted, in a quite irregular procedure, the license of Mitre radio. At the end of this period, the Alfonsín administration was defined more by turning over the page after a dark military dictatorship and its censoring structure, than by the generation of new structures, including the media matrix.

Co-option of markets

Transformation took place when Carlos Menem took office in 1989, and it was marked by the privatization of television channels and radio stations, as well as by the establishment of an openly neoliberal model that decidedly defined this second stage. If the Alfonsín administration represented the first steps of the transition, the Menem administration enabled its fulfillment.

Soon after taking office, Menem achieved the passing of the state reform law, which modified essential aspects of the dictatorship's broadcasting Law Decree No. 22,285. In some other aspects, several restrictions were eliminated like those that constrained concentration and cross-ownership, those that prohibited print media owners to hold broadcasting licenses, and those that limited participation in the broadcasting market only to businessmen related to journalism (Rossi, 2009). As a result of these changes, there began a fast transformation process with the merging of printed and broadcasting groups at a time when cable and satellite services were just around the corner to be explored as fruitful businesses. Clarín, already involved with Mitre radio, took over Channel 13 and afterwards created cable operator Multicanal; while Telefe, controlled by Editorial Atlántida, acquired the licenses for Channel 11 and Continental radio, entering shortly afterwards into the cable television business. These groups achieved the introduction of foreign capital – something that was restricted by Law Decree No. 22,285 – through the strong promotion of an international treaty concerning the Reciprocal Encouragement and Protection of Investment that was signed with the United States.

At this stage, the media map was redesigned and the main media groups emerged with large margins of action and limited regulatory restrictions to expand into new markets. Unlike previous years, throughout the 1990s, the private sector became very powerful and began to set the terms of the relationship with the political power. Due to the neoliberal and strong market reforms implemented by the Menem administration, the state withdrew almost entirely as a key participant in the media scenario, and as regulator and generator of contents (Mastrini and Bolaño, 2000). It became an age of private commercial expansion that did not build a pluralist democratic system but a model strictly ruled by economic factors. Particularly during Menem's first term up to 1995, a strong relation existed between the private sector – benefited by a concessive and flexible national administration – and the government, benefited by a soft press, even when at the end of Menem's term the media began to look closer at several cases of corruption. The resulting trends were both the expansion of media business in the hands of groups with interests external to journalism, and a growing concentration of existing media corporations, since there was no incentive by the state to establish an harmonious and balanced framework (Mastrini and Becerra, 2006).

Dealing with the crisis

The administrations of Fernando De la Rúa and Eduardo Duhalde, in the period between the unstable end of the Menem administration in 1999 and the beginning of the Kirchner administration in 2003, did not have enough strength, capacity and time to implement critical transformations in the relationship with the media. Moreover, the economic crisis created a common front in the media – heavily indebted in dollars through the convertibility system in place – of being aligned with the government to share the need that the news does not deepen the unsettled social scenario.

De la Rúa, in his crusade against the corruption and arbitrariness typical of the Menem administration, drove the regulatory process in the radio electric spectrum, flooded with transmissions by broadcasters whose licenses were not short of irregularities. As a hint of a possible communication policy, he made progress toward the creation of a National System of Public Media (Sistema Nacional de Medios Públicos – SNMP), bringing together under the same direction the already existing state channel (rebaptized as Channel 7 after many years known as ATC), Nacional Radio, and the Telam official agency. Moreover, the De la Rúa administration drafted a project to reform the dictatorship's broadcasting law decree that did not substantially modify the structure of the media but that was not passed anyway. Therefore, his tenure lacked a clear political will to deeply revise the relationship between the political power and the media, and instead tended to be in agreement with the media companies.

His successor Eduardo Duhalde, on the other hand, only managed to remain in office for a year and a half in the middle of one of Argentina's deepest economic, social, and political crises that brought to an end the De la Rúa administration. The Duhalde administration was therefore weak, devoted to rebuilding internal peace, and to guiding the economy to a post-convertibility stage. In this context, his scope of action with the media was poor and his action restricted to the renewal of broadcast licenses that were to expire (América TV), the approval of transferring broadcasting signals – Channel 9 was passed to Fernando Sokolowicz and Daniel Hadad, who started a new holding company – and mainly to support the so-called law for the Protection of Cultural Heritage and Property (Preservación de Bienes y Patrimonios Culturales). It must be said, however, that the passing of this law occurred during the early days of the first Kirchner administration in 2003. Such legislation is noteworthy because besides restricting to 30 percent the participation of foreign companies in the media, it eliminated the mechanism known as cram down, thus preventing creditors from keeping the property of the media in case of bankruptcy or payment inability. Taking into account that most large communication companies were indebted in U.S. Dollars during the convertibility period, the law meant an insurance to avoid the loss of possession. The situation was particularly severe in the case of the Clarín Group, with a debt of US$ 1 billion.

A post crisis atmosphere also marked the first years of President Néstor Kirchner's rule. He arrived to the presidency with only 22 percent of the votes (Menem withdrew from the second round of the elections facing the evidence of a sure defeat) that turned him into a weak president who required consensus to maintain governability. At the beginning of his administration, the media were not part of Kirchner's agenda. However, eventually President Kirchner agreed with them not only in the government's steady provision of exclusive information and scoops, but also an unrestrictive respect to the media's *status quo*. A decision made on May 20, 2005, to extend and renew the main broadcaster's licenses in advance (including those belonging to the Clarín Group) for ten years from their expiration dates – in some cases until 2025 – was a clear sign of this new relationship.[1] Moreover, President Kirchner even accepted – just before transferring the presidential office to his wife – the merger of the cable television companies Multicanal (from the Clarín Group) and Cablevision, although in most parts of the country this merger actually became a monopoly (Sirven, 2011). Later, when the relationship with the media turned unfavorable, Kirchner tried to stop the process. That was the reason why in September 2009, the Federal Communications Commission, *Comfer,* denied the merger between both companies and a legal process began without a conclusive decision to date.

The transformation of Kirchnerism

The consolidation of Kirchner's power that materialized in votes – with the categorical victory of his wife Cristina Kirchner in the 2007 presidential election – paved the way to a third stage in the relationship of the media with the political power. This was a period marked by a high level of stress and a deep polarization that journalism promptly reflected (Sarlo, 2011). Even when as early as 2006, the couple had begun to openly criticize some sectors of the press (the criticism was most frequently addressed to La Nacion newspaper), it was not until 2008 when profound changes appeared and a new strategy was adopted. After consolidating their rule, the Kirchners decided to struggle for power against the media moguls, since they were considered to be a risk factor due to their strong influence on public opinion (Mochkofsky, 2011). That is to say, they moved from an initial situation in which both presidents required to recognize and to negotiate with other powerful actors and interests, like those represented by the largest media corporations, to a situation where they were capable of defying these interests and groups due to their accumulation of power.

This strategy coincided with the political discourse that the Kirchners adopted. On the one hand, it was based on the promotion of a higher intervention of the state in the functioning of the economy and society, and on the other, on the need to strengthen the role of the public media. The strategy was to strengthen the state participation in an environment dominated by the private sector, and also to balance the nature of messages and to decentralize production focus. There was a healthy will to provide the state with the instruments that had been weakened by the faults of previous national administrations and by the excessive concessions made to the largest media corporations (De Moraes, 2011).

On the other hand, the Kirchners' administration developed a discourse that placed them as an oppositional force challenging the system (despite being in the presidency and coming from Peronism, one of the main political parties in Argentina since the middle of the 20th Century) and justifying their actions as a struggle against powerful 'corporations,' the name given not only to the big business but also to the traditional partisan political structure (including sectors of the Peronist party and its historical opponent, the liberal Radical party). The Kirchners appeared then as opponents of an economic establishment that allegedly benefited from the governments since the dictatorship and committed to change the 'Justice,' which was defined only as an instrument to defend the powerful, according to this interpretation. This world view was nurtured by the contributions of intellectuals such as Ernesto Laclau and Chantal Mouffe, who worked on the idea of permanent conflict as a dynamic mechanism for political construction and antagonistic of hegemonies (Mouffe, 2012; Laclau and Mouffe, 2004). Their perspective had a strong influence on large sectors of society and had a late but effective extension toward the media, considered to be responsible for 'naming and destroying governments' and 'having dismissing attitudes' in the Kirchners' words. Consequently, it was necessary to provide the state with the capacities to rebalance the biased media landscape and to oppose any kind of disagreement or criticism coming from 'the ruling hegemonic model.'

The novelty of this stage, that continues to this day, is that there seems to be room only for confrontation, not for negotiations as in past administrations. The Kirchner administration's goal was to reduce the power of the media in different ways, to corner them in terms of information and business, to discredit them before society, and to directly co-opt a group of media entrepreneurs to develop a solid propagandistic machinery (Califano, 2009). In short, the government did not resort to censorship, but justified its actions as a battle against concentrated media corporations that limit freedom of speech, defining itself as a 'national and popular' government that defends the right of the civil population to listen to multiple voices.

Nevertheless, evidence shows that the process was not guided by a genuine devotion to develop a pluralist system, similar to the democratic model mentioned by Hallin and Mancini (2004), beyond the passing of a new media law supposedly inspired on those principles. Thus, in Argentina in the past years, the media system has moved from a concentrated model of business participants with low regulatory efficacy, to another concentrated model but in the hands of the state according to the aims of the political leadership and not necessarily to those of the public interest.

Polarization strategy

In order to achieve its goals, the Kirchner administration deployed a gradual strategy, which did not seem the result of preconceived planning but of specific answers to political demands. In this context at least five mechanisms through which the government generated a deep polarization with the media can be identified.

(a) Infiltration of the market

It was set up through the acquisition of media outlets by entrepreneurs who were close to the government; this included the print media, as well as radio, television, and digital companies and ended up in the creation of a real pro-government multimedia front funded with public advertising and shaping a favorable pro-government editorial coverage.

Journalist Edi Zunino defined the model as 'guerrilla warfare.'[2] At the beginning this strategy led only to the multiplication of content broadcasting channels, since the low audience share of most of them did not produce the expected results. At a second stage nevertheless, the government tried to reach a mass audience with new alliances not so ideologically pure but instead more effective regarding audience penetration.[3]

At present, this structure counts among its main participants the business group led by Sergio Szpolsky;[4] the group of Cristóbal López, one of the most relevant businessmen in the Kirchner period;[5] the group Vila-Manzano,[6] the group Olmos,[7] the holding Moneta;[8] the group Pierri;[9] the group Electroingeniería;[10] the newspaper Página 12; the magazine Debate; and Channel 9, belonging to Mexican Ángel González.[11]

The practical outcomes of this front could be summarized as follows:

- Most of the informative spaces on television have been colonized by the pro-government structure, with the exception of Channel 13 and cable channels Todo Noticias and Metro, belonging to the Clarín Group and emphatically critical of the government. Some programs in other cable channels (e.g., Channel 26 and America 24), funded by independent producers, have also remained on the sidelines.
- Regarding radio broadcast, something similar has happened: among the main radio stations, overt criticism of governmental policies can only be heard on Mitre radio (also property of the Clarín Group) and on some programs on Continental radio (belonging to Spanish Prisa Group). There are also some isolated radio programs hired by independent producers.
- The penetration of the pro-government media has not been so successful in newspapers. The two best-selling newspapers, Clarín, with an average print run of 270,444 copies, and La Nación, with an average print run of 165,166 copies, have been critical of the government. Also the bi-weekly newspaper Perfil, with a print run on Saturdays and Sundays of 32,645 copies, could be sided with the critics thus making a triad with high power for agenda definition. Among the pro-governmental print media, the only one with an important print run is Página 12, although we cannot be precise with figures since it did not accept the monitoring of the Instituto Verificador de Circulaciones – IVC (Circulation Verification Institute). Regarding magazines, the situation is similar. The best-selling newsmagazine is Noticias, published by Perfil Editorial, opposes the government. The rest of them, mainly pro-government, do not boast of high levels of sales.

(b) The expansion of the State media structure

Public and state media are Channel 7; Nacional radio, its repeaters in the provinces; and Telam news agency. The Kirchner administration expanded these media with the new music FM radio stations such as FM Rock, FM Clásica, and FM Folklórica; with the participation in the Telesur network promoted by Venezuela; with the new TV channel Encuentro, devoted to cultural and educational contents; with INCAA TV channel (INCAA is the National Institute of Cinema and Audiovisual Arts) for broadcasting national films; with children's channel Paka-Paka; and with Argentina Satelital (ArSat), service provider of telecommunication and radio broadcasting, and with fiber optics installation through the Argentina Conectada plan. A separate case is Televisión Digital Abierta (TDA) system that is a free service created in 2009 as an attempt to compete with paid television. Although it was highly promoted with the distribution of over a million free decoders and a $3 billion investment (around U$D 576 million), its importance in the television world has been irrelevant to date.

Another controversial project was Fútbol para Todos (Football for Everybody), with the nationalization of the premier league broadcasting through a compulsory termination of the contract that the Asociación del Fútbol Argentino – AFA (Argentine Football Association) held with Torneos y Competencias, a company in which the Clarín Group was a shareholder. Although this change enabled the free broadcasting of football matches, the mechanism was questioned because of its high costs (in a three-year term, some $ 4 billion, that is to say U$D 769 million,[12] in public funds have been invested) and because broadcastings have been saturated with pro-governmental advertising and have been scheduled at the same time as TV shows critical to the government.[13]

Besides the increase in the structure of the media, the government developed an effective mechanism regarding content production, allowing for the elaboration of high impact television spots, interactive videos for public events, and high aesthetic and technological quality reports. This spread of it own 'story' has been a priority of the highest concern for the government in order to contrast the message diffused by the oppositional media.

(c) The use of State advertising with political purposes

It is necessary to identify two aspects pointing at the same objective. In the first place, the exponential growth of funds allocated for public advertising and propaganda that transformed the state into the main advertiser of the country with 9 percent of the total advertising pie.[14]

In the five years of the Cristina Kirchner administration, the amount increased from over $ 381 million (around U$D 73 million) in 2007 to $ 1.1 billion (around U$D 211 million) in 2012, that is to say almost three times as much.[15] Journalist Maria O'Donnell (2007), author of a book on the subject, pointed out that in the Kirchner administration there has been a 'lack of will to regulate the distribution of the state advertising' and it has been used 'for personal promotion and as a tool for rewarding and punishing both the media's editorial line and individual journalists' (Zanoni, 2007).

This is linked to the second aspect: the discretional nature of the distribution of those funds, one of the first steps taken by the Kirchner administration in its relationship with the media, even when the battle against the press had not yet been declared. In the first stage, a fierce rage against Perfil Publisher was applied. This company filed a lawsuit and at the last stage of the proceedings it got a favorable verdict from the Supreme Court, which ordered the executive to balance the distribution of state advertising funds. The government not only did not comply with the sentence. But when the relationship with the media was definitely damaged in 2008, it discriminated against the outlets belonging to the Clarín Group and La Nación newspaper. With the argument that the state should favor a variety of voices, the outlets that benefited from state advertising were those close to the government to the detriment of those other media critical to the government. This could be seen in the distribution figures of the advertising fund in the last few years, where all business groups close to the Kirchner administration appear in privileged places.

(d) The audiovisual media law

The most important communication policy during the Kirchner administration was the passing of the Audiovisual Service Law No. 22,522 in 2009, which replaced Law Decree No. 22,285 dating from the dictatorship.[16] The regulation, approved in both legislative houses after a profound debate all over the country, set up a new regulatory regime for the functioning of the broadcast media and defined the limits regarding the number of radio stations and channels that each group of the media could own by coverage area. The law's main goal was to guarantee a wider representation in the media system through the distribution of the radio electric spectrum in thirds: one for state actors, another one for private licensees, and the last one for nonprofit sectors (Sel, 2013). It also tried to guarantee a higher volume of national production and to regulate advertising times on television and radio (Mastrini, 2009).

In spite of common aims in the law shared by most political and social participants, its implementation was distorted since the government showed an almost exclusive interest in enforcing the law to dismember the Clarín Group, disregarding other aspects of the regulation. Thus, the debate of the law was focused on the legal dispute on Articles 41, 45, 48, and 161 that limit the number of stations and market share per business group with the possibility of dividing and parting companies trespassing those limits. The Clarín Group brought up the issue of unconstitutionality and finally in October 2013, the Supreme Court upheld the constitutionality of the law and put an end to the controversy (See Chapter 10 in this book). Few days later, the Clarín Group presented a plan for splitting the company into six parts to adjust to the judiciary decision, a step considered a victory for the government. However, some scholars are skeptical that this fragmentation could represent a real change in the nature of the Argentine media map since the owners of the holdings could arrange a division of shares in order to allocate a fraction of the group for each one.

At the same time, while the government has made an effort to apply all of the articles in the case of the Clarín Group, on the other hand it has accepted without discussion the direct transfer of licenses belonging to the Hadad group to the Kirchnerist businessman Cristobal Lopez. Not only was there no debate regarding concentration here, but also there was a blatant violation of the law, since direct transfer between private individuals is not allowed. In those cases, the licenses should be returned to the state so that it could call for a new public tender before re-awarding them. In this obscure process, the government gave reasons to all those claiming the selective application of the law and its political use. In fact, there are still many articles of the law that have not been enforced.

Another important fact when analyzing the application of the regulation is that 94 percent of the new media stations created since the passing of the law belong to governmental institutions (1,176 out of 1,256, most of them FM stations), which results in even more pro-governmental voices.[17]

(e) Public pressure to the media and journalists

Kirchnerism developed a strategy of everyday criticism against the media with the president herself as the main stoker. The print press has been one of the topics she usually addresses both in a general and broad way and in specific terms referring to particular journalists and individuals. The Kirchner administration has been also very active in spreading its message through state media and the programs produced by PPT, belonging to businessman Diego Gvirtz, with panelists commenting on the every day information from the government's perspective. A case in point is the TV program '6,7,8' by Gvirtz, broadcasted on the state channel. Recently, the government tried to prohibit the main private advertisers to publicize in the critical media. The measure, informal of course, has been carried out since February 2013 when the Secretary of Domestic Trade, Guillermo Moreno, informed supermarket and home appliance chains. Many advertisers have succumbed to the official pressure, and the impact has been very strong, particularly for the pockets of Clarín, La Nacion, and Perfil newspapers.

The impact on journalism

The passing from co-option to polarization has had a direct impact on the role of journalism in Argentina. For many journalists, a heritage of many years of censorship under military rule has been a fragile and precarious sense of independence and autonomy, although during the 1980s there was an explosion of freedom in the entire society. After military rule, the need for backing up democracy was so strong that, with some exceptions (Página/12 and Noticias, e.g.), there was an implicit agreement not to be disruptive and excessively critical with the new political system. At the same time, Argentinian journalists were very determined to reveal the atrocities committed by the dictatorship and to endorse the trial against their main leaders.

As mentioned earlier in the chapter, the first half of the 1990s was marked by a certain acquiescence from the media vis-à-vis political actors, and many companies benefited from the privatization process. This directly affected the role of journalism. In this period, many professionals undertook their own private projects, while still working for big media outlets, that in turn contributed to reshaping the profile of modern journalists. In the second part of that decade, the traditional watchdog role improved with some investigations about corruption and wrongdoing, which coincided with the demise of the Menem administration. There was a growing social demand for transparency, and the press filled the gap. The dominant position of media in this period favored such function, and the Clarín Group led the trend, which in turn strengthened its position in the political arena. It was a time of romance between journalists and their media organizations.

With the turn of the century, a new type of young and multimedia journalist emerged, who renewed the professional field and challenged traditional media. The Kirchner administration contributed here to journalism by decriminalizing slander and libel. Nevertheless, the new era was marked by a deep polarization in reporting, with an important sector of the media groups siding with the government, motivated by state advertising and with increasing impact on the audience; and with another sector of the media, led by Clarín Group, clearly opposed to the Kirchners and facing a hard economic onrush. This extreme polarization negatively affected the quality standards of information since the opinions on the media were subjected to a binary logic that impoverished the analysis of political life and contributed, as a consequence, to a certain delegitimation of journalism before the eye of public opinion.[18]

Journalists have been trapped into this conflict. In many cases, they have participated in this media dispute by stating clear support for one or the other positions in conflict.[19] This has given way to the concept of 'militant journalism' that was popularized in Argentina to define those journalists who take sides without any critical reflection.[20] This in turn has led to an increasingly aggressive rhetoric between journalists from both sides, bringing them into the center of the media-government battle and severely exposing them to criticism.

However, not all journalists have fallen into the trap. There are segments of professionals who decided not to support the media-government struggle, and in some cases their decision has contributed to stress internal labor relationships in companies. For example, the employees of Channel 7 publicly defended the work of their work-mate, journalist Juan Miceli, who had come under official fire for making Kirchnerist representative Andres Larroque feel uncomfortable on air with a series of sharp questions. On the other hand, in the Clarín newspaper, unsigned articles are now very frequent, since journalists do not wish to be linked to information coming from the company's resistance to the official onrush.[21]

In this context, any sign of moderation or balance could be understood as a concession by the opposing party, and this has aggravated polarization. Public opinion has also been deeply divided regarding the government, thus contributing to the loss of objective parameters for the media in its criticism (CPJ, 2012). As a consequence, intolerance has spread and spoken (and sometimes physical) aggression has increased. This situation has been particularly worrying in the provinces, where media are more dependent on public funds, and journalists are more exposed to political pressures. Nevertheless, the situation has not reached dramatic levels so far and according to international reports in Argentina, freedom of the press is still at work.[22]

Variables of political evaluation

In this section, the chapter briefly discusses some of the variables in the political system that affect the conformation of the media system, defined by Hallin and Mancini (2004).

(a) The role of the State

According to the three stages previously mentioned, Argentina went through a period where the role of the state was crucial both in politics and economics, not only for constantly affecting the economic performance, but also for controlling most of the economic production model (Rapoport, 2006). The Argentinian state was not a welfare state based on the European tradition, but an interventionist state affecting the production matrix (Romero, 2001). This model was absolutely undermined since 1989 through Menem's neoliberal policies, which became the fastest and deepest privatization experience in the world (De Titto, 2009). In politics, the US democracy was the role model. A swing came with the second term of the Kirchners where decisions have been taken to strengthen the state, to bring it back into the economy and the public services. Some of these measures have been the re-statization of oil services (YPF), of the water supply (Aysa), of the national airlines (Aerolineas Argentinas), and the control of the pension fund system (AFJPs).

These swings have also defined the relationship between the state and the media: immediately after transition, in the midst of deep liberalization and privatization processes, the media reached the peak of their influence over politics; now with a renewed role of the state under the Kirchners, the situation with the media can be defined as one of polarization instead of co-option.

(b) Political history and the type of government

Going back to the distinction made by Arend Lijphart, Hallin and Mancini (2004) work on the distinction of 'democracy by consensus' and 'democracy by the majority.' Argentinian political tradition is clearly based on the second category as a result of its hyper presidential system where the image of the president is the axis on which the whole organization of the state spins around (O'Donnell, 1995). The model with paternalistic and populist characteristics sets aside the importance of the Congress as the place for plural representation and disolves the Supreme Court's independence so that if a president fully exercises the authority granted, a concentration of power with poor limitations is achieved. Strong presidents such as Menem and the Kirchners could impose their stamp on the system. Thus, in Argentina, governmental stability is the outcome of a full imposition of the executive other the rest of the political actors and institutions. Nevertheless, those presidents whose governments were constrained, either by remaining military power enclaves such as Alfonsín or by economic crisis such as De la Rúa and Duhalde, could not overcome their weakness by searching for consensus among other political actors and thus had to leave power in advance.

Guillermo O'Donnell crafted the concept of:

delegative democracy, based on the idea that whoever wins the presidential elections will have the right to govern the way he (or she) considers to be appropriate, only restricted by the hard reality of existing power relationships and by a term limited by the Constitution. The president is considered as the personification of the country, the main guardian and interpreter of its interests (O'Donnell, 1993).

The experiences on the coalition of parties have not been successful, as can be seen in the emphatic failure of the Alliance between the Radical Party (UCR) and Frepaso that ended up with the unsuccessful experience of De la Rúa (Cheresky, 2008). The exercise of power is only understood from the domination of the political system without the need to make consensus or political agreements under the logic of a zero-sum game where the incumbent achieves all its goals at the expense of the outsiders. The Kirchner administrations have developed this strategy with ability, working also on the creation of an enemy that allowed for confrontation and for power increase. Nestor and Cristina Kirchner polarized against the military, the Church, and the agricultural sector, the trade unions, the justice, the 'neoliberal right-wing' and, in particular against the media, considered to pose a menace to their power supremacy. The government takes credit for an instructive mission through the discretionary distribution of state advertising, the restrictions to private advertisement, the domination of regulatory agencies (such as AFSCA), and the colonization of the media. From their point of view, there is no liberal democratic approach in which the media are vital civil actors for institutional functioning.

(c) Regulatory problems and the trend toward patronage

Argentina's rough institutional way has prevented the crystallization of a truly consolidated democratic system. The constant regulatory changes, the military coups, and the state's repeated defaults on its basic obligations have led to a cultural structure with poor respect for laws and regulations. Guillermo O'Donnell points out that the effectiveness of the rule of law brings certainty and accountability.[23] But common citizens do not find any encouragement in law enforcement, since laws can change at any moment or because the state can at any time subvert the rules. Many think that the state that during the last military dictatorship installed an illegal system of persecution and torture, lacks any legitimacy to restrict the people's rights during democracy. Moreover, the state that seized saving funds in the 2001 crisis, today has lost all moral authority to ask taxpayers to pay their taxes. The state incapable to protect the institutional system in every crisis, has lost enough strength to set the rules. In sum, many people do not feel compelled to obey.

The lack of tradition of an effective rule of law derives into a weakening of legal and regulatory mechanisms, thus the effective application of rules depends on arbitrary criteria moved by political, economic, or personal interests (Hallin and Papathanassopoulos, 2002). Argentina has a long history in that sense, with an apparent legal structure, that instead of being applied, dissolves in favor of a patronage system, or of intimidation.[24]

Regulation problems, lack of regulatory capacity, and patronage make up a noxious triangle for the link between political power and the media system. For example, the media privatization process began in the Alfonsín administration with a serious number of irregularities. Next, during Menemism, concessions were awarded to the large multimedia groups who also obtained enormous tax benefits and exemptions. And now, during Kirchnerism, the patronage logic increased, although much more selectively, as shown in the example previously mentioned regarding the strictest application of the audiovisual media law in the case of the Clarín Group, but circumventing its mandates in the case of the sale of part of the Hadad group to Kirchnerist businessman Cristobal Lopez. Another case was the announcement made by the AFIP (Federal Administration of Public Revenue) in March 2013 to apply a tax moratorium for private debts, a measure that specifically excluded the media. Much more oppressive has been the implementation of the so-called 'advertising clamp.' In this case there was neither a formal measure nor a public announcement to introduce it. The government set the restriction to supermarkets and home appliance stores at a meeting, and stores stopped advertising.

Conclusion

The absence of an effective rule of law, the tendency toward patronage and clientelism, as well as the lack of state regulatory capacities have all prevented Argentina from creating a balanced, stable, and truly pluralistic media system. On the contrary, a communication ecosystem dependent on the constant changes in the logics of the political system and on taking advantage of legal permeability has been created. During dictatorship, the state took over the media without creating, of course, basic conditions for an institutionalized democratic model; and then when liberalism became the dominant paradigm, the private sector profited from higher concentration and unregulated business possibilities.

All these factors have had a negative effect on the quality of Argentinian journalism and on the professional ability to answer to the growing audience demands. For fear (during the dictatorship), for a lack of proper regulation (during Menem administration), or for excessive polarization (during the Kirchners administration), journalism has not been empowered by the regulatory, social, or political environment to advance toward better quality standards of information. This does not exclude the fact that there are professionals who do an excellent job with a strong devotion to research and to critical journalism. But these kinds of journalists are not the product of an unstable system, but of a long professional tradition. The Argentinian media system still has many challenges to face, as does its democratic system.

Notes

I appreciate the contributions of Mariano Ure, Mariano Chretien and Gaston Trelles.

1. 'We are absolutely aware that the hurricane devastating Argentina also hit the owners of the Argentine national media strongly. In many cases they were left in a serious vulnerability situation. This decision was to generate the opportunity to strategically design the framework wanted for investment,' said Kirchner in the act where the measure was announced (Editorial, *Cronista.com* [May 20, 2005] Available at: http://bit.ly/1azOa2v).
2. In his book, he describes the situation by saying 'Menem before, as well as Kirchner now, stimulated the creation of official multimedia in order to, if necessary, split up the overwhelming Clarín Group and reorganize the whole social communication map according to their political interests. Their differences are just in tone. While the man from La Rioja [Menem] in his second term fostered a kind of conventional guerrilla warfare thus strengthening banker Raul Pedro Moneta's CEI Citicorp Holdings, Telefónica de Argentina, and Werthein Group; the man from Patagonia [Kirchner] wagered for a sort of guerrilla warfare in several simultaneous fronts, where the "partners" would act separately' (Zunino, 2009).

3. It is in this context where we need to understand the privileged link that the government developed with channel Telefé, or the promotion in the purchase of cable Channel C5N and Radio 10 by businessman Cristobel Lopez, all of them with a high level of audience.
4. Mr. Szpolski is the main shareholder of the newspapers Tiempo Argentino, The Buenos Aires Herald, the free newspaper El Argentino, and the Sunday newspaper Miradas al Sur; magazines Veintitrés and Newsweek, cable channel CN23, Radio América, among others.
5. In 2012, Mr. López bought cable channel C5N; Radio 10, by that time the radio with the highest level of audience; and FM radios Vale, TKM, Pop and Mega.
6. Vila-Manzano owns channel America TV; cable channel America 24; newspapers Uno in Santa Fe, Parana, and Mendoza; newspaper La Capital de Rosario; and radio La Red, among others.
7. It owns the newspapers BAE, Crónica, and Atlántico in Mar del Plata; and channel Crónica TV.
8. Owner of the magazines El Guardian – recently discontinued – and El Federal; radios Belgrano, Splendid, Rock and Pop, Blue, and Metro, among others.
9. Grupo Pierri owns Channel 26 and cable operator Telecentro.
10. Holder of radio Del Plata and 360 TV.
11. To this conglomerate, Telefe could be added – controlled by the Spanish group Telefónica for over fifteen years. One out of the two over the air channels with the highest level of audience together with Channel 13 belonging to the Clarín Group that has been one of the media with the highest funding from the state as regards advertisement and that has kept an ideology very close to the government.
12. Including the fee agreed with the AFA, advertisement and production (Casar-González, 2012).
13. The Executive Branch also tried to tighten the control over production and commercialization of newsprint. First, in 2011, a law was passed through which the production, distribution, and sales of this supply was declared of public interest, thus enabling its import and export regulation. Moreover, in 2013, the official party representatives, with the support of the government, drafted a bill so that the state could add an extra 24 percent of ownership of Papel Prensa (the print paper company) thus keeping 51.5 percent of stock, which allowed for the control of the company.
14. In 2011, the NGO Poder Ciudadano presented the report 'Nación y Ciudad Unidas por la Publicidad Oficial,' made by the media specialist Martin Becerra (http://bit.ly/19BunFd).
15. According to journalist José Crettaz (2013, September 2), the public expenditure has benefited mostly five large media corporations: Veintitrés (Grupo Szpolski-Garfunkel), Telefe (Telefónica), Uno (Manzano-Vila), Albavisión (Ángel González), and Página 12 (Sokolowiccz).
16. The complete text can be read at: http://bit.ly/1a1lDGy.
17. Apparently with the new law, most of the new media to be created will be dependent on public funds (Crettaz, May 2, 2013).
18. A survey conducted by the Forum of Argentinian Journalists (FOPEA, 2011) shows that journalists admit the existence of a lack of accuracy, low salaries, and a dependency on state advertising. Seventy percent admitted

not to work with an ethical code in their companies, 51 percent said that the professional rigor is unsatisfactory, and 63 percent branded the credibility of Argentinian journalists as standard (FOPEA, 2011).

19. The Rapporteur for Freedom of Expression of the OAS Inter American Commission pointed out in the last annual report that 'the context of an extreme confrontation, by which constant disqualifications and stigmatization are produced, generate an atmosphere that does not allow plural and reasonable debate on every political matter.' It also states that the 'sharp polarization closes doors for patient debate and does not help neither authorities nor the press to better fulfill the role given to them by a strong, open and deliberative democracy.'

20. In 2010, Telam's then president Martin Garcia, said: 'Professionals are like prostitutes, they write lies in defense of the interests of those who pay for them. Nevertheless, we, the militants, write the truth at the service of the population. First of all I am a militant, then I am a journalist.' From then on, the debate on the existence of 'militant journalism' was made official.

21. There is not a freedom of conscience clause in Argentina. Senator Norma Morandini is promoting a bill with this right, but it has not been debated in the Congress yet.

22. Freedom House classified Argentina as 'free' in the 2012 global report about freedom of expression (Freedom House, 2012); whereas Reporters Without Borders considered the freedom of the press as 'satisfactory' (Reporters Without Borders, 2012).

23. O'Donnell states: 'The accurate enforcement of the law is an obligation of the competent authority: the same kind of decision should be made in similar situations and, when this is not the case, another qualified authority could penalize the lawbreaker and try to solve the consequences. This is similar to say that the rule of law is not simply a group of legal regulations, not even if all of them were correctly passed; it is a legal system, a group of rules with several main characteristics apart from having been correctly passed' (O'Donnell, 2002).

24. Carlos Nino shows Argentina as a nation on the fringes of the law, where 'dull anomia' or 'the practices of behavior in illegality make the rule paradoxically, while the spontaneous adaptation to rules, make the exception' (Nino, 2005).

References

Becerra, M. (2011) 'Nación y Ciudad Unidas por la Publicidad Oficial,' *Poder Ciudadano*. Available at http://bit.ly/19BunFd (accessed September 2013).

Califano, B. (2009) 'Comunicación se escribe con K, la radiodifusión bajo el gobierno de Néstor Kirchner,' pp. 341–374 in G. Mastrini (ed.) *Mucho ruido, pocas leyes* (Buenos Aires: La Crujía Ediciones).

Casar-González, A. (2012, July 9) 'El fútbol para todos costó $ 4000 millones en tres años,' *La Nación*. Available at http://bit.ly/1doLntF (accessed September 2013).

Cheresky, I. (comp.) (2008) *La política después de los partidos* (Buenos Aires: Prometeo).

CPJ (2012) *En la confrontación entre el gobierno argentino y la prensa, pierde el periodismo* (Buenos Aires CPJ). Available at http://bit.ly/1cneXys (accessed: December 2013).

Com, S. (2009) 'Alfonsinismo, contexto sociopolítico y medios de comunicación,' pp. 185–210 in G. Mastrini (ed.) *Mucho ruido, pocas leyes* (Buenos Aires: La Crujía Ediciones).

Crettaz, J. (2013, May 2) 'El 94% de los medios creados con la nueva ley es estatal,' *La Nación*. Available at http://bit.ly/1azOv5h (accessed September 2013).

Crettaz, J. (2013, September 2) 'La pauta oficial benefició a cinco grandes grupos,' *La Nación*. Available at http://bit.ly/1lsR8xr (accessed September 2013).

De Moraes, D. (2011) *La Cruzada de los medios en América Latina, gobiernos progresistas y políticas de comunicación* (Buenos Aires: Paidós).

De Titto, R. (2009) *Breve historia de la política argentina* (Buenos Aires: El Ateneo).

Editorial (2005, May 20) *Cronista.com*. Available at http://bit.ly/1azOa2v (accessed December 2013).

FOPEA (2011, September 6) 'Bajo nivel salarial, falta de rigor profesional y dependencia de la pauta oficial,' Foro de Periodismo Argentino. Available at http://bit.ly/1g1dyCf (accessed December 2013).

Freedom House (2012) *Freedom on the Net 2012* (Washington, DC: Freedom House) Available at http://bit.ly/KjqQ30 (accessed December 2013).

Hallin, D. and Mancini, P. (2004) *Comparing Media Systems. Three Models of Media and Politics* (Cambridge: Cambridge University Press).

Hallin, D. and Papathanassopoulos, S. (2002) 'Political clientelism and the media: Southern Europe and Latin America in comparative perspective,' *Media, Culture and Society*, 24(2): 175–195.

Laclau, E. and Mouffe, C (2004) *Hegemonía y estrategia socialista, hacia una radicalización de la democracia* (Buenos Aires: Fondo de Cultura Económica).

Mastrini, G. (ed.) (2009) *Mucho ruido, pocas leyes. Economía y políticas de comunicación en la Argentina* (Buenos Aires: La Crujía Ediciones).

Mastrini, G. and Becerra, M. (2006) *Periodistas y magnates. Estructura y concentración de las industrias culturales* (Buenos Aires: Prometeo).

Mastrini, G. and Bolaño, C. (2000) *Globalización y monopolios en la comunicación en América Latina* (Buenos Aires: Biblos).

Mochkofsky, G. (2011) *Pecado original. Clarín, los Kirchner y la lucha por el poder* (Buenos Aires: Planeta).

Mouffe, C. (2012) *La paradoja democrática, el peligro del consenso en la política contemporánea* (Barcelona: Gedisa).

Nino, C. (2005) *Un país al margen de la ley* (Barcelona: Ariel).

O'Donnell, G. (1993) 'Estado, democratización y ciudadanía,' *Nueva Sociedad*, 128: 62–87.

O'Donnell, G. (1995) 'Delegative Democracy', *Journal of Democracy*, 5(1): 55–69.

O'Donnell, G. (2002) *La (in)efectividad de la ley en América Latina* (Buenos Aires and Barcelona: Paidos).

O'Donnell, M. (2007) *Propaganda K, una maquinaria de promoción con dinero del Estado* (Buenos Aires: Planeta).

Rapoport, M. (2006) *El viraje del siglo XXI: Deudas y desafíos en la Argentina, América Latina y el Mundo* (Buenos Aires: Norma).

Reporters Without Borders (2012, January 25) *Clasificación Mundial de la libertad de la prensa 2011–2012* (Paris: RSF). Available at http://bit.ly/1eqCjGH (accessed December 2013).

Romero, L. (2001) *Breve historia contemporánea de la Argentina* (Buenos Aires: Fondo de Cultura Económica).

Rossi, D. (2009) 'La radiodifusión entre 1990 y 1995: exacerbación del modelo privado-comercial,' pp. 235–256 in G. Mastrini (ed.) *Mucho ruido, pocas leyes, 2da edición* (Buenos Aires: La Crujía Ediciones).

Ruiz, F. (2010) 'Fronteras móviles: Caos y control en la relación entre medios y políticos en América Latina,' pp. 17–60 in B. Sorj (comp.) *Poder político y medios de comunicación, de la representación política al reality show* (Argentina: Siglo XXI Editores).

Sarlo, I. (2011) *Kirchner 2003–2010. La audacia y el cálculo* (Buenos Aires: Sudamericana).

Sel, S. (2013) 'Actores sociales y espacio público,' pp. 183–209 in S. Sel (coord.) *Políticas de Comunicación en el capitalismo contemporáneo* (Buenos Aires: Consejo Latinoamericano de Ciencias Sociales).

Sirven, P. (2011) *Perón y los medios de comunicación. La conflictiva relación de los gobiernos justicialistas con la prensa: 1943–2011* (Buenos Aires: Sudamericana).

Ulanovsky, C. (1997) *Paren las rotativas: una historia de grandes diarios, revistas y periodistas argentinos* (Buenos Aires: Espasa Calpe).

Zanoni, L. (2007, August 27) 'Kirchner gasta más plata que otros presidentes,' [Blog Entry]. eBlog cibercultura, medios, periodismo. Available at http://bit.ly/KkU1BW (accessed September 2013).

Zunino, E. (2009) *Patria o medios, la loca guerra de los Kirchner por el control de la realidad* (Buenos Aires: Sudamericana).

6
Pluralism, Digitalization and the Contemporary Challenges of Media Policy in El Salvador

José Luis Benítez

Introduction

This chapter focuses on some of the contemporary challenges of media policy that El Salvador faces in the context of both the digital age and in the need to advance to a more democratic society. First, the chapter delineates a brief characterization of the Salvadoran media landscape in the traditional, digital, and telecommunications industries. In each sector, the text highlights issues of media property concentration and the consequences in terms of diversity and pluralism in El Salvador. Second, it discusses several considerations regarding a pluralistic media system and individual rights to communication, taking into account the UNESCO (2008) indicators to evaluate media development in each country. The rights to communication include a variety of rights and possibilities to ensure people's participation and expression in society. Third, the chapter then considers the potential of digital television transition to strengthen pluralism in the national media system, and its actual developments both in El Salvador and in Central America as a whole. Finally, the chapter outlines five major proposals for media and cultural policies to tackle the current challenges to promote the right to communicate and a multicultural democracy in the digital age.

Salvadoran media landscape

One important limitation for characterizing the Salvadoran media landscape is precisely the lack of public information, systematic academic research on this issue, and the updated statistics from governmental

Table 6.1 Central American media

Country	Newspapers (per 1,000)	Radio sets (per 1,000)	TV sets (per 1,000)	Computers (per 1,000)
El Salvador	28	481	679	25.2
Guatemala	33	79	61	14.4
Honduras	55	411	96	13.6
Nicaragua	30	270	68	27.9
Costa Rica	94	816	144	197.2
Panamá	62	300	183	52.8
Average	50	393	205	52.8

Source: World Bank (2013).

sources. Moreover, as Salzman and Salzman (2009) argue, the role of the media in Central America cannot be grasped without understanding the interrelations among the media industry, government, and civil society. Thus, some researchers conclude that the 'majority of the Salvadoran media have had a reputation of being biased in favor of the government, the military, and the powerful economic actors throughout most of the twentieth century' (Lawrence, 2004: 22). Table 6.1 offers a general overview of the Central American media landscape.

Newspapers

The first Salvadoran newspaper appeared in July 31, 1824, and was called El Semanario Político Mercantil. It included official news, stories about the activities of the federal provinces of Central America, and controversial political and religious issues (López, 1987). Today, El Salvador has the following major newspapers: Diario CoLatino, La Prensa Gráfica, El Diario de Hoy, Diario El Mundo, Más, El Gráfico, and Mi Chero. Likewise, with the development of the Internet, there are new online newspapers such as: El Faro (www.elfaro.net), Contrapunto (www.contrapunto.com. sv), La Página (www.lapagina.com.sv), among others.

In recent decades, the most important Salvadoran newspapers such as La Prensa Gráfica and El Diario de Hoy have had connections with powerful families in the country. For example, the newspapers La Prensa Gráfica and El Gráfico belong to the Dutriz family who also has important investments in media-related business such as printing, publishing, cable operation, broadcasting, telecommunications, advertisement but also in sectors as diverse as real state, property development, retail, steel structures, painting and decoration, law firms, and several others (Becerra and Mastrini, 2009: 88).

The Altamirano family, an important landowning group with coffee and cotton plantations, owns the newspapers El Diario de Hoy and Más. Moreover, the Altamirano family, defined by its very conservative political ideology, has had strong links with the right-wing political party Alianza Republicana Nacionalista, ARENA. This group fervently opposes all initiatives and discussions about the need for media policies and the democratization of the broadcast spectrum in the country.

Currently, the newspaper industry is mainly concentrated in these two families, Dutriz and Altamirano; and their newspapers La Prensa Gráfica, El Gráfico, El Diario de Hoy, and Más represent 92 percent of newspapers' total circulation in the country (Becerra and Mastrini, 2009: 89). Other newspapers such as Diario El Mundo belong to the Borja Nathan family, also with investments in coffee and sugar plantations. For its part, the CoLatino newspaper is administered by a workers cooperative and is considered to be the only print media that stands for popular interests, but with a very limited readership of 7.7 percent in the country (Freedman, 2012; Becerra and Mastrini, 2009).

With the development of the Internet and the emergence of digital investigative newspapers such as El Faro (founded in 1998) and Contrapunto (launched in 2007), there emerged a more pluralistic news agenda over public issues in the national media sphere. Nevertheless, wider pluralism and diversity are still needed in the digital print landscapes, particularly in terms of giving voice and visibility to a variety of social actors like children, youth, and marginalized groups in the Salvadoran society.

Radio

The first radio station in El Salvador began broadcast transmissions on March 1, 1926; its name was AQM (the acronym of the president of that moment Alfonso Quiñónez Molina). According to the General Superintendence of Electricity and Teleccomunications (Superintendencia General de Electricidad y Telecomunicaciones, SIGET), El Salvador has 71 radio stations on the AM band, and 196 radio stations on the FM band. This amounts to a total of 267 radio stations in the country (SIGET, 2008). Undoubtedly, in Central America the radio stations have enormous relevance because sets are relatively cheap, they can work with batteries, the transmissions reach the furthest corners, and audiences that do not 'need to be literate to use radio' (Salzman and Salzman, 2009: 51).

The radio industry in El Salvador is concentrated in five major media groups: SAMIX (its principal investor is the former Salvadoran president

Antonio Saca), Corporación FM, Grupo radial YSKL, Grupo Radio Estéreo and Grupo Megavisión (Freedman, 2012; Becerra and Mastrini, 2009).

Other important radio networks are the Christian Radio Corporation, the radio stations of the Catholic Church, and two radio stations administered by the state (Herrera, 2013). The majority of private commercial radio stations are united in the Asociación Salvadoreña de Radiodifusores, (Salvadoran Association of Broadcasters, ASDER by its Spanish acronym). ASDER defends the auction of the broadcast spectrum and noticeably opposes the debate on, and the need to, revise the current 1997 telecommunications law in order to recognize the community radio stations in the country.

The Asociación de Radios y Programas Participativos de El Salvador (Association of Participative Radios and Programs of El Salvador, ARPAS) was founded in 1993. It currently includes 23 mostly community radio stations located in rural and urban communities and six content production associations. The majority of these community radio stations broadcast on the same frequency, 92.1 FM, and face several economic limitations to compete with private media groups for new frequencies. Even though community radios have a growing sociocultural recognition in the country, they lack legal status recognition. Hence, ARPAS has become 'one of the main forces in civil society in the struggle for the democratization of access to radio frequencies' (UNESCO, 2003: 90).

Television

The first television channel in El Salvador was launched in 1956 with the name YSEB La Voz Latinoamericana, and it covered just a limited area of the capital, San Salvador (López, 1987: 435). According to SIGET, in 2008, there were 47 terrestrial broadcast television stations in the country. In addition, there are 91 TV channels carried by cable operators and only one satellite television operator (SIGET, 2008). Television is dominated by the private sector with the exception of one channel owned by the state (Salzman, 2008).

Boris Eserski, who holds the licenses for Channels 2, 4, 6, and Channel 35 in UHF, mainly controls private TV in El Salvador; although Megavisión is a far second and owns Channels 15, 19, and 21. The Eserski group, the strongest opponent to any change in the actual distribution of frequencies, holds enough economic and media power to influence politicians and the government. Thus, the possibilities for diversity and ideological pluralism in Salvadoran television are very limited, particularly for civil society organizations and the leftist party

Frente Farabundo Martí para la Liberación Nacional, FMLN. In their analysis of media concentration in El Salvador, Becerra and Mastrini (2009) conclude that the Eserki group not only dominates the television industry but also an important part of the advertising market and public relations agencies in the country. Consequently, 'this indicates a particularity almost unique in the world, a media outlet that also controls the distribution of publicity' (Becerra and Mastrini, 2009: 96, my translation). The Eserski family through the MedCom Group has investments not only in television but also in radio, cable, movie theaters, advertising, and public relations. Moreover, this group participates in other business sectors such as mills, storing, and banking (Freedman, 2012; Becerra and Mastrini, 2009). Although there have been some investments from transnational capital such as the Mexican TV Azteca that in 1996 acquired the majority of Channel 12's assets in El Salvador; the Eserski group, with strong ties to the ARENA party, has also promoted the implementation of several barriers to international competitors in the media markets (Rockwell and Janus, 2003).

With regard to state-funded and administered media, Channels 8 and 10, previous governments have paid scarce attention and allocated few resources. These channels have operated since 1971 when there was an important educational reform in the country and television was used to deliver educational content and classes. Currently, Channel 8 is in concession to AGAPE, a Catholic church organization, and Channel 10 is under the supervision of the Secretary of Communications of the president of El Salvador. The government is now working on a new media law that, if approved in the Legislative Assembly, will transform the status of Channel 10 and Radio El Salvador from state-owned into public media in similar mission to European public broadcasting service.

Internet and telephone

El Salvador was officially connected to the Internet in February 1996, after the former National Administration of Telecommunications (Administración Nacional de Telecomunicaciones, ANTEL) and SVNet[1] signed a memorandum for adopting this new technology in the country. Two private universities were the first to be connected: Universidad Centroamericana José Simeón Cañas (UCA) and Universidad Don Bosco. Currently, the Internet penetration in El Salvador is still low, about 16.1 percent according to the International Telecommunications Union (ITU). Table 6.2 shows the evolution of Internet users and penetration rates in the past decade in the country.

Table 6.2 Internet users and penetration rates in El Salvador

Year	Users	Population	% Penetration	Source
2000	40,000	5,963,800	0.6%	ITU
2003	550,000	6,281,600	8.5%	ITU
2005	587,500	6,467,548	9.1%	ITU
2008	700,000	7,066,403	9.9%	ITU
2009	975,000	7,185,218	13.6%	ITU
2010	975,000	6,052,064	16.1%	ITU

Source: Internet World Stats (2010).

In terms of fixed telephone lines, there is a density level of 15.94; this means that there are almost 16 fixed phones per 100 inhabitants. On the other hand, the density level of mobile phones is at 126.53, meaning a bit more than 126 mobiles per 100 inhabitants (SIGET, 2010). The adoption of mobile phones is certainly related to the processes of migration and the Salvadoran diaspora to the United States (Benítez, 2012). Both fixed and mobile phone markets in El Salvador are predominantly controlled by the following five corporations: Movistar (owned by Telefónica, Spain), Claro (Mexico's Telecom, property of Carlos Slim), Tigo (Telemovil, a unit of Millicon International Cellular or MIC), Digicel, and Red. Because of the dominant influence of the telecommunications corporation Claro, some researchers argue that, 'Slim adds up another country where he controls the fixed telephone market almost at his total will' (Becerra and Mastrini, 2009: 92, our translation).

Pluralistic media system and the right to communication

The reality of the media system in El Salvador and the other countries in Central America reveals the limitations of pluralism and diversity. As Salzman and Salzman (2009) argue, 'a mix of oligarchic ownership, unstable regime types, economic and technological development, and deficient user adoption policies cause Central America to stand alone as a uniquely comparative region for studying the media industry in Latin America' (Salzman and Salzman, 2009: 47). This characterization also implies the possibilities to analyze the interrelations between economic elites, national governments, and transnational media and telecommunications corporations; and how the participation of civil society organizations and citizens' communication needs are diminished in the public sphere.

The 'Media Development Indicators: a framework for assessing media development,' proposed in 2008 by UNESCO constitutes a key document to evaluate the articulations between media, democracy, and development. As UNESCO (2008) emphasizes, media outlets are crucial for the exercise of freedom of expression and democratic debates, and they serve as platforms for information and news. Moreover, the media can be considered as a vehicle of cultural expression and cohesion within and between nations, a means by which a sense of community is configured, and a mediated space where people recognize and appropriate collective identities.

UNESCO (2008) underlines the critical need to measure both independence and access to the media in particular countries, because 'it is not just the absence of restrictions on the media that matters, but the extent to which all sectors of society, especially the most marginalized, can access the media to gain information and make their voices heard' (UNESCO, 2008: 4). Conversely, the usual argument of those who oppose the democratization of media and communications is that regulation limits the freedom of expression. Curiously, from this point of view, the exclusion of marginalized communities, sociocultural groups, and civil society organizations is not considered to be a serious limitation to the freedom of expression. Thus, of outmost importance is to socialize in public debates the dissenting views in order to conform a more democratic society (Miralles, 2011).

Democracy, particularly in post-conflict, war-stricken societies like El Salvador – the country underwent a civil war from 1981 to 1992 – requires work in three fundamental dimensions: free elections, free media, and human rights (De Zeeuw and Kumar, 2006). To date, various projects and international cooperation programs in El Salvador have promoted free elections and the advancement of human rights. Nevertheless, there is still much to be done to tackle the culture of impunity in the country and the promotion of human rights in general. Likewise, the state and the media group elites have not been receptive to ideas of promoting a more pluralistic and democratic media system in the country.

Today the development of democracy cannot leave aside multiculturalism and its implications for the national media system. In this sense, García-Canclini suggests that:

> A democratic multicultural development will be realized in each nation only if there are favorable conditions for the expansion of regional, ethnic, and minority radio and television stations; or at least of programming designated for the expression of different cultures, subject to collective public interest rather than commercial profitability. (2001: 133)

The access and use of the media are crucial for the exercise of the collective dimension of freedom of expression and ideological pluralism, and also for the cultural rights for producing our own media representations and collective identities. UNESCO (2008) also highlights the relevance of the media to promote access to information, literacy, and knowledge, particularly for the poor and the marginalized in our countries. Accordingly, UNESCO (2008) calls for state intervention in order to promote:

A media environment characterized by freedom of expression, pluralism and diversity, with laws restricting media freedom narrowly defined and limited to those necessary in a democracy, and with legal provisions that ensure a level economic playing field. This requires provisions for public and community-based media as well as private media. (2008: 5)

Then, what we need to promote is a national media system that recognizes and allows equal conditions for the existence of public, private, and community media. However, in El Salvador, private commercial media whose proprietors consider public and community media as unnecessary dominate the prevailing media system. If we take into account the Media Development Indicators proposed by UNESCO, we should evaluate the five key categories included in these indicators: (1) a system of regulation conductive to freedom of expression, pluralism, and diversity of the media; (2) pluralism and media diversity as well transparency of ownership; (3) media as a platform for democratic discourse; (4) professional capacity in institutional building and support that enable freedom of expression, pluralism and diversity; and (5) enough infrastructural capacity to support independent and pluralistic media (UNESCO, 2008).

In this context, wider recognition of pluralism requires a dialogue and, if possible, consensus among dissenting viewpoints on how to build a truly democratic media system (Rodríguez and Moreira, 2011). Nevertheless, the process of building consensus over media reform requires an informed and widespread public debate (McChesney, 2004). A diversity of social, cultural, economic, and political sectors of the country should participate in this debate because the construction of a democratic media system based on the UNESCO Media Development Indicators requires a real process of participation, debate, and inclusion.

This is a critical dimension of the right to communication, a concept that in recent years emerged as a notion that embodies different rights: freedom of expression and the right to know or the right to have access to public information (Herrera, 2013; Busso, 2011). Following García-Canclini's (2001) findings, it is urgent to also include cultural rights for ethnic and marginalized groups and communities. In short, the right to communication implies the exercise of the freedom of expression and the access and real possibilities to establish public, private, and community media; and the possibility for the people to appropriate and to use the Internet and other information and communication technologies (ICTs).

At present, there is an emerging social movement promoting a wide public debate on the need for a democratic media system in the country. The movement is spirited by diverse organizations, like ARPAS, the aforementioned university UCA, the Foundation for the Study and Application of Law (Fundación para el Estudio y Aplicación del Derecho FESPAD), and other civil society organizations. On August 23, 2012, representatives of these three organizations, FESPAD, ARPAS, and UCA, pleaded a case of unconstitutionality in the Supreme Court against the bidding system as the only mechanism for allocating radio and television frequencies according to the current telecommunications law. The promoters argue that the auction system runs contrary to Articles 3, 6, 101, 110, and 144 of the Salvadoran Constitution by limiting democratic access to the broadcast spectrum. In January 2013, the Supreme Court of El Salvador agreed to hear this case of unconstitutionality, although the final decision is still pending.

While the role of the state is crucial for setting the conditions of a democratic media system, there has not been a government that assumes this challenge of promoting pluralism and diversity in the Salvadorean media. Likewise, only in the final term of the current president Mauricio Funes (a former television journalist), a proposal for a public media broadcasting system law was submitted to the Legislative Assembly. It is very unlikely that this proposal will advance in the context of the presidential elections and the end of the presidential term. Nevertheless, as McChesney (2004) points out, 'managing a viable public broadcasting service can be difficult in a democracy, but the international experience shows that it can be done, if there is a political commitment to make it happen' (McChesney, 2004: 241).

In the community media sector, ARPAS has worked on a proposal for a community radio bill that was sent to the Legislative Assembly on July 24, 2013, and it is still pending discussion. The proposal defines community media as broadcast stations that provide a public communication service where the ownership and management belong to nonprofit associations or foundations and that are oriented by values of the freedom of expression, the right to information, and to communication. In addition, the proposal establishes that at least a third of the broadcast spectrum available should be awarded to these kinds of stations and that the process for obtaining a license must be through public competition instead of auctions, as it is currently the case according to the telecommunications law. However, a reform like this is not enough. Likewise, we need to develop media literacy education for children, the young, and other sectors that may support a more pluralistic and democratic society (Sorj, 2012). In this regard, as Jenkis argues:

> The fight over media concentration is only one struggle that should concern media reformers. The potentials of a more participatory media culture are also worth fighting for. Right now, convergence culture is throwing media into flux, expanding the opportunities for grassroots groups to speak back to the mass media. (2006: 259)

This perspective highlights that a struggle for a democratic and pluralistic media system in the digital age should be accompanied by a media and digital literacy education strategy and the promotion and appropriation of the right to communicate, because this perspective and these skills will allow people, especially children and youth, 'to think of themselves as cultural producers and participants and not simply as consumers, critical or otherwise' (Jenkis, 2006: 270).

Digital television and new opportunities for media pluralism

The transition to Digital Terrestrial Television (DTT) allows for new opportunities and decisions to be made. In El Salvador, we expect that the DTT will be in place by January 2019, which means that the analogical blackout will take place at the end of 2018. The digitalization of television entails the possibilities for a better use of the broadcast spectrum, better signal quality, more options for asynchronous television consumption, and new services not directly related to television (Albornoz and García, 2012). Up to date governments have paid a lot of attention to the specific technical standard the country has adopted or will adopt in the future. However, the risk is to leave the debate on digitalization only at the technical level without considering its implications.

Until now, there were four international Digital Terrestrial Television standards: North American (ATSC), European (DVB-T), Japanese-Brazilian

Table 6.3   Digital television standards in Central America

Country	DTT standard	Analogical blackout
El Salvador	ATSC (in evaluation)	2018
Guatemala	ISDB-Tb	2018
Honduras	ATSC	2020
Nicaragua	ISDB-Tb	Undecided
Costa Rica	ISDB-Tb	2017
Panama	DVB-T	2020
Dominican Republic	ATSC	2015

Source: elaborated by author with sources from (www.siget.gob.sv) and (www.internetworld stats.com/am/sv.htm).

(ISDB-Tb), and Chinese (DMB-T). Several countries in Latin American have evaluated the possibilities and qualities of most of these standards and tend to conclude that the Japanese standard is in general better (Angulo, Calzada and Estruch, 2011). In the case of El Salvador, in April 2009, the SIGET announced that the country will adopt the North American DTT standard (ATSC), but this decision happened just a few weeks before the presidential transition from former president Antonio Saca to president Mauricio Funes took place. However, the Funes administration resolved to revise the DTT standard the country will adopt, although so far (December 2013) there is no final decision. So far, the transition to DTT in El Salvador and the other Central American countries reveals the lack of integration in the region in terms of technological adoptions and media policies for the digital age. Table 6.3 shows the DTT standards to be adopted in the Dominican Republic and Central America.

In contrast to the South American region where through MERCOSUR and other mechanisms of coordination the countries promoted the adoption of the ISDB-Tb standard, in Central America there have been no agreements or initiatives for bringing together the different needs and expectations for the DTT transition and adoption of the standard. Moreover, in the view of some researchers, 'the adoption of the ATSC standard in Mexico, Honduras, and El Salvador responds to a similar pattern of technological, economic, and political dependency with respect to the U.S.' (Angulo, Calzada and Estruch, 2011: 786).

Nonetheless, what is at stake in the digital transition process is much more than the simple adoption of a particular DTT standard. It implies also the financial alternatives to support the transition to digital terrestrial television; the negotiations between the government and the television media groups; the geopolitics of cultural industries; and the role of these industries in terms of cultural diversity, digital inclusion, and political pluralism (Albornoz and García, 2012). Precisely, for these reasons the United Nations Special Rapporteur on Freedom of Opinion and Expression along with the other rapporteurs from the Organization of American States (OAS), the Organization for Security and Co-operation in Europe (OSCE), and the African Commission on Human Rights and People's Rights (ACHPR) launched a joint declaration on: 'The protection of freedom of expression and diversity in the digital terrestrial transition.' This statement was adopted on May 3, 2013, in the context of the UNESCO International Free Press Day, in San José, Costa Rica. After meeting in Pretoria on April 5, 2013, to discuss digital transition, the four special rapporteurs expressed in this declaration their concern about the following fact:

> In many countries, commercial and political considerations have dominated discussions and policy making regarding the transition to digital terrestrial broadcasting (switchover or digital transition), to the detriment of human rights, and particularly freedom of expression considerations, including diversity, and the protection of the rights of viewers and listeners. (Joint declaration on the protection of freedom of expression and diversity in the digital terrestrial transition, 2013)

In a similar vein, this joint declaration emphasizes the role of the state in order to promote and protect the right to the freedom of expression and media diversity. The state, suggest the rapporteurs, must assess the risks of media ownership concentration along the digital transition process. Finally, the declaration highlights that the decision-making process relating to the digital terrestrial transition should take place in a 'transparent and fully consultative manner, allowing for all stakeholders and interests to be heard' (Joint declaration on the protection of the freedom of expression and diversity in the digital terrestrial transition, 2013).

Eleven months before the publication of this joint declaration, a group of Salvadoran civil society organizations sent a letter to President Funes. In this letter, delivered to the Secretary of Communications on February 19, 2013, the organizations proposed the creation of a national commission where different stakeholders should participate and discuss the implications of the digital television transition. One of the main concerns of these organizations is that the digital transition could enhance the possibilities for either a democratic access to the broadcast spectrum or a greater concentration of media ownership. Until now, there has not been an official response to this letter. The lack of response may be interpreted as an unwillingness of the government to commit with the recommendations of the Joint Declaration referred to above.

This moment, when the decision is yet to be made regarding the standard El Salvador will adopt, is an opportunity for opening up the debate on the challenges the country faces in terms of the freedom of expression, the digital divide, and the promotion of a pluralistic media system in the country. The digital transition process also requires looking at the relocation of the spectrum freed up by the switch-off from analogue broadcasting; what has been called 'the digital dividend.' Thus, this digital dividend, as the freedom of expression rapporteurs point out, has to take into account the need to include cultural and linguistic minorities and the possibility for providing public funding for the development of new media content and television channels, particularly for marginalized communities. Hence, the discussion on the digital transition is much more than just a technical matter, but in El Salvador there seems to be no political will to start up this debate and even less to follow up on the recommendations of the Joint Declaration.

Conclusion: challenges for media and cultural policies in El Salvador

There are several challenges for media and cultural policies in El Salvador and Central America in general. It is important to establish a close relationship between media and cultural policies, because as García-Canclini (2001) argues, the state tends to develop cultural policies mainly for the protection of monuments and folkloric expressions (García-Canclini, 2001: 128). It also tends to pay less attention to media policies, the development of cultural industries, and the promotion of the use of ICTs and Internet within a broader understanding of democratic development. The following five considerations entail some of the key contemporary challenges Central America faces today for building more democratic and pluralistic media systems.

The state's role in developing media policies in dialogue with the private sector, civil society and international actors

The state has to assume responsibility for promoting a participatory process where various stakeholders can contribute to the development of media policies in terms of the distribution and access to the broadcast spectrum, the technical and sociocultural implications of digital transition, and the conditions for a transparent media market according to international standards, such as the UNESCO proposal. The state is key for articulating the different ideological, economic, political, and cultural interests and powers among the variety of stakeholders. In this vein, I argue that El Salvador needs a new and independent institution specialized in the area of media and new technologies that can provide leadership for media policies and respond to the information and communication needs that emerge from academia, the civil society, and the national and international markets. This institution must ensure the transparency of these decision-making processes and the distribution of the official publicity budget among the different media outlets. The government cannot use public advertising funds to privilege or punish private and community media.

Media and cultural policies for social cohesion and regional integration

We need to think more of media and cultural policies from the perspective of social cohesion at the national and transnational levels, particularly in El Salvador that can be defined as a transnational state with a large population of over 2 million people living in the diaspora, especially in the United States and Canada. Thus, we have to develop media and cultural policies that include diasporic Salvadorans with their political and cultural rights and their information and communication needs. Likewise, regional bodies such as the Central American Integration System (SICA) should have a more relevant role in the creation of a regional audiovisual space, a common Central American market for books, movies, television programs, and favor the free circulation of cultural commodities (García-Canclini, 2001). In addition, the SICA should contribute to generate a minimum consensus on fundamental issues such as the digital television transition in the region, the recognition of public and community media in Central America and Dominican Republic, the development of common policies for tackling the digital divide, and collaborative initiatives to improve the access and uses of the Internet for more pluralistic societies and open governments.

Media and cultural policies that ensure a pluralistic and diverse communication system

Following the UNESCO (2008) recommendations in the Media Development Indicators proposal, the state has to ensure that the national media system formally recognizes in legislation the existence of the three communication sectors: private, community, and public media. In order to fulfill this requirement it is necessary to have an evaluation and public discussion on the current laws and regulations, and the concentration levels of media ownership and control. Since the broadcast spectrum is a public resource and the media are fundamental for the exercise of the right to information and freedom of expression, it is incongruous with international standards of human rights that only economic elite groups have the possibilities to operate broadcast stations. Recently, in Latin America, there are examples of new media laws such as in Argentina, Uruguay, and Ecuador; but the key point is how each country finds the most appropriate proposal combining international standards on freedom of expression with its own historical conditions and communicational reality.

Media and cultural policies that promote multicultural productions

There is a need to design and implement cultural public policies that include the production of multicultural and multimedia productions: radio series, television programs, movies, documentaries, music, and video games, among others where we can express and recognize our hybrid and transnational identities. In Central America, we have little media production that truly expresses the diversity and complexities of our countries: history and voices of indigenous communities, African-American cultures, and a variety of immigrant communities within Central America, and now, in the diaspora. For instance, several media policies include quotas for including local content on radio and TV in order to give visibility to domestic media and cultural productions (García-Canclini, 2001). In El Salvador we have to take into consideration the transnational media programs that circulate for Salvadorans in the diaspora. Here it is necessary to promote the diversity of cultural expressions and not just media content full of nostalgic tourism and folklore. We need to approach national and collective identities from multicultural perspectives, particularly to give voice to the youth that are looking for spaces to communicate their sociocultural identities and forms of political participation.

Media and cultural policies for digital and communication literacy

The government and civil society organizations, particularly universities and communication and journalism associations, should develop a variety of digital and media literacy educational strategies. These digital and media literacy programs may target different sociocultural groups but should give priority to children, youth, women, and marginalized sociocultural groups. One of the key aspects of media literacy is that people need to be aware of their dual condition of consumers and producers of content in the digital age, particularly through digital social media. This is also another way people can appropriate the right to communicate, demand a more pluralistic media system in the country, and exercise their right to freedom of information in everyday life. Similarly, I suggest that civil society organizations, universities and professional associations should support the creation of the role of an ombudsman to defend the interests of media audiences. In this way, audiences can have another mechanism to exercise their right to information and entertainment with quality, based on ethical principles assumed by the media, and to ensure the protection of the fundamental human and cultural rights of vulnerable groups such as the children and women. Ultimately, only if people believe and take responsibility over their right to communicate can we expect to construct a multicultural democracy in the digital age.

Note

1. SVNet is the company that registers the names of websites under the '.sv' dominion in El Salvador.

References

Albornoz, L. A. and García, M. T. (2012) 'Televisión digital terrestre: caracterización, antecedentes e importancia,' pp. 23–42 in L. A. Albornoz and M. T. García (eds) *La televisión digital terrestre. Experiencias nacionales y diversidad en Europa, América y Asia* (Buenos Aires: La Crujía Ediciones).

Angulo, J., Calzada, J. and Estruch, A. (2011) 'Selection of standards for the digital television: the battle for Latin America,' *Telecommunications Policy*, 35(8): 773–787.

Becerra, M. and Mastrini, G. (2009) *Los monopolios de la verdad. Descifrando la estructura y concentración de los medios en Centroamérica y República Dominicana* (Buenos Aires: Prometeo Libros).

Benítez, J. L. (2012) 'Salvadoran transnational families: ICT and communication practices in the network society,' *Journal of Ethnic and Migration Studies*, 38(9): 1439–1449.

Busso, N. (2011) 'Derecho a la comunicación: conceptos clave y contexto internacional,' pp. 7–12 in N. Busso and D. Jaimes (eds) *La cocina de la ley. El proceso de incidencia en la elaboración de la Ley de Servicios de Comunicación Audiovisual en Argentina* (Argentina: FARCO).

De Zeeuw, J. and Kumar, K. (2006) *Promoting Democracy in Postconflict Societies* (Boulder, CO: Lynne Rienner Publishers).

Freedman, E. (2012) 'El mapa de los medios de comunicación salvadoreños,' *Envío*, 358. Available at http://bit.ly/1bzU3fE (accessed September 10, 2013).

García-Canclini, N. (2001) *Consumers and citizens. Globalization and multicultural conflicts* (Minneapolis: University of Minnesota Press).

138   *José Luis Benítez*

Herrera, L. (2013) 'Aportes para una ley que transparentice y democratice los medios de comunicación en El Salvador,' Master's Thesis in Communication (San Salvador, El Salvador:Universidad Centroamericana).

Internet World Stats (2010, July 13) 'El Salvador: search engines, reports and internet usage,' *Internet World Stats*. Available at http://bit.ly/1dotnDd (accessed January 2012).

Jenkis, H. (2006) *Convergence Culture. Where Old and New Media Collide* (New York and London: New York University Press).

Lawrence, M. D. (2004) *Freedom of Expression in El Salvador. The Struggle for Human Rights and Democracy* (North Carolina: McFarland and Company, Inc.).

López, I. (1987) *El periodismo en El Salvador* (San Salvador, El Salvador: UCA Editores).

McChesney, R. W. (2004) *The Problem of the Media. U.S. Communication Politics in the 21st Century* (New York: Monthly Review Press).

Miralles, A. M. (2011) *El miedo al disenso. El disenso periodístico como expresión democrática de las diferencias y no como provocación de violencia* (Barcelona: Gedisa).

Rockwell, J. and Janus, N. (2003) *Media Power in Central America* (Urbana and Chicago: University of Illinois Press).

Rodríguez, M. and Moreira, C. (2011) 'La calidad democrática y la lógica mediática. Un modelo teórico,' pp. 317–352 in C. M. Rodríguez and C. Moreira (eds) *Comunicación política y democratización en Iberoamérica* (México, DF: Universidad Iberoamericana).

Salzman, C. C. (2008) 'Central American Media: a comparative study of media industries in Guatemala, Nicaragua, Honduras, El Salvador and Costa Rica,' Master's Thesis of Science (Denton, Texas: University of North Texas).

Salzman, C. and Salzman, R. (2009) 'The media in Central America: Costa Rica, El Salvador, Guatemala, Honduras, Nicaragua and Panama,' pp. 47–62 in A. B. Albarran (ed.) *The handbook of Spanish Language Media* (New York: Routledge).

SIGET (2008) *Boletín estadístico de telecomunicaciones 2008*. Available at http://bit.ly/1dosAly (accessed September 10, 2013).

SIGET (2010) *Boletín estadístico de telecomunicaciones 2010*. Available at http://bit.ly/1dosGd1 (accessed September 10, 2013).

Sorj, B. (2012) 'Medios de comunicación y democracia: más allá de la confrontación entre gobiernos y empresas,' pp. 5–31 in B. Sorj (ed.) *Democracia y medios de comunicación. Más allá del estado y el mercado* (Buenos Aires: Catálogos).

United Nations (UN) (2013) *Joint Declaration on the Protection of Freedom of Expression and Diversity in the Digital Terrestrial Transition* (Pretoria: UN/OSCE/OAS/ACHPR).

UNESCO (2003) *Legislation on Community Radio Broadcasting. Comparative Study of the Legislation of 13 Countries* (Paris, France: UNESCO).

UNESCO (2008) *Media Development Indicators: A Framework for Assessing Media Development* (Paris, France: UNESCO).

World Bank (2013) *World Development Indicators and EconStats*. Available at http://bit.ly/1cvoAPe (accessed December 2013).

7

Media and Politicians in Guatemala: A Marriage that will Last Until Money Do Them Part

Silvio René Gramajo

Introduction

Guatemalan history, especially in the past 50 years, accounts for the forms and contents that define the relationship between the media and the political systems. As observed by Guerrero and Luengas (2013), it is the political system that shapes the legal and operational context in which the mass communications industry flows. However, in the case of Guatemala, one must take into account that transition to democracy initiated in the midst of an internal armed conflict that, as noted by Kruijt (1998), marked socially, economically, and politically the whole nation. This conflictive frame in which democracy was born is key to understanding the transition and negotiation of the new rules of the game (Munck, 1994, 2002; Mazzuca, 2002).

While democracy has opened the possibilities for more pluralistic and open communicative practices and a deeper, critical exercise of investigative journalism (as compared to the civil war period), these have not led to a more dialogic public sphere, or to a deliberative democracy (Sampedro, 2000). As in other Latin American countries, clientelism, corporatist, and patrimonial kinds of relations have prevailed between political, social, and economic groups in Guatemala, the media among them. These relations have seriously hindered both the development of professional journalism practices and a proper regulation framework that promotes pluralism while effectively protecting fundamental rights, including the right to information. Instead, they have favored a highly concentrated local media industry (Mastrini and Becerra, 2006) where the authorities selectively apply regulation, and the media selectively exposes governmental mismanagement (Hallin and Papathanassopoulos, 2002). This reflects a relationship based upon simulation and perversion, rather than independence and autonomy. The first part of this chapter outlines a brief historical configuration of the political system in Guatemala. The second part assesses how this political system has shaped a quite inefficient regulatory framework for the media enabling undue profits and extreme market concentration. The last part discusses how the political system has negatively affected the emergence of a true watchdog role in the media and of professional journalistic practices.

The burden of the past marks the present

In Latin America, transition processes in general have shaped the development of media structures. Most transitions have been similarly classified in the literature (O'Donell, Schmitter and Whitehead, 1994; Linz and Stepan, 1996; Colomer, 1998). However, Guatemala does not fit completely into these models, and it becomes necessary to define its particularities because they are crucial to understanding the logic and operation of the Guatemalan state and today's democratic institutions.

After decades of military dictatorship, Guatemala's transition of the mid-1980s ascribes to what is known as the third wave of democratization (Huntington, 1998). Certainly transitions have led to governments invested in the formalities of democracy, but with strong authoritarian legacies supported by codes, laws, rules, symbols and, of course, the interests of conservative actors as indicated by Poitevin and Sequen (2002).

However, what are the particular features of Guatemalan transition and democratization? And how to understand them in the context of an armed conflict? The transition literature assumes the end of any armed conflict before the creation of foundational agreements and pacts that define the new rules of the game (O'Donell et al., 1994; Linz and Stepan, 1996). Guatemala is one of the few exceptions to this assumption. Here the regime changed 12 years before the end of the armed conflict, inaugurating a formal democracy that, in the words of Torres-Rivas, 'erupted from a canyon' (Gramajo, 2009). The Guatemalan experience shows that the organization of elections and the creation of other institutions of democracy may prove to be only a façade to a regime where the authoritarian nature of power survives through rules and practices. The transition was not effective in dismantling authoritarianism.

In fact, transition and democratization have been uneven and unstable. The former was gradual and incremental. In addition, as noted by Schirmer (1996) and Urrutia (1999), it was marked not only by apparent deadlocks that were overcome by quantum leaps but also by the process of peace negotiations. While Guatemala has not undergone any dramatic regression threatening democracy, it has not fully consolidated. Democracy is not exempted from idiots and demagogues as Sampedro indicates (2000).

The challenge has been to build check and balance mechanisms and solve the problems left by the previous regime. As Mazzuca (2002) says, the mechanisms to access power are already defined and accepted by most players. The problems are in the mechanisms to exercise political power, many of them inherited from the old regime and still intact. The transition left a series of legacies and inertia that have not been discussed and properly solved. As noted by Colomer (1998), the virtues of transition have become the addictions of democracy.

This context has decisively molded the relationships between the actors who participate in the political dynamics, especially, among those who exert power whether political, economic, social, or symbolic. For the purpose of this chapter, the question is how has this context affected the media system in Guatemala? The following sections focus on regulation and journalistic professionalization.

The regulatory efficiency

Guerrero and Luengas (2013) assert that there is a low degree of regulatory efficiency in Latin America assessed through either the irregular application of legal frames or the inexistence of adequate laws promoting more open and pluralistic media markets. In Guatemala, democratization did not alter the mechanisms to exercise power – including the media property structure – and it instead focused only on creating new institutions to compete for power and access to it. Not only the media property structure was left untouched, but also its role during the military dictatorship was never put into question. This enabled the media to keep its benefits and even to consolidate its market position by strengthening its monopoly systems and leveraging the technological resurgence.

Many are called, few are chosen

Although the Constitution of Guatemala results from a transitional pact and it prohibits monopolies in Article 130, they currently exist, and the media is an example. If a state has been as permissive in this regard as to reach the extremes, it is Guatemala. The authoritarian tradition in which information and communication were fundamental to the exercise of power not only permeated the political agenda, but also attitudes and practices. The management and manipulation of information and of the media industry were essential to the counterinsurgency policy instituted during the armed conflict where mistrust and secrecy practices became very handy. Despite democracy, secrecy has become one of the strongest institutions of the Guatemalan state (Gramajo, 2009); therefore, data collection – especially related to economic activities – is an almost unattainable task. As pointed out by Mastrini and Becerra (2009), in the country, it is almost impossible to obtain relevant information about the state of cultural industries.

There are seven printed national newspapers published in the capital, Guatemala City. Among them, there are five morning newspapers (Prensa Libre, Nuestro Diario, Siglo 21, Al Día, and elPeriódico), one evening newspaper (La Hora), and one governmental paper (Diario de Centro America). The concentration of the incoming population around the capital has formed a major urban circle divided into several municipal districts; they are called 'ciudad dormitorio' (bedroom city). Some of these locations have already developed local newspapers, such as El Metropolitano (printed in various cities) and El Quetzalteco, published in Quetzaltenango, the second largest city in the country and the largest economic and media center after the capital.

Mastrini and Becerra (2009) account for the disappearance, in 2001, of Revista Crónica, a leading weekly magazine; although it has been just re-launched. In a few months, other magazines are expected to be published, including Contrapoder that is a weekly newspaper the majority of whose staff migrated from El Periódico en masse. However, as the market in this area is uncertain, so is the future of these new outlets.

The strongest publishing group is Prensa Libre, which also owns Nuestro Diario and El Quetzalteco. Combined, these three outlets stand for almost 80 percent of daily newspaper circulation. The rest of the newspapers mentioned above are published in the metropolitan region, and their circulation is limited compared to the editions of Prensa Libre. The newspapers Siglo 21 and Al Día belong to Corporación de Noticias, which is a corporation initially founded by traditional elite families. Today this company belongs to a cooperative in Guatemala. Despite readerships being relatively low in Guatemala, according to Mastrini and Becerra (2009), advertising revenues are not related to the volume of circulation. For example, Prensa Libre tops advertising sales with Siglo 21 a distant second, but they are second and fourth respectively in terms of circulation, where Nuestro Diario is number one. This confirms what Sampedro (2000: 13) says: 'the media entrepreneur is interested in either large majorities or wealthy minorities. The formers provide sales revenue, and the others expensive advertising.'

For its part, the radio industry has lost popularity to television, but still has presence in almost all Guatemalan households (Mastrini and Becerra, 2009). Satellite or cable TV and the increasing literacy rates in the country account for the declining popularity of radio, though it is still the medium with the widest reach in the country. According to Berganza (2004), 54 percent of the radio frequencies are owned by a handful of proprietors, including the Aliu's group; the Central de Radio Group (which includes El Tajin group) that owns Radio Sonora, one of the most listened stations; the Emisoras Unidas group; and the Nuevo Mundo group. Other important groups in this sector are Radio Corporación Nacional; Corporación de Radio Vision of the El Shaddai Church – whose leader, Harold Caballeros, was a presidential candidate and former foreign minister of the current government; and El Consorcio de Radios Nacionales, with a strong presence in the countryside. It is noteworthy that the Catholic and the Evangelical churches also hold a good number of radio stations. As it is evident, these private groups concentrate the highest percentage of advertising. Besides the private radio groups, there is an undetermined number of local and community stations that transmit in 23 Mayan languages and operate in legal or 'allegal'[1] frameworks.

As for TV, Guatemala is one of the few countries with a total monopoly on the VHF television system, belonging to Mexican businessman Ángel González. He has four frequencies: Channels 3, 7, 11, and 13. The remaining frequencies in the spectrum have no impact and in fact one of them (Channel 9) assigned to the National Congress has never been used, and the other (Channel 5), in the hands of the Academy of Mayan Languages, has a very limited schedule in both transmission and hours of coverage.[2] Almost the entire market programming and advertising revenue have been secured by the monopoly of González. It is worth mentioning that Channel 31 – acquired by TV Azteca, another Mexican group – has broadcast for some years on the UHF frequency. The other channels do not represent any weight in the media agenda, much less in the generation of public opinion.

Due to its configuration, cable TV should be analyzed in a separate paragraph, though there are some similar variables to what occurs in broadcast television. In Guatemala, cable TV has become increasingly important not only due to economic reasons, but also due to its relation with politics throughout the country. As pointed out by Berganza (2004), television has become the primary means by which citizens learn from political information. TV formats are attractive to politicians and to those who want to build a political career.

Cable TV is rapidly growing. In Guatemala there are currently 480 cable companies registered in the Supervisory Control Unit of the Ministry of Communications, Infrastructure and Housing (see Figure 7.1). This means that most of the territory is covered by TV cable systems. Due to its increasing relevance, politicians seek the support of the cable networks in their constituencies. Moreover, some want to become shareholders and, once there, use their power to deny the access to political opponents and to any other company that wants to get a license for operating cable TV services.

In the recent research on the relationship between politicians and local media in the seven municipalities of Guatemala, Naveda (2013)[3] notes that it is very common to find informal ties of political or ideological and even kinship affinity between politicians, journalists, and communication businessmen. The main relationships are established in the workplace (journalist-source) but also on the business front: from the legal to the fraudulent means, from preferential governmental advertising to bribing, Naveda says.

This research makes evident that today's political competition in inland Guatemala implies also a competition for media property. In this case, cable TV is not only a business where economic profits are sought, but also electoral benefits. In the words of Naveda: 'Although to obtain conclusive results it would be necessary to multiply the sample of municipalities studied, the research prompts us to mention, as a hypothesis [...] that the domain of the media by certain political and economic actors depends largely on the ways in which local authorities evolve and are structured' (Naveda, 2013: 209, my translation).

The media operate under a monopoly structure that achieves extraordinary dimensions. If this couples with a weakened state that is unable or unwilling to change this reality, then the shaping of public opinion is orientated not by the debates on public interest issues, but by the blatant interests of politicians and businessmen. Media pluralism and dissension from mainstream opinion do not penetrate the news agenda. In this regard, only in the digital landscape is there some space for diversity.

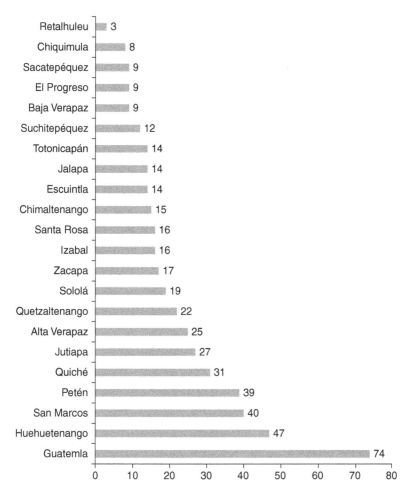

Figure 7.1 Cable companies in Guatemala: number of cable operators by region

Source: Ministry of Communications, Infrastructure and Housing – Ministerio de Comunicaciones, Infraestructura y Vivienda.

The goose that lays the golden eggs

Guatemala lacks a proper regulatory frame on governmental advertising, which enables discretionary practices in funding amounts and formats. Due to the requirements of the procurement law and the state's contracts, public advertising expenditures must be published. Moreover, the Law on Access to Public Information forces the state to publicize all contracts made with the private sector, including the media. However, there are ways to circumvent the law and allocate public funds without considering the criteria of price, coverage, or impact. There are forms of simulating public biddings that reintroduce old practices in the relationship between public power and the media: reward or punishment. As properly pointed out by authors like Mastrini and Becerra (2009) or Naveda (2013) public advertising revenues are key to the media's survival in Guatemala.

Even when governmental advertising refers to airtime bought with public funds to promote, theoretically, information relevant to the public, the truth is that it is in fact correlated to the struggle for power. Since the financing of the political parties is mostly private, the public funds transferred to the parties – dependent on previous electoral outcomes – are really eager to finance a whole campaign based upon media messages and distribution. This exemplifies the relationship between media and politics that strengthens during election campaigns. In that sense, even though there are regulations limiting electoral funding, political parties seldom comply with them given that the sanction mechanisms by the electoral authorities are ineffective due to weaknesses in the institutional design of the Supreme Electoral Tribunal.[4]

A weakened and deformed electoral sanction mechanism implies serious difficulties for democratic consolidation. And even though some political groups have made efforts to discuss this topic in the amendments to the Law on Elections and Political Parties, it has not been passed in congress. Moreover, the media do not invest much editorial effort in covering the problems of public advertising funding to the media. And for politicians, quoting Baires (2013), 'more (media) presence, more votes.'[5] Thus, the issue is not discussed.

Media and politics, a profitable duo

The media have gained prominence in the political arena presenting politics as spectacle. Berrocal (2003), Canel (2006), and Del Rey Morato (2008) all acknowledge a kind of coverage where politics lose content and the focus is on the 'performing' capacity of the leader or candidate. Here politicians no longer strive to improve their mediation skills, ideological leadership, or argumentative conviction. What is important for them is to develop acting skills, which turn citizens into mere spectators.

We mentioned earlier the interest of politicians to participate and co-opt local cable companies. This interest now extends to local and community radio stations as well. From the study of Naveda (2013), it is possible to infer that politicians are even willing to participate in community radio stations, since the logic of production and transmission in indigenous languages has become a great attraction to the candidates for local representative offices.

One of the most significant cases is Petén, the largest province in the country, with a natural and incalculable historical wealth, but the smallest population. In Petén the media belong to two political families who have even reached provincial and national political positions in their respective political parties. Even more, one of them, Manuel Baldizon, was presidential candidate in 2011 and came in second place; now his party is the largest oppositional force. It is taken for granted that he will run again in the presidential elections of 2015.

This situation is not exclusive of the provinces. In the central district of Guatemala, politicians manifest an increasing interest in participating in the centralized national media business. However, here it is not necessarily an easy road. The concentration of the media system and the long tradition of family ownership have been a difficult bulwark to evade. The high levels of advertising revenue due to the conditions of monopoly in TV, of strong concentration in the print industry, and of the advantageous situation for radio groups make it unlikely that these corporate groups will share the business. Apparently, media owners are better off establishing healthy distanced and mutually convenient relationships with politicians. Everybody wins: proprietors earn electoral and advertising revenues, and politicians get votes and uncritical news coverage that rarely questions the form of the exercise of power.

This does not mean that media owners are unwilling to participate in politics, as the case of Petén shows. Juan Alcázar, from the Radio Corporación Nacional group, participated with the Partido Patriota – current ruling party – and is a representative to the congress. Also, the actual Minister of Energy, Erick Archila, is a member of Emisoras Unidas, and he recently acquired the ownership of a cable channel, Canal Antigua, which has a news program highly influential on public opinion. Apparently President Otto Perez Molina appointed Mr. Archila as a way to pay the 'political debt' to the corporation during the elections. Roberto Alejos, former president of the Congress, head of the political group 'Todos,' and with presidential aspirations for the coming elections seems also to support different media outlets.

With the arrival of democracy, the bridges between politics and media have been kept open, especially since the latter have become privileged spaces to maintain or gain power. According to the scholar Marques de Melo, 'new subjects quickly emerge without being clearly perceptible if they are situated in the territory of politics or in the media [...] it is a political and media androgyny' (2009: 122).

They run the business without saying a word

If there is any country where interests perfectly converge to create institutional frameworks that benefit corporate groups, including privileges from the state, it is Guatemala. The origins of the foundational agreements and of the constitution itself that inaugurated democracy contain such frameworks (Gramajo, 2009). Examples are the laws guaranteeing freedom of expression and the regulation on print and broadcasting, as well as the rights of rectification and reply.

The National Constituent Assembly established the right to freedom of expression and of thought together in Article 35 of the constitution. However, it determined some provisions that invested in apparent protections for those who exercise the informative and journalistic activities. At the end, they became prerogatives for the corporations to maintain the *status quo*. For instance, the law states the obligation to conform special courts and juries for resolution of disputes in the freedom of expression domain. The problem is that the institutional design of these regulators has made it virtually impossible to integrate properly, and benefits the corporations – and not necessarily the journalists – in the sentences.

Moreover, the legal and constitutional tradition in Guatemala establishes the rights in the Carta Magna, which are then developed in secondary regulation. In the case of freedom of expression, the law still in force dates back to 1966. In 1985, when the actual constitution was adopted, that law was not updated – and it still is not – in spite of its obvious obsolescence. Later developments such as the jurisprudence of the Inter-American Court of Human Rights regarding the right to information lack a proper legal framework in Guatemalan laws. Thus, cases involving the right to information are virtually impossible to litigate in the country.

There have been only a few attempts to update the rule in congress. The media corporations close ranks and create a climate of opinion contrary to any possible modification, arguing that the freedoms of speech and the press are under threat. Censorship and political pressure are the discursive elements evoked by the corporations to keep the current situation. It is noticeable that the whole media regulatory framework has not experienced significant changes even in democracy. The only shift has been the approval of the Telecommunications Act, which involved a number of perks for television business, radio, and telecommunications.

As said at the start of the chapter, democracy was inaugurated in the context of an armed conflict. Negotiations extended for several years. In 1995, one of the peace agreements called 'Agreement on Identity and Rights of Indigenous Peoples' was signed. It states that the government must provide media spaces for indigenous peoples, promote reforms to legislation in order to make frequencies available for indigenous projects, and ensure compliance with the principle of non-discrimination, as well as define and support a system of programs to promote indigenous culture in their own languages.

However, as Guerrero and Luengas (2013) mention, during the 1990s Guatemala favored economic neoliberal reforms, privatized public services, and gave better conditions for capital accumulation. The 1996 Telecommunications Act was approved in this context. Also, according to the Movimiento de Radios Comunitarias (2012), the Guatemalan state has not only unfulfilled the provisions of the above referenced agreement of 1995, but the Telecommunications Act has left indigenous peoples out of any consideration. The new law regulates matters concerning amateur radio frequencies, the frequencies of the state, and the frequencies of commercial radio companies. There are no precepts regarding indigenous peoples and their rights to transmit and disseminate in their own cultural, social, economic, political, and spiritual contexts.

Reality shows that legislation on telecommunications has generated a series of processes that have favored private enterprises at the expense of other social sectors, like the indigenous people. In this regard, the Special Rapporteur for Freedom of Expression of the Inter-American Court of Human Rights has recommended the State of Guatemala to revise the broadcast regulations to promote a more pluralistic access both to the broadcast media and to ICTs.

As icing on the cake, in November 20, 2012, the Congress approved reforms to the Telecommunications Act with the votes of all of its representatives. These reforms maintain the current model favoring media ownership concentration; increases the period of the licenses from 15 to 20 years; and facilitates continuity of usufruct. Regardless of the deadline of broadcasting licenses granted after the adoption of such standard in 1996, after the approval of the actual reforms, the owners could ask for a renewal of 20 more years just through a single exchange of letters with the authority.

The main beneficiaries are the current broadcasters and cell phone companies, such as Tigo, Claro (in which the Mexican tycoon Carlos Slim holds a stake), and Telefónica. According to some observers, the only change here is that the monopolist position of Mexican Ángel González may be at risk because the cell phone companies who also benefited from the almost automatic renewal of their licenses control the technological progress and the emergence of digital satellite television (Perez, 2012).

The 'watchdog role' of the media

It is worth mentioning that since the end of the armed conflict and since the arrival of democracy, patterns of harassment and political persecution to media and journalists have changed, but have not ended. They moved from the logic of war to the logic of politics. Politicians and journalists may not be enemies anymore, but it does not mean in any way that the freedom of expression is exercised freely and without pressures.

Besides continuous political pressures, in Guatemala there are many other risks to professional journalism: the increase in drug trafficking activities, their embedding in state structures, as well as the excessive growth of organized crime have generated other forms of pressure and censorship. As pointed out by the journalists' Observatory Center for Informative Reports in Guatemala (CERIGUA), in 2012 alone, there were 36 violations against the freedom of expression reported, highlighting physical and verbal abuse, intimidation, threats, harassment and restriction of access to sources, among others. It is to be noted that there were no murders, unlike other countries in the region. However, the lack of proper protections for journalists continues. The general attorney created the Unit for Crimes against Journalists, but the unit's resources and funding fall short from its objectives and aims.[6]

Also, in 2012, the Human Rights office received a total of 47 reports of acts of aggression against journalists. The diversity of data only gives the certainty that there is underreporting. Obviously, the number of threats and attacks against journalists' unions are larger, especially in Guatemala's inland where the rule of law is weaker and local journalists are trapped at the crossroads of politicians, drug cartels, mob bosses, and other *de facto* powers. Understandably there is a lot of fear in making these situations public that constitutes a clear hindrance to the watchdog role of journalism.

Additionally, a second hindrance to the watchdog role of journalism has to do with the professional development of the industry. Though the level of professional education of journalists is still uneven between those in the capital and in the rest of the country, the general formal educational standards have improved. Since the early 1980s when the training of journalists and communicators had a boost, it became part of their profile for recruitment. Nowadays, there is no one in the national media that would not hire a university educated journalist.

In the capital, educational provision has improved considerably. From three college programs that existed in the 1980s, now eight universities currently offer such training. Some of them even replicate such programs in other regions. As for the salary structure, contrary to what happens in many other places, in Guatemala the printed press pays better wages and offers more benefits to journalists. The lowest wages are paid in radio, in spite of arriving with a university degree.

In any case, the increase in the supply of journalism and communication professionals does not necessarily mirror an increase in the quality of what is reported and of how it is reported. Also, the recruitment of university educated journalists is not a widespread geographical trend. Especially in the countryside, professionally educated journalists are still scarce in comparison to the actual number of individuals doing journalistic work on cable channels, local and community radios stations, and other digital media that have begun to emerge. As referred to by Guerrero and Luengas (2013), Guatemala has not escaped the controversy generated between journalism training versus the versatility offered by training in communication sciences and the impact that it generates not only in the recruitment process, but especially in the elaboration and structuring of messages' contents, as noted by Lozano (2007).

The media labor market in Guatemala has another characteristic: a large number of media companies resort to various legal maneuvers to avoid the observance of labor obligations regarding their employees, including journalists of course. This factor is crucial for determining quality and professional journalism.

In the case of radio organizations, if one adds here the low salaries paid to journalists, it is possible to understand the low quality news programming. Here newscasts are based on the statement of official sources and official releases transforming the anchor into a spokesperson and legitimizing the message without critical reflection and discussion. A common feature of these programs is that the news contents presented are seldom based upon journalistic investigation. The myth of 'immediacy' and a distorted idea of 'competition for getting the story first' are the perfect excuses for maintaining radio journalism trapped in the sound bite, the 'say-stories'[7] type of reporting. Of course, low wages are not an incentive for journalists to alter this model.

In television, due to new technologies, there have been some improvements. The growing popularity of cable TV and the new technologies for downloading content from the Internet have forced traditional TV to change. For instance, in the past ten years, three news programs launched in cable television that targeted an audience slice that had been so far only addressed by the news and current affairs programming aired by the traditional TV monopoly of the Mexican Gonzalez. It is true, however, that most investment here has been allocated to production and display than to the content quality.

One of the consequences of pay TV is that traditional and cable TV now wrestle for governmental and private advertising. Here one must note a particularity: traditional network television advertisers require customers to sign exclusive contracts with their channels. Otherwise, they violate the contract and are vetted. In spite of cable penetration, network television has managed to convince the advertising agencies of their higher ratings. Many point out that in this game advertising agencies play a complicity role, as they make profits ranging between 16 and 25 percent of the incomes billed by the media.

Finally, the printed media have made the most visible efforts regarding investigative and professional journalism. However, it has been insufficient to gain autonomy from the political agenda and promote their own. Recently, elPeriódico created an investigative unit, but – except for the publications of 2012 – the experience turned out to be unfortunate in terms of technical quality and the depth and scope of investigation. Instead of covering public interest stories, the topics responded more to the economic interests of the corporation and of powerful interest groups or politicians who have been able to co-opt the media and transform it into an arena to settle their own disputes. It is worth remembering that the financial structure of newspapers in Guatemala, except for Nuestro Diario (the widest-circulating newspaper), lives off of advertising sales. This factor has been used several times to blackmail the press. The disappearance of Revista Crónica in 2001 due to financial starvation caused by the withdrawal of advertising has been a case in point. The strong dependence on advertising has been used to make the press and professional journalism if not supportive of governments and corporations, at least silenced accomplices.

A final aspect that must be mentioned here is that this precariousness of labor markets, the specific conditions in which journalists are hired, and the lack of proper legal protections to journalism performance combine not only to hinder professional journalism, but end up promoting unethical practices and a blatant lack of commitment to the profession's values. Given this context, in Guatemala bribes, gifts, and underhanded salary compensations are common resources to subdue the enthusiasm and the good will of journalists, editors, and media owners.

Epilogue

In general terms, the relation between the media and the political systems in Guatemala can be defined within the 'captured liberal' model proposed by Guerrero in Chapter 2 of this book, and previously advanced by Guerrero and Luengas (2013). In spite of some peculiarities of the Guatemalan transition and democratization processes, the relation between the media and the political systems share most of the characteristics defined in the 'captured liberal' model.

The weakness of the state, combined with the convenience of political actors, for not regulating or not applying the existent regulation regarding the media is evident. In these terms, the monopoly in the ownership structure of the media is one of the strongest in Latin America. Finally, as suggested by Hallin and Mancini (2004), it is undeniable that in the country, the concept of 'instrumentalization' in journalism fits perfectly. The influence of powerful actors is crucial for the formation of an agenda, but also for the shaping of journalistic coverage. While politicians successfully keep the media as part of their patronage networks (with the economic convenience of media owners), professional journalism will have few chances of flourishing. Journalists will keep on covering on the go statements and other topics imposed by extra journalistic interests, maintaining and legitimizing the actual *status quo*; a situation beneficial for politicians and media owners alike. Unfortunately, while profit for both groups exist, the relationship will endure and the cohabitation will last until the money do them part.

Notes

1. This term refers to radios that operate outside of legal regulations. Indigenous and social organizations working in this area refuse to be called 'illegal' or 'pirate' radios because they consider it a discriminatory and racist name.

2. It is worth noting that the frequency was delivered to the Academy of Mayan Languages to comply with the peace agreement. However, the government's attitude was highly questionable, since in effect, it gave the frequency but not the resources necessary for this channel to work and operate effectively. In fact it has had to rely on international aid. Another problem this channel is facing is the inability to sell advertising, as the law states that this type of media has a social purpose, noncommercial, that the private media have taken advantage of in their favor and that has stifled both the television and community radio in general.
3. The research includes all types of media, and it is clear the weight cable television has.
4. The NGO Acción Ciudadana published the study, *How expensive was the election campaign? Analysis of expenditure and accountability of political parties in the electoral process.* Guatemala (2011).
5. The report, published in *Plaza Pública*, indicates that the proposed reforms to the Electoral Law promote some new rules for media advertising expenditure during the campaign, which is clearly inconvenient for both media and politicians. For the media, they would never accept losing more than $ 70 million every four years.
6. This unit has been controversial, since it was created to follow up on all complaints against attacks and threats, among other offenses, contrary to the practice of journalism. However, it is at this instance chasing all those working in 'allegal' radio communicators, primarily backed by the organized sector of commercial radio.
7. British journalist David Randall (2000) brands 'say-stories' as stand-alone articles about what people are saying. Thus sources, normally well-placed within the government apparatus, make a statement or comment on a story and the resulting reporting is titled with verbs such as 'warns,' 'urges,' 'calls,' or 'denies.'

References

Baires, R. (2013) 'Cinco razones por las que no caminará la reforma electoral,' *Plaza Pública* (Guatemala: Universidad Rafael Landívar). Available at http://bit.ly/1bA3dbR (accessed December 2013).

Berganza, G. (2004) *De verdad, influyentes: los efectos de los medios en las elecciones presidenciales de 2003* (Guatemala: Asociación DOSES).

Berrocal, S. (2003) *Comunicación política en televisión y nuevos medios* (Barcelona: Ariel Comunicación).

Canel, M. (2006) *Comunicación Política. Una guía para su estudio y práctica* (Madrid: Tecnos).

Centro de Reportes Informativos sobre Guatemala (CERIGUA) (2012) *Estado de situación de la Libertad de Expresión en Guatemala* (Guatemala:CERIGUA).

Colomer, J. (1998) *La transición a la democracia: el modelo español* (Barcelona: Anagrama).

Del Rey Morato, J. (2008) *Comunicación política, internet y campañas electorales. De la teledemocracia a la ciberdemocracia* (Madrid: Tecnos).

Guerrero, M. A. and Luengas, M. (2013, May) *Sistemas mediáticos en America Latina: entre la captura corporativa y la audiencia participativa.* Conference paper presented at International Days on Diversity, organized by the High Authority of Telecommunications of Morocco and UNESCO Chairs in Communication, Rabat.

Gramajo, S. (2009) *Un pasado que aún pesa. Los legados autoritarios imprimen su huella en la ley de acceso a la información pública en Guatemala*, PhD Thesis in in Social Science (México: FLACSO).

Hallin, D. and Mancini, P. (2004) *Comparing Media Systems. Three Models of Media and Politics* (Cambridge: Cambridge University Press).

Hallin, D. and Papathanassopoulos, S. (2002) 'Political clientelism and the media: southern Europe and Latin America in comparative perspective,' *Media, Culture & Society*, 24(2): 175–95.

Huntington, S. (1998) *La tercera ola, la democratización de finales del siglo XX* (Madrid: Paidós).

Kruijt, D. (1998) 'Reflexiones sobre Guatemala,' pp. 9–36 in B. Arévalo, *Sobre arenas movedizas: Sociedad, Estado y Ejército en Guatemala* (Guatemala: FLACSO).

Linz, J. and Stepan, A. (1996) *Problems of Democratic Transition and Consolidation. Southern Europe, South America and Post-communist Europe* (Baltimore: Johns Hopkins University Press).

Lozano, J. (2007) *Teoría e investigación de la comunicación de masas* (México: Pearson).

Marques De Melo, J. (2009) *Pensamiento comunicacional latinoamericano. Entre el saber y el poder* (Salamanca: Ediciones Comunicación Social).

Mastrini, G. y Becerra, M. (2006) *Periodistas y magnates. Estructura y concentración de las industrias culturales* (Buenos Aires: Prometeo).

Mastrini, G. and Becerra, M. (2009) *Los monopolios de la verdad. Descifrando la estructura y concentración de los medios en Centroamérica y República Dominicana* (Buenos Aires: Prometeo Libros).

Mazzuca, S. (2002) '¿Democratización o burocratización? Inestabilidad del acceso al poder y estabilidad del ejercicio del poder en América Latina,' *Araucaria*, 4(7): 23–47.

Movimiento De Radios Comunitarias (2012) *Radio comunitaria, su historia ante un Estado racista en Guatemala y sus fundamentos jurídicos* (Guatemala: PaxilKayalá).

Munck, G. (1994) 'Democratic transitions in comparative perspective,' *Comparative Politics*, 26(3): 355–375.

Munck, G. (2002) 'Una revisión de los estudios sobre la democracia: temáticas, conclusiones y desafíos,' *Revista de Ciencias Sociales*, 41(164): 579–609.

Naveda, E. (2013) *Reyes de cartón o por qué las elecciones se cuentan como se cuentan.* Master of Arts Thesis. Guatemala: Universidad Rafael Landívar.

O'Donell, G., Schmitter, P. and Whitehead, L. (1994) *Transiciones desde un gobierno autoritario* (Barcelona: Paidós).

Perez, A. (2012) 'El beneficio es para todos...los que ya tienen su frecuencia' *Plaza Pública* (Guatemala: Universidad Rafael Landívar). Available at http://bit. ly/1doH8Sc (acessed December 2013).

Poitevin, R. and Sequen, A. (2002) *Los desafíos de la democracia en Centroamérica* (Guatemala: FLACSO).

Randall, D. (2000) *The universal journalist* (London: Pluto Press).

Sampedro, V. (2000) *Opinión pública y democracia deliberativa. Medios, sondeos y urnas* (Madrid: Ediciones Istmo).

Schirmer, J. (1996) 'La otra cara de la dimensión internacional: el saqueo del discurso democrático por parte de los militares guatemaltecos,' pp. 97–110 in E. Jelin and E. Hershberg (coords.) *Construir la democracia: derechos humanos, ciudadanía y sociedad en América Latina* (Venezuela: Nueva Sociedad).

Urrutia, E. (1999) 'Recuento de la transición a la democracia,' pp. 77–117 in E. Torres-Rivas and J. Fuentes (comps.) *Guatemala: las particularidades del desarrollo humano; Democracia, etnicidad y seguridad* (Guatemala: Naciones Unidas).

8
The State in Pursuit of Hegemony over the Media: The Chávez Model

Andrés Cañizález

Public policies today

In the past 15 years, Venezuela has become one of the flagship states in Latin America in regaining and sustaining a strong dominance and presence in the shaping of media policy. But as a starting point, it is first necessary to clarify the concept of public policies and the process they entail in order to proceed to review the specific experiences related to communication and to study the events that occurred in Venezuela under Hugo Chávez's administration (1999–2013).

According to Alejandro Oropeza, when the state designs public policies, it seeks one of the following goals: '(a) to deal with public problems, (b) to satisfy a social need or preference, (c) to fulfill the goals of the state, (d) to comply with a legal mandate regardless of its hierarchy' (2008: 2, my translation). The creation of public policies, in any field, may arise from one or many of the aforementioned elements, which are defined in terms of needs that require attention for the state to take action. For this author, there is a combination of factors that differentiate this process: on the one hand, grounds for political action, summarized in the previous four items; and the search for social or public utility improvements, on the other, which should result in an alternate situation, that is, in visible change.

It is important to specify that the state is not the sole actor in the generation of public policies, and its actions do not stand alone. William Dunn points out three components in permanent interaction as he considers policies as resulting from a process: (a) public policies on their own, (b) the actors and/or decision-making participants who are interested in political results, and (c) the political environment (Dunn, 1994 cited in Oropeza, 2005: 13). As stated by Oropeza, policy systems 'are realities with particular characteristics, limits, and dynamics resulting from decision-making processes with the ability of being redesigned in their components' (2008: 13). When we discuss public policies and place them within the context of a process, we cannot see them as static decisions, immovable in time. On the contrary, their nature includes daily reviews or evaluations with their corresponding readjustments. On the other hand, public problems may have different interpretations and approaches. Thus, diverse actors may interpret the same fact differently due to the multiple conceptions about human nature, government, and social opportunities (Dunn, cited in Curcio, 2007: 64.) On this subject, public problems and, consequently, public policies issued as their responses 'must be understood as systems' and therefore 'require a holistic approach and must be treated inseparably.' This means the planning of 'a feasible intervention of the government from the legal, economic, administrative, and political point of view' (Curcio, 2007: 64).

Grindle and Thomas (1991) give importance to the interaction of different activities in a model that crafts public policies, making it dynamic and variable over time. These authors consider evaluation to be very significant, even vital, within the framework of a democratic decision-making and social consensus-building processes. Moreover, this way of crafting of public policies not only includes the social participation of the sectors involved (Meentzen, 2007: 30), but goes beyond since 'they are created from the logic of their interaction with the accepted social practices and own cultural traditions' (Segal, 2006: 15).

To sum up, it is naïve to think that the decisions regarding public policies only take place within sociopolitical contexts of wide and free deliberation. However, Latin American in general and Venezuelan history in particular show an opposite trend: long record of arbitrarily made official decisions with great impact on citizens' lives. Lindblom (1997) emphasizes several examples about how it is possible to force the acceptance of policies issued from a state that may appeal to terror, authoritarianism, and the imposition of a 'government of the majority' (241). This chapter departs from analysing the nature of public communication policies in Latina America where the interests of the governments have prevailed over truly public conceptions. In the second part it discusses how presidential political systems, like those prevailing in Latina America (and the US), favor conditions that make the president the key communicator, in order to show in the third part how in Venezuela Hugo Chávez took advantage of these conditions to redefine public communication policies in the interest of his government in an unprecedented way in Venezuelan history. The fourth part shows how private media have been cornered while at the same time communication policies have confused the understanding of 'public' to a limited state's media hegemony.

Public communication policies from Latin America

During the 1970s and 1980s, the National Communication Policies (Políticas Nacionales de Comunicación, PNC) were promoted in Latin America as part of the debates of the international communications order during the Cold War and the widespread observation of unequal flows of cultural exchange on the part of developing countries that were typical of the day. These policies brought public communication policies to the region at a time when different regional or national initiatives surfaced to set up a legal framework for the overall media system, laid ground for the inception of the public broadcasting system, and promoted communication for social development in rural and urban areas. Back in the day, international organizations, high-ranked government officials, and academic specialists all agreed on the need to implement these policies in Venezuela. For some years, when most Latin American governments were mainly experiencing a consolidation of the market economy and the shrinking of the state, public communication policy-making was absent from the discussion agenda. During the 21st century, with the growing presence of governments with strong populist features that began to question the role of the private media corporations, the debate on the nature of public communication policies has resurfaced. For this reason, it was necessary to revisit Latin American tradition on this subject and enrich it with the democratic – though uneven – development in the region during the last decades.

The 1990s in particular, persistently emphasized the idea that globalization and its increasingly common inclusion in many aspects of social interaction meant the 'end of politics' and, in consequence, of the state.

> Turned into an ideology, a unique school of thought, globalization – a historical process – has become globalism, i.e., the imposition of unification of markets, and the reduction of political and cultural differences to the market. If we subordinate these two scenarios of differences to a single vision of economy, politics become blurred and the state seems unnecessary. (García-Canclini, 1999: 50)

This process was accompanied by the promotion of communications in corporate and global terms. As in other Latin American countries, existing global corporations converged with or made alliances with the biggest Venezuelan groups with consequences at different levels in the markets and the economy. For instance, symbolic productions were increasingly broadcasted internationally, and the use of 'franchises' became more frequent in local productions, for example, in television, with clear directions as to which sort of contents should or should not be broadcasted. From my perspective, this process has always been political. Deep down, financial transactions and media broadcasts are political constructions because they are ways to interfere in the public scenario, that is, in society. It is important to remember, as stated by Martín-Barbero (2001), that communication is not merely the object of a policy; but rather a fundamental scenario for politics to find a space for its symbolic development, because the media can represent a link among citizens. According to another author,

> The media has become a crucial space in shaping public spaces and even citizenship – we say crucial to point out that although this is not a new phenomenon, it is intense and fundamental –, because of their importance in the definition of public agenda and in the definition of legitimacy of a given debate. (León, 2002: 2)

Given its importance for social life, it is necessary from the state and citizens' point of view to define public policies for this liaising space that has transformed our understanding of politics. Some societies, like the Venezuelan, need to consolidate the state rather than replace it, because there are social gaps evidenced in the access to new information technologies and the lack of a legal framework that provides tools for the citizens' exercise of cultural and communication interaction. Building a state that facilitates and promotes citizen participation arises from political democratic activities that are related to the inclusion of the variety and diversity found in the social and media scenarios that in turn are related to the public policies issued by the state.

An important debate about PNCs took place in Latin America throughout the 1970s and the beginning of the 1980s. As mentioned before, PNC was the name given to public communication policies in the region. At the time, these measures were harshly attacked by commercial media networks and, in many cases, there were contradictions in governments and public offices due to a lack of political will and administrative coordination in the states. Nowadays, as the need for public policies in the communication sector emerges, it is important to thoroughly analyze PNCs. In the same way that we needed to set a new approach to study the cultural processes derived from the cultural industries, we also require new ideas to avoid repeating mistakes from the past and to open the door to new realities.

Peter Schenkel, who at the time was devoted to the study of this area, had already highlighted three decades ago the difficulties in defining public policies in communications. Its presence, he claims, could be found 'in agriculture as well as in the industry, and in all areas, in executive, legislative, global and local branches, and are manifested both collectively and individually' (1981: 16). The same author mentions the classic definition of PNCs developed by Bolivian Luis Ramiro Beltrán who considered PNCs an integrated, explicit and long-lasting set of communication policies reconciled in a coherent body of principles and regulations aimed at guiding specialized institutions to handle the general process of communications in a country. In this context, PNCs are guidelines for public policies from which a new set of plans, actions, and strategies should emerge. In the 1970s, authors pointed out the need for planning, hoping to 'organize the communications system according to society's main needs' (Schenkel, 1981: 16). A sample of this viewpoint is presented in the book Planificación y Comunicación (Planning and Communication) by Bordenave and Carvalho in 1978.

However, it is imperative to study the Latin American debate on public communication policies in previous decades, particularly because some governments in the region, including Venezuela, currently appeal to – and sometimes distort – concepts and proposals from the past without considering the historical and political contexts. For this purpose, an article published by Jesús Martín-Barbero (2001) is useful as a guide in this brief but necessary review of these policies according to the current social dynamics. The experiences in creating public communication policies in Latin America gathered together government and specialists (from the official and academic spheres and from international organizations like UNESCO). Although the proposals were generally aimed at guaranteeing the rights of the majority of the population in their relation to the media, in reality, governments responded to this dynamic with a greater presence in the communications space. Evidently, these purposes (which moved at parallel levels) weakened the original proposals because governments failed to understand that such policies were intended to empower citizen voices in their own media spaces not necessarily aligned with the government in the national mass media universe.

A second restrictive aspect of public communication policies in the 1970s and the 1980s is that they were limited to the governmental sphere, ignoring that the construction of a truly public sphere must be set up on an inclusive and pluralistic logic. After reviewing those experiences, we can conclude that factors like the state, citizens, market, institutions, political parties, and everyday life interact in the generation of public policies. In this context, we must emphasize the following:

> It is not advisable to leave these matters in the hands of politicians and entrepreneurs, since these matters are related to basic human rights and communication and comprehension among nations. They include education as the instructor of the view towards others, and cultural policies as the place where some patrimonies are selected and others excluded, discriminations are transmitted, or the appreciation of diversity is promoted. (García-Canclini, 1999: 55)

During the 1970s and in the following debate in the 1980s, these proposals were mostly generated from the executive branches, and the starting point was that good intentions (in theory guaranteeing citizen rights) were enough for fostering citizen appropriation. This appropriation was crucial for the long-term viability of the proposal (which basically stayed on paper), especially when PNCs were severely criticized by private communication companies.

Most recently, public communication policies have suffered precisely from what they once criticized. The conception of what is national in these proposals was based on a culturally uniformed conception of the nation, disregarding differences and pluralism. This vision repeated the cultural homogenization it deservedly criticized, due to the predominant presence in Venezuelan television of American audiovisual productions. While it is valid to review PNC proposals nowadays, such process must address inclusive practices of diverse representations while building national culture. In practice, this can be guaranteed by different levels of citizen participation in the concept of visualizing, designing, and executing plans in the communication sector. Today's public policy cannot be reduced to merely guaranteeing diffusion of content or broadening their reception, because even if the messages are conceived from a different cultural view, they are equally unilateral. For this reason, I agree with Martín-Barbero when he stresses the necessary activation of axes in the different social scenarios where citizens go through experimentation, appropriation, and invention in a bidirectional relationship with the communications universe with which they have so far only been able to be passive recipients. This requires communication to be transferred from the media to social mediation and acknowledgment; and in this regard, these public policies must keep in mind that society is formed by the state, citizens, market, political parties, as well as social movements and organizations. It is not enough to include the institutions; everyday life must be considered as well (Martín-Barbero, 2001).

Moreover, in Latin America, the states are in debt with the development of a true public media model because, under official management, public media have either exclusively mirrored the government's interests or reproduced unfortunate copies of the commercial formulas of the private media. These public broadcasters should have had policies seeking to reinforce their role 'as spaces to promote wide, plural and open debate of the different perspectives, ideas, and cultural expressions of society' (León, 2002: 2). But in most Latin America, this was not the case. However, the case where it did happen in Latin America is the Public Television of Chile. Once democracy was reinstalled in the 1980s, the Public Television of Chile was reestablished under the principles of information and opinion plurality, editorial independence, and administrative autonomy (Fuenzalida, 2006).

Media Presidency

As pointed out by the expert Roberto Izurieta from the George Washington University, 'the main communication resource of the governments is the president. And the best communication resource of the president is to turn directly to the public' (2002: 206). This direct communication between governor and governed has different nuances depending on the media-related qualities of the chiefs of state and their relationship with the media system in their country. For the author, presidents have a direct communication platform with the citizens due to different opportunities: 'the annual speech to the nation, ceremonies, trips, any kind of speeches and, in the case of the United States of America, Saturdays on the radio' (206). The later practice has been somewhat inherited from generation to generation among American presidents since Franklin Delano Roosevelt started his fireside chats. Roosevelt had great instincts for political communication that led him not only to establish these radio dialogs but also to open the gates of the White House for Americans to let their president know about their problems and demands through letters and telegrams.

At the same time, Roosevelt completely changed the public information office created by Woodrow Wilson in the White House by establishing distribution networks for press articles among hundreds of regional or local papers. This was a wonderful campaign of governmental communication: '...toward the end of his administration, government's publicists would send a thousand newspaper articles written by expert former journalists with their own style and format, which needed very few or no changes at all' (Vega, 2002: 142). As stated by Izurieta, the image of a direct dialog between the head of state and the citizens was reinforced with television, thus entering into the era of the image. Nixon's address as vice president in 1952, known as the Checkers Speech, set a milestone in this regard. This speech was aired directly in a blanket television broadcast, and it was considered to be 'the salvation of his political career at the moment and the beginning of the practice and later trend of all presidents to turn directly to the public without going through journalists' (Izurieta, 2002: 206).

The discussion about the role of a head of state in communications is not an exclusive to recent years, or to the particular case of Venezuela with a president like the late Hugo Chávez. Not only did Chávez host an extremely long show, *Aló, Presidente* ('Hello, Mr. President') every Sunday, but he also made frequent and lengthy national blanket broadcasts that were a mandatory transmission for the country's broadcasting system. The communicational role of a president was reflected on by the American president Harry Truman (1945–1953) in a letter written to his sister: 'All what the president is, is a glorified public relations man who spends his time flattering, kissing and kicking people to get them do what they are supposed to do anyway' (Izurieta, 2002: 216). Modern society, characterized by the increase of mass media, reinforces the communicational feature of a nation's presidency. For Izurieta (2002), 'it is difficult to know if a president's labor will be measured by his/her rhetorical ability (or public relations) or by his/her administration; so far, the evidence suggests both' (216).

According to Izurieta (2002), the time devoted to communication media by presidents and successful ministers is over 15 hours per week, without including the trips outside the capital or abroad, when normally the president travels accompanied by journalists and media representatives. Izurieta cites data issued by the Organization for Economic Cooperation and Development (OECD) to show that, 'many presidents organize their daily work agenda around the media' (2002: 216). Aside from the time invested in direct contacts with the press or in public appearances, the president also invests a significant amount of time with his or her team in analyzing 'how to communicate a policy, or if a state policy should or not be implemented based on its correct communicability to the public' (Izurieta, 2002: 216). For Izurieta, whose theories are supported by reports and documents from other authors such as Samuel Kernell (2007) or Philip Lesly (1998): '...most part of a president's time is spent in doing public relations' (Izurieta, 2002: 216). An American president who has awakened interest in investigations about communication politics is Bill Clinton (1993–2001). Some authors claim that his first government lacked effective communication strategies. However, during his second term, he was able to structure them, which ultimately enabled him to complete eight years in office with a high level of popular acceptance despite the scandals in which he was involved. According to the Spaniard José Sanmartín, Clinton reinvented himself by using some of Roosevelt's resources:

> When attacks against his administration, and even himself, intensified, Roosevelt assumed an impeccably constructive position: to ignore, mostly, the negative comments and, in due time, deploy great activities for solving pending and new problems; give response to the demands that awakened a special sensibility in the public opinion. (Sanmartín, 2008: 142)

As previously stated, Roosevelt's fireside chats have been passed on among American presidents with radio transmissions on Saturdays. Clinton modernized the media message to turn this Saturday radio space into 'a manifestation integrating two basic elements for the president: a combined image of professional competency as a manager with a personal human touch' (Sanmartín, 2008: 142). During Ronald Reagan's administration (1981–1989), the mise-en-scene of the White House press conferences was transformed by 'modifying the set design, but not the set' (Sanmartín, 2008: 143). To avoid contact with journalists, a central hallway was set up for the president to walk through in a well-established ritual. The president went through the hallway to its end where the press conference room was located. Everything was related to symbols:

> The walk through the hallway can confer public visibility and political credibility to the president's address: a steady and firm walk, standing up straight, decisive gestures [...] Symbols before words. America is in good hands. (Sanmartín, 2008: 143)

Naturally, these symbols cannot be easily extrapolated to other countries without taking into account that there is an important dose of local political cultures that are tied to particular national histories that help explain the phenomena of politics, personalization, and its communication symbols in different historical moments.

Hegemony as the official proposal

Transferring the notion of *Media Presidency* to Venezuela requires some considerations on how President Hugo Chávez used the private and public media space with unprecedented facts and figures in the country's democratic history. The official discourse discouraged the political role of the private media while simultaneously promoting the 'State's media hegemony,' a term coined by former minister Andrés Izarra in January 2007. Naturally, this directed all political and government action to the media area (Weffer, 2007).

The number of public television networks administered by the government increased significantly by 2004; going from one single channel, Venezolana de Televisión, to seven: Venezolana de Televisión, TVES, Vive, ANTV, Ávila TV and Telesur (with two channels: one national and one international). The state endorsed three radio circuits with national broadcasts (Radio Nacional de Venezuela, YVKE Mundial and Rumbos) and 'over 250 community radio stations, most of which are simple relays of the official line' (Petkoff, 2010: 1). In addition, there are three newspapers financed with public funds: Vea, El Correo del Orinoco, and Ciudad CCS. According to Teodoro Petkoff (2010), editor of the journal Tal Cual, the strategy of establishing a communication hegemony was aimed at two different goals: on the one hand, to set up 'an enormous communication machine property of the state,' handled at President Chávez's discretion; and on the other hand, 'to crush the independent media' (p. 1).

Based on a text written by Marcelino Bisbal, the following pages will present a summary of the principal trends in the subject of communication policy carried out by the government of President Hugo Chávez in the period 1999–2013. Altogether, these trends could provide us with a different perspective: Venezuela's government has indeed defined public communication policies, but they are aimed at supporting the goal affirmed by Andrés Izarra: building the 'state's media hegemony.' These policies refer to a series of actions sustained over time:

> Uncontrolled use of blanket broadcasts by the president; degrading or threatening journalists and media owners; aggressions to reporters and camerapersons; direct attacks to media facilities; use of financial resources as means of pressure; ignorance of the interim measures in

favor of communicators issued by the Inter-American Commission on Human Rights; elimination of official propaganda from the media adverse to the government; lack of access to public information; information bias in the state's media. (Bisbal, 2006: 63)

Silvia Cabrera (2010) explains how in Venezuela the audiovisual media have suffered a sort of metamorphosis by going from a mixed-unauthentic system to a mixed-authoritarian system.[1] According to different media monitoring studies (Cañizález, 2008; Hernández, 2007; Izurieta, 2002), official channels have had a noticeable political bias, which could even be considered as political discrimination. Even though these media are owned by the state, and are therefore public, they ignore an important segment of Venezuelan society that opposes or disagrees with the 'Bolivarian Revolution' project led by Hugo Chávez. A study carried out in 2004 by Bernardino Herrera from the Communications Research Institute of the Universidad Central de Venezuela (ININCO-UCV, for its Spanish initials) confirmed that more than 70 percent of a regular day of programming in Venezolana de Televisión (VTV), the main state channel, was constituted with biased and opinionated informational pieces, party-government propaganda, and reruns of presidential addresses (Cañizález, 2008: 69). Furthermore, a month after government-led TVES was founded (the substitute for the private RCTV on Channel 2 of the open television spectrum)[2] with the promise of creating a public service television channel, a two-day program analysis demonstrated that a new space had been added to the government's communication model:

The national government uses this channel with the purpose of spreading its political doctrine through the news, promotions and propaganda from public institutions. This propaganda, which is constantly repeated in all the programs, is aimed at promoting the political indoctrination of the population, as well as aggravating the cult of Chávez's personality. (Hernández, 2007: 28)

Aside from the consolidation of a state media machine unknown to Venezuelan democratic history, President Chávez appeared to rule through the media. According to the figures issued by Reporters without Borders, between February 2, 1999, and December 31, 2008, President Chávez addressed the nation via national blanket broadcasts of television and radio for a total of 1,179 hours, which equalled 49 uninterrupted days of speeches (Reporters without Borders, 2009). This calculation did not include the broadcast hours of the TV show *Aló,*

Presidente, that was only aired on the official media network. However, the total on-air time was estimated to be a similar number to that of the national blanket broadcasts. In his televised speeches, the president made announcements and even made spontaneous decisions related to his administration, changed his ministers, scolded his collaborators, designed his party's strategic guidelines, indoctrinated his followers, and so forth. Chávez's overexposure seemed to go against the recommendations of political communications experts: 'One should not abuse the political blanket broadcasts, because the audience will get tired and they can become counterproductive' (Izurieta, 2002: 206).

In another unprecedented fact in Venezuela as in the rest of the democratic Latin American countries, President Chávez literally ruled through the media (during the decade of the 1960s and the 1970s, Cuban president Fidel Castro also used the media extensively). It is important to emphasize that, with his show *Aló, Presidente* and his blanket broadcasts, 'Chávez has become sort of a "showman" who sings, recites, and tells anecdotes about his life' (De la Nuez, 2002: 29). Additionally, as stated by some experts, he showed visible personality features reflecting narcissism and an obvious trend to use the first-person personal pronoun: the characteristic 'me-ism' of President Chávez's discourse (Bolívar and Kohn, 1999 in Koeneke, 2002: 73). The investigation carried out by Bolívar and Kohn in 1999 analyzed the speech during the Venezuelan head of state inauguration ceremony and compared it to his predecessors (Carlos Andrés Pérez and Rafael Caldera). The results evidenced a more frequent use of the first-person personal pronoun than any other pronoun form: 44.8 percent of time, compared to 20.7 percent in the case of Perez and 29.4 percent for Caldera (Bolívar and Kohn, 1999 in Koeneke, 2002: 73).

The statements made by Bolívar (1994) regarding the use of personal pronouns in the political arena must be mentioned in this subject. Quoting Wilson (1990 cf. Bolívar, 1994: 95), the former prime minister of Great Britain, Margaret Thatcher, only used the 'I' pronoun in mainly three kinds of occasions: (1) to tell anecdotes and establish some rapport with her listeners, (2) to express 'honesty,' and (3) to express positive things. On the other hand, the use of 'we' appeared when associated to organizations, persons, and concepts. At the same time, the results obtained from analyzing other politicians indicate that 'we' is used exclusively to indicate abstract concepts related to ideals, strength, justice, and beliefs. Moreover, linguistic analysis indicates that the use of the first-person personal pronoun ('I') is more frequent in oral than in written speeches (Chafe, 1982 cf. Bolívar, 1994: 95). In Venezuela, I agree with Koeneke in considering this 'me-ism' as a narcissistic feature (Koeneke, 2002: 73).

In several occasions during his extended administration, the head of the state set out the guidelines, announced decisions, and changed state strategies that seemed to take even his closest collaborators by surprise. From our point of view, this is an official trend devised by the president: many decisions affecting public policies are not necessarily included in the previously designed plans and programs; these decisions appear to be included within the logic of a television setting where the program's host (president Chávez himself) had enormous power to change the script, make announcements, and make decisions without previous consensus with the governmental team. Personality politics in Venezuela became evident under the aegis of Chávez, and his natural scenery of exposure was the small screen. The government's actions were developed starting from the symbolic in the media space that led to important decisions for the nation.

Before Hugo Chávez arrived in office, the use of blanket broadcasts in Venezuela was limited to several messages from the head of state throughout the year, the transmission of official acts on national holidays, and the arrival of foreign dignitaries to the country. On February 2, 1999, the same day Chávez took office, an unprecedented record was established in the country. Four presidential blanket broadcasts were transmitted for a total duration of 8 hours and 14 minutes in the daytime, afternoon, and prime-time schedule (AGB Nielsen Media Research, 2009).

When President Chávez spoke in blanket broadcasts, he annulled any other message, for example, he limited Venezuelans' possibility to freely choose which viewpoints, information, or opinions to follow. The blanket broadcast is a unique message (from the president) that must be compulsorily followed by the rest of the country. As stated by the Inter-American Commission on Human Rights (IACHR) in its report *Democracy and Human Rights in Venezuela* (2009), during Chávez's administration there was 'a large number of blanket government broadcasts in the media' that 'force media stations to cancel their regular programming and transmit information as ordered by the government' and 'many of them were of a duration and frequency that could be considered abusive in light of the information they conveyed, not always intended to serve the public interest' (IACHR, 2009: 406).

An evident result of what has been discussed here regarding Hugo Chávez's government was the creation of a new communication model in television, a particular Media Presidency that shares many of the mixed-authoritarian trends presented by Cabrera (2010), and whose characteristics are summarized in the following Figure 8.1.

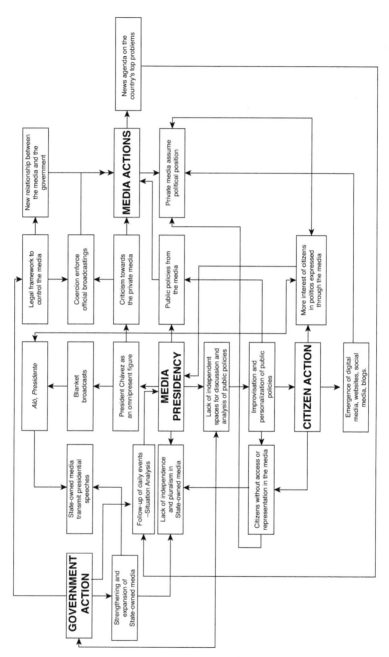

Figure 8.1 Map of the 'Media Presidency'

I contend that this new communication model in Venezuela was strictly linked to a particular dynamic of exercising the presidential power through the media characterized by the gradual restriction of criticism in radio and television through laws and administrative decisions, by the strengthening of governmental media that reinforce the president's voice, and by a recurrent official discourse questioning the work of media and journalists in order to socially discredit them.

Restriction and coercion as policies for the media

From our previous discussion regarding the events in the complex relationship between the media and the government in Venezuela and the making of public policies, it could be concluded first that there were no true public policies on communication – in accordance to their current definition – in Venezuela during the Hugo Chávez administration.

The executive branch implemented a set of official actions and decisions that failed to provide answers to concrete citizens' problems and were rather aimed at creating a legal-institutional siege to restrict the freedom of speech with direct consequences on the work of the media and journalists. These official decisions were not a space for democratic and plural discussion, nor were they preceded by a genuine citizen consultation.

From the very beginning, President Chávez put into question the way private media covered his administration. Between 2001 and 2003, the private media were extremely critical of the Chavez government and his policies. These reciprocal critical attitudes of the media and the government must be understood within a context of growing social and political polarization. One cannot blame the private media for fostering this tremendous polarization, though it is undeniable that they explicitly sided with the political opposition to Chávez. In retaliation, under Chávez's command, the state unilaterally decided to penalize the private media. In this context, the government also failed to develop a coherent plan to turn state media into spaces for public service, while using the radio-electric spectrum (an asset belonging to us all, according to UNESCO) at its own discretion with the presidential blanket broadcasts. These signs ratify the official view on the matter: official communication hegemony.

Outlined through the different viewpoints set out by Marcelino Bisbal (2006), Figure 8.2 shows the dimensions characterizing communicational hegemony. It comprises sustained operations from different areas in the Hugo Chávez government to siege and restrict the work of media and journalists in Venezuela. When analyzed as a whole, these trends

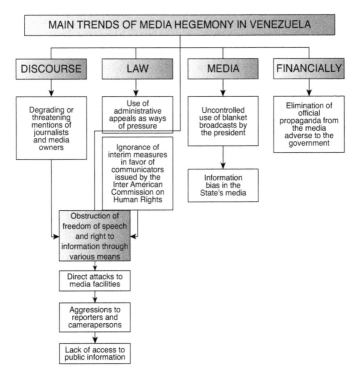

Figure 8.2   Concept map about the main trends of Venezuelan media hegemony
Source: Personal compilation.

make evident the actions sustained across time from different official branches with the inclusion of the recurring public discourse from President Chávez that aimed at judging communicators.

The closing down of the private RCTV channel in 2007 evidenced the lack of independence of the Supreme Court of Justice (TSJ, for its Spanish initials). The TSJ ruling enforced what many commentators interpreted as a discriminatory measure to punish the channel's critical coverage of the government. It was also said to validate the seizing of the channel's property, including technical equipment, infrastructure, and facilities that the government later transferred to the newly launched public network TVES for its broadcasting needs. It became a sort of 'mandatory loan' without severance or compensation, while the repeated appeals by the network were simply disregarded or responded to in an untimely fashion (Cañizález, 2008). The assessment on this subject made by organizations like Freedom House, with its worldwide press freedom index, or

Reporters without Borders, with its annual ranking, also agree with our previous statements on the negative consequences of this communication hegemony held by the Hugo Chávez government on media and journalism and, in consequence, on Venezuelan democracy. One of the last presidential decisions made by Chávez was separating Venezuela from the Inter-American human rights system; however, in the midst of this process, the Inter-American Human Rights Court accepted RCTV's claim against the Venezuelan government of ceasing its broadcasting service.

The RSF analysis on the country's situation sets out a distinct breaking point in 2007 regarding the cessation of RCTV's signal. The decision to not renew the license, legally called 'concession,' of this channel as a punishment for its critical editorial line (Correa, 2007) was announced by President Chávez a few weeks before his reelection in December, 2006 –an extraordinary time in his government due to the significant number of votes he obtained for a new term of six years in office.

For Chávez and his government, the need to readjust the media system preceded the political-institutional crisis in the period of 2002–2003.[3] The public policies program called the General Guidelines of the Nation's 2001–2007 Financial and Social Development Plan (*Líneas Generales del Plan de Desarrollo Económico y Social de la Nación 2001–2007*), published in September 2001, already set some guidelines in terms of the need to promote 'true and convenient information.' According to this document, 'the media should become strategic instruments of participatory democracy' (República Bolivariana de Venezuela, 2001: 102) since they are mobilizing agents. The document also prioritizes the 'strengthening of community media' (108). This guideline was successfully fulfilled through the creation of growing numbers of community communication media that were often financed by the state, particularly since 2002.

Evidently, Hugo Chávez's government succeeded in creating a legal framework to control critical private media, while consolidating a major system of official media, especially when compared to previous governments in Venezuela. However, the communication hegemony had serious problems in connecting with the Venezuelan audience without forcing the circumstances, which may help explain the recurrent use of blanket radio and television broadcasts as a coercive mechanism to oblige people to listen or watch official messages.

As for the private media, their strong political criticisms and the controversial role they played between 2002–2003, particularly during the crisis of April 2002 and the national strike at the end of 2003, served the Chávez's administration as pretexts to impose strategies of greater control. These controls were enhanced in view of the president's ratification in office after the referendum of August 2004. It soon became evident that official actions had no interest in promoting pluralism and transparent public policies in communication, or in turning the state media into true examples of public services. It is reasonable to believe that Chávez's model was aimed at imposing one single voice, the president's, over all other actors in the Venezuelan public sphere.

By way of conclusion

In Venezuela, the Chávez's administration implemented a hegemonic model of official communication in response to the media and freedom of speech. This plan had two lines of action: to limit public criticism with higher control over the private media, particularly in radio and television, and to significantly increase the official media machinery to spread its propaganda and the president's personal image. It has been often affirmed that the idea of hegemony as presented by Hugo Chávez's government derives from Gramsci's school of thought. However, this is a mechanical comparison lacking any serious analysis of the Italian socialist's ideas: '... in reality, Gramsci carefully used this concept (hegemony) to distinguish elements of pluralism and competence, persuasion and consent, among the most coercive and repressive forms of domination' (Kohn, 1995: 53). Thus, in Venezuela, conversely to what Gramsci said, the concept of hegemony has been implanted in terms of pure state control and dominion.

Moreover, when comparing the data on the television audience, for example, the dominion of this model of communication was effective in controlling the media, but failed in handling audiences. The controls were established, but the effective persuasion was not, confirming the ideas of Gramsci summarized by Kohn. This contradiction could be related to the actual sociopolitical context defined by a diminished democratic governability – according to the World Bank parameters – causing a decrease in government credibility as well. Venezuela is undoubtedly a complex scenario, but thanks to it, the close relation between full governability and a freedom environment for the press has become evident. Governability and the media are closely related. Both dimensions are pillars to a democratic system. Weaknesses in these dimensions also imply a weakness in democracy.

I use the term *Media Presidency* to refer to the Hugo Chávez government in Venezuela. Not only did the president dedicate long hours to his public speeches, which were mandatorily broadcasted in public and private radio and television, but he literally ruled and executed his power through the media because he analyzed situations, made decisions, allocated public funds, set strategies among other actions in the exercise of government while the mise-en-scene was broadcasted live to the country.

Moreover, the *Media Presidency* was in reality a presidential monologue where citizen participation slowly decreased (in fact, at the beginning the idea was to create a space for dialog between the chief of state and the citizens; hence, the name *Aló, Presidente* – Hello, Mr. President), while the closest and highest-ranked presidential collaborators went on to assume a secondary role.

After this analysis, I may conclude that the *Media Presidency* model exercised by Hugo Chávez in Venezuela had key characteristics. First of all, the model was applicable because there was a legal and administrative framework limiting the action of radio and television media causing them to subjugate to the president's will through blanket broadcasts. In addition, the public broadcasters functioned as a supplementary platform for the *Aló, Presidente* program and other 'special' broadcasts. The president used the radio and television networks in Venezuela, both public and private, intensively and extensively with broadcasting records unprecedented today in any other nation in the Western Hemisphere. Through all these means, Chávez managed to implement his communication hegemony.

Notes

1. For Silvia Cabrera (2010), the Venezuelan media system used to be mixed (public and private), but unauthentic, since the commercial media were dominated only by two big corporations – Grupo 1BC and Grupo Cisneros. With the arrival of Chavez, the authoritarian dominance of the media has prevailed in a context where not only public and private media are found, but also community media.
2. In an extremely controversial measure, private RCTV channel was closed by the government.
3. The private media in Venezuela had played a very salient role in the context of the 2002 coup d'etat against President Chávez. Although there is insufficient evidence to back the claim that media proprietors masterminded and orchestarted the coup – as the government often acussed them – many observers accept that the private media had covered events prior to the coup, such as demonstrations and clashes, in a biased way. They argue that news coverage appeared to legitimize the coup and champion the brief leadership that ensued, giving no space to Chavista followers and collaborators in those moments. Once Chávez was restored to power, this episode was widely

used as his main reason to discredit the private media and their foreign allies abroad. According to Cabrera (2010), this moment became a breakpoint for institutional life in Venezuela, the media's protagonistic role in public life, and their commitment to democracy. For Chávez, the overt support that the media provided to the coup would become a perfect alibi to justify the hegemony of state-owned media.

References

AGB Nielsen Media Research (2009) *Horas de transmisión de las cadenas presidenciales y del programa Aló, Presidente* (Caracas: AGB).

Bisbal, M. (2006) 'El Estado-Comunicador y su especificidad,' *Comunicación: Estudios venezolanos de comunicación* (134): 60–73.

Bolívar, A. (1994). *Discurso e interacción en el texto escrito* (Caracas: UCV).

Bolívar, A. and Kohn, C. (1999) *Análisis del discurso político venezolano. Un estudio multidisciplinario* (Caracas: UCV).

Bordenave, J. and Carvalho, H. (1978) *Planificación y Comunicación* (Quito: CIESPAL).

Cabrera, S. (2010) 'La agenda informativa de la televisión venezolana durante el golpe de Estado de abril del 2002. Un análisis bajo la dimensión informativa del proceso de Agenda Setting.' Unpublished Doctorate Thesis (Germany: Rostock University).

Cañizález, A. (2008) 'Venezuela: El lejano servicio público,' pp. 67–78 in M. Albórnoz and M. Cerbino (eds) *Comunicación, cultura y política* (Quito: Latin American Faculty of Social Sciences).

Chafe, W. (1982). 'Integration and involvement in speaking, writing, and oral literatura,' pp. 35–53 in D. Tannen (ed.) *Spoken and written language: Exploring orality and literacy* (Norwood, NJ: Ablex).

Correa, C. (2007) *Informe 2006: Venezuela Situación del derecho a la libertad de expresión e información* (Caracas: Espacio Público).

Curcio, P. (2007) 'Metodología para la evaluación de políticas públicas de salud,' *Politeia*, (38): 59–85.

De la Nuez, S. (2002). "Héroes y Villanos", *Tal Cual*, (Venezuela), May 3. Available at http://bit.ly/1iHXSb2 (accessed December 2013).

Dunn, W. (1994). *Public Policy Analysis: An Introduction* (Englewood Cliffs, NJ: Prentice Hall).

Fuenzalida, V. (2006) 'Pluralismo informativo: El caso de la televisión pública chilena,' *Comunicación: Estudios venezolanos de comunicación*, (134): 54–59.

García-Canclini, N. (1999) *La Globalización imaginada* (Buenos Aires: Paidós).

Grindle, M. and Thomas, J. (1991) *Public Choices and Policy Change: The Political Economy of Reform in Developing Countries* (Baltimore: John Hopkins University Press).

Hernández, G. (2007) 'Gubernamental TVES,' *Comunicación: Estudios venezolanos de comunicación*, (139): 26–31.

IACHR (Inter-American Commission on Human Rights) (2009) *Democracy and Human Rights in Venezuela* (Washington: IACHR).

Izurieta, R. (2002) 'La comunicación política en la era del entretenimiento. Un estudio de la comunicación y las relaciones públicas para gobiernos,' pp. 187–225 in R. Izurieta, C. Arterton and R. Perina (eds) *Estrategias de comunicación para gobiernos* (Buenos Aires: La Crujía).

Kernell, S. (2007). *Going Public* (Washington, DC: Congressional Quarterly Press).

Koeneke, H. (2002) 'Personalidad presidencial y medios de comunicación social: el caso de Hugo Chávez,' *Nuevo Mundo*, (91): 64–80.

Kohn, C. (1995) 'Praxis política comunicativa y participación política: apuntes para la construcción de un espacio público democrático,' in C. Kohn (ed.) *Discurso Político y Crisis de la Democracia: reflexiones desde la filosofía social, la ética y el análisis del lenguaje* (Caracas: UCV/FHE).

León, O. (2002) 'Hacia una agenda social en comunicación,' *América Latina en Movimiento*, (353): 2–6.

Lesly, P. (1998) *Lesly's Handbook of Public Relations and Communications* (Chicago, IL: NTC/Contemporary Publishing Company).

Lindblom, C. (1997) 'Cómo adecuar la política en el análisis de las políticas públicas,' *Gestión y Política Pública*, 6(2): 239–255.

Martín-Barbero, J. (2001) 'De las políticas de comunicación a la reimaginación de las políticas,' *Nueva Sociedad*, (175): 70–84.

Meentzen, A. (2007) *Políticas públicas para los pueblos indígenas en América Latina* (Perú: Fundación Konrad Adenauer). Available at http://bit.ly/1ipn0Di (accessed January 21, 2013).

Oropeza, A. (2005). *Política pública y demanda cultural en Venezuela* (Caracas: CENDES-UCV).

Oropeza, A. (2008) 'Economía de la cultura y proceso político.' Unpublished Doctorate Thesis. Universidad Simón Bolívar.

Petkoff, T. (2010, February 2) 'Miedo a los medios,' *Tal Cual*, 1.

Reporters Without Borders (2009, February 13) 'Referéndum constitucional: un paisaje mediático ensombrecido por la polarización y el exceso de alocuciones presidenciales.' Available at http://bit.ly/KfQFQG (accessed January 21, 2013).

República Bolivariana de Venezuela (2001) *Líneas Generales del Plan de Desarrollo Económico y Social de la Nación 2001–2007* (Caracas: Government of the Bolivarian Republic of Venezuela).

Sanmartín, J. (2008) 'La retórica política del presidente Clinton,' *Utopía y Praxis Latinoamericana*, (43): 135–148.

Schenkel, P. (1981) *Políticas Nacionales de Comunicación* (Quito: CIESPAL).

Segal, A. (2006) *Experiencias nacionales de políticas de provisión de materiales curriculares* (Buenos Aires: CEPP/Fundación Konrad Adenauer). Available at http://bit.ly/KfR1XA (accessed January 21, 2013).

Vega, H. (2002) 'La comunicación de gobierno e Internet,' pp. 131–186 in R. Izurieta, C. Arterton and R. Perina (eds) *Estrategias de comunicación para gobiernos* (Buenos Aires: La Crujía).

Weffer, L. (2007, January 15) 'El socialismo necesita una hegemonía comunicacional,' *El Nacional*, A-4.

9
Clashing Powers in Bolivia: The Tensions Between Evo Morales's Government and the Private Media

Víctor Quintanilla

Introduction

On the evening of December 9, 2008, Bolivian President Evo Morales used a ceremony to commemorate the International Day Against Corruption as a platform to publicly accuse the national newspaper La Prensa of lying. During the event, the president rebuked the invited representative journalist of the newspaper on national public TV broadcast. The president's reaction was in response to allegations in the reporter's paper. That morning La Prensa had titled its headline 'Evo authorized "green light" to smugglers two months ago' – therewith directly involving the president in a notorious smuggling case with extensive news coverage that occurred in the border town of Cobija.[1] In spite of this grievous phrasing, the president's involvement was not proved in the article. In the following days, the reactions polarized Bolivian public opinion. Many journalists, union leaders, communicators, and media entrepreneurs condemned the public humiliation suffered by the journalist. Some politicians and a few other journalists in La Paz questioned the newspaper's editorial line of accusing the president without proper evidence.

This episode accurately mirrors the tense atmosphere that surrounds the actual relations between the media and the government in Bolivia, where the media are considered not just as an adversary but as an straightforward enemy (Sorj, 2010; Bravo-Gallardo, 2012). In this chapter, this conflictive relationship serves as a framework for analyzing the media regulation in Bolivia, characterized by governmental efforts to gain control over very powerful media organizations (Torrico, 2007; Ruiz, 2010). The chapter emphasizes actual efforts to apply and reform existing regulation and to adopt new standards that may strengthen the government regarding public information. Some brief historical context is presented regarding Bolivian democracy, the media ownership structure, and the state media relations before President Morales's administration. One must recall here that in many ways today's oppositional media react to the conformation of new regional political alliances that include Venezuela and Ecuador.

A close relationship sharply in change

Before examining the media-government dynamics, it is important to understand the general context of Bolivian politics in the last decades. After a period of different sorts of authoritarian rules since the 1960s, in 1982, Bolivia transitioned to uninterrupted democratic government. Previously, the electoral system had been very complex, as it was established that in presidential elections, only the candidate who obtained 50 percent of the votes plus one could take office directly. Instead of resorting to a system of *ballotage*, that is, a two-round presidential vote when no single candidate gets 50 percent plus one of the votes similar to the French system (Duverger, 1990), the president was appointed by two thirds of the congress. The law stated that if no agreement was reached, the majority must make the appointment. To avoid this, party leaders always chose to agree and decided among the first and second most voted candidates. Candidates were then forced to forge different political alliances that included the largest three political parties – the National Democratic Action (ADN in Spanish), the Revolutionary Leftist Movement (MIR in Spanish), and the Revolutionary Nationalist Movement (MNR in Spanish). The result was called the 'protracted democracy,' as Torrico points out:

> This feature [of Bolivian democracy] caused dynamics of power reproduction for the same circle and soon produced a lack of representation and engendered corruption. Corporate interests, and even those personal and small group interests, were permanently privileged, which favored patrimonial, privileged, nepotistic and clientelistic practices. These practices simultaneously promoted a growing gap between politicians and citizens. The outcomes of democracy never reach the population; and the political opacity increased. (2007: 4)

According to the author, along with the decay of the image of political institutions and actors, a media 'pseudo-empowerment' was taking place. The author identifies three stages in this process. In the first one, Torrico explains, the media – particularly the privately owned TV and the newspaper organizations – were spaces of political display: they brought the facts and actors of politics to the citizens regularly, not only during electoral periods. In a second stage, the media became increasingly engaged in political activity 'intervening explicitly in orienting public decisions, in conflict management and in promoting or disqualifying actors and groups during national and local electoral processes or even once governments were already in office' (2007: 5). Finally, after assuming not only a watchdog role over politics, but in fact an active role determined by direct continuous exchange with politicians and policy-makers, a third stage consisted in the media becoming a strong protagonist in politics (Torrico, 2007). Apparently this trend toward media empowerment seems to be replicated in other Latin American countries (see especially Chapters 5 and 10 on Argentina in this volume).

Another scholar, Sáinz (2010) agrees with Torrico that the Bolivian media has become 'a political battlefield' where journalists and social movements are the new actors. However, important differences can be noted in the media before and after the presidency of Evo Morales. In 2000, when the Bolivian indigenous conflict erupted – led by peasant leader Felipe Quispe and coca farmers' leader Evo Morales – it shook a centennial *status quo* slightly modified by the National Revolution of 1952.[2] According to Sáinz (2010), it was only during this period that the big media networks began to include the stories of these social movements in their news agendas.

> [...] the emblematic figure of Evo Morales in their daily media coverage, along with the strength and mobilization capacities of the social movements, functioned as a contrast to the weakness of traditional parties in the political system. Such was the formula that catapulted the leadership of Morales, that he became the main reference of change at a time of deep political and institutional unrest. (Sáinz, 2010: 89, my translation)

Torrico (2007), referring to this crisis between 2000 and 2005, says that both politics and media were responsible for generating an atmosphere that increasingly favored coherent and organized social protests. In those years, state authority was rapidly losing efficacy and legitimacy, and it became clear that the political and economic model implanted at the beginning of the transition was absolutely exhausted. At the same time, the media, already transformed into a central political actor, lacked any true capacity of anticipation, preparation, and commitment to democracy and ended up acting at times reactively and, in other cases, with sensationalism.

> The crisis permeated and conditioned the journalistic narrative, which fed both a certain social and regional polarization. The political crisis came later as uncertainty gripped the public sphere until the results of the general elections [of the presidential elections of 2005] were known, that is, until the triumph of the MAS coalition [MAS in Spanish: Movimiento al Socialismo] and its candidate Evo Morales with 53.74% of the vote was known. (Torrico, 2007: 4, my translation)

Actually, Evo Morales was the first ever politician to get more than the 50 percent plus one vote, which enabled him to claim his direct right to the presidency without passing through congressional sanction (Quintanilla, 2012). According to Sáinz, it is quite possible that the media contributed to the historic triumph of Morales due to their constant positioning of 'the history, the causes and the struggles of social movements in the collective imagination' (2010: 91). While the political crisis had worsened the regional gap between Eastern and Western Bolivia, until then, it had been kept off the media agenda. However, the arrival of President Morales brought the geographical conflict on to the stage once again. From the very start, President Morales's speech did not appeal to all of the population and contributed to a quick polarization between the new government, supported by social and indigenous movements, and middle and upper classes that had benefited from the existing establishment. These latter social sectors are mostly concentrated in the eastern region of greater industrial and economic development and quickly organized under the slogan of regional autonomy. According to Zárate (2005), the geographical division of the Bolivian territory locates the indigenous population in the west, where the high levels of poverty and the dominion of the traditional political ruling elites have given way to communitarian leaderships that have frequently radicalized. Conversely, the eastern side of the country is the richest and most vibrant in economic terms, populated by the wealthier businessmen, the most important political leaders, and the dynamic migrants and colonizers. The ethnic, racial, regional, and class differences between those two regions, existing since colonial times, widened their gap due to the free market and liberalization policies of the

1980s. This, in turn, engendered an atmosphere of popular insurrection and indigenous groups' uprisings in search for a historical vindication against traditional political and economic elites. In this new scenario, the formerly supportive attitude of the media changed. For Sáinz (2010: 92), the same news outlets that originally contributed to Evo Morales's leadership and championed him to power had suddenly became strong opponents to his government and his project of change, giving way to a conflictive relationship where the government delegitimizes the media and the media retaliates with constant attacks.

While the new government began to insist on structural reforms and talked about the nationalization of natural resources, state intervention in the economy, and the legitimacy of indigenous claims, the private media reacted by mostly devoting their coverage to the political opposition. Since the media ownership structure in Bolivia resembles that of the rest of the economic sectors, very close ties between the business elites and the traditional political system existed. Property concentration, explains Sáinz, has not generated powerful monopolies as in other countries of the region, like Mexico, Brazil, or Argentina, but media consortiums have tended to side with the rest of the economic elites. In this regard, the more than 1,800 media outlets operating in Bolivia mostly belong to family groups historically close to the traditional economic and political elites, though new groups have invested in the media in the past 20 years.

Precisely with the neoliberal wave of the 1990s, the number of private TV stations greatly increased from 35 in 1985 to 109 in 1990, many of them belonging to multimedia groups (including newspapers, magazines, radio, telephony, and other companies in the field). By the beginning of this century, foreign capital also entered the media landscape and reconfigured ownership (Giavedoni, 2010). Family, business, and political groups joined the Catholic church clustering into more than 100 communication facilities (including radio, television channels, radio programs producers, news agencies, and others) making it 'one of most important information producers in Bolivia' and one who 'enjoys more institutional credibility' (Giavedoni, 2010: 6).

According to Archondo (2003), media concentration affects in varying degrees the public and political life. The author states that, 'against a generalized hypothesis about an increasing subordination of political systems to the media logic, the history of media tends rather to put in evidence a long term collaboration among them' (2003: 76, my translation). Archondo examines the relationship between the media, politics, and business in the cases of two big consortiums: Garafulic Group and Canelas/Rivero Group. Since 1998, both groups have been characterized by strong horizontal media concentration (mostly, newspapers and television channels). The Garafulic Group in particular also shares interests with political groups and other economic sectors different from the media. Archondo concludes that,

> [...] at the same time that media entrepreneurs expand their interests to other economic sectors, their dependence on the decisions and actions of politicians also increases. At the same time, this parallel strengthening of political and economic systems has negatively affected journalism, making it more vulnerable. In this sense, the most encouraged informative actions are those oriented to reinforce the pursuit of higher earnings external to journalism. (2003: 319, my translation)

The relationship between media and politics in Bolivia can also be explored through the coverage of the electoral processes. The National Media Observatory (Observatorio Nacional de Medios, ONAMED) is in charge of this task. Recently, it analyzed the coverage of the 2009[3] and 2010[4] elections on radio, TV, and the printed press (Sandoval, 2011) to conclude that the news did not appropriately report on the analysis of governmental proposals, citizens' demands, and other similar issues that could have defined a more interesting agenda. The report states that information was turned into spectacle and that debate was excessively simplified and opinionated. Such findings could be explained if we consider, as Peñaranda warns (2003), that media and Bolivian journalists see themselves as a Fourth Power. For most journalists it is unthinkable to refrain from giving their own opinions and stick only to reporting on the debate among the political and social actors. One of the consequences of these practices, according to the author, has been the substitution of informational genres for journalists' opinions. The predominance of opinion in Bolivian media is also attributed to the discredit of both politicians and the Supreme Court representing the whole law administration and enforcement systems, plus the poor education level of the population and the structural weakness of public institutions.

The fight to regain policy control

The media-politics scenario of confrontation is not exclusive to Bolivia. Ruiz (2010) argues that such conflicts define one of the features of democracy building in Latin America. The democratic agenda in the region, following Ruiz (2010), faces two problems: a great heterogeneity in professionalism among the different media systems, and the harshness of some recent policies designed to control what is perceived as an excessive influence of media in political life. For Ruiz, media are political institutions. Quoting Cook (1997: 86), he mentions that journalism is formed by media groups sharing behavior patterns, routines, and informal procedures and controlling certain areas of the social and political life that enable them to be decisive in 'organizing public life.' The media are incarnate forms of political representation and they are, by their nature at the center of all political activity. Politics cannot be understood without studying the modes of communication dominant in each place and time. Thus, media and politics are always intertwined. And that is why Ruiz speaks of a dominant perception about media influence:

> The democratic wave of eighties and nineties in Latin America has coincided with a growing perception that media influence has overextended, exceeding or equaling in influence to institutions such as parliaments, judiciaries, political parties and even to popularly elected governments. (Ruiz, 2010: 33–34)

The author traces the origin of such perception to the process of democratization in Latin America during the 1980s that propelled a strong freedom in media content at a time of major technological changes. In other regions, Ruiz (2010) explains, the technological revolution in the media occurred in contexts where this liberty of expression was already settled. In Latin America, it took place simultaneously: when most countries were undergoing processes of political democratization, the media were also in the middle of a technological transformation. On the other hand, these developments in the media coincided with the rise of economic neoliberalism in Latin America, as many observers link the consolidation of the media with this ideology. Ruiz (2010: 37–38) claims that the conception of powerful media with strong and perverse influence on policy is sustained on the following perceptions: the bad image of professional politicians, the weakness of actual political identities, the loss of functions of political parties, the lack of centrality of congresses, and the belief that today's governments govern less. It is not difficult to imagine that parallel to this conception of powerful media, voices have risen stating the need to liberate politics from this illegitimate 'media colonization.'

Stigmatization of journalists as political/economic actors

In the past decade, a majority of presidents in Latin America have made reference, some way or another, to the need for media regulation. In some cases, like Ecuador, Argentina, Venezuela, and Bolivia, the private media have been frequently stigmatized as 'enemies' weapons.' This confrontational discourse coincides with the Bolivarian Alliance for People Of Our America (Alianza Bolivariana Para Los Pueblos de Nuestra América, ALBA), a regional integration initiative created in 2004 that sees private media as instruments of neoliberalism and international economic interests (Bravo-Gallardo, 2012). According to Kitzberger (2010), a constant confrontation with the media is precisely one of the most prominent features of left-leaning governments that emerged in the region with the turn of the century, including Bolivia. The arguments of both sides reduce to the following: on the one hand, the populist styles of presidents such as Evo Morales, Cristina Fernández de Kirchner (Argentina), or Rafael Correa (Ecuador); and, on the other, the use of media as battlefields to attack the legitimacy of governments by those who oppose the reformist agendas (O'Schaughnessy, 2007; cited in Kitzberger, 2010). In the case of Morales, his confrontation with the media began as soon as he took office. President Morales questioned all media whose coverage, in his own view, attempted to protect the interests of groups linked to traditional political parties. Indeed, in his own inaugural speech on January 22, 2006, President Morales accused the owners of the private television channel UNITEL to be part of the oligarchy and to be naturally inclined to oppose the changes his government wanted to promote, like the nationalization of hydrocarbons (Bravo-Gallardo, 2012). UNITEL began to report on all negative issues related to governmental performance in its programs *Telepaís* and *Al despertar*. Citing Peñaranda, Molina (2010: 203) asserts that with the arrival of Evo to power and the collapse of the previous neoliberal consensus, the media tried to sort out the economic crisis by siding directly with traditional political interests.

However, unlike Bravo-Gallardo, Kitzberger affirms that the confrontation between government and media is prior to the coming to power of the indigenous movement and the MAS. Since the episodes known as 'The Water War'[5] and 'The Gas War'[6] says Kitzberger, most of the TV networks and the major newspapers in La Paz, Cochabamba, and Santa Cruz [cities that compose the backbone of the country] 'privileged their corporate, social and political interests over journalistic standards in the covering of the popular mobilizations and protests in 2003' (Kitzberger, 2010: 78–79). After the triumph of MAS in 2005, private media coverage focused on attacking the governmental project and its policies, like the nationalization of hydrocarbons. Nevertheless, the polarization is rooted in the unsolved ethnic, regional, and class divisions in Bolivia. And the largest corporations, especially television, are strongly linked to the elites from the so-called 'Media Luna,' the eastern Bolivian lowlands that lost political influence when President Morales took office (Kitzberger, 2010: 80).

Polarization spread to most professional media practices where normative journalistic standards were sacrificed, generating even some criticisms from international press organizations and NGOs (Kitzberger, 2010). However, President Morales took advantage of every chance to criticize the media as the instrument that gave voice to 'a resentful racism that yearn for a domination now relegated to the past' (2010: 81). Initially, President Morales differentiated between media owners and journalists, attributing to the former the campaign against him. From 2006 to 2008, it was the period of greatest tension between Morales and the media: his speeches encouraged social movements and groups to harden their positions against the press. The result was an atmosphere of intimidation that was not exempted from physical attacks, harassment, and even the eventual murder of journalists for their alleged offenses (Bravo-Gallardo, 2012). Morales formalized the rupture with journalism when he declared, according to a report by the Inter American Press Association (IAPA), that 'only 10% of journalists have dignity' (Kitzberger, 2010: 82).

However, this rupture with traditional media in Bolivia differs from that of countries like Venezuela and Ecuador 'because not even in the worst moments of polarization the Bolivian government ceased to interact with the private media, and never tried to close down any outlet' (Bravo-Gallardo, 2012: 73). Despite this distinction, the relationship between the media and political power in Bolivia is defined by the constant interference of political and economic interests on the watchdog role of the media and the difficulties to enforce proper formal rules. One can label the Bolivian media as a captured liberal system as posed by Guerrero (Chapter 2 in this book), though in certain ways its features are more extreme than other cases in the region. This points to the colonization of the media spaces by the new political class, a strategy that does not seek the destruction of private commercial media, but only their alignment with the interests of those in charge of political power.

Reform of the regulatory framework

According to Ruiz (2010), in many countries of Latin America, a renewed political debate is taking place regarding the media; and, in many cases, new regulatory frameworks are being approved. In Bolivia, regulatory changes in this area are based on the new constitution, approved by referendum on August 25, 2009, just a few months before the end of President Morales's first term in office. The constitution includes the right to information and communication in the legal system (Sandoval, 2011). Article 106 provides that 'the State shall guarantee to Bolivians the right to freedom of expression, opinion and information, to rectification and reply, as well as the right to freely express ideas through any media, without previous censorship' (Constitution, 2009: 29). Moreover, the constitution also establishes the state's obligation 'to guarantee to all those who work in the media their freedom of expression and their right to communication and information, according to the principles of responsibility, and by the standards of ethics and self-regulations of the journalists and media organizations, and the correspondent laws' (2009: 30).

Furthermore, Article 107 of the constitution states that the media should help promote ethical, moral, and civic values from the different cultures of the country through the production and dissemination of multilingual educational programs and through alternative means and language for disabled people. However, it also mandates that the information and opinions issued by the media 'respect the principles of truthfulness and responsibility' (2009: 30). Obviously, this statement complicates the picture. Finally, the constitution prohibits the direct or indirect creation of media monopolies and oligopolies, and delegates to the state the task of supporting the creation and maintenance of community media under equality of conditions and opportunities. In addition to the constitutional regulations, the ruling party promoted in congress the creation of the National Council on Ethics (Consejo Nacional de Ética) and the Media Observatory (Observatorio de Medios) to watch over media contents. Most journalists criticize both organs as *de facto* limits to the freedom of expression (Bravo-Gallardo, 2012).

A major tort to Bolivian media was the Law Against Racism and All Forms of Discrimination issued in October 2010. The main controversy lies in the provisions of Articles 16 and 23 that establish sanctions to all those who promote, authorize, or publish racists and discriminatory ideas. Article 16 says, 'media that authorize and publish racist and discriminatory ideas will be liable to financial penalties and even the suspension of their operating licenses, subjected to regulations' (Law Against Racism and All Forms of Discrimination, 2010: 10). Article 23 incorporates racism and discrimination, called Crimes Against Human Dignity, into the criminal code. According to Bravo-Gallardo (2012), although this new debate constitutes another front of tension between President Morales and the private media, so far there are no cases of closure. However, what has in fact been achieved is the moderation – some say self-censorship – of the media discourse and the strengthening of President Morales's position vis-à-vis private media. President Morales's habit of identifying by name the journalists and broadcasters who are critical to his administration have caused several media to cease publishing their journalists' opinions on their websites and to become more careful in conveying their editorial policies, since the Law Against Racism establish severe sanctions from fines to license suspensions – a law that for many has been directed to silence certain journalists and media (Bravo-Gallardo, 2012: 98).

As Guerrero states in his definition of the captured liberal model (See Chapter 2) when comparing Bolivia, Ecuador, Venezuela, and Argentina: the aim of regulations in these countries is neither to destroy commercial market media, nor to promote true pluralism, but to force them to align with the interests of the new political actors in power, to have a grip on the media. So, in the case of Bolivia (as well as in Ecuador and Venezuela, at least) it is the political sphere – more than the corporate – what is capturing the social and watchdog roles of the media and of journalism, forcing them to comply with its interests.

Efforts to continue the enacting of new media regulation have not ceased in Bolivia. In July 2011, inspired by the Argentinian Media Law, congress passed the Telecommunications Law, dividing the spectrum into thirds: one awarded to the state; another to the private sector; and the last one to indigenous and social organizations allied to the government. According to its critics, President Morales will control, in practice, up to 66 percent of the spectrum due to his close relationship with the indigenous and social organizations, with the risk that private media will be displaced and lose their licenses (EFE, 2011). According to Giavedoni, this is one of many laws that 'congressmen of MAS will be issuing after its clear electoral victory in 2009 [which resulted in the second term of Morales's mandate] with 63 percent of votes, the absolute majority in congress (2010: 4). In this regard, the government announced in January 2012 that it would soon present for approval a new Media Law that, based upon the constitution, will respect freedom of expression (Galindo, 2012).

Co-option of community media and the development of State media

In countries like Venezuela and Bolivia, supporting community media is sometimes part of a strategy to conform a pro-government media front vis-à-vis commercial private media. For instance, in July 2006, President Morales inaugurated Radio Orinoca in the town of Andamarca (Oruro), the location of the first station of what was called the National Radio System of Native People (Sistema Nacional de Radios de los Pueblos Originarios, RPO). RPO is a project that derives directly from the constitution and it is sponsored by a cooperation agreement with the government of Venezuela (Ramos-Martín, 2011). By 2010, RPO included 31 radio stations across the nine provinces (*departamentos*) of the country. Though they are referred to as community radio stations, in reality they are not. In principle, all the stations should belong to each of the community's unions that agree on an installation contract with RPO. However, the contract establishes that the state is not only the financial supporter, but also through a series of bailment clauses remains as the ultimate owner, transferring the control to the communities for periods of five years (Ramos-Martín, 2011). Moreover, the contents are also subordinated to a centralized governmental system. For the broadcasting of information, the central public radio Patria Nueva supervises the interconnection of all these stations and hitches them to its own news contents. The National Directorate of Social Communication (Dirección Nacional de Comunicación Social, DINACOM), a governmental office, is the second instance that supervises the news and information contents of the RPO stations. Thus, these stations end up being part of the government informational network (Corrales, 2010: 84). In Bolivia, there was an important tradition of community radios that began in the 1940s and 1950s when different groups established broadcasting facilities in factories, railway stations, and mining sites. In those decades, the Catholic church also developed a network called Broadcasting Schools of Bolivia (Escuelas Radiofónicas Bolivia, ERBOL). The actual governmental project, with its centralizing aims, sacrifices precisely the autonomous and alternative character that had distinguished such kinds of radio stations. According to the author:

> Community radio stations can no longer be distinguished as alternative media, contributing to pluralism and democracy from the rural area. They are now part of a governmental media block for promoting and defending its interests, actions and policies, following the path of Venezuela and Cuba. This block is intended to promote a discourse to confront the private media networks, and everyone who opposes the regime of MAS. (Vargas, 2011: 1)

Bolivia seems to have privileged the expansion of community radio instead of other practices of direct communication, as regular presidential broadcasts on radio and television, something that do occur in Venezuela (Kitzberger, 2010, see also Chapter 8 in this volume). This decision has to do with the fact that local radio stations have had a strong rooting in the country compared to the relatively low territorial penetration of television. Nevertheless, despite its limited scope, Televisión Boliviana, the state television network, has been strongly supported by the government. Along with the Bolivian Information Agency (Agencia Boliviana de Información, ABI) and the newspaper Cambio (launched in 2009), it is part of the modern governmental media structure. It becomes evident that the government of President Morales has reconfigured the media scenario by creating or strengthening a network of state-funded media, defined by a clear promotional and propagandist editorial line. The justification for these media is that they are needed in a context where private media are negatively biased against the government. However, sceptics argue that these other media are no better: not only do they fail to comply with basic journalistic standards regularly mixing opinion with information, but they also end up feeding political polarization by giving uncritical coverage to the official discourse (Sandoval, 2011: 61).

The result of this reconfiguration is a disproportionate growing of the governmental hegemony in most topics of the public agenda and a silenced acceptance of an atmosphere of journalistic self-censorship (Molina, 2010; quoted in Bravo-Gallardo, 2012). The government has strengthened vis-à-vis a private media structure once regarded as all-powerful, and it has retaken the political initiative in that relation. The resulting problem, as one observer puts it, is that current news today is mostly defined by what 'Evo's government does or decides' (Bravo-Gallardo, 2012: 75).

Conclusions

In Bolivia, under President Evo Morales, regulation has been oriented to regain state control over the once perceived all-powerful private media. The antecedents of the conflict are actually rooted in Bolivia's political history where strong ethnic, regional, and social gaps have never been closed. After authoritarian rule, a succession of different governments all holding similar ideological orientation toward neoliberalism lost popular support as they had mostly concentrated power in the hands of historically privileged social and economic groups. In this process, the media transitioned from being a space for debate to becoming part of the central political actors. This coincided with a growing property concentration that, though it did not lead to the emergence of strong media monopolies, did link media elites with other economic sectors and with the traditional political class. The transformation of the private media in Bolivia can be seen in the way they first reported and covered the indigenous social movements giving them – and their leaders – a national platform from which Evo Morales jumped to the presidency. Once in power – with a media structure already linked to traditional economic and political interests – they immediately backed off their support and aligned again with political opposition discourse to discredit the government's social and political project.

Thus, the relationship between the media and the government has developed in an atmosphere of constant conflict and tension. However, this situation is not exclusive of Bolivia. Some other countries have been following the same confrontational path: Ecuador, Venezuela, and Argentina. The justification is the same in all cases: private media have illegitimately gained uncontrolled and unaccountable power in public life, therefore the states see it as their duty to limit such power in the public interest and to promote true media pluralism. In any case, the situation coincides with Guerrero's model of captured liberal media system where government efforts are intended not to destroy the private media, but to limit their autonomy by forcing them to align with its interests. In this way, the regulatory efforts in Bolivia follow the same path as in Venezuela and Argentina to regain control over media policy.

This view coincides with that of the ALBA, the regional bloc led by Venezuela and Cuba that regards private media as instruments of economic neoliberalism. However, President Morales's discourse adds the local tones of ethnicity and class where private media appear as vehicles of racist groups who yearn for past domination. Constitutional reform and regulations have drastically diminished criticism against his government and policies. At the same time, through information control of community radio, the Morales administration has redesigned the media landscape, therewith strengthening a supportive media framework. In this way, the government not only controls the public agenda, but also becomes the major focus of news. In that way, he dominates the public agenda and has become the focus of the news. However, following Ruiz's (2010) assertion, this scenario may bring up a positive unintended consequence: that private media may take the chance to professionalize its journalistic practices and, given the actual legal constraints, become an impeccable watchdog not only of government, but of all public actors.

In a context of polarization a voice critical to all may be a welcomed credible information source.

Notes

1. In July 2008, a convoy of 33 trucks with smuggled goods illegally crossed the boundary of the free-zone in Cobija on the grounds that they had the permission of the Minister of the Presidency, Juan Ramón Quintana, and the then Head of the Anti-Smuggling Joint Command, Rear-Admiral Rafael Bandeiras. Customs tried to retrieve the cargo on three occasions: on July 29, when trucks were in the port of Santa Rosa del Abuná; on July 30, when they received a call from La Paz indicating that there was a negotiation in place; and on August 22, when there was no support from the Joint Command and eight members of the Customs Control (COA in Spanish: Control Operativo Aduanero) were in charge of the merchandise.
2. Historical period in which, during the MNR government (1952–1964), there were fundamental changes in citizen participation, distribution of land, and state control over the natural resources.
3. In that year, general elections were held in which Evo Morales won reelection with 63 percent of the vote.
4. On April 4 of that year, governors for all nine departments of the country, members of the Departmental Legislative Assemblies, and representatives of indigenous and native peasant people to the Departmental Assemblies, were elected directly for the first time.
5. This name refers to all of the social protests that, in 2000, triggered the attempt to privatize the water municipal service in the city of Cochabamba.
6. Political and social crises occurred in October 2003 and were caused by the governmental decision to export gas through Chile. It ended with at least 67 people dead and the end of Gonzalo Sánchez de Lozada's administration.

References

Archondo, R. (2003) *Incestos y blindajes: una radiografía del juego político-periodístico* (La Paz: Plural).
Bravo-Gallardo, C. (2012) *Nueva integración entre gobiernos progresistas y los medios de comunicación: Los casos de Venezuela, Ecuador y Bolivia.* Unpublished Master Thesis (La Paz: Universidad Andina Simón Bolívar).
Cook, T. (1997) *Governing with the News: The News Media As a Political Institution* (Chicago: University of Chicago Press).
Corrales, C. (2010) 'La radiodifusión en tiempos de cambio en Bolivia,' *Chasqui*, 110: 81–90.
Duverger, M. (1990) *Los partidos políticos* (México: Fondo de Cultura Económica).
EFE (2011) 'Asamblea Legislativa sanciona proyecto de Ley de Telecomunicaciones,' *Página Siete*. Available at http://bit.ly/o6N6Q1 (accessed July 27, 2013).
Galindo, C. (2012) 'Dávila dice que habrá nueva Ley de Medios,' *La Razón*. Available at http://bit.ly/19wl9IH (accessed July 26, 2013).

Giavedoni, D. (2010) 'Los medios en Bolivia: mapa y legislación de los medios de comunicación,' *La revista del CCC (Centro Cultural de la Cooperación Floreal Gorini)*, 9(10): 1–17.

Kitzberger, P. (2010) 'Giro a la izquierda, populismo y activismo gubernamental en la esfera pública mediática en América Latina,' pp. 61–100 in B. Sorj (comp.) *Poder político y medios de comunicación: de la representación política al reality show* (Buenos Aires: Siglo XXI).

Molina, F. (2010) 'De la polarización a la hegemonía,' pp. 199–216 in O. Rincón (ed.) *¿Por qué nos odian tanto? Estado y medios en América Latina* (Bogotá: Centro de Competencia en Comunicación para América Latina).

Morales Ayma, Evo (2010) 'Ley Contra el Racismo y Toda Forma de Discriminación,' La Paz: *Gaceta Oficial de Bolivia*.

O'Schaughnessy, H. (2007) 'Media Wars in Latin America,' *British Journalism Review*, 18(3): 66–72.

Peñaranda, R. (2003) 'Los periodistas frente al poder: el eterno recelo,' pp. 18–35 in C. Rojas and R. Peñaranda (eds) *Prensa y poder en Bolivia: Relaciones entre el mundo político y los medios de comunicación* (La Paz: Fundación Konrad Adenauer).

Quintanilla, V. (2012) 'Bolivia, entre la vitalidad democrática y la sombra del autoritarismo,' *Translatin*, 21: 36–43.

Ramos-Martín, J. (2011) 'Políticas públicas y radiodifusión comunitaria en Bolivia: proceso de cambio, control del proceso,' *Redes.com: Revista de Estudios para el Desarrollo Social de la Comunicación*, 6: 249–270. Available at http://bit.ly/13lBf46 [accessed April 22, 2013].

Ruiz, F. (2010) 'Fronteras móviles: caos y control en la relación entre medios y políticos en América Latina,' pp. 17–60 in B. Sorj (comp.) *Poder político y medios de comunicación: de la representación política al reality show* (Buenos Aires: Siglo XXI Editores).

Sáinz, L. (2010) 'Los medios de comunicación, campos de batalla política en Bolivia,' *Diálogo Político*, 1: 79–98.

Sandoval, F. (2011) 'El Observatorio Nacional de Medios (ONADEM) de Bolivia, por el ejercicio del Derecho a la Información y la Comunicación,' *Chasqui*, 116: 60–63.

Sorj, B. (2010) 'Introducción,' pp. 5–15 in B. Sorj (comp.) *Poder político y medios de comunicación: de la representación política al reality show* (Buenos Aires: Siglo XXI Editores).

Torrico, E. (2007) 'La narrativa periodística desorganizadora,' *Diálogos de la Comunicación*, 75: 1–9.

Vargas, A. (2011) 'La distorsión de la diversidad en radiodifusión: las radios comunitarias en Bolivia como instrumento de propaganda política,' paper presented at the XII Iberoamerican Congress of Communication. Santa Cruz, Bolivia: Universidad Privada de Santa Cruz de la Sierra.

Zárate, C. L. (2005) 'El conflicto social en Bolivia: a la búsqueda de una interculturalidad incluyente,' *Papeles de cuestiones internacionales*, 91: 125–131.

10
State Intervention and Market Structures: The New Overview of the Argentinian Audio-visual Sector

Guillermo Mastrini, Martín Becerra, and Santiago Marino

Introduction

Private, for-profit companies that feature concentrated property owner-ship and centralized production in large urban centers have traditionally dominated the media structure in Latin America. Much of its print and audiovisual content comes from the United States, rather than being domestically or locally generated. The size of the domestic markets and the low per-capita consumption of culture have created a profitable media model in which the state plays a major role. In a number of Latin American countries, governments have largely subsidized the privately owned media system, either directly or indirectly through state adver-tising. An unwritten arrangement takes place: in return, the media turn a blind eye to government excesses or abuses, in effect giving up their watchdog role.

For many years, Argentina has been a good example of what happens when efforts at media reform collide with the media's economic inter-ests. The government has played a decisive role in broadcast media by granting licenses, awarding subsidies, granting tax exemptions to selected media, and allocating official advertising to favored stations and holdings. Far from conveying a consistent state policy, though, these efforts have been typically intended to advance whatever party happened to be in power.

In Argentina, private companies have controlled the broadcast stations in the country's principal cities. But with the launch of digital television in 2009, the number of state-led TV stations increased. There were no examples of cross-ownership among press and broadcasting outlets until the 1990s, when President Carlos Menem initiated reforms that enabled the creation of multimedia groups. As a result, media ownership in Argentina has become increasingly concentrated in the media sector. For example, media group Clarín now not only owns the national newspaper with the largest circulation as well as papers in some important regional capitals such as Córdoba (La Voz del Interior) and Mendoza (Los Andes). It also operates one of the main TV channels in Buenos Aires (Channel 13) and others in major cities (such as Channel 12 in Córdoba and Channel 7 in Bahía Blanca), a chain of radio stations (led by Mitre and FM 100), the biggest cable TV distributor (Cablevisión), and various cable TV channels (such as Todo Noticias, Volver, Metro, and TyC Sports).

The Clarín Group also holds stakes in related industries, such as the manufacturing of newsprint for journals and newspapers (an area in which the conglomerate has partnered with the state since the last military dictatorship), and related media ventures such as film, radio, and TV production (it has shares in Pol-Ka Producciones, Patagonik Film Group, and Ideas del Sur); a news agency (DyN); and an Internet service provider (Fibertel). Clarín's media dominance is only challenged in the communications sector by telephone companies such as Spain's Telefónica, which is also the largest provider of cellular telephone service and broadband Internet, that operates nine TV stations in Argentina.

But the country's concentrated media landscape abruptly changed following passage of the 2009 Audiovisual Communication Services Law (ACSL). It was first major effort to regulate the media since 1980 when the military dictatorship banned not-for-profit groups from participating in the media system to ensure greater control over media access and content.

The military-era regulations were modified partially during the governments of Carlos Menem (1989–1999), Fernando de la Rúa (1999–2001), Eduardo Duhalde (2002–2003), and Néstor Kirchner (2003–2007) (See Chapter 5). But ACSL transformed the system. It reflected both the emergence of new media technologies and the emerging efforts to link the concept of freedom of expression with human rights by reserving space on the radio spectrum for civil society groups. The law not only allowed nonprofit organizations, groups, and communities to obtain radio and TV licenses, it set aside 33 percent of the broadcast spectrum for such groups. It also established limits on the concentration and domination of the market to increase the number of groups that could participate.

And for the first time in Argentinian history, the bodies that regulate the media are able to include different political parties, the public universities and civil society organizations, rather than being appointed only by the executive branch.

Moreover, the law demanded pluralism and diversity from state media, recognized explicitly the right to freedom of expression, and required television and radio stations to produce a local content quota where they were licensed to broadcast. The ACSL ruptured what had been a close relationship between Clarín and the president's predecessor and late husband, Néstor Kirchner, who on his last working day authorized the merger of two of the main cable TV operators that, combined, gave the Clarín Group 60 percent stake in the market. At the time, Clarín's reporting had been noticeably pro-government.

ACSL: a new law from a democratic perspective

The regulation of the media system in Argentina has a specific rule for broadcasting and another one for telecommunication services, and this characteristic has not yet been modified in spite of the opportunities for convergence between both systems that is enabled by digitization.

National Law No. 19,798 on Telecommunications was passed in August 1972.[1] It regulated all forms of broadcasting and electronic communication. In 1980, with the introduction of Decree-Law No. 22,285,[2] radio broadcasting (AM and FM), free-to-air television, and cable networks were excluded from the application of that general standard for telecommunications. Since then, they have been governed by sector-specific legislation with several changes implemented during the democratic period, especially since 1989, on the issue of licenses.

Audiovisual media are regulated today in accordance with Law No. 26,522 on SCA Law passed in October 2009 after an intense and lengthy debate to repeal the Decree-Law of 1980, including a series of forums for citizen participation and spaces for public discussion. The debate was characterized by strong confrontations between the highly concentrated media groups owned by national and international capitals and the government and sectors that supported the project. As we mentioned in a previous paper:

> Democratic values are at the heart of the SCA Law, guaranteeing freedom of expression, reserving a portion of the spectrum for the not-for-profit private sector on all bands and frequencies, defining mechanisms to thwart the emergence of highly concentrated

oligopolies, defending radios and small channels in provincial towns, and requiring local production quotas from all operators in the system. Its objectives propose advances like creating an authority for federal regulation, with autarchic powers, and inclusive of members from the political parliamentary minorities; establishing rules to prevent cross-ownership in the audiovisual market (free-to-air and pay TV) so as to facilitate new entrants; and prohibiting telephone companies to hold media licenses (thus preventing powerful operators from potentially monopolizing the system). (Marino, Mastrini and Becerra, 2011: 8)

The law created the Federal Authority of Audiovisual Communication Services (Autoridad Federal de Servicios de Comunicación Audiovisual, AFSCA),[3] the agency charged with the allocation of radio-electric spectrum licenses, both digital and analog (except for cities with more than 500,000 inhabitants where licenses are granted by the NEP). The only article of the recently introduced law that defines TDT-related matters states that existing terrestrial TV licensees will receive the so-called 'mirror signal,' that is, space for one broadcasting signal out of the six or eight possible signals that can be carried on the 6 MHz used by an analog signal.

In connection with the distribution of spectrum, it should be noted that the democratizing intentions of the law encounter a significant limit in the fact that the licenses for cities with more than 500,000 inhabitants will be granted directly by the National Executive Power, and not by AFSCA. As a result of this provision, the decision as to the allocation of top spaces in the ether – located in large cities, thus having the greatest advertising potential – is in the hands of an individual (the president of the nation), rather than a collegiate body formed by representatives from multiple sectors of communication and culture (i.e., the regulatory authority, AFSCA). This is coupled with the concrete fact that the spectrum in several of those cities had been saturated before the application of the new SCA Law.

The law recognizes three types of licensees: public (governmental), commercial private, and non-commercial private. An original aspect of the SCA Law is that it reserves 33 percent of the spectrum for nonprofit civil society organizations. This reservation applies to both the analog and the digital environments and is a positive development in terms of diversity, since economic considerations are no longer an obstacle or a definer of who obtains a broadcast license. Other groups receiving special treatment, and included under the public category, are national universities, the Catholic church, and indigenous peoples. These groups are to receive directly assigned frequencies with a maximum of one AM radio, one FM radio, and one free-to-air television (as it happens with municipalities and regions). The remaining spectrum, which is estimated to be far more than 50 percent, is available for commercial private operators.

It should be remarked that this process has just begun, and it is evolving slowly due to the judicial actions that commercial groups have initiated in order to stop the application of the law coupled with certain political sloppiness and indecision on the part of the government and the refusal of opposition parties to join the decision-making bodies created by the law. In October 2013, the Supreme Court (SCJN) backed the complete constitutionality of the law and put an end to all of the judicial actions. So now, after all the judicial arguments have been cleared, the government must ensure the application of the law.

The most important thing about the Supreme Court's ruling, is that it establishes a new concept on how to understand freedom of speech in Argentina. The ruling considers that there are two dimensions of freedom of speech: one individual that is based on the personal right to publicly express ideas that may translate into economic rights; and a second, social dimension that should grant the exercise of freedom of speech for the population at large. In a time where media have a key role, the CSJN expressed that freedom of speech is indivisible from the possibility of spreading ideas, thus stressing the importance of the legal regime applicable to the media in order to ensure both aspects.

The CSJN does not assess the quality of the ACSL because it understands that this is the job of legislators. The CSJN highlights that the act 'aims to promote competitive and antitrust policies to preserve a fundamental right to life in a democracy such as freedom of speech and information' (SCJN, 2013: 89). The Supreme Court analyzes whether the rule is proportionate and reasonable from the legislative will, markedly respecting the separation of powers.

The ruling is grounded on the need to promote and ensure a strong public debate as the American constitutionalist Owen Fiss, who was supported in Argentina by Carlos Nino, advocated it. That is why the court states that the principle that the ACSL aims to ensure is the plurality of voices and that the state has the right to set limits to media concentration when that does not affect the subsistence of the companies.

The decision recognizes a fundamental issue, that is, the specificity of the communication sector whose diversity must be protected, especially because this is the cornerstone of a democratic society: 'Unlike other markets, in the media industry, concentration has social consequences that manifest themselves on the right of information, essential for the individual liberties.' And the CSJN adds: 'restrictions strictly related to assets are not disproportionate to the institutional weight of the goals of the Act' (SCJN, 2013: 97).

Since October 2013 Argentina has gone one step further in developing state of the art jurisprudence on freedom of speech, prioritizing the social right to have a public and plural debate over the economic rights of companies. The law introduced in 2009 implies major changes in terms of ownership, since one of its objectives is to promote the de-concentration of the media markets by lowering the threshold on the number of permitted media companies owned by the same proprietor and by encouraging more diversity, both in ownership and contents.

The SCA Law sets major limits in terms of the number of audiovisual service licenses that an individual operator can hold. For satellite TV services, an operator may hold only one license that reaches the entire territory. Furthermore, such a license disqualifies the holder from holding any other license to any other broadcasting service. However, there is no restriction on cross-ownership between broadcasting companies and newspapers.

For terrestrial TV and radio broadcasting services, there is a maximum limit of ten licenses. In Argentina, there are no broadcast licenses for national coverage, and permits are granted for coverage areas in a radius of approximately 70 km. For cable TV services, a maximum of 24 licenses is established. Cable TV licensees may not hold terrestrial TV licenses in the same coverage area.

In parallel, the law sets a cap on the market share that a single licensee can reach: it determines that no individual operator may provide services for more than 35 percent of the population or of the market for a service covered by the law. This restriction represents in fact a limitation for those having licenses in the Buenos Aires Metropolitan area (Area Metropolitana de Buenos Aires, AMBA). Considering that approximately 33 percent of the Argentinian population resides in the AMBA region, the regulation effectively precludes license holders in that region from holding licenses in other regions.

A maximum of three licenses may be held in a single area of coverage. Cable TV operators have the obligation to provide a signal with local content but can only distribute a signal owned by the operator, while all others have to be purchased by external producers.

Finally, the new regulation introduces a number of limitations on the establishment of broadcasting networks. The most important requires operators that become part of a chain to ensure that content produced by other operators within the network is limited to 30 percent of airtime. In all cases, as said above, there are no restrictions on cross-ownership between audiovisual and print media.

Considering that the previous law established the overall maximum limit at 24 licenses, permitted chains without restrictions, and had even fewer cross-ownership limitations, the change has been quite significant. More importantly, Article 161 of the SCA Law granted all media companies exceeding the new quotas at the time the law was passed a one-year term to adjust to the new regulatory framework. The article has stirred up much controversy, and Grupo Clarín (the group most affected by the SCA Law) filed at the end of 2009 a complaint in court. In 2010, it obtained two court decisions ordering the interim suspension of this article until it was resolved whether or not the retroactive enforcement of the law was constitutional. The suspension order applies to Grupo Clarín only. Due to the court ruling in October 2013, Article 161 now also applies to Clarín.

Four years after the law was passed, and after overcoming legal obstacles that hindered its immediate application, it is too soon to make a complete evaluation of its impact on the media landscape. So far, no substantive modifications have been observed in the media markets' structure. The newly appointed authority, AFSCA, created by Law 26,522, has the power to force owners to sell those media outlets that exceed the legal ownership quota. Originally, a transition period of one year was introduced to allow owners to adapt to the new regulation. However, due to the legal challenges by media owners, this deadline is not being enforced. It may be assumed however, that if the provisions of the law are honored, there will be a positive result for pluralism and diversity and increased national and regional content production.

The LSCA law established the inception of the Federal Authority for Audiovisual Communications Services (AFSCA for its Spanish acronyms) to enforce the norms against concentration and to run the process of granting licenses. This body is composed of seven members, two appointed by the executive power (PEN), three by Congress (two of the appointed by opposition parties), and two by the Federal Council of Communication. Four opposition parties have refused to appoint any members in solidarity with media owners in the first two years, and AFSCA has as a result been functioning with only five members. In 2011, one director appointed for the opposition parties occupied its chair. It is expected that for the next period beginning in December 2013, AFSCA´s directory will be fully represented.

The institutional design of AFSCA might in theory promote a radical shift in the traditional balance of power between the government and the regulatory authority. But as a result of the constraints outlined above, so far the new regulatory agency has not been legitimized by the political opposition. This problem is compounded by the fact that the present administration has deviated from the principles of the SCA Law by, for instance, ensuring a consistent majority of its own representatives among AFSCA members.

All this means that even though the original legal design seemed to promote independence, in practice, and due to the government's maneuvers and the opposition's inaction, the regulator is not independent.

It should also be remarked that in the original drafting of the bill it was allowed for telecom companies to enter the media sector – though with severe limitations to prevent them from becoming dominant players. However, the government removed that provision during the parliamentary debates in order to secure the votes of center-leftish parties – which ultimately supported the law. In the privatization process of the former state telecom, Entel, in 1990, it was established that companies would have a monopoly in the telephone market but were forbidden from entering the broadcasting market. Laws 22,285/80 and 26,522/09 prevent companies that provide or distribute public services like gas, energy, or telecommunications from entering the audiovisual sector. Still, taking advantage of the ambiguous dispositions of some laws (25,750/03 and 26,053) and the inactivity of government, Telefónica of Spain owns one of the most prominent channels in the city of Buenos Aires, and a few more in the provinces. It should be remarked that Telefónica keeps separate company structures and does not provide convergent services in order to avoid obvious conflict with the telecoms' regulatory framework (decree PEN 764/00) that prohibits the ownership of communication media by telecom service providers.

Other important issues of the law are linked with content production. Chapter V of the SCA Law is devoted to content regulation. Article 65 establishes that holders of licenses and authorizations that provide audiovisual communication services must comply with certain rules regarding content:

- All non-public radio stations must broadcast at least 70 percent of national production and a minimum of 50 percent of production of their own that must include news.
- State, municipal, and university radio stations must broadcast at least 60 percent of their own and local programming, which must include

newscasts with local news, and at least 20 percent of educational, cultural, and public service programming.

- Free-to-air television stations must broadcast a minimum of 60 percent of national production of which at least 30 percent must be production of their own including local newscasts. In cities of more than 1.5 million inhabitants they must also broadcast 30 percent of independent local production, 15 percent in cities of between 600,000 and 1.5 million inhabitants, and 10 percent in smaller cities.
- Pay TV services (cable and satellite) must include an open signal with all channels in which the state has participation, all free-to-air channels in its coverage area (must-carry and must-offer), and all public regional, municipal and university channels within its coverage area. They must organize their programming guide so that all channels belonging in the same genre are side by side, and they must include at least one local channel that satisfies the aforementioned conditions for free-to-air stations.

Besides Article 68, the law aims at protecting children, and mentions that all content (including advertising) must be child-friendly from 6 a.m. to 10 p.m., while from 10 p.m. to 6 a.m. adult content is allowed. The law forbids the participation of children under the age of 12 in programs that are broadcast between 10 p.m. and 8 a.m., unless they have been recorded before in which case it must be mentioned during the broadcast.

While deregulation and content homogeneization have been global trends worldwide as far as TV programing is concerned, the Argentinian case poses a contrasting example. Generally, it may be claimed that the orientation of the new law is not aligned with mainstream trends worldwide because it does not include the loosening of limits to ownership concentration, and it does not encourage cross-ownership. As a result, the Argentinian law has received a lot of attention in the region. In several South American countries, moderately leftist political forces have taken it as a beacon of social action in the media sphere.

What has been undoubtedly observed is an unflinching resistance by media proprietors against the new regulation through both national (ATA, ATVC, ADEPA, CEMCI)[4] and regional (SIP, AIR)[5] organizations. The argument presented by the business sector is that the intervention of the state regulating the functioning of the media operates as a restriction on the freedom of the press. And while the law can be considered an improvement toward a more democratic and pluralistic media system, it must be acknowledged that the government has so far not applied the law in a way consistent with the law's objectives.

The debate continues from both the business and social sides of the argument. In a general evaluation of the law, the United Nations Special Rapporteur on the Promotion and Protection of the Right to Freedom of Opinion and Expression, Frank La Rue, has frequently praised the Argentinian government's media policy, calling it 'exemplary,' particularly in reference to the SCA Law. Similar feedback has come from such organizations as Reporters without Borders and the World Association of Community Broadcasters (AMARC). On the contrary, the media owners assembled though the pro-business Inter-American Press Society have reiteratively condemned the Argentinian government on the same account.

TDT implementation

The implementation of digital TV only began in 2010, and the analog switch-off is anticipated for 2019.

In August 2009, the government adopted the Japanese-Brazilian ISDB-T TV standard and one month later, it issued the decree 1148/09, introducing SATVD-T. At the same time Decree No. 1785/09 established the Advisory Council of SATVD-T, all within the sphere of the PEN. It also introduced a ten-year term (2019) for the analog switch-off. Consequently, operators and users still have plenty of time to migrate. A broader switch-off policy was enshrined in the SCA Law passed in 2009, which began to be implemented in 2010.

Since then, the government has assumed leadership in the deployment of digital TV, so far with feeble support from commercial players. The government has made – and is making – the first digital signal transmissions; it funds the purchase of the infrastructure, including transmitter and repeater towers; it is handing out set-top boxes free to low-income sectors of the population (it is estimated that some 1.2 million set-top boxes were distributed to beneficiaries of social welfare plans and pensioners from early 2010 to September 2013); and it assigns provisional licenses to some carriers willing to carry out trials (licenses are granted under provisional terms because the SCA Law includes a provision requiring licenses to be awarded as a result of competitive bidding processes) and subsidizes content production.

There have been positive aspects to intervention. The set-top box distribution program was unprecedented and gives priority to the most socially disfavored sectors in the introduction of new technological platforms as part of a public policy. Digitization seems to be totally unrelated to the changes that have occurred. Digitization was not a driver in any sense for the 2009 legislation. More so, it was implemented in parallel with other areas of government, different from those that manage media policy. And while the digitization process has been led by the state through SATVD-T, which depends on the Ministry of Federal Planning (Ministerio de Panificación Federal), the Broadcasting Law is being implemented by AFSCA.

Indeed, the digital TV implementation process has not yet included consultation and engagement mechanisms similar to those used to introduce the media law. The permits for digital experimental transmissions have not followed the procedures required by the law creating a contradiction between the goals of the law and the actual policies being implemented. According to Carla Rodríguez Miranda, '...in this setting, the state assumes a leading role in the development of TDT but fails to agree on a strategic and transversal position with the other social sectors. Private broadcasters are waiting for the 6Mhz allocation for the simulcasting process, still pending definition, so their investments in TDT contents and networks are frozen.' (Rodríguez-Miranda, 2011: 115).

There are no binding obligations for state or privately managed operators beyond the provision of free-to-air transmission. However, there is no rule or law supporting this situation; rather, it follows the course of customary free-to-air transmission in the history of terrestrial analog broadcasting. There are no indications of how spectrum allocated to each operator is to be utilized. Nor is there certainty over whether the current licensees of terrestrial analog TV will simply enjoy a mirror channel – a digital reproduction of their analog signal that would permit the remaining bandwidth to be used for the benefit of nonprofit social sectors or whether they will be granted the full bandwidth so they can decide if they will broadcast in HD or in a lower definition.

All operators, however, have to comply with a set of obligations set forth by the SCA Law, including respecting the hours of special protection for children, the length of advertising blocks (12 minutes/hour), inclusion of the closed-caption service, and percentages of own production and local production, among others.

As noted above, the government launched a scheme for the distribution of 1.2 million set-top boxes that were delivered free of charge to low-income sectors. This scheme is funded through the national budget. The rest of the population can buy their set-top boxes at home appliance stores or access digital TV through mobile telephony, though the stock of mobile telephony equipment enabled for digital TV reception is still limited. Penetration of digital TV in the population is still very low compared with cable and satellite TV.

Final remarks

Four years after the law was passed, its goals have not been reached. In the face of Clarín's judicial appeals, the Argentinian government has been dedicated to dismantling the group's domination of the market. In this dispute, the ACSL has been shoved aside and, contrary to what the law prescribes, the government has effectively turned state TV into an arm of partisan politics. Government subsidies are also directed at rewarding friendly stations and withhelding from those that oppose the government.

Moreover, the government has tolerated the concentration of large, pro-government media groups; arguing that until Clarín relinquishes some of its market share, it would be asymmetrical for other groups to do so. The government has not even put into place a system to determine what percentage of radio frequencies are being used by current media as part of its stated aim of ensuring that 33 percent of the radio frequencies are being used by nonprofit groups. Without this information it is impossible to open up the spectrum to public tender so that new operators might diversify the Argentinian media system.

The government's quarrel with Clarín, in effect, has distorted the entire Argentinian media environment. Its attacks against the media giant have been accompanied by overt efforts to strengthen Clarín's competitors through state advertising and exemptions from key elements of the law, including the social investment requirements, limits on concentration of ownership, and restrictions on granting licenses to foreign companies.

Until now, though, government efforts to bolster Clarín's adversaries against the government's vowed enemy have been futile. Clarín continues to dominate Argentinian media, with 35 percent of the print market, 60 percent of the cable TV market, and two of the leading broadcast channels in Buenos Aires. Meanwhile, pro-government competitors such as the newspapers *Tiempo Argentino* (Szpolski Group) and *Página 12* (Soklowicz Group); the TV Channel 7 (state television) and Channel 9 (owned by Mexican national Remigio Ángel González); the radio station 10 (owned by Cristóbal López); and Del Plata (Electroingeniería) are far behind, despite government favoritism.

Freedom of expression is real in Argentina. Government actions to decriminalize libel and slander are an example. There is still a lot of work to be done, not least on the part of the media groups that complain most vociferously while engaging in anti-competitive practices that restrict media diversity. The law did not, as its supporters promised, lead to immediate democratization of the media market through the expansion of access to new actors. One major failure was the government's inability or lack of will to implement some of the law's most important initiatives, such as the establishment of the technical plan cited above to assign one-third of the broadcast spectrum to nonprofits. Since 2009, the government has granted only a handful of licenses to nonprofits. And the government has yet to announce a public auction for new licenses that would bring the country closer to the media diversity promised by the law.

However, media regulation has been submitted to an open and head-on debate with positive consequences. This open debate, unprecedented in Argentinian history, has increased the country's awareness of its media system, its interests, and the rules of the game. No single law can transform a media culture created over several decades. But the ACSL has established a foundation for new communications policies that can increase cultural and information diversity in Argentinian society. Building on that foundation, however, will not be easy. Like the rest of Latin America, Argentina needs to overcome the systemic weakness of its regulatory bodies to implement the kinds of rules that can protect an open, diverse, and impartial press. The ultimate question is whether the powerful media groups that have been fighting to protect their monopolistic access will regard this in their own interests as well.

Notes

1. This law was issued during the military dictatorship that claimed to be the 'Argentinian Revolution' and remained in power from 1966 to 1973.
2. This rule was introduced during the civil-military dictatorship called 'National Reorganization Process' that lasted from 1976 to 1983.
3. This agency is made up of seven members: two are designated by the Executive Power, three by the National Congress (two of them from political minorities), and three by the Federal Council on Audiovisual Communication (Consejo Federal de Comunicación Audiovisual, CFC), also created by this new law.
4. Association of Argentinian TV Broadcasters (Asociación de Televisoras Argentinas, ATA) Cable TV Association (Asociación de televisión por cable, ATVC), Association of Argentinian Journalistic Entities (Asociación de Entidades Periodísticas Argentinas, ADEPA), Entrepreneurial Commission of Independent Communication Media (Comisión Empresarial de Medios de

Comunicación Independientes, CEMCI). Given their high levels of multi-media concentration, some media groups are members in all of the foregoing associations. Grupo Clarín and Grupo Vila-Manzano are two examples.
5. Inter-American Press Association (IAPA), Inter-American Radio Broadcasters' Association (AIR).

References

Marino, S., Mastrini, G. and Becerra, M. (2011) 'El proceso de regulación democrática de la comunicación en Argentina,' *Derecho a Comunicar*, 1(1): 1–17. Available at http://bit.ly/JnJMg7 (accessed June 2013).

SCJN (Suprema Corte de Justicia de la Nación) (2013) 'Fallo Grupo Clarín y otros c/Poder Ejecutivo Nacional.' Disponible en http://bit.ly/1bwq2xa (accessed November 2013).

Rodríguez-Miranda, C. (2011) 'La implementación de la TDA en Argentina,' Master Dissertation in Cultural Industries (Argentina: Universidad Nacional de Quilmes).

11
Public Service Broadcasting and Media Reform in Brazil in Comparative Perspective

Carolina Matos

Introduction

Public service broadcasting (PSB) has been under threat in Europe for both ideological and technical reasons since the 1980s. The threat is the result of the expansion of media commercialization, the proliferation of new technologies, and the impact of the deregulation trends in the United States and throughout the world that resulted in the rapid growth of cable and satellite television. Following Jakubowicz's (2006), it seems that a key role for PSB in democratization is one of assisting globalization and contributing to wider international dialog and understanding between countries, as well as functioning as a national public sphere for debate.

The question then is what precisely is the role of the state in communications in the digital age, in a scenario of multi-channels and new technologies, and what should it be in the future? As Santos and Silveira (2007: 76) have correctly affirmed, the reasons why the state should still have a role include its capacity to organize the use of limited resources, stimulate technical advancements, guarantee fair competition, and favor national development. This chapter gives an overview of the role that PSB has in European democracies and its relationship to the public interest. I argue here that there is much to learn from the tradition of PSB in Europe and that, in a moment when it is in serious crisis in advanced democracies like the United Kingdom, it is a source of inspiration for countries like Brazil in their attempts to fortify the democratic project. This assessment is done in a comparative perspective to the ways in which Latin American countries are aiming to strengthen their public service broadcasters and conduct media reforms in favor of the public interest and in line with international demands.

This chapter starts by defining PSB and its relationship to the public interest, moving on to the assessment of European PSB and the current problems it is facing. The second half of the chapter pursues an assessment of Latin American media systems and their tradition of misuse of public communication structures, before focusing on the case of Brazil and the challenges regarding media reform, broadcasting policy, and democratization of communications more generally.

Defining PSB and the public interest

There has not yet been a standard and precise definition of what PSB is, but many theories and debates on what PSB should stand for in a democratic society, and the relationship it has and should have with the public interest, has been developed extensively by various UK academics (i.e., Keane, 1995; Scannell, 1989). The classic arguments have been mainly grounded on the assumption, as correctly highlighted by Keane (1995: 59), that the public service model is the main forum that permits the whole nation to talk to itself. This view has also been influenced by the *Habermasian* concept of the public sphere. Writing in the context of the 1980s, academics like Scannell (1989: 85) emphasized how public broadcasting and its programming served as a public good, contributing to the democratization of everyday life in the United Kingdom. Scannell (1989) stated in his examination of the BBC that the United Kingdom's PSB has helped voice the opinions of all members of society regardless of class and socioeconomic status. This is still precisely the role that is required of the public media in democratic societies, and the one it is destined to have in developing countries.

Other critical voices have pointed out that the initial motivation behind establishing PSBs in Western Europe has been one more aligned with a paternalistic stance and view of broadcasting. As the critical argument goes, the necessity of PSB comes from an *elitist* (bourgeoisie public sphere) conception or desire to see the media function in a specific way in our democratic societies, thus establishing a particular type of relationship with the public and audiences deemed at worse as patronizing. This more paternalistic stance claims that the intellectual intelligentsia knows best and is better equipped to feed 'high-brow' programs to unwilling audiences. Some of these critiques have been made by sectors of the left also in the context of the debates on the 'crisis' of PSB in the United Kingdom, and its need to rapidly adapt to a digital environment and to the changing needs and tastes of contemporary global as well as national audiences.

Comparative analyses and data taken from different European countries also reveals variations among PSB and public service media cutting across time and space and differing according to nation and to specific historical factors and types of pressures. In an age of excessive commercialization of the media and growing global economic and social inequality, the abandonment of the ideal of a media system that can cater to the public interest, be socially inclusive, boosting educational and cultural levels, and helping a society discuss its problems is a vital error. As Seneviratne (2006: 22) affirms, the audiovisual techniques, multimedia formats, and the possibilities of interactivity that PSB offers, of which the BBC and its investment in online platforms and other forms of interactivity are good examples, stresses the centrality still of its role as an educational force alongside libraries and other information resource centers. It also signals to the fact that public communication systems *can* adapt to digital technologies and new audience consumption habits and are not simply old dinosaurs which must suffer a slow death.

Jakubowicz (2006: 95) also affirms that the debate on the role of PSB in the democratic polity is a discussion about the 'values and principles governing society and social life.' It is above all an 'ideological and a sociological discussion about *the kind* (my emphasis) of society we want to live in.' It is precisely the contestation of this fact that makes the engagement with the different ideological understandings of the role of PSB so vital a task. In the current digital age context, as Jakubowicz (2006: 101) states, the concept of PSB should be understood by taking on boarder technological aspects, such as PSB's growing presence on *all platforms* (i.e., online transmissions). According still to Jakubowicz (2006: 104), to keep up with the changes in user behavior and in the media environment, PSB must be able to offer all types of services, ranging from national, generalized channels to an Internet-delivery 'personalized public service.'

Public forms of communication media undoubtedly have certain characteristics that distinguish them from commercial market media. Further, these forms can have a role in national development as well as providing a means of dialog between countries in an age of globalization. In this rapidly changing technological environment, PSB is also being obliged to refocus its aim regarding both the local *and* the global (Raboy, 1996: 5). It is precisely PSB'srole in contributing to globalization, in fostering more mutual understanding between countries and more cooperation in the fight against global and economic injustices, that makes it the more worthwhile. I will first give an overview of some of the successes of public communication policies in Europe and the United Kingdom, and their relationship to democratization and the public interest, before moving on to look at Latin American broadcasting and the current challenges to broadcasting regulation and further media reform in Brazil.

Public communication policies and regulation in Europe and the United Kingdom

The state's participation in the ownership or regulation of the broadcast media in liberal democracies has been largely based upon the need to guarantee standards of neutrality, minimizing political bias, and working to secure democratic standards. As Baldwin and Cave (1999: 9–13) state, many of the rationales behind the philosophy of regulation can be described as focusing on correcting market failures and function as attempts to produce results in accordance with the public interest. These can also be conceived as being positive examples of regulation and should be understood in opposition to censorship practices applied by the state. Notably, even in an age of globalization, the fact that states can still have a role in regulating for the public interest attests to their continuous importance in shaping the very structure of media markets. This includes their capacity to continue to be able to put legislation through that affects national media industries.

Without a doubt the search for emancipation through regulation is a delicate issue that must be rethought in the current context of multiple channels, increasing media commercialization, and the concentration and legitimacy of a market-based understanding of the public interest. Attempts at regulation in favor of the public interest nonetheless need to be differentiated from censorship, associated with the practices of authoritarian regimes. Hardy (2008: 239) argues that it is through comparative analysis that one can overcome the simplistic evaluation of the merits of the state versus the market in media regulation. It can also be seen as worthwhile in assisting in the construction of agendas for democratic media reform at both national and transnational levels. The state can have a role in assisting in the extension of the public sphere through regulation and subsidy (Hardy, 2008).

In the case of the United Kingdom, Dunleavy and O'Leary (1987) have argued that PSB regulation in the country has managed to act as a counter-weight to the press, neutralizing or balancing the biases of the partisan British newspapers and tabloids by offering more trustworthy information. Thus, the role that regulation has had in broadcasting is seen as one that is tightly connected to the public interest and to the uses of public media for educational and cultural services (Santos and Silveira, 2007), securing political coverage that is impartial between parties and in favor of the collective good.

British television with its mixed PSB tradition and commercial channels has been considered to be somewhere between the United States and the European continental model. When it comes to broadcasting regulation, the United Kingdom has also been seen as having established a sophisticated system of PSB funding that has made it easier for broadcasters to be less obsessed with audience numbers and more preoccupied with the public interest. Set up under the 2003 Communications Bill, the United Kingdom's broadcasting regulator, *Ofcom*, has set an example for media regulation in Europe.

Further, according to Forgan and Tambini (2000: 3, in Santos and Silveira, 2007: 73), regulation in the United Kingdom developed over time. With technological expansion, a system based on complaints post-transmission began to emerge while self-regulation by the sector increased (Forgan and Tambini, 2000 in Santos and Silveira, 2007). Regulation bodies, with established codes of conduct, nonetheless have traditionally supported regulation. Gradually, rules began to be created to attend more to the expectations of consumers.

The regulator *Ofcom* for instance states on its website that its main duties consist of furthering the interests of citizens *and* consumers. It also says that it is not swayed by party politics and wants to ensure fair competition.[1] *Ofcom* is further responsible for limiting publicity, establishing gender quotas, independent production, protection of privacy, combating offensive content, as well as establishing impartiality criteria. It also organizes audience consultations with the aim of analyzing content that permits a critical view of the media for the public.[2]

The ideology toward television regulation nonetheless changed from the 1980s onward with the governments of Thatcher and Reagan. These governments paved the way for the expansion of deregulation trends and the commercialization of television with the growth of cable and satellite TV. The deregulation trends that began to take place in the United Kingdom did not necessarily mean relaxing controls over program content. The commercial broadcasters in the United Kingdom for instance have onerous PSB obligations in the same way as the public broadcasters that are set out in their licenses with the ITC (Independent Television Commission).

As Gunther and Mughan (2000) affirm, TV deregulation has gone further in the United States than in the United Kingdom. The proliferation of cable and satellite were largely encouraged in the former country. The Reagan government in 1987 rejected the Fairness Doctrine on the grounds that spectrum scarcity did not justify it anymore. The Federal Communications Commission (FCC)'s allocation of the spectrum and assignment of TV licenses in the early 1950s had been initially intended to promote localism. The FCC from the 1990s onwards relaxed the Fairness Doctrine, which required broadcasting to devote a 'reasonable percentage' of broadcast time to public issues in a way that presents contrasting viewpoints.

The objective of state regulation in broadcasting has been generally defended with the view of favoring the public interest and securing an independent media. The Fairness Doctrine in the United States and the public service obligations imposed on the BBC and on other commercial (PS) broadcasters are thus quintessential of this public service ethos and their principles. Government regulation has been deemed necessary by many liberals and democratic theorists in order to ensure that the media provide the kind of information and debate required for an informed electorate (Lichtenberg, 1990). According to this argument, robust debate should be achieved more fairly through government regulation, with the state sometimes required to interfere and install measures so as to enrich public discussion and guarantee pluralism. Nevertheless, this is not to say that broadcasting regulation does not have its limits. Iyer (2006: 140) makes the case for defining regulation as being either negative or positive, where the former involves the restriction of certain types of content and the creation of loopholes for censorship or wider forms of control in opposition to the democratic public interest concerns of the latter.

Thus, broadcasting regulation can be successful overall, as it has managed to be, largely because it has been attentive to citizens and consumers' needs by responding to the public's urge for regulation around issues such as diversity, plurality, political balance, and educational purposes (Petley, 1999). The next section looks at the contradictory scenario in Latin America and the reasons for the absence of a strong public media in Brazil and a sophisticated regulatory framework for broadcasting and media regulation.

Broadcasting policy and media regulation in Brazil

In most Latin American countries, the regulation of broadcasting clashed with national and international forces standing behind commercial broadcasting. The history of PSB in the whole of the region has had a troubled life. There have been attempts at constructing a public media platform to serve the public interest that governments since the decade of the 1920s have pursued. Given its political stability in the 1930s, Uruguay managed to finance culture and its public service media (Fox, 1997). Politicians have also traditionally maintained an interest in using the state (public) media to reach out to voters and to gain political support, starting from the Vargas period in Brazil in the 1940s to the Peron years in Argentina (Fox, 1997: 13).

Since its origins in the 1920s, Latin American broadcasting has not managed to have a role in social and economic development (Waisbord, 2000). Due to largely state sponsorship, countries like Mexico and Brazil were capable of developing the largest broadcasting industries in the region. In most Latin American countries, the state performed both an arbitrary authoritarian role as well as serving as an investor in the construction of the telecommunication infrastructure and a supporter of the private media. State intervention in South America has had the main aim of reinforcing governmental powers rather than promoting democratic communications (Waisbord, 2000; Matos, 2008). The assumption that the state could have a role in promoting national development and education did exercise some influence, and these positions were mainly predominant during the 1960s and 1970s in the context of wider discussions on development.

Notably, the broadcasting model that developed in Latin American countries was very similar to that of the commercial-inspired, entertainment style encountered in the United States (i.e., Straubhaar, 2001). It consisted of privately owned television and radio stations and private newspapers financed by both private and public (state) advertising. Few companies controlled wider shares of the market, and there were very few under-funded public (state) television channels dedicated to educational interests.

In countries like Brazil and Chile, public television has had a historical record of failures. Broadcasting in Brazil has been largely built on a combination of political control and limited regulation. Various efforts have been made to strengthen the public media system since the return to democracy. Fox and Waisbord (2002: xxii) point out how the whole Latin American region has had a weak, anti-trust tradition of legislation and a culture of promiscuous relationships established between governmental officials and the media that undermined aspirations for the democratization of the media. Educational and state channels are mainly owned by sectors of the Catholic church and oligarchic politicians. National broadcasting policies in Brazil have also been traditionally aligned with political interests and state control. Broadcasting regulation has been under the control of the Ministry of Communication, with presidents using the distribution of radio and television licenses as a form of political patronage. According to the 1988 Brazilian Constitution, the executive body has the power over television and radio concessions, with congress having to ratify or not the decision. Because of this, state interventionism in Brazil has been characterized by a mixture of *clientelistic* practices, political patronage and censorship control, and less by democratic concerns.

Guedes-Bailey and Jambeiro-Barbosa (2008: 53) have underlined how Vargas's *Estado Novo* government saw broadcasting as a service that needed to be regulated by the state, as the electromagnetic spectrum was public property. Since 1932, when the first Broadcasting Act was signed, radio and television licenses were subject to federal government approval (Guedes-Bailey and Jambeiro-Barbosa, 2008). According to the authors (2008: 53), the educational purposes of Decrees 20.047 and 21.111 served to set the standards for the nationalistic ideologies that influenced policy-making in the country. Caparelli (1986 in Fox, 1997) point out that between 1965 and 1978, the code enabled the military government to distribute almost 60 percent of the television channels in Brazil to their friends.

Thus, the relationship between the public media and the state has always been an uneasy one in the history of broadcasting in Brazil. The president still has control over radio and television concessions, although current civil society pressures are for a more transparent system. Former president Jose Sarney in the mid-1980s was accused of granting radio and television concessions to Congressmen in exchange for a longer term in office (Guedes-Bailey and Jambeiro-Barbosa, 2008: 54). Brazil has also traditionally had a weak public media sector, composed mainly of the respected but fund-starved TV Cultura in Sao Paulo and its counter-part TVE in Rio, as well as other regional outlets controlled by local politicians and by sectors of the evangelical Church.[3] Other stations include legislative television (Senate TV), community channels, and television stations linked to state and federal governments as well as to universities.

In their fear of a stronger public media sector that poses a threat to the commercial media, market liberals in Brazil have pointed to the bad state of the structures of the public media. The promiscuous relationships shared between the weak and partisan state media with politicians stand as among the main reasons to condemn the restructuring of the PSB platform. Lima (2007) has underlined how at least 50 percent of the more than 2,000 community stations permitted to operate by the Ministry of Communications in Brazil belong to people linked to politicians. Further, according to the journalists Felipe Bachtold and Silvia Freire in a report published in the Folha de Sao Paulo newspaper, local stations of the private main television channels, Globo, Record, SBT and Bandeirantes and small radios are owned by 61 politicians elected during the 2010 elections. Of the 61 elected MPs, at least two participate in the Congressional Communications Commission. In the State of Maranhao, the four biggest television stations are in the hands of politicians, including the local TV Globo that belongs to the Sarney family, SBT that has links to Senator Edson Lobao (PMDB), Record that belongs to the MP Roberto Rocha (PSDB), and Bandeirantes that is connected to Manuel Ribeiro (PTB).[4]

As Azevedo (2006: 34) claims, although the current legislation limits to five the number of television channels per group, the national television stations explore loopholes in the law. They associate themselves with stations owned by others that merely repeat the channels or the national program. Thus, PSB does not have a democratic history or a genuine commitment to the public interest because the market media has largely taken on this role and being allowed to develop unregulated. When one looks at the series of communication policy measures in the country, one is dazzled by the complexity and the number of laws and regulations that change in accordance to the political mood and market pressures (Santos and Silveira, 2007: 50).

The ties with the state were weakened from the 1990s onward but are still somewhat maintained. The state continues to control and to regulate vital legislation concerning the media system, many of which benefit the private media. The 1988 Federal Brazilian Constitution confirmed the government's authority as well as congress' co-responsibility in licensing radio and television broadcasting services, as stipulated in Article 223 (Guedes-Bailey and Jambeiro-Barbosa, 2008: 99). Certain legislations that were of interest for the media market were approved in the last few years by the federal government, including the privatization of the telecommunications system and the permission for the participation of foreign capital in the national market after the revision of articles in the Constitution.

As Saravia (2008: 72) reminds us, the whole notion of communication rights by itself is a relatively new phenomenon in the country. The first investigations of the concept occurred in the 1960s. The right to communication was established in the 1988 Constitution, mainly in Article 220 that prohibits restrictions on the freedom of expression. Although the 1988 Constitution has contained advancements, critics have argued that not much has been done to actually make these rights effective (Saravia, 2008: 75). The constitutional articles that deal with social communications to start with have not all been officially regulated.

Political liberalization in Latin America has undoubtedly opened the avenue in the continent to revisit debates on media democratization and public communications in a changed atmosphere from the New World Information and Communication Order (NWICO) discussions of the 1970s. In Brazil, pressure has been applied in favor of the formulation of a media regulatory framework capable of providing wider access to citizens to the means of media production. Debates on the necessity for media reform and regulation in Brazil culminated in the realization of a conference on the theme in December 2009, Confecom (National Communication Conference).

Notably, the formation of a sharply divisive and black and white scenario of 'big business and media barons' on one side and 'trade unions' on the other during the conference regarding the creation of media regulation policies exacerbated the ideological tensions between the camps, making negotiations difficult and impeding further advancements during Dilma Rousseff's administration. Civil society groups are currently defending the ratification of the articles of the 1988 Constitution that deal with regional programming and that suggest a preference for cultural and educational television outputs. The Confecom debates also included proposals on the adoption of new broadcasting regulation, wider transparency in TV, and radio concessions and an end to the marginalization of community radio.

New media policy measures aimed at stimulating diversity and the public sphere have begun to be slowly implemented throughout the region with Argentina emerging as a model for countries like Brazil. The Law of Audiovisual Communication Services was presented by president Cristina Kirchner and approved on September 17, 2009, by the Chamber of Deputies. This law proposes limits on the power of media conglomerates and limits any private television station to only 35 percent of the media. It demands official publicity to be regulated and licenses to be renewed every ten years, with no firm alone having more than ten radio and television concessions. It also allocates a third of the electronic radio spectrum to nonprofit organizations, prohibits horizontal and vertical concentration, and establishes minimum quotas for national productions. Experts are seeing it as ground-breaking and a sign that the whole region might follow this example soon afterwards (Moraes, 2009).[5]

As Moraes (2009) has argued, the debates taking place in Brazil in the last few years concerning the communication field and the role of the state can actually contribute to revitalize the public sphere and the regulation capacity of the state in socioeconomic and cultural life, reinforcing in the state a social-democratic ethos. Some of the key governmental initiatives that have encountered some level of success, as well as other proposals and challenges for media democratization in Brazil, are explored next.

Challenges for the Brazilian public media and future reforms

The former government of Luis Inacio Lula da Silva (2002–2010) has been accused by critics as not having done enough to change more sharply the concentrated media environment in Brazil (Moraes, 2009; Lugo-Ocando, 2008) beyond the realization of the Confecom debates at the end of 2009 and the creation of TV Brasil in 2008. Political commitments in the area of democratic communications were announced by the government nonetheless, with the program for the social communications sector that the Lula candidature presented in 2006 underscoring that the democratization of communications was a necessary step for further democratization. It underlined knowledge as an important tool in the development of a nation, envisioning two main strategies of action, including the modernization of the current fragmented legislation through the creation of a more adequate model suited to the convergence era. It also defended the ratification of measures set forth in the constitution aimed at guaranteeing a market where three communication systems (public, private, and state) can operate.

Confecom emerged as an important milestone in the recognition of various sectors of society of the urgency of discussing public policies on communications. The debates resulted in the approval of 672 proposals put forward by representatives of the former government, social movements, and entrepreneurs. The ratification of the constitutional articles on the production of regional, educational, and cultural programming, as well as Article 220 that prohibits the formation of monopolies, were some of the key proposals. These initiatives were met with hostility from key media players, with newspapers like O Globo and Estado de Sao Paulo classifying the measures of Confecom as an attempt to control the press by radical sectors of the government.[6] A key novelty of the debates was the significant presence of both progressive bloggers and entrepreneurs. The outcome of the proposals ranged from solid propositions, such as the necessity of more technical rigor in the system of granting concessions to radio and television stations, legislation on media concentration, to other more controversial suggestions that many deemed less realistic and that could either open loopholes for censorship or raise tensions with the already reluctant market-driven media, such as proposals that argue for wider systems of 'control' of the media and punishment for journalists.

Various scholars (e.g., Saravia, 2008) also defended the strengthening of community media as a means of democratizing further social relations in Brazil, the registration of all of the concessions in order to evaluate if those given to particular entities were not operating against the law, the implementation of Internet regulation, and the ratification of Article 221 of the constitution that obliges television stations to prioritize national content. The initial official commitment toward the adoption of a new regulatory framework for the media and telecommunications committed to the public interest, and intending on explaning the outdated laws created before the dictatorship, was taken on by sectors of the government during the First National TV Forum debates held in 2007 and shortly afterwards in the Confecom debates held in 2009 in Brasília.

Civil society players and organized groups have underscored the necessity of building a solid regulatory framework capable of replacing outdated laws such as the Codigo Brasileiro de Telecomunicaçoes (1962), following from some of the initiatives of the 1990s that include the creation of the Cable Law (1995) and the Lei Geral de Telecomunicaçoes (LGT, 1997). The latter two were seen as having mainly benefited commercial groups. According to Bolaño (2007), the public policy laws for the communication sector mainly consist of the Codigo de Telecomunicaçoes and the 1997 LGT. Broadcasting is still controlled by the old law, whereas cable television and other forms of paid television are linked to the telecommunications sector.

The LGT law was created during the presidency of Fernando Henrique Cardoso. According to Bolaño (2007: 41), the then Minister of Communications, Sergio Motta, implemented a broadcasting concession decree (Law 8,666) that altered the procedures with the intention of moralizing and modernizing them. This did not impede the Cardoso government from making political use of the radio and television concessions. The separation between radio and television regulation from telecommunications was also attempted in vain by the former Minister of Communications, Pimenta da Veiga, in 2001.

Proposals were put forward that favored the de-politicization of the process and the adoption of more technical criteria, such as those carried out by Anatel (National Agency of Telecommunications). These however were also defeated (Bolaño, 2007: 47–93).[7] According to Bolaño (2007), during the first Lula administration there were clashes within the government's own forces: the Ministry of Culture supporting the democratization of culture and communications, while the Ministry of Communications took a more right-wing stance.

Thus the Cardoso years mainly saw the passing of liberal reforms in the area of telecommunications, such as the LGT. Some of the proposals on the strengthening of competition came close to the progressive stance and its defense of cultural diversity. A proximity between the two camps occurred during the end of the Cardoso government around the defense of Anatel (Bolaño, 2007: 90–92). Conservative forces in congress however managed to further impede advancements during the Cardoso administrations (1994–2002).

In an article about the clashes between the Lula government and the media ahead of the 2010 elections, Lima (2010) argued that the eight years of the Lula government did not represent a threat to the media. The only project of public policy, already indicated in Article 223 of the 1988 Constitution, was the implementation of Empresa Brasileira de Comunicaçao (EBC), which can be seen also as a complement to the mainstream media. Similarly to the ways in which many Americans oppose an active regulatory role for the state because of their fear that state intervention will encourage partisan manipulation, in Brazil similar worries were expressed at the time of the emergence of the EBC, which is responsible for TV Brasil. Nonetheless, many argued that attacks on the EBC died after the organization managed to show commitments to professionalism.

Lima further underlined how the former Lula government backed down on various issues, including the creation of the Federal Council of Journalism (in 2004), the rejection of the ratification of the new regulation for community radio (2003 and 2005), the project concerning the General Law of Mass Communications, and the withdrawal of proposals on communication rights. In the last six months of its administration, the former Lula government prepared a series of proposals for the communication sector, including the idea of creating a new regulatory agency, the National Agency of Communications (ANC), to regulate the content of radio and TV. The text stipulates that firms can charge for broadcasting programs considered offensive, also prohibiting politicians with mandates to be owners of radio and television stations as well as advocating improvements in the current process of new station channel concessions, making them more transparent to the wider public.

After conducting a seminar with regulators and experts from across the world on the topic, the Brazilian government announced its intention to implement new regulation policies, which were put on hold and given to the government of Dilma Rousseff (2011–2014) to evaluate. The Ministry of Communications of the Dilma government hinted at the possibility of establishing two communication agencies:[8] Anatel will continue monitoring technical aspects, whereas the other agency will ensure that the articles of the Brazilian Constitution will be respected. The proposals on media reform have also been abandoned by the Dilma government, with many civil society players seeing this move as a step backward from the commitments on media democratization assumed by the previous administration.

How then should public policy be developed in a way that guarantees commitment to the public interest while also not 'suffocating' but complementing the market? This is currently a core dilemma that civil society players and others interested in media democratization need to tackle as a means of undermining the resistance of the market to media reform and regulation. To start with, there must be more debate on the differences in regulation for the public interest in democracies and attempts of censoring the media, as I discussed briefly in this chapter. For there are differences between a democratic public service model from one of direct government control and interference, more associated to the practices upheld by authoritarian regimes. The former requires the placement of regulatory structures that institutionally guarantee balance and quality in programming and information that safeguard public communications from political and economic pressures.

Many Brazilian journalists and academics however have expressed doubts in regards to the real intentions of politicians to deepen media democratization. They hope that this not a distant dream and that change will inevitably come in the midst of the persistent pressure for the advancement of the democratization project. In the light of the massive protests for further reforms in health, education, public services, and transport that occurred all over Brazil in June 2013, it remains to be seen how requests for media reform can add to these wider demands in a persistent way that results in more signs of reform in the years to come.

Conclusion

Since the 1980s, countries like the United Kingdom have seen a decline in the reliance on the state and PSB, including ties with communities and political parties, shifting toward a resurgence of the market forces in all spheres of social, political, economic, and cultural life. Changes in European societies have had a direct effect on the media: political scientists, journalists, and academics have been engaging in ideological debates on the role that the media, and especially public communication structures and PSB, still have in advanced democracies. Questions arise regarding how public communication structures should be preserved in an age of increasing economic pressures, commercialization, and shifting consumer habits. In contrast to Europe, public communications are emerging as potential tools for development in Latin American nations like Brazil.

Many Brazilian academics have underscored how the country has advanced less in media reform in contrast to other Latin American nations. In the eight years of the Lula government, as some scholars have stressed, there has been little concrete advancement in the area of media reform and broadcasting, with the media scenario continuing to be heavily concentrated and affecting the strengthening of media pluralism in the country. The Internet has emerged as a space for the proliferation of debate, stimulating an incipient but growing potential for a more vibrant media environment. Nonetheless, the realization of the Confecom debates and the implementation of TV Brasil, followed by the unification of various state and educational channels, the granting of some funds to support regional players, and the commitment assumed by the government in favor of media reform and broadcasting regulation, have been some key achievements when it comes to media democratization.[9] It seems evident that the debate regarding public communications in Brazil needs to move beyond the more straightforward issue of 'to regulate' or 'not to regulate,' or both being understood as a form of censorship, to one of *how* to design a model of broadcasting regulation and media reform that can be capable of contemplating the interests of the country's multiple publics.

Notes

1. The broadcasting duties include the licensing of all United Kingdom commercial TV and radio services, such as (1) TV channels; (2) digital TV services like Sky and Virgin Media and digital radio; (3) Internet TV services including Home Choice, and (4) community radio.

2. In Portugal, the regulation agency ERC is independent and monitors the written press as well as broadcasting. It also has the National Authority of Communications, which regulates the market of telecommunications.
3. The other public television channels in Brazil are: TVE-RS, Parana Educativa, TV Cultura SC, TVE-ES, TVE Bahia, TV Ceara, Rede Minas, TV Brasil Central, TV Rio Grande do Norte, TV Cultura PH, and TV Palmas. The public sector platform and decision-making organ comprises the state radio station, Radiobras, Radio MEC, the Cabinet of the Presidency and the Rio state television, TVE Brasil.
4. See '61 politicos eleitos sao proprietarios de radios e TVs' – (61 politicians are owners of radio and TVs' – Bächtold and Freire (2010). The law permits politicians to be partners in radio and TV stations, but not to manage them.
5. Will Cristina do what Lula could not do? – 'Conseguira Cristina fazer o que Lula nao fez?,' Lima (2009). Another editorial published by the newspaper *Estado de Sao Paulo* (15/10/09) criticized the measure and accused it of being an attack on press liberty. The law nonetheless has been supported in the country by various sectors of society, including the opposition, as well as social organizations and universities. It was also approved by the Freedom of Expression section of the Organization of American States (OEA) and by Unesco.
6. See 'O Estado de Sao Paulo e O Globo criticam documento da Conferencia de Cultura' – *The State of Sao Paulo and O Globo criticize document of the Conference of Culture*, Rosa (2010).
7. During the decade of the 1990s, various independent regulation agencies with state functions and public interest commitments emerged. Anatel incorporates mechanisms such as public councils, present also in the cable legislation. It is an organ that perhaps can be seen as the Brazilian equivalent to Ofcom, although its duties relate to telecommunications and not broadcasting. Some of the key public interest principles that are stated in the mission of Anatel could be applied to the regulation of the media, including its intention of developing a competitive environment for Brazil telecommunications (we could substitute 'communications').
8. 'Bernardo diz que discussão caminha para ter duas agências na área de comunicação' – *Bernardo says that discussion is about having two communication agencies*, Ministério das Comunicações (2011).
9. See 'Novas leis e projetos na America Latina esquentam polemica entre midia e governos' – *New Laws and projects in Latin America heat polemic between media and governments*, Viana (2010).

References

Azevedo, F. A. (2006) 'Democracia e Midia no Brasil: um balanço dos anos recentes,' pp. 23–46 in J. O. Goulart (ed.) *Midia e Democracia* (Sao Paulo: Annablume Editora).

Bächtold, F. and Freire, S. (2010, October 17) '61 políticos eleitos são proprietários de rádios ou TVs,' *Folha de S. Paulo*. Available at http://bit.ly/1dodn4b (accessed August 2013).

Baldwin, R. and Cave, M. (1999) *Understanding Regulation: Theory, Strategy and Practice* (Oxford: Oxford University Press).

Bolaño, C. (2007) *Qual a Logica das Politicas de Comunicaçao no Brasil?* (Sao Paulo: Editora Paulus).

Dunleavy, P. and O'Leary, B. (1987) *Theories of the State: The Politics of Liberal Democracy* (Handmills: MacMillan Education).

Fox, E. (1997) *Latin American Broadcasting: From Tango to Telenovela* (Bedforshire: University of Luton Press).

Fox, E. and Waisbord, S. (eds) (2002) *Latin Politics, Global Media* (Austin: University of Texas Press).

Guedes-Bailey, O. and Jambeiro-Barbosa, O. F. (2008) 'The media in Brazil: a historical overview of Brazilian broadcasting politics,' pp. 47–59 in Jairo Lugo-Ocando (ed.) *The Media in Latin America* (Berkshire: Open University Press).

Gunther, R. And Mughan, A. (eds) (2000) *Democracy and the Media: A Comparative Perspective* (New York: Cambridge University Press).

Hardy, J. (2008) *Western Media Systems* (London: Routledge).

Iyer, V. (2006) 'Legal and regulatory aspects of public service broadcasting,' pp. 133–149 in Indrajit Banerjee and Kalinga Seneviratne (eds) *Public Service Broadcasting in the Age of Globalization* (Singapore: Asian Media Information and Communication Centre).

Jakubowicz, K. (2006) 'Keep the essence, change (almost) everything else: redefining PSB for the 21st century,' pp. 94–117 in Indrajit Banerjee and Kalinga Seneviratne (eds) *Public Service Broadcasting in the Age of Globalization* (Singapore: Asian Media Information and Communication Centre).

Keane, J. (1995) 'Structural transformations of the public sphere,' *Communication Review*, 1(1): 1–22.

Lichtenberg, J. (1990) 'Foundations and limits of freedom of the press,' pp. 102–135 in J. Lichtenberg (ed.) *Democracy and the Mass Media* (New York: Cambridge University Press).

Lima, V. A. de (org.) (2007) *A Mídia nas eleições de 2006* (Sao Paulo: Fundacao Perseu Abramo).

Lima, V. A. de (2009, March 10) 'Conseguirá Cristina fazer o que Lula não fez?,' *Observatório de Imprensa*. Available at http://bit.ly/1dodNr7 (accessed July 2009).

Lima, V. A. de (2010, September 25) 'Razões para a hostilidade crescente entre mídia e governo,' *Núcleo Piratininga de Comunicação*. Available at http://bit.ly/1epcMO0 (accessed June 2013).

Lugo-Ocando, J. (2008) (ed.) *The Media in Latin America* (New York: MacGraw-Hill).

Matos, C. (2008) *Journalism and Political Democracy in Brazil* (Maryland: Lexington Books).

Ministério das Comunicações (2011, February 15) 'Bernardo diz que discussão caminha para ter duas agências na área de comunicação.' Available at http://bit.ly/1doeQYd (accessed May 2012).

Moraes, D. de (2009) *A Batalha da Midia: Propostas e Politicas de Comunicacao na America Latina e Outros Ensaios* (Rio de Janeiro: Paes e Rosas).

Petley, J. (1999) 'The regulation of media content,' pp.143–157 in J. Strokes and A. Reading (eds) *The Media in Britain: Current Debates and Development* (Basingstoke: Palgrave).

Raboy, M. (ed.) (1996) *Public Broadcasting for the 21st Century* (Luton: University of Luton Press).

Rosa, T. (2010, January 19) 'O Estado de Sao Paulo e O Globo criticam documento da Conferencia de Cultura,' *Portal Imprensa*.

Santos, S. dos and Silveira, E. da (2007) 'Servico publico e interesse publico nas comunicacoes,' pp. 49–83 in M. C. Ramos and S. dos Santos (orgs.) *Politicas de comunicacao – buscas teorias e praticas* (Sao Paulo: Paulus).

Saravia, E. (2008) 'O novo papel regulatorio do Estado e suas consequencias na midia' pgs. 59–71 in E. Saravia, P. E. Matos and O. Penna Pieranti (orgs.) *Democracia e regulação dos meios de comunicação de massa* (Rio de Janeiro: FGV).

Scannell, P. (1989) 'Public Service Broadcasting and Modern Public Life,' *Media, Culture & Society*, 11(2): 135–166.

Seneviratne, K. (2006) 'Definition and History of Public Service Broadcasting,' pgs. 9–59 in I. Banerjee and K. Seneviratne (eds) *Public Service Broadcasting in the Age of Globalization* (Singapore: Asian Media Information and Communication Centre).

Straubhaar, J. D. (2001) 'Brazil: the Role of the State in World TV,' pp. 133–153 in N. Morris and S. Waisbord (eds) *Media and Globalisation – Why the State Matters* (Oxford/New York: Rowman and Littlefield Publishers).

Viana, N. (2010, September 29) 'Novas leis e projetos na America Latina esquentam polemica entre midia e governos,' *Última Instância*. Available at http://bit.ly/1dofqF9 (accessed January 2013).

Waisbord, S. (2000) *Watchdog Journalism in South America: News, Accountability and Democracy* (New York: Columbia University Press).

12
Globalization and History in Brazil: Communication, Culture, and Development Policies at a Crossroads

César Bolaño

Introduction

Content production has recently become a matter of policy concern in Brazil. In this country, significant advances have been registered in the areas of Information and Communication Technology (ICT), technological convergence, and the Internet. It is possible to affirm that a historic shift is underway that calls into question the hegemony of the symbolic production of culture. As it is argued, the configuration of cultural production and the media structure in Brazil have responded to accommodations and impacts from external and globalized processes throughout history.

In the first section, this chapter very briefly reviews Celso Furtado's ideas on the genesis and development of Brazilian culture, which serve as a theoretical and historical framework. Then, within a broader context of international hegemony, the chapter defines the contentious relationship between culture and development in 20th century Brazil. This is compared, in the third section of the chapter, with the case of India since it shares with Brazil similar trends, stages, and problems of development, though in terms of cultural and communication policy the latter country has followed a more consistent and self-determinant path. And, in the last section, the chapter ends with a reflection on the general structural changes and their future prospects in Brazil.

Celso Furtado and Brazilian culture

According to Furtado (1984), to understand the roots of Brazilian culture, one must focus on Portugal during the 16th century, a time of intense cultural creativity in Europe wherein two trends were prominent: the secular rationalization of life and the expansion of the world's borders. Whereas these two trends decisively strengthened the base of the accumulation process in Europe, Portugal played a key role especially in the first stages of the second one. In this sense, Furtado regards the expansion of Portuguese language, culture, and technology as:

> A remarkable anticipation of modernity [since it implied] a coordinated effort [directed by the state] on multiple fronts, given that it involved simultaneously developing boat-building techniques suited to long-distance ocean travel, training navigators and other specialists, developing navigation skills on the high seas, accumulating cartographic knowledge, opening new sea and land routes. (Furtado, 1984: 19)

The threat of unification of the Iberian Peninsula under the command of Castile triggered an 'early alliance' between the Portuguese monarchy and the bourgeoisie of Lisbon that enabled this first ambitious project of European commercial expansion.

Brazil is a direct outcome of this process of articulation between the state and commercial capital, which according to Furtado foreshadows the creation of the English and Dutch trading companies – institutions of private law performing public functions. Portugal's constant concerns to preserve and expand vast territories translated into a model of exploitation based on export-focused agricultural enterprises, which became a key component of the Atlantic System. By providing a bridge between Africa, Europe, and America under the control of big Portuguese commercial capital and the latter's hegemonic ownership of the slave trade, this exploitation constituted a powerful lever of primitive accumulation in the Old Continent (Novais, 1979), which eventually benefited England and the First Industrial Revolution.

As a result of this process, two elements characterize Brazilian culture, according again to Furtado (1984). Firstly, the formation of the Brazilian people was extremely asymmetrical, given that Portuguese immigrants not only brought with them substantial technical superiority but 'continued to feed on European cultural resources,' while 'aborigines and Africans had been isolated from their respective cultural roots and subsequently deprived of their own languages, whereupon they lost their sense of cultural identity' (Furtado, 1984: 20).

Secondly, trade – the heart of the economic model – continued to be mediated by metropolitan agents, thus preventing the establishment of a local merchant class in Brazil capable of challenging the central power (in Portugal), as was to occur in Spanish America where this local mercantile bourgeoisie eventually helped to bring about the independence movements. In contrast, Brazil´s independence in 1822 was the work of experienced public officials, like José Bonifácio de Andrada e Silva, while large-scale commercial activities continued in the hands of Portuguese traders.

Thus, 'in the absence of a powerful merchant class, everything depended on the State and the Church. Cultural creation reflected the preeminence of these institutions [...] The historical context in which Brazil was formed [...] maintained its features previous to pre-humanistic Europe' (Furtado, 1984: 20). The result of this near-stagnation was dramatic: 'the extraordinary performance of the Brazilian cultural process in this period was marked by increasing estrangement from a Europe undergoing rapid cultural change' (Furtado, 1984: 21).

Europe's Industrial Revolution boosted a massive increase in labor productivity, intensified capital accumulation, and enhanced the amount and diversification of consumption. At the same time, it favored the emergence of a country like Brazil that specialized in agricultural products for export and allowed it the 'access to modern technology in the form of consumer products without having to modernize labor productivity' (Furtado, 1984: 22). The cultural asymmetry of Brazilian society was maintained by the rapid expansion of international demand. Its ruling elites accustomed to the constant importation of luxury goods and completely identified with external values.

This imitative behavior of the national elites, in thrall to 'dependent modernization,' reduced the popular cultural expressions that were forming into 'a symbol of backwardness, giving no importance to any non-European cultural heritage and refusing to value homegrown artistic creativity' (Furtado, 1984: 23). However, during the three centuries of colonial rule, local cultural manifestations developed. As the author claims, they were 'although Portuguese in theme and style, incorporated to local motifs a whole range of values held by the dominated peoples and cultures' (Furtado, 1984: 20).

Culture and Empire: the general issue of development in the 20th century

In Latin America, industrialization and capitalist expansionism arrived in the last decades of the 19th century at a time when monopoly capitalism was already fully entrenched in the central countries. During the 1930s, industrialization strategies based on import substitution were launched in countries like Brazil, Mexico, and Argentina. With the end of World War II, many of the external constraints that had forced Latin American economies to initiate industrialization through import-substitution programs were overcome, and the majority retreated to their former status. In some cases, particularly in Mexico and Brazil, state planning was instrumental in completing the industrialization process, internalizing the conditions for capital reproduction but without either eliminating social inequalities (quite the contrary) or terminating their dependence on financial capital and technological flows from the core countries (Cardoso de Mello, 1982).

In the case of Brazil, the aforementioned dichotomy between the ruling class and the popular sectors (despised by the elites) allowed the latter to continue 'their process of development with considerable autonomy. This allowed the non-European elements of popular culture to consolidate, and helped creative forces to expand in a more uninhibited fashion, regardless of the culture of the ruling classes' (Furtado, 1984: 23). During the years of industrialization, the political class that arrived with the Revolution of 1930 decided to use these features to create a new political hegemony based on a national popular culture consonant with other Latin American populisms. This culture, especially from the Revolution of 1930 onwards, was expressed principally in music, but also in a wide variety of other cultural manifestations, such as *fiestas*, football matches, and kick-dancing performances (capoeira), all of which represent behavior patterns and lifestyles typical of the complexities of Brazilian popular culture, its mixed-race population, and its regional peculiarities. This discourse, reflected in cultural and media production, was to be shattered in the late 1970s and 1980s by new global transformations whose initial traits emerged after the war.

In the postwar years, with the world divided into two antagonistic power blocs, development became a key issue. In the case of Latin America, the cultural imitative model of traditional elites was abruptly shaken by a devastated and divided Europe. Moreover, within the framework of the Cold War, the Soviet-style option adopted by Cuba rang alarms for the United States and for most local elites that made them aware of the urgent need to set an agenda focused on new dependent development strategies.[1] At this time the United States cultural industry consolidated in the world with links both to its military and academic establishment.

The theoretical framework of communication projects designed to benefit development (e.g., diffusionist approach) was advanced by the American sociological approaches based upon the so-called 'Communication Sciences' discipline. These ideas led to the creation of a new hegemonic structure that favored the new material and spiritual culture of North American monopoly capitalism over the European tradition of economic or sociological thought. In this respect, US hegemony encompassed technological elements emanating from the country's dynamic military-industrial complex, as well as cultural elements that determined the patterns of production and consumption, behavior models, lifestyles, and so forth, which taken together ensured social reproduction. A complete cultural, material, and spiritual revolution took place in the scientific and social areas in the United States. Its news agency networks befitted a model of political organization, representing a world view imbued with certain values and behavior patterns and even influencing the building of science and technology systems in which the humanities were beginning to play an increasingly vital role.

The cultural industry and the major mass media systems form part of the plethora of innovations that have flowed from the new international capitalist hegemonic structure under the aegis of the United States, colonizing what Habermas (1984) calls the *Lebenswelt* or lifeworld, This capitalist hegemony intensively resorts to propaganda for legitimizing capitalist accumulation (Bolaño, 2000a). After the war, it quickly spread throughout the world, manifesting significant local peculiarities but always ensuring the global hegemonic features of the *American Way of Life*. Such hegemony is achieved by forging links between national TV and radio broadcasting oligopolies and monopolies and Hollywood's global oligopoly, the American music industry and its show business. The collapse of Communism deepened and globalized these US models.

Communication, cultural hegemony, and development

Since the 1980s, the economy of the culture and communication industries has experienced a fundamental shift caused by the restructuring of capitalism arising from the major breakdown in the postwar pattern of growth. It is interesting to compare Brazil's situation with a country like India, whose trajectories of economic development and the culture and communication industries can be seen as an alternative paradigm to that adopted in most Latin American countries following the end of the industrialization through import-substitution policies and the beginning of the authoritarian cycles of the 1960s and 1970s.

The model of regulation (in the broad French Regulation School sense) of the so-called 'Glorious Thirties' (1945–1975) was characterized throughout the world by the remarkable stability of market structures and of the hegemonic actors involved, especially in the telecommunications and television sectors. The latter was the core of an entire system of cultural industries that had rapidly evolved since the advent of mass written media at the beginning of the 20th century that set the pace for the emergence of brand new industries. Products such as black and white movies, then color movies, radio, monochrome TV, color TV, LPs, cassette tapes, VHS, DVDs, and the like generated an entire new range of entertainment, culture, and leisure that made very substantial global inroads into the way of life of whole populations.

Although constrained by the available frequencies or the cable network monopolies, two paradigms (one American and one European) existed in the audiovisual and telecommunications sectors. These sectors, especially in the case of telecommunications, effectively complemented each other and were instrumental in upholding the regulatory powers invested in national states and local industries. Thus, the global cultural industries, dominated by the U.S. 'majors,' were unable to undermine the power of the state monopolies or the national oligopolistic radio and TV markets. However, by the 1980s, the United States restructured its policy in support of the expansion of the corporations and global markets dominated by its own gigantic corporations. The new policies brought into question the telecommunications models that have been in force since the postwar years.

As a result, the entire global telecommunications system was forced to adapt and conform to this US strategy. In Europe, the public television monopoly was already suffering heavy pressures for reform, on the one hand from those who wanted more democracy and participation in the telecommunications sectors, and on the other from the corporate sector seeking more profitable investment opportunities. These questionings were supported by the United States and shattered the stability of local markets in different ways (Bolaño, 2000b; Bolaño, 1997).

As for the cultural and communication industries, particularly since the privatization of the Internet in 1995, the number of actors entering the field grew rapidly – including small specialist firms as well as the new capitalistic oligopolies representing powerful interests in sectors such as telecommunications that were eager to exploit opportunities for financial gain from the new advances brought about by technological convergence. The challenges were, and remain, manifold (as are the different approaches).

Brazil radically changed– and unfavorably, one must say, regarding countries like Spain – its telecommunications policies. While Spain decided to keep Telefónica to compete in the international markets, the Brazilian government of Fernando Henrique Cardoso preferred to split up Telebrás and sell it to foreign capital. Unfortunately, the process also undermined an important telecommunications research and development center that could have proved crucial to improving Brazil's competitiveness in the so-called knowledge economy. In the end, Telefónica, based in Madrid, eventually replaced Telebrás in the global ranking of telecommunications firms, drawing strength from its natural market (Spain) and from the old São Paulo subsidiary of Telebrás.

It is however perhaps more interesting to draw a comparison with India, another BRICS country like Brazil.[2] In India, education as a driving developmental force is also based on the emergence of television, which was introduced in 1959 as part of a UNESCO educational experiment. While initially confined to the area around Delhi, transmissions were gradually extended to other areas in the 1960s and 1970s. By 1965, a regular public television service was established and in 1976 the Doordarshan appeared, a public agency (separated from All India Radio) that controlled all TV broadcasting until 1990. The Doordarshan focused on public service and 'education for development,' with little entertainment content. Entertainment was left to the popular and well-endowed movie market, whose *star system* was implanted in the 1920s and 1930s with the advent of India's first major film studios (Deprez, 2006).

An important element worth considering in any comparison between Indian and Latin American TV is Indian television's strong links with the aforementioned powerful and popular film industry. This industry was born largely as an entertainment outlet for a society heavily leveraged toward, and fascinated by, strong imagery (as are many Latin American societies). Thus, while Indian TV was initially conceived almost exclusively as an educational means in pursuit of the developmental aims of successive Indian governments – centered on culturally unifying a multiethnic and multilingual population – the national homegrown cinema now popularly known as 'Bollywood' succeeded in constructing a parallel form of unity through popular entertainment by exploring the traditional rich iconography of India. Along this process, the Indian filmmaking industry consolidated a unique and powerful *star system,* comparable only to Hollywood.

Eventually, however, TV moved closer to Bollywood, and it is possible to affirm that the growing popularity of Indian public television from the 1980s (and especially from the 1990s) owed much to the integration of the two industries, whereas, in Latin America, the situation is the opposite:

> Latin America, throughout its history, has not possessed the capacity to establish a genuine film industry, able to compete with US movie production in its own domestic markets and even less so internationally. It is true that at given moments domestic film industries have made their mark in Brazil, Argentina, Mexico or Cuba, but in general they never evolved, with the possible exception of Mexico in the 1950s, into a powerful industry, as in other places such as India or Japan. (Bolaño, Moreno Domínguez and Santos, 2006)

However, the strongest spot of Latin America in cultural industries has been television. Brazilian television is a prime example of a successful Latin American private TV industry. Unlike the Indian model, this success is acutely related to the concentration and centralization of powerful economic resources in a handful of TV companies, among which the dominant one is Globo. As a result, competitiveness has been reduced, while decisions on communications policy (as well as constant interference in national policy) have always tended to serve the particular interests of the hegemonic Globo corporation. Curiously, Globo has come to be viewed internationally as a 'national flagship' for Brazil in the global television industry.

Conversely, in India, state public television has since Nehru been regarded as the instrument of a consistent developmental policy, influenced not only by Soviet socialism, as Camille Deprez avers (2006: 34), but also by the public service traditions inherited from Britain, and perhaps surprisingly by an additional boost provided by developmental concepts emanating from Latin America.

Indian media developments were marked by the presence of two essential elements: First, a strong 'local' culture influencing the emergence of a particular techno/aesthetic pattern (Bolaño, 2000a) in different areas of television production. The links between TV and the national film industry in India is key. The filmmaking industry provided a substantial barrier (a kind of cultural resistance) against the incursion of foreign, especially American, program content, and at the same time it projected the Indian products onto the international stage. Second, the local developmental strategy, unlike Latin America in the 1960s and 1970s, ensured a degree of autonomy in economic policy that was not affected by the liberalization of the 1990s. The process was conducted, as in China, in a controlled manner consistent with the consumption patterns of the newly emerging urban middle class – the basis for any sustainable development project and which only occurred in Brazil from 2002 onwards. Thus, while increasing the competitiveness of its television production, in line with the country's growing success in the global economy, India has unified and expanded its domestic consumer market and is now able to offer its population a broad, rich, and diverse range of television contents, drawing substantially on local cultural inputs.

Under these conditions, it is no surprise that in such a country a broad social consensus exists on maintaining the public television broadcasting system, which successfully coexists (and competes favorably) with national and international private broadcasters with local community and neighborhood channels. It is interesting that Indian state television has succeeded in ensuring systemic competitiveness and maintaining cultural resistance in the face of the hegemonic global cultural industries, while the route chosen in the Latin American countries has generated giants with feet of clay, such as Globo in Brazil or Televisa in Mexico, dependent on favors from the state and unavoidable alliances with foreign capital.

It is ironical that many of the theories that drove India's communication, education, and development policies originated in Latin America, such as the ECLAC development theories, NOMIC dependency theories, and the 'pedagogy of the oppressed' notion mooted by Paulo Freire – all of which were eventually execrated, first by military governments in the name of their National Security Doctrine, and subsequently by neoliberal economists who assumed power throughout the continent during the transitions to democracy. Brazil is a country with similar development challenges to India's, but as discussed below, it responded in very different ways in terms of cultural and media policies.

Culture and development in Brazil: structural change and prospects

Compared to India, the Latin American story is very different. At the end of the industrialization process through the import-substitution strategy – the 30 yearlong postwar developmental phase in the case of Brazil – a major structural crisis put the country at a difficult crossroads. During the late 1970s, while the military cycle still continued to produce significant growth through the so-called authoritarian modernization, including the resolution of certain bottlenecks remaining from the previous process of industrialization (such as telecommunications), the external debt strategy nevertheless eventually proved disastrous.

Throughout Latin America, the coincidence between the transitions to democracy and the adoption of neoliberal structural adjustment policies, in addition to the weak democratic political culture of both the population and the political class, made it difficult to establish a broad social pact to bring the masses to the center of the political process. By the beginning of the 21st Century, most Latin American economies were growing slowly, but steadily, after a period of painful orthodox adjustments implemented by popular, democratic, and leftist governments. However, in spite of this growth, most countries are still hampered by increased crime rates and intractable levels of social exclusion. Brazil is a case in point.

The problems of development as posited by Furtado's dependency approach are still on the agenda. Key sectors of Brazilian ruling classes do not accept that democratic consolidation involves distributing wealth and power, which will only be possible with the creation of a new social pact. Here communication and cultural policies are essential. Regarding communication one must recall that in those countries that transited from authoritarianism and want to enjoy full democratic modernity, the previous mass media system has undergone a radical overhaul, as can be seen in postwar Germany and Italy, and more recently, in Spain and Portugal.

The 20th century mass media have so far played a key role in building political and cultural hegemony. In Brazil, for example, the modern state building process after the Revolution of 1930 and during the industrialization process used radio as a fundamental component in the consolidation of a hegemonic new industrial bourgeoisie that replaced the agrarian oligarchies of the Old Republic. Mass culture served to build a sense of nationhood by retrieving the popular cultural traditions of non-European origin, molding them into a national identity and finally sealing the rift between the elites and ordinary people that was so accurately identified by Furtado. As said before, such a rift perpetuated 'marginalization' on the one hand and imitation on the other and undermined the vast potential of Brazil's cultural heritage created over the centuries, which the intellectual elite so shrewdly perceived.

During the military regime that followed the 1964 coup, television moved to the center of a process of consolidation of the domestic market due to the reform and expansion of the country's telecommunications infrastructure resulting from the nationalized and centralized organization of the system. From a pure industry point of view, this outcome was extremely ingenious, ensuring state control of transmission, research, and development. This also favored the internalization of technical knowledge based on a model that replaced the European notion of a national champion producing all the equipment domestically with a series of preferential arrangements awarded to a group of international companies to supply equipment for the state sector. In return these companies agreed to conform to national content goals and, as in other sectors, to adopt technologies originated in publicly owned laboratories, such as CPqD Telebrás, in joint ventures with the academic sector.

This infrastructure, serving the interests of industrial policy, gave rise to propaganda, advertising, and program content produced and broadcasted by private companies. Through TV concessions, these companies were responsible for an undeclared cultural policy aimed at consolidating the hegemony of the new political-military elites who focused on the ideology of national security and were also enthusiastic of the concept of 'imported modernity.' This only involved national popular culture when framed in industrialized models of commercial production at the service of the capitalist accumulation of cultural goods. From the 1970s onwards, commercial production followed an extremely rigorous techno/aesthetic pattern (Bolaño, 2000a) with respect to technical and financial resources. This in turn led to unprecedented market concentration headed by a particular company, Globo, who back in the day was deemed by the government as the epitome of modernity in terms of production and management copied from the United States.

Globo not only dominated the domestic market, but it soon went international based on a strategy of extremely competent – albeit centralized – content production, which met the international hegemonic formulas. This was particularly true in the classic genre of the soap opera (telenovela) favored by Latin Americans. Telenovelas manage to incorporate elements of Brazilian popular culture by recruiting skilful intellectuals – authors, actors, and directors, many of them left-wing and trained in the fine traditions of Brazilian theater and cinema. In the 1970s, Globo had evolved into a national network, similar to US networks, through a system of affiliated companies – effectively bypassing the law restricting the number of concessions allowed in Brazil and establishing too close of a relationship with local politicians who were often the lucky recipients of TV and radio broadcasting concessions. Thus over the years, this national network became the hegemonic actor in the economic field of cultural production, as well as the vector of a powerful lobby in national politics.

The internationalization of Globo depends upon a concentration of production and knowledge that dramatically reduced systemic competitiveness. In addition to importing methods, models, and formats, Globo and the national broadcasting oligopoly allied themselves closely with the Hollywood global oligopoly and the American music industry. This results, for instance, in the exclusion of Brazilian-made films from TV screens. Until very recently they were regarded as a kind of outsider techno-aesthetic competitor. Here one must recognize the efforts of the government of President Lula da Silva who inaugurated a program called Cultura Viva (Live Culture) through the Ministry of Culture aimed at rescuing and supporting cultural production of groups and communities who have been traditionally excluded from the mainstream media production and diffusion. One of the areas of this program is called Pontos de Cultura (Culture Hotspots) orientated toward the provision of distribution and access to communities and social groups for their cultural production. This program is still supported by the government of President Dilma Rousseff.

However, the powerful 'cultural factory' that Globo represents has exerted a kind of colonization on peoples' lives, given that its power impacts heavily on viewers' tastes and effectively educates them to be in thrall to the medium. This represents the true power of Globo corporation: its acceptance by the widest audience thanks to the company's skill in transforming national popular culture and identity into commodity. This is not presented quite so blatantly, since the advertising model masks the role of the viewing audiences as reproducers of cultural capital. However, those same audiences ensure, from the economic standpoint, the company's access to the advertising pie; and from the political viewpoint secure Globo the exclusive right to determine the form and content of the messages addressed to the Brazilian people. Through communication and advertising techniques, skillfully backed up by modern research and planning tools, Globo assumes in the process a paramount role in the building of consensus and hegemony, with ample power to exert pressure on the government of the day.

In a fully democratic system it is not admissible that certain companies, or a few families or businessmen should be in a position to wield such power. The new cultural policy mentioned above is of course important, but nevertheless insufficient and ends up only appealing to a minority of already organized groups. It could only ever be anti-hegemonic with the establishment of a fresh model of regulation of the sector to reflect the new set of social and political forces that have been apparent since the introduction of the 1988 Constitution.

The recent history of innovations in the media landscape reveals a disturbing trend toward deeper internationalization. This is a worrying development, captained once again by the Globo empire that in the cable TV market alone, has allied with the global oligopoly run by major international television companies. Even though according to the ruling of the 1995 Law, public channels must be carried on all cable and satellite TV services, they still do not pose any true challenge to the dominant position of the private channels.

Alliances with foreign capital in the cultural field cannot be justified from the standpoint of national interest. It is not a question of internalizing technical know-how produced abroad as used to be the case in the old telecommunications model. What is vitally important is to preserve and defend Brazilian popular culture, which is only possible with the existence of a public media service and a cultural policy that could provide the adequate funding and know-how for popular creativity to blossom. Access should also be guaranteed to the most modern broadcasting delivery systems so that local, regional, independent, and community-based productions could truly channel the voice of a pluralistic and complex society, granting the right to communication as an inalienable human right.

Throughout the democratic world,unrestricted media power is recognized as a problem for democracy. Two alternatives generally put forward to try and prevent the state being hijacked by the 'fourth estate': the parallel existence of a competitive and democratically structured public broadcasting system, as in Europe (e.g., in the United Kingdom), or a robust system of state regulation applicable to the private sector as in the United States. In Brazil, in contrast, broadcasting companies are able to operate free of any type of control and are given a free hand to exploit the media commercially with no obligation whatsoever to provide a public service.

The solution eventually found by the Lula government was to reorganize the public system by introducing, although in a limited way, the new TV Brazil channel. To ensure a balance between public, private, and state systems in accordance with the Brazilian Constitution it is necessary to balance the supply of open private channels – many of them subcontracted to *telemarketing*, Evangelistic interests and others with program contents of dubious quality – and public channels focused on fostering a genuine policy of culture and sustainable economic and social development.

One may think, for instance, of a public television system with three channels: the first one such as that created under the Lula government as a centralized 'general interest' channel; a second decentralized regional channel operating at individual state levels, possibly in a network configuration, targeted at around a 15 percent slice of viewers; and a third channel totally devoted to local, independent, community, university sponsored, and experimental productions that could be broadcasted at certain times of the day and that could potentially be capable of attracting ratings of about 5 percent. The latter is close to the European standard model but uses existing Brazilian inputs reflecting production and organizational traditions already developed in this country.

A public system organized democratically with management councils, independence from government, and following best international practice, does not prevent private TV from fulfilling, by regulation, 'public service' commitments (in return for its concession). The existence of a democratically run public television service able to attract 50 percent of the viewing public by applying top editorial and technical standards also serves *inter alia* as a useful quality benchmark, as is common in Europe.

The growth of the Internet and the restructuring of regulatory models of communication are linked to three processes at global level: the restructuration and reorientation of production that began in the 1970s, the revolution in microelectronics, and the development of ICTs – all of which have had significant destabilizing effects on the cultural industries. On the demand side, these technological innovations have led to a profound change in culture consumption habits. On the supply side, the outcome for hegemonic companies running the old cultural industries (including TV) has been a lowering of the barriers to entry, accentuated by technological convergence and a potential influx of substantial capital resources into content production and delivery in the telecommunications area.

In this new landscape, Globo network presents itself as a representative of 'Brazilian national culture' as opposed to the cult of 'internationalization' that the company itself promoted in its early days and expanded with the advent of Pay-TV in the 1980s. It did so in the expectation of reaping the benefits of the new market then opening up as the result of telecommunication privatization, soon forming an association with Carlos Slim's Telmex.

The growing demand for content boosted by the new technologies and digital convergence signaled a veritable potential explosion in national production, which on the one hand justifies a broadcasting policy as suggested above and, on the other, foreshadows the continuing transformation of Globo into a truly global production company. It is obvious that if this happens, Globo will not be able to retain control over mass TV delivery (for an indefinite period and with no regulation or restrictions) and will lose its hegemonic status in the segmented TV market, radio, and newspapers in Brazil, since cross-ownership is limited.

A final question to be addressed

According to Furtado (1984), the constitution of a mass culture could be boosted not only by the greater visibility of the popular culture whose creativity is more 'difficult to conceal' at the present stage of Brazil's modernizing development, but also by the country's process of urbanization coupled with the emergence of a middle class of increasing economic importance. This middle class' cultural leanings are generally 'too close to the people' and tend to favor the formation of a mass culture representing 'the end of the isolation of the popular sectors, but also the beginning of its dismemberment as a creative force' (Furtado, 1984: 24).

Under these circumstances 'the rise of the US economy, driving a mass culture endowed with powerful means of delivery, serves [...] as the principal destabilizing factor of a cultural framework based on the elite-people dichotomy' (Furtado, 1984: 24). However, the problem resides not only in the quantity of American content reaching Brazil, as Furtado makes clear when referring to the Brazilian crisis in the 1980s,

The crisis is not simply the product of readjustments in the world economy. To a large extent it is the manifestation of an impasse that is present in our society, where the material culture of the most advanced capitalist societies seeks to be reproduced here while most of our population is deprived of essential goods and services. Although the dissemination, in one form or another, of certain patterns of behavior adopted by high-income minorities, cannot be avoided, a counter-faction of mass society is emerging, which enjoys sophisticated forms of superfluous consumption while people in the same social stratum, and even within same families, suffer shortages. (Furtado, 1984: 30)

It is worth asking what effects a quarter century of social, economic, and cultural policies in Brazil have had on the situation described by the quotation above. Could, for example, the social and cultural policies inaugurated by the Lula government and continued today have made any significant difference to the equation? During Lula´s second mandate, an alternative national project was presented focusing on a growing domestic market driven by so-called inclusion policies; a program that apparently is being followed by Lula's successor. The final question is: can this really gain major significance as an effective Brazilian developmental project, as posited by Furtado, while the current symbolic power structure remains untouched?

Notes

A much longer and modified version of this chapter was published earlier in Portuguese: *Produção de conteúdo nacional para mídias digitais*. *Brasília: Presidência da República*, Brasilia: Presidency of the Republic, Secretariat for Strategic Affairs 2010.

1. Dependency theory is an approach developed at the end of World War II that focuses, first, on the unbalanced nature of trade between core and developed nations and periphery and underdeveloped nations, where the former benefit the most and enrich themselves at the expense of the latter. Second, this approach also recognizes the emergence of a local elite in peripheral countries that not only takes the lion share of political and economic power, concentrating the benefits of trade and resources, but also shares similar cultural values to those dominant in the core nations. In Latin America, leading scholars of dependency theory are Argentinian Raúl Prebisch – who played a key role in the U.N. Commission for Latin America (UNCLA) – and Brazilian Celso Furtado. One of Prebisch's theses was that in order for a peripheral nation to cope with the core nations, local developmental policies to foster and protect local industry and commerce must be implemented. Among these policies were the famous import-substitution strategies practiced in most Latin American countries between the 1940s up to the economic crises of the early and mid-1980s, when privatization and liberalization policies replaced them as a global trend in policy-making.
2. With antecedents in 2006, it was not until June 2009 when the BRIC group, constituted by Brazil, Russia, India and China – all of them fast growing economies – held its first official Summit in Yekaterinburg in Russia. In 2010 South Africa joined the group and now it is called BRICS.

References

Bolaño, C. R. S. (1997) *Privatização das Telecomunicações na Europa e na América Latina* (Aracaju: Editora UFS).
Bolaño, C. R. S. (2000a) *Indústria Cultural, informação e capitalismo* (São Paulo: Hucitec).

242   *César Bolaño*

Bolaño, C. R. S. (2000b) 'Notas sobre a reforma das Telecomunicações na Europa e nos EUA até 1992,' Texto para discussão 1, Aracaju. Available at http://bit.ly/18YSv3Y (accessed November 2013).

Bolaño, C. R. S., Moreno Dominguez, J. M. and Santos, C. A. (2006) *A indústria cinematográfica no Mercosul: economia, cultura e integração*. Presentation at Colóquio Brasil-Espanha de Ciências da Comunicação, Málaga.

Cardoso de Mello, J. M. (1982) *Capitalismo Tardio* (São Paulo: Brasiliense).

Furtado, C. (1984) *Cultura e desenvolvimento em época de crise* (São Paulo: Paz e Terra).

Habermas, J. (1984) *Mudança estrutural da esfera pública* (Rio de Janeiro: Tempo Brasileiro).

Novais, F. A. (1979) *Portugal e Brasil na crise do antigo sistema colonial (1777–1808)* (São Paulo: Hucitec).

13
The Publishing Industries in Ibero-America: Challenges and Diversity in the Digital World

Stella Puente

Introduction

In the past fifteen years, the concept of cultural diversity has gained renewed relevance – even if it has had a late arrival – both in the field of cultural industries and in the public policies orientated towards safeguarding such diversity as a result of strong processes of concentration and trasnationalization in the cultural field. In fact, diversity is the correct word nowadays, and by extension, the compulsory concept of discussion in the cultural field, be it on the discursive side of cultural policy, the researching of cultural policies, or in cultural management (Puente, 2011). While the concept of diversity has an immediate antecedent in 'cultural exception,' its use nowadays refers to the importance of plurality of actors, particularly local and regional, in the production and circulation of cultural goods, such as books.

It is yet to be seen whether this concept of cultural diversity shall really translate into the digital world – as diverse as it is per se – and if it becomes a predominant aspect of digital policies and regulation in the publishing field, both at the global, regional, and local level. There are several clues that suggest a widespread anxiety on the matter: some authors warn about the ever-growing predominance of the English language in Latin America and Spain: 'I want tomorrow's world to be shaped by diversity and not by the English-speaking hegemony' (Arana, 2007, my translation). Others note the prevalence of unfair competition in the digital world: 'Nowadays the whole world is sick of Amazon, a company that, by dumping its prices penetrates other markets, lowers its prices, and then, as if it were a near-monopoly, makes prices go up again' (Peces, 2013, my translation).

Similar concerns have been openly expressed elsewhere in the world. Jean-Noël Jeanneney, former president of the National Library of France, and Aurélie Filippetti, current Culture and Communication Minister of France, both agree on the fact that the specific weight of a few big companies in the publishing industry have severely undermined other companies. The monopolization and concentration that already existed in the analogue world replicate their battles in the digital world, for instance, against Google's decisions to digitalize about fifteen million books and to make the world's most important English-speaking book collections available online. In the case of the French National Library president, his opinions are meant to expose the situation; in the case of the public servant, it has worked as the underlying argument to back a 9 million Euro program to aid independent publishers and book shops that have been damaged by Amazon's penetration of the market.

The French Minister's words imply that the risk posed to cultural diversity will be a continuing challenge for the publishing industry, and thus, state intervention in order to preserve smaller companies will be crucial to their survival. One could think of other countries outside Europe, with gigantic corporations other than Google and Amazon, and one will find the same maneuvers and the same predicament: the market conditions endanger both the development of a productive sector with a diverse set of participants and the production and circulation of a diverse set of contents. Even if this is not a new[1] issue, it's interesting to note the way in which this takes place in a digital environment.

Digitalization of the book industry: the challenge of conversion

Some editors do not consider the monopolization of content in the hands of big companies to be a big deal. On the contrary, those same editors relativize that fact and claim that new technologies could have a positive impact, creating new space for those who were originally left out by the traditional publishing business. The process of digital conversion that cultural industries are undergoing has been filled with uncertainty, faced resistance, and modified the rules of the game in terms of production, business models, and cultural consumption. However this situation, first experienced in the music industry, has spread throughout the cultural industries. While displaying particularities in the different sectors, the changes brought about by digital conversion are here to stay.

Editor Mike Shatzkin has put it this way: 'Anything that can be digital will no longer have materiality. There are things that have to be material – such as food and clothing – but everything related to information or content, makes more sense to exist in digital form' (Shatzkin, 2013). Yet, in most publishing industries across Latin America, the reaction has been to face the new phenomenon with resistance, distrust, and denial. That reflects on their delayed reactions before the conversion demanded by the new digital era.

However, as recommended by Argentinian publisher Alejandro Katz, instead of envisioning a dim future for the book industry, his fellow publishers should sharpen their wits and adapt what they know well in the non-digital world: 'it is strategic to know how to adapt old knowledge to a new environment. It is not about acquiring new knowledge, but instead about giving value to what we know' (Katz, 2013).

Further deepening this argument in his essays on mutation entitled 'I Barbari' (The Barbarians), Alessandro Baricco reflects about the importance of books in this new civilization inhabited by digital natives.[2] He suggests that humans' relationship with the book is bound to change. He argues that, conversely to what happened with the enlightened bourgeoisie, books will make no sense on their own but will instead have value as long as they can recreate stories whose signification takes place in other fields, such as the movies, newspapers, and television. 'The barbarians tend to read only those books who's user manuals can be found elsewhere' (Baricco, 2008).

The aforementioned reflection gains special importance for understanding the current ways in which the perception of new readers might be configuring. Obviously, this situation becomes unacceptable for – and it is thus simply denied and neglected by – actors pertaining to the traditional world of publishing. He adds:

> Naturally this bothers people and provokes that widespread and prevailing feeling of rubbish, but it is also true that therein, in its more vulgar form, a non-vulgar principle begins to unravel: the idea that the book's value resides in offering itself as an installment of a broader experience, as the episode of a sequence that started elsewhere and will probably finish somewhere else. (Baricco, 2008, my translation)

Anyway, it is hard to offer an accurate outlook on a process that is constantly being redefined, wherein there exist few systematized data, tons of uncertainty, and great asymmetry between countries and regions.

This chapter is thus meant to explore some of these issues, with a special focus on the Ibero-American region – the Hispanic markets – wherein diversity challenges are particularly evident.[3] The Spanish-speaking world is one of the most disputed by the biggest digital distributors as it is a market of nearly 500 million speakers. One recurring question in the region has been why, given the Hispanic market size and potential, there has been so little presence of both actors and regional contents in the global markets. As García-Canclini asserts:

> The figures for audiovisual sectors show that Ibero-American countries get as little as 5 percent of the global markets' revenue, but we do know that if we add up the number of Latin American residents, Spaniards, and Spanish-speaking residents in the USA, we amount to more than 550 million people. To think on globalization means to also think on why we get so little a share of revenue, and at the same time, we should imagine how could we take advantage of being one of the linguisitc groups with the higher levels of literacy and cultural consumption. (García-Canclini, 2000, my translation)

It is in the aforementioned issue where public policies and regional strategies become especially important. The global corporations of digital distribution now represent what the major publishing houses used to represent in the analogue world. In this new landscape, the former could have the better conditions to grow and gain positions, as digital is their natural field. According to an executive of Grupo Planeta, one of Ibero-America's leading publishers: 'The six biggest publishing houses in the West had a turnouver of 25,000 million euros, while Internet giants managed a 160,000 million euro turnover, that's six times as much' (Manrique-Sagobal, 2013, my translation).

Diversity in the book's world

According to the Independent Publishers Alliance: 'Bibliodiversity is cultural diversity applied to the world of books [...] While big companies, with their massive level of production do create a certain editorial market supply, bibliodiversity is closely related to the production of independent publishers' (Alianza Internacional de Editores Independientes, 2013). A few years ago, we had tried to account for the existing relation between concentration in the book market and diversity in book catalogues. While we have no doubt about the strength of this relation, we found no factual data or indicators that could account for such a relation (Puente, 2011).

As a first step in that direction, we decided to begin our measurements of that relation by using the book exports in the Ibero-American region as our first parameter. We could see that the European Union, together with North America, concentrated almost three thirds of the world book exports (73.1 percent). Distribution by region is as follows: European Union with 54.8 percent, Asia with 20.1 percent, North America with 18.3 percent, Latin America with 2.9 percent, the rest of Europe with 2.5 percent, Oceania with 0.9 percent, and Africa with 0.5 percent (CERLALC, 2008).

That situation of unequal exchange was also replicated within the same geo-linguistic zones. In the Spanish language, Spain exported to Latin America more than what it imported from Latin America, Canada, and the United States altogether. Eight publishing houses concentrate this market, among which we can highlight Oceano, Santillana, Norma, and Planeta (Enríquez Fuentes, 2008). From Latin America's total of book exports, Spain concentrated 63 percent of exports, 35 percent went to fellow Latin American countries, and the remaining 3 percent to Portugal. We also find that out of Latin American exports, Mexico and Colombia are the biggest exporters and concentrate 66.4 percent.

Meanwhile, there has been a constant rise in terms of the amount of titles produced in the region. In 2006, in all of Ibero-America (Spain plus Latin America, including Brazil), 163,000 titles were produced vis-à-vis 118,000 in 2001 (up by 38 percent). In Brazil, the increase was 71 percent in the period, Argentina 50 percent, and Spain 19 percent. This could be interpreted as follows: there is no doubt of the protagonist role of some countries in the book market – their productive actors lead the largest share of the market – but there are no sufficient data and indicators to help us analyze the way in which that has affected the diversity of published content, or *bibliodiversity*.

Even if the sole existence of an heterogeneous universe of publishing houses – regarding size and legal status and private, public, and NGOs – led us to assume the existence of a diversity of interests and political, cultural, and social affinities; this has not been measured and therefore insufficient data prevents us from determining how diverse the publishing industry actually is.

So far, we do certainly know that there is widespread concentration from the point of view of the publishing houses, we also do know which Ibero-American countries top the exports league, and we do know the composition of publishing houses in terms of ownership status. We also know that there has been a considerable increase in book production in recent years, which may lead us to think that there is, at least, some diversity of contents.

In this respect, we have highlighted elsewhere the need to analyze the markets according to the size of their editorial publishing houses and to explore within the different segments of the industry how diverse they are regarding the amount of titles, genres, and authors most published and read. One of the challenges is now to measure these dimensions and variables both with regard to supply – how many titles are offered and by whom – and to demand, which books and from what companies are bought, what are their titles, and to which genre do they belong.

The creation of these indicators can then be related to the development of public policies towards the sector. The systematization of this information, in line with a certain criteria, is vital to making a diagnosis of the field and to evaluating then the effect of the actions taken by the governments. This systematization is also important in order to assess the behavior of regional markets and to train the eye to identify the extent to which these patterns are reproduced in the new scenarios of technological convergence. The more professionalized and developed the systems of cultural information or satellite accounts in each of the countries, the more common parameters of diagnosis and evaluation we will have. All of the above might positively impact on devising appropriate public policies orientated towards the book. It might also impact on the adoption of regional strategies to better face the challenges posed by the current technological battlefield wherein the global market reinforces a terrain for the major players to impose the rules of the game.

The only certainty of the foreseeable future is that the digital world is here to stay. The great question is whether the digital world is here to fuel the sale of bestsellers, to generate survival conditions for small print runs, or to target specific niches in favor of diversity, following Chris Anderson's 'Long tail' theory. He argues that sales and trends show that new digital economies will continue to radically differ from today's mass market. While the entertainment industry throughout the 20th century centered around products that garnered success and popularity, the 21st century will be about a focus on niches (Anderson, 2007).

How are publishers and editors facing the new scenario in Ibero-America? What is the subjective construction of readers and what will be their reading experience in the digital environment? These questions have yet not been sufficiently addressed from the perspective of publishing houses in the region.

Diversity and the digital environment

According to many of the productive actors in the book industry – as has been aforementioned – the digital environment, far from affecting diversity, actually promotes its conditions of existence and development. The drop in production costs and storage as well as the entrance of new local players are some of the recurring arguments used to defend this view.

> The only path for an independent Latin American publisher facing a big corporation is the e-book. The costs of launching a new book have fallen and now it's mostly about having good promotion in specialized networks and the circles of potential readers. In the digital world, the difference between a small publisher and a transnational corporation are no longer as important. (Kulesz, 2013, my translation)

Once again, this is an ongoing subject of discussion without visible certainties, and where uncertainties are connected to the shortage of solid evidence. Kulesz (2011) claims that so far it has not been easy to identify a successful system of digital publishing in Latin America. Even in the Western world, Amazon's Kindle Store and Apple's iBooks sales figures are relatively unknown, hence global publishers are still uncertain on whether these platforms are as lucrative as self-proclaimed. In fact, the author notes, the constant variance of fixed pricing or format definitions shows that even the mayor players are still testing the waters.

However, the major international platforms of book distribution have begun to lead the global markets, and more precisely the Hispanic markets. As a result – as we have seen with the aforementioned conflict between Amazon and the French government – they wield the power to fix market prices, thereby compromising the survival of small and medium-sized publishers. It is not that Amazon prices its products much lower than what the fixed book price agreement establishes. But French editors argue that somehow their competition is unfair when they add as 'discount' the gratuity of delivery and shipment.

Even if it is so, there are a number of things we do know: the production chain of books is being transformed fundamentally with regard to the part played by its main actors; the most endangered link of which seems to be book shops. Also, in this new environment, digital infrastructure and digital divide are key problems; migration of funds towards the digital environment and the generation of new contents that cater for the demands of new markets are both as important; as well as the development of aggregators and commercialization platforms to upload local and regional content are of vital importance.

In a recent publication by CERLALC (2012),[4] which is UNESCO's regional body to increase book reading in Latin America, there are some interesting figures and data on e-books. For instance, it is no surprise that the latest transformations in digital publishing are taking place in the United States. The report is based on research carried out in 2009. Back then 53 percent of publishers claimed to be producing e-books, but by 2012 the percentage had climbed up to 80 percent.

As for Spain, the CERLALC report shows how the top book producers of the Spanish-speaking world are reaching similar rates of digital publishing to those of the English-speaking world. The Spanish ISBN agency database shows that between 2008 and 2011 the recorded digital publications rose from 2.4 percent to 17.9 percent, while paper books decreased from 91.6 percent to 73.4 percent in the same period.

That same report notes that there is a similar trend going on in Latin America, if we take into consideration that in 2003 the share of e-books compared to the total book registration was only 4 percent, that number went up to 15 percent by 2011. If we consider the numbers within the region, we observe an unequal trend, as 90 percent of the e-book publishing is concentrated in Brazil, Colombia, Argentina, and Mexico.

On a further note, the digital edition per se does not guarantee the regional circulation of contents on its own. Kulesz (2011) again notes how most e-books sold by Latin American stores proceed from foreign aggregators, mostly Spain, the United States, and England. He observes how in Spanish-speaking countries, the existing online libraries get their funding from Publidisa (Spain), whose online store focuses on e-books in the Spanish language and holds more than 20,000 titles in its catalogue. In general, the lack of proportion between local and foreign content is very significant. One of the most important issues regarding this new context, which we can find throughout the history of the publishing industry, is that besides the need for an ongoing supply of publications in Spanish we also need the means to guarantee their circulation and visibility.

In this respect, the commercialization network of books is still very poor in Latin America. Libraries run the risk of disappearing: they are increasingly dispersed and located in the larger cities. Their technological modernization is thus a key factor to their possibility to cope with competition in digital networks.

Conclusions: future and diversity

I have argued elsewhere (Puente, 2012) that creativity and digitalization are the two operating concepts in the contemporary reality of cultural industries. The emergence of the concept 'creative economies,' as well as the irruption of digitalized contents turning into quicksand the formerly solid foundations that underpin this ever-changing field. In the past few years – no more than a decade – these industries have undergone several stages. Doubtless we are witnessing a change of paradigm in cultural production that has been expressed and experienced in the entire chain of production: from the first traces of creative work, to its circulation, stage, and consumption. The irruption of digitalization and social media has disorganized a field that was beginning to configure steadily in terms of actors, products, sectors, and competition.

Thus, the irruption of the digital platform in the book industry must be carefully analyzed and comprehended in depth. In this industry coexist both the aspects that originally shaped the history of printing, and new features that will delineate its fate. Thus, we witness trends from the analogical era that are being accentuated in digital times: the concentration of the industry, the predominance of certain economic actors, the existing frailty of some of the links in the value chain, and the asymmetry between countries and regions.

Likewise, the emergence of powerful digital players such as Amazon, Google, and Apple is also not new. After all, they are the contemporary versions of what major publishers such as Random House and Barnes and Noble used to be; and, like their predecessors, digital giants also notice the potential of a regional market of close to 500 million inhabitants.

Perhaps this new environment may boost the development of the book industry as long as new actors emerge and old ones face, with a new perspective, the characteristics presented by this new context. In this regard, as it is the case in other cultural industries, audience segmentation – specialization of supply or content selection for niche audiences – is the key to the new business model. Here, the role of editors will be crucial, and new technologies will constitute an unrivaled tool to identify the expectations of a contemporary society more interconnected through social networks.

As final remark, I can highlight that new technological development involves a change in cultural frames that confronts us with the challenge of reshaping practices that are strongly tied to our ways of life. Culture does not escape the norm that – at different times and as depicted by various examples – we have seen through history. The press, the automobile, electric power, the airplane, and the personal computer all completely transformed the way in which we have conceived and experienced our most genuine habits. Reading, the access to knowledge or mere pleasure, and above all, the availability of a diverse set of publications, are the current challenges that cultural industries have to face and that public policies must urgently face.

Notes

1. As stated earlier, the concept of cultural diversity makes evident the failure of cultural industries to represent diverse voices, social actors, expressions, territories, and what that failure means in terms of the construction of a nation's or a given territory's social imaginaries. Its first steps at the General Agreement on Tariffs and Trade (GATT) Rounds, as a cultural exception, and its posterior development under UNESCO shows the extent to which this concept has gained central relevance and spread through local and global cultural management (Puente, 2007).
2. 'I Barbari' is a series of 30 essays published by Italian writer Alessandro Baricco in the prestigious newspaper La Reppublica between May 12 and October 21, 2006. The essays can be consulted in Italian at the newspaper's website at the following address, where the newspaper also opened up a blog for participating in the debate: http://bit.ly/18YWgqb. Here the author uses the collection of essays published in Spanish as *Los barbarous* by Anangrama Editores in 2008 (Note of the editors).
3. As Chávez and Guerrero note: 'In English-speaking countries the very word "Ibero-America" sounds quite unfamiliar and, actually, there is no natural term to define the world comprised by the Spanish – and Portuguese-speaking worlds. The most common used and larger term is that of "Latin America" – a term crafted by the French in the 19th century – or the "Americas" if it encompasses all the countries of the continent. Instead, for Spanish – and Portuguese-speaking countries, the term "Ibero-America" has the meaning of encompassing the countries of Latin America plus Spain and Portugal, or the Iberian Peninsula in Western Europe. Ibero-America is, thus, a term that underlines a common cultural heritage among the Spanish- and Portuguese-speaking countries on both sides of the Atlantic. Such heritage cannot, by any means, be considered in narrow and homogeneous ways, though it can still be recognized broadly in terms of the language, dominant religion, customs and traditions' (Chávez and Guerrero, 2009: 19–20).
4. The Centro Regional para el Fomento del Libro en América Latina y el Caribe (CERLALC, by its Spanish acronym) is located in Bogota, Colombia, and stands for the Regional Center for the Book in Latin America and the Caribbean, and intra-governmental body funded by UNESCO.

References

Alianza Internacional de Editores Independientes (2013) 'Nociones clave: Bibliodiversidad.' Available at http://bit.ly/1dVkpv7 (accessed December 2013).

Anderson, C. (2007) *La Economía Long Tail* (Barcelona: Ediciones Urano).

Arana, P. (2007, January 17) 'No se puede dejar a Google todo el manejo de la cultura,' *La Nación*. Available at http://bit.ly/18YWZHP (accessed September 2013).

Baricco, A. (2008) *Los Bárbaros. Ensayo sobre la mutación* (Barcelona: Anagrama).

CERLALC (2008) 'El espacio Iberoamericano del Libro 2008,' *CERLALC*. Available at http://bit.ly/1dVkSO1 (accessed December 2013).

CERLALC (2012) 'El libro electrónico: tendencias y recomendaciones,' *CERLALC*. Available at http://bit.ly/18YWVYs (accessed November 2013).

Chávez, M. and Guerrero, M. A. (2009) 'Conceptualizing journalism, information, entertainment, and citizenship: applications for Iberoamerica,' pp. 11–38 in M. A. Guerrero and M. Chávez (eds) *Empowering Citizenship through Journalism, Information, and Entertainment in Iberoamerica* (Mexico City: University of Miami, Michigan State University and Universidad Iberoamericana).

Enríquez-Fuentes, E. (2008) 'El comercio de libros entre España y América Latina: disonancia en la reciprocidad,' *Alianza internacional de editores independientes*. Available at http://bit.ly/18YWUDX (accessed November 2013).

García-Canclini, N. (2000) *La Globalización Imaginada* (Buenos Aires: Paidós).

Katz, A. (2013) *Editar y vender en el mundo digital. Cómo aprender del pasado para dar de leer*. [Web log post]. Available at http://bit.ly/1dVkBL2 (accessed September 2013).

Kulesz, O. (2011) 'La edición Digital en los países en desarrollo,' *Alianza Internacional de Editores Independientes*. Available at: http://bit.ly/1dVksaf (accessed December 2013).

Kulesz, O. (2013, June 13) 'Entrevista con Javier Sepúlveda Hales, director de Ebooks Patagonia (Chile),' *Alliance Lab*. Available at http://bit.ly/1dVkwaa (accessed December 2013).

Manrique Sabogal, W. (2013, October 23) 'La batalla por el futuro del libro se dirime en Latinoamérica,' *Diario el País*.

Peces, J. (2013, June 4) 'La ministra de Cultura de Francia avisa: "Estamos hartos de Amazon",' *El País*. Available at http://bit.ly/18YWEox (accessed December 2013).

Puente, S. (2007) *Industrias culturales* (Buenos Aires: Prometeo).

Puente, S. (2011) Bibliodiversidad: Indicadores y Debate. Bibliodiversity Indicators. Bibliodiversity: publishing and globalization (January 2011). Retrieved from www.bibliodiversity.org (accessed September 2013).

Puente, S (2012) Industrias Culturales y Después,' pp. 87–91 in F. J. Piñón (ed.) *Indicadores Culturales. Cuadernos de Políticas Culturales* (Buenos Aires: Eduntref).

Shatzkin, M. (2013, May 26) 'Todo lo que pueda ser digital, dejará de ser físico,' *La Nación*. Available at http://bit.ly/18YWDAY (accessed December 2013).

14
The Global Notion of Journalism: A Hindrance to the Democratization of the Public Space in Chile

Rodrigo Araya

Introduction

In the Chilean case, there has not been strong enough questioning on the relevance that a prevailing idea of journalism, one that has certainly become the global standard – along its professional practices, norms and values – may hold on the social reality of the country. Hence, the interest in identifying the basis of this constituent discourse is based in its use as the standard and legitimizing force for the professional practice in Chile. By discussing deontological codes and also interviews with community broadcasters in Valparaíso, Chile, this chapter identifies core components of what I call here Eurocentric conception of journalism that henceforth will be referred to as '*Reporterística.*' In looking at the core components of such dominant model of reporting and journalism, the chapter first identifies the aspects that underpin the univocal conception of journalism that the chapter traces back to the European Enlightenment and the Independent movements, and then calls for a 'situated' perspective of journalism that considers other possible models of reporting other than '*Reporterística*'. The chapter argues that the discussion on media democratization and pluralism needs to address the very core of the constitutive discourses with which journalism came into being in Chile.

With the end of Pinochet's dictatorship, there were renewed hopes for a media system that would automatically favor a strong democratization of the public space. However, with political democratization

254

the opposite occurred: key newspapers and magazines disappeared and ownership of radio stations concentrated. Moreover, with the growth of private television – until then TV networks had been in the hands of the state and universities – new stations emerged, fueling hopes of pluralism and debate. However it soon became clear that save for very few exceptions, most of them displayed a clear-cut conservative leaning. In short, despite the apparent advance of political democracy, the ideological plurality of the media reduced instead of increasing, and thus the public space weakened rather than strengthened (Mönckeberg, 2009; Dérmota, 2002). All of this took place as an accompanying force to democracy rather than under dictatorship as we would have been expected.

That was, undoubtedly, an unexpected phenomenon. Although the accepted wisdom had been to trust in the positive impact of democracy in the quality of the mediated public space – 'to greater democracy corresponds, greater plurality of information' – it was not fulfilled in Chile. The resulting disillusionment attracted both academic and political efforts not only to understand the reasons for what happened, but also to intervene and rectify the course of events. All in all, this attempt sought to identify the appropriate ways to contribute to the democratization of the public space.

Thus far, most studies dealing with that period of recent Chilean history have mainly centered on the material dimensions of the phenomenon. This means that the configuration of a highly ideological media concentration has been explained through the focus on the economic model within which the media industry operates. This trend is justified in the context of an existing neoliberal model, inherited from Pinochet's dictatorship, with inherent forces such as commercialism, media privatization, and deregulation.

So far a dominant strand of scholarship in Latin America has denounced imbalances in the concentration of media property in the region and the resulting manipulation and bias of information. The argument is that if the material conditions of journalistic production become democratic – such as media ownership – then the inevitable consequence should also be the democratization and pluralism of the public space. However, as I argue throughout this chapter, this perspective is misleading and limited because it fails to account for a more invisible but equally fundamental aspect beyond media property: the (Eurocentric) dominant ideology of journalism. An approach that merely focuses on the analysis of the material conditions of news production overlooks the important implications of practitioners' cultural concepts of journalism in their professional exercise within a context of dominant ideology. In other words, the critical political approach neglects the fact that existing journalistic practices have a guiding or constitutive discourse that legitimizes a certain way of exercising the profession, in benefit of elites and an Eurocentric thought – to the detriment of alternative of alternative views – which could be as equally or probably more democratic or pluralistic practices of journalism.

Existing approaches that deem journalism as professional ideologies are extremely useful for our argument here, as they at least acknowledge the coexistence of multiple, and sometimes contesting, professional ideals, norms and practices (Deuze, 2005; Hanitzsch, 2007). Other studies also view journalists as members of an 'interpretive communities' (Zelizer, 1993) that function within a similar and located cultural framework, which in turn allows its members to coincide in their conceptualization of the profession.

In this chapter, however, the argument goes beyond merely acknowledging the existence of several communities of journalists that share local-based cultural frameworks that shape their professional norms, values and practices. Instead, we support the view that when journalism is treated as a constituted product without constituent principles (Ricoeur, 1989), it favors a homogeneous understanding of its nature. Therefore, neglecting the study of journalism's discourse of legitimation contributes – although unintentionally – to the preservation of a predominant practice of the profession, one that precisely arises from such legitimizing discourse. As we argue here, the discussion on media property therefore overlooks entrenched cultural practices, news routines and discourses within the profession of journalism that favor the visibility and agendas of elite groups while ignoring the marginalised groups and the community concerns. This is why Argentinian journalist Pedro Brieger (2007) asserts that even if media ownership is democratized, the same reporting practices, reliance on news sources, and discursive frames remains as the staple feature of journalism. This is due to a largely because of a Eurocentric view that underpins journalism education in Latin America – an educational model to be analyzed in forthcoming paragraphs – and even the news practices of community media meant to be alternative and oriented towards the citizens, as this chapter shows. As a result, the long-awaited democratization and pluralism of the public space is not achieved and the reasons go beyond pure governmental censorship, ineffective regulation, market logics or media concentration.

There are various reasons to support the view that a Eurocentric discourse of professional journalism also hinders the public space. In fact, the predominant conception of journalism in Chile today has been reinforced by globalizing forces that expand a univocal notion of the profession – objectivity, fact-based reporting, individual work, hierarchical and vertical dissemination of information – which then becomes the universal framework, with negative consequences to be explained throughout this chapter. Needless to say, in a radical critique to globalization, we consider it not as only as a production model capable of operating geographically distant production units in real time, but predominantly as a force with an ideological dimension that has acquired a hegemonic condition and thus has settled as the commonplace, along sociopolitical values and expectations, of contemporary society (Lander, 1993). Within the latest strand journalism research, globalization has become an analytical comparative dimension concerned with the identification of universal traits of the profession (Hanitzsch, 2007) or with the comparison between journalistic roles and professional values across contrasting geographies. Their aim has been to identify shared macro and micro forces that impact journalism production. However, there are also remarkable efforts performed in the opposite direction, namely those striving to 'provincialize' the conceptualizations of journalism, to borrow Chakrabarty's (1992) expression. A number of initiatives in this direction can be observed, for instance, in Africa, where scholars have attempted to identify situated or locally-shaped journalism practices (Mano, 2007; Israel, 1992; Skjerdal, 2012). For example, upon analyzing the African case, Israel (1992) argues that the concept of news focused on the individual, and not on the community, is closer to the Eurocentric perspective than to the Afrocentric one, which according to the author undermines the culture of the continent.

However, despite the strong presence of indigenous groups and civilizations in the region, the same has not happened in Latin America. Although the cultural criticism to globalization (i.e., to Eurocentrism) has begun to acquire academic renown and in fact has been a steady concern in several disciplines – which is expressed, for example, in the configuration of research networks such as *Modernity/Coloniality* (Escobar, 2006), the Group of Sub-Altern Latin American Studies (Sandoval, 2009), or in the emergence of indigenous and intercultural universities (Mato, 2009) – journalism studies still remain impervious to this academic production. Hence, I propose to refocus the academic reflection of journalism in the necessity to generate Latin America's own current of thought, or what I shall call henceforth a 'situated' – that is, locally engendered and practiced – concept of journalism that could, in turn, strengthen citizenship in the region. So far, however, from its very emergence and named as such, journalism has serviced the expansion of the Enlightenment ideals and, by extension, Eurocentric modernity. This establishment of Eurocentric thought in the Chilean case occurred with special strength in two foundational moments of journalism. The first one, as becomes evident in forthcoming paragraphs, occurred during the process of independence from Spain, when journalism emerged as the instrument to bring modernity to the entire population, through which the transition from monarchy subjects to post-independent citizens was materialized. The second one took place in mid-20th century, a period when journalism education was institutionalized, and university-level schools of journalism opened. At this time journalism was viewed as an effective instrument to expand developmental ideas to the entire population, ideas newly arrived from the post-war United States; wherewith to bring development to the Latin American countries so social conditions could proliferate, and thus achieve autonomy. In all this aims and goals, this model based on foreign projects often clashes with situated perspectives of journalism.

Journalism and the social present

The importance of having a situated concept of the profession lies in the fact that journalism makes a key contribution to the construction of the social present (Rodrigo-Alsina, 1989; Gomis, 1991) and, consequently contributes to the construction of Benedict Anderson's (1983) well-known concept: the imagined community. The kind of journalism that a given society envisions and eventually puts into practice defines the type of shared social present of that society and also contributes to the construction of the community in which we live in. So far it may seem to be an obvious question. However, the issue becomes more complex if we consider that the type of journalism that emerges in Latin America as a discourse and as a professional practice – objectivity and neutrality, elite-centred information, fact-based reporting – stems from a model originated elsewhere in the world (Chalaby, 1996; Schudson, 2001, 2005) and brought to Latin America by processes of colonization. This model appears vastly disconnected not only from the local realities and histories of Chile and many local communities, but, as observed in several newsrooms across the country, is taught, applied, and practiced by journalists without critically questioning its origins.

The fact that press histories in Chile only go back as far as the Colonial days, amounts to the argument that no other existing practices – those from indigenous communities, for instance – qualify as 'journalism' and for that reason the later have merited little theorisation or historisation as valid and equally important models of journalism. Indeed, among journalism scholars there exists a broad agreement to trace journalism's origins to the independent Republic in 1810 (Silva-Castro, 1958; Valdebenito, 1956; Ossandón and Santa-Cruz, 2001). The argument to link the emergence of journalism to the Independence ideals – therefore Enlightenment ideals – is that the Spanish Crown did not bring any printing presses whatsoever to Chile, since the Republic acquired the first one in 1811 after Chilean independence. In fact, a pro-independence faction devised the model of journalism back in the early 19th century, when this faction constituted nearly exclusively by educated creoles – not by the illiterate masses of peasants and indigenous communities – had a clear vision of the benefits that journalism and the print press could bring to the new Republic of Chile and its project of modernity. In such perspective, the press was the instrument for the dissemination of the Enlightenment ideals and the rationales – and hence the ideals of the educated elites. In accordance to the Enlightenment project and following a Kantian public use of reason, this model of the press would come to assume the autonomy of the Monarchy' subjects, and their transformation from Colonial subjects into the rational citizens of the nascent Republic of Chile. The press would then be the ally to the project of modernity and the necessary tool to achieve the autonomy of the newly born Republic and its inhabitants, now regarded as citizens (Silva-Castro, 1958).

Journalism's inception in the country occurred under the influence of the Eurocentric modernity and its project of autonomy. Historical accounts of press development across the region show a similar path in other countries on the continent (Marques de Melo, 2009; Aguirre, 1998; De Marco, 2006).

So far, in the history of Chilean journalism, apart from the model that stemmed from the Enlightenment project, we find no other that departs from a different epistemological – that is, situated – approach; one that, for instance, searches for a different notion of journalism within the native ethnic groups that undoubtedly must have had their means of information, probably in connection with their oral traditions. In fact, those who have studied journalism's inception in Chile assume it as inseparable from the printing press and from a literate practice of the profession, therefore our arguments that the existing notion of journalism, as well as their professional norms, were originally essentially foreign. Apart from the epistemological perspective with which Chilean journalism has been historicized, a similar issue occurred with the foundation of university schools of journalism in the country. The first appeared between 1953 (Universities of Chile and Concepción) and 1961 (Catholic University of Chile). Journalism schools began their activities under the inspiration of the Eurocentric influence area – the United States, primarily. Their founders attended training centers in those countries to get acquainted with their experiences in order to replicate them in Chile. They translated into Spanish the texts and handbooks circulating there, their reporting practices, their values, and their methods.

Both journalism history and journalism schools thus present us with such a univocal – universal – understanding of journalism that addressing a situated concept appears unnecessary by the parties involved: journalism educators, practitioners, students, or scholars. On the contrary, the univocal model appears to be the standard and norma-tive template of professional practice, unquestioningly taken to all the places and corners to be practiced and taught. That is what probably lies within Blood's assertion that 'journalism, it seems, is like pornography. The specific definition varies from person to person, but in general you know it when you see it' (Blood, cited in Mano, 2007).

The need to identify the core components of the constitutive discourse under which the prevailing model of journalism came into being and continues to function as the global normative standard is therefore crucial. After conducting a hermeneutical analysis (Araya, 2006) of the media industry's deontological codes (newspapers, radio, and televi-sion); collegial ethical codes, such as that of Colegio de Periodistas de Chile; the entity that brings together professionals in the country as well as the most cited journalism handbooks, manuals, and primers; I can clearly identify core components of this Eurocentric conception of journalism in Chile that henceforth will be referred to as '*Reporterística*.' The shared components revolve around four issues: (1) the contribution that journalism makes to society, (2) the communication model that supports such activity, (3) the type of citizen that it addresses, and (4) its relationship with the existing institutions.

First, *Reporterística* – as contained in the Eurocentric epistemology of journalism – means that journalism's contribution to society is the provi-sion of information. However, there is no greater questioning about the definition of information. It is rather assumed that information equals the publicizing of the activities carried out by those in charge of the state, or who carry out activities regarded as public – businessmen, reli-gious leaders, athletes, etc. This conception of *Reporterística* thus involves an understanding of information that is natural and therefore universal; despite the fact that as early as 1910, Max Weber (1992) claimed that what was to be understood as news in the United States and in England at that time varied due to cultural patterns.

More recently, Miquel Rodrigo-Alsina defines news as 'a social representation of everyday reality produced institutionally that manifests itself in the construction of a possible world' (Rodrigo-Alsina, 1989: 185, my translation). According to this, news has no universal value or significance but is rather acquired through the existence of interpretative communities capable of attributing value to a particular event, and who qualify it as worthy of being publicly known. Unlike what *Reporterística* does, a cultural and situated perspective of newsworthiness could allow a locally positioned concept of journalism because it is in a given place where information acquires its value, according to the signification modes of a particular audience. In a situated model of journalism, news need not to be about elites and officials and the formal institutions of the State, but about meaningful events for the community involved.

The second issue is that *Reporterística* assumes journalism as sustained by the well-known 'sender-message-recipient' model. Although vast, I will not address here the widespread critiques made by the Latin American school of reflection toward this model of communication (Pasquali, 1990). I only want to highlight two aspects: on the one hand, that this concept of communication places the sender in a position of preeminence with respect to the recipient that then feeds the assumption that the sender is the only actor capable of producing messages, since the recipient's role is limited to that of providing feedback, at best, or remaining passive and distant, at worst. The feedback acts as the acknowledgment that the sender requires to assess whether or not he or she fulfilled the goal of intentionally provoking an effect, that is to say, if he or she managed to dominate (Berlo, 1969). On the other hand, the sender-message-receipt model fails to problematize reception because the model assumes a universal or homogenous understanding of the message and, therefore, that there is only one possible reading of the message. This ignores – as claimed by seminal works in Latin American cultural studies (Martín-Barbero, 1987) – the existence of cultural mediations that influence the appropriation of messages.

This idea of *Reporterística* based on the sender-message-receiver model has three consequences:

• It leads to the assumption that the journalist is in a situation of preeminence and superiority over his or her audience – that is the reason why the journalist is a sender and the citizen only a passive recipient. This idea then justifies the journalist's position as the privileged witness of power center, a position that stems precisely from being a self-assumed representative of passive citizens.

- This view sees journalism's audience as universal without any internal diversity whatsoever. That is, it understands journalism audiences as culturally homogeneous without questioning the pluriculturalism of nation-states or their current state of multiculturalism (Kymlicka, 1996).

- And finally, *Reporterística* understands that in order to accomplish its mission effectively, journalists require certain knowledge and skills but which are restricted to the spreading and disseminating of messages, not to the understanding of reception processes.

A further issue underlying *Reporterística* places the citizen as a passive spectator; namely, as a person busier with his or her private activity than with the life of the polis. For this reason, *Reporterística* considers that the main duty of journalism consists of disseminating information to a citizen so that he or she eventually becomes the privileged spectator of the activities carried out by those responsible for making the decisions that affect the destiny of the territory. The consequence of this idea is that *Reporterística's* conception of news assumes that its main interest consists in publicizing the activities of public people, somewhat similar to the representative public sphere that Habermas (1994) describes. Understood in those terms, *Reporterística* estimates that it is up to citizens to approve or disapprove the actions of elected representatives and civil servants through polls, and, fundamentally, through votes. As it stands, it appears to be ultimately a democracy of voters and not a democracy of citizens.

Consequently, *Reporterística* does not question itself about journalism's contribution to citizen empowerment. Among other reasons, because it is not distanced enough from the conception of public space as the place wherein people debate rationally to achieve the common good. This view prevails despite arguments that the public space is a place of disputes over recognition (Fraser, 1997). Two issues are at stake in these disputes for recognition: one is the ability to be able to legitimately appear in the public space without fear of being penalized by either the speech or by stylistics conventions. The other one is to be able to deploy in public space the topics that affect a certain identity and that, for its resolution, such topics are required to be understood as public issues. This can be illustrated with gender inequalities, which at first were understood as women's private issues. Ultimately, it is a question of understanding journalism as a constructor of the social present (Gomis, 1991), or as the socially legitimized activity in order to produce publicly relevant constructions of reality (Rodrigo-Alsina, 1989).

In short, the type of journalism that contributes to the transformation of a formal citizenship into a substantive citizenship (Sojo, 2002) in our Latin American societies should pose the question about the most appropriate concept of news to reach this goal. And this not only entails the publicizing of state affairs, as it is understood by *Reporterística*, but also to move toward a concept that emphasizes the circulation of social representations that account for the diversity of actors existing in the territory, their concept of publicness, and agreements and disputes about these ideas. Therewith we can imagine a state more occupied in coordinating these actors than in imposing a certain societal project (Lechner, 1997).

Further, another issue has to do with the way in which *Reporterística* understands that journalism is at the service of a given social order. Namely, it presupposes that representative or liberal democracy, as we know it, is a natural institutional order. Therefore, it understands that journalism's role consists of strengthening that order, wherein the journalist plays a dual role: (1) the journalist is a guide for citizens on how to effectively play their part in this kind of democracy, therefore justifying the journalists' role of publicist for public and political actors, and (2) the journalist's role of purveying democratic values to a citizenry that is still not completely qualified to perform satisfactorily in the existing social order. In this new respect, this vision of *Reporterística* has further limitations.

To begin with, *Reporterística* does not assume what in Latin America has been called the discontinuity between state and nation (Martín-Barbero, 1987), that is, the cultural fracture caused by a literate state and a nation that is mostly constituted by an illiterate popular culture (García-Canclini, 1990). Therefore, *Reporterística* understands that the role of the state is, precisely, to turn Latin Americans into enlightened people and sees journalism as an irreplaceable contributor to this project without questioning the pertinence of this proposal. Also, *Reporterística* understands politics as the discussion of the means to reach an end: democracy as well as the achievement of development to overcome underdevelopment. It opens a deep gap between subjectivity and institutionality because it disregards politics as the conflictive and never accomplished construction of the desired order (Lechner, 2002). Moreover, this takes away from politics the ability to produce social integration because it is reduced to a question of means and ends efficiency that prevents us from seeing human action as a channel of the deliberate construction of a social order.

Since *Reporterística* spreads the conception of journalism typical of Eurocentric modernity, so far, all of the above allows us to understand why its model of journalism is univocal and universal, thereby closing the opportunities to devise and produce a 'situated' journalism. Consequently, a critique to this perspective would allow the provincializing of Eurocentric thought (Chakrabarty, 1992) while simultaneously opening the dialog with other regional thoughts to endorse diversity. Walter Mignolo considers this dialog crucial for the abandonment of 'universality' in order to endorse 'diversality'. According to Serequeberhan (2001), the first step in this direction consists of carrying forward a negative critical project to dismantle the existing categories in order to build up Social Sciences that let us see reality from the position that Latin American societies occupy: a colonial one.

In the project of epistemic independence that the aforementioned authors call for, there would need to be not only an overt criticism to the predominant conceptualization of journalism, but a straightforward denaturalization of its comprehension as univocal. An epistemic independence, would then need to acknowledge the role that journalism has played in the establishment of the Eurocentric hegemonic thought in Latin America, as claimed by the post-colonial theorists in the region (Mignolo, 2001).

The idea of journalism and community radio

The argument in this chapter has been a call for action to produce and promote another journalistic practice – situated journalism – whose different discourse of legitimation challenges the hegemonic condition of *Reporterística*. However, the overarching importance of the prevailing model of journalism lies in that *Reporterística* has such an influence that it affects the way in which even traditionally situated experiences such as community radios and their broadcasters understand the work they carry out.

This is one of the main findings of a research project implemented in the school of journalism of the Pontificia Universidad Católica de Valparaíso.[1] This was an investigation carried out in 29 community radio stations in the province of Valparaiso, Chile. In each of them, there was a team of broadcasters in groups ranging from 5 to 15 people that were divided into executives, reporters, anchors, and technical staff. Members of each of these teams were interviewed to know their perceptions about community radio.

For the purpose of the research, community radio was conceptualized with the definition that broadcasters themselves utilize. This methodological choice prevented researchers from deciding which one is a community radio or which one is not. Because, had the research team decided a priori what community was meant to be for the purposes of research, we risked reifying a certain conception of community radio – in vogue in the 1970s and 1980s – that did give appropriate responses to the contextual experiences of Latin America in general, and Chile in particular back in the day, but which is nowadays not as conceptually useful nor obvious in its pertinence given the current changes. Community radios were conceived in much of the existing literature as alternative yet clandestine spaces to give voice to rural, deprived and marginalised communities as well as indigenous groups and give them voice vis-a-vis dictatorial regimes and the middle classes that ruled Chile and monopolised the discussion in the press (see Ramírez, 2004 for a review). Theoretically, both 'alternativity' and 'situated discussion' were paramount to the conception of community radio. However, by taking for granted the operationalization of both ideals we would be precisely blinding ourselves of the overpowering influence of *Reporterística*. Instead, the advantage of leaving the definition of community radio to broadcasters themselves is that it invites a new knowledge of the broadcasting models that arise precisely from those involved, and the notions and assumptions of what they mean by community and whether those conceptions fit with their definition and practices of community radio. In most cases, the apparent and self-assumed goal of community radios was said to help improve the quality of life in a certain territory and foster community engagement. Alternative communicational practices aimed at achieving those goals could then be expected within this conception.

However, our study detected four issues that illustrate the expanding influence of *Reporterística* on community broadcasters and their understanding of 'alternativity': the concept of communication being used, the conception about the broadcaster, the role of community radio in the relations with the state and the community, and on the diagnosis that helps vindicate the creation of a community radio.

First, I will review the concept of communication as visualized by community radio teams. Almost all of the consulted teams understand, just as *Reporterística*, that communication is equivalent to the sender-message-receiver model. Therefore, they seem not to share the understanding of communication as a dialogic relationship inherent to human beings (Pasquali, 1990), that is, as an activity that enables people to share subjectivities, and in that way, strengthen identity and invigorate community life. In their view, the transformative power of the radio is attributed not to the linkages or social networks that it contributes to generate and strengthen in the territory – or in other words, to the community as a whole – but to the messages that the radio – and therefore the broadcasters – is able to transmit: messages that acquire greater strength if they are alternatives to the prevailing hegemonic model, yet still devised and planned by a reduced number of staff. The design of radio programming, therefore, mainly focuses on the contents of the programs, and the broadcasting teams barely mention as relevant the need for formats that encourage the active participation of the audience.

Consistent with this conceptualization is their understanding about the community broadcaster and thus who they are. Since they believe that the radio achieves its objectives thanks to the alternative messages being transmitted, community radio staff believes that the fundamental responsibility of the anchor holding the microphone is to have an in-depth knowledge of the topics being covered. This parameter defines the recruiting and hiring decisions. Conversely, while talent is valued in individual terms – what staff can do and achieve based on skills – these radio journalists do not immediately appear to see the need for staff who are able to use effective communication to establish or strengthen communal networks or to generate programming aimed to build or strengthen inter-subjectivity in the community.

The above is linked to their portrayal of their listeners. In interviews, staff noted that their audience's role is to listen to the radio and merely react to its messages. Expected expressions of such reactions include feedback sent in through telephone calls or attending the activities promoted by the radio. In this conception of their audience, again anchored in the concept of *Reporterística*, there appears to be no greater concern to incorporate audiences into the radio management or in programming decision-making.

The third aspect on the influence of *Reporterística* in community radios can be assessed in that broadcasters estimate that, to fulfill their mission, their radio stations must be recognized by the state so that they can command greater influence and authority to intervene in favor of their community demands and needs. Hence participants in the study expressed with pride that they are called upon by state institutions to discuss issues related to the territory or that governmental institutions express interest in making the most of community radio coverage to spread their messages. This effort to achieve state recognition leads them to view their audience (the community, in short) as the backing that the station needs to achieve this recognition. In this way, they attribute to their stations the position of preeminence in relation to the audience. The equation is simple: when the community gains prompt attention from the state, it is assumed that this happened because of the existence of the community radio and because of the work carried out by staffers. And, as stated earlier, community radios do not assume as their role the creation or strengthening of existing networks in the territory, but instead there is a certain clientelistic conception of citizenry. In this perspective, the community radio station assumes a self-given role of performing as the agent or representative of the citizens without which, staff believe, the community could not satisfy their demands.

The foregoing is coherent with a fourth issue: certainly, radio teams do share a diagnosis about the current media system that prompted them to launch their community radios in the first place. It is the disenchantment with the work carried out by commercial radio stations, which they do perceive as the antagonistic model to the kind of work they do. The disenchantment stems from what they consider to be the commercial radio's silencing or omission of various topics, musical trends, age groups, certain news, or the silencing of criticism toward the prevailing model of development and the institutional framework in the country.

In other words, their complaints are addressed towards the lack of content diversity and plural voices in existing commercial formats, not to the predominant way of doing radio, rife with formats that – whether commercial or alternative – do not encourage, but rather restrict, community participation. Accordingly, it makes sense that the reason behind the launching of community radios is to broadcast alternative contents to end the commercial radios' silence. In doing that, they do seem to achieve their self-assumed role. However, community radio staff do not perceive the need to work with formats that do succeed in generating a radio station capable of dynamizing the community life in a territory. This even translates into a lack of interest in generating any linkage between the different radio teams, a connection that might allow them, for example, to produce and broadcast joint programs, such as a communal or provincial news program. They do not envision spaces that make the most of the community radio stations' reach in order to constitute a much larger public space that addresses the concerns that arise from their respective communities.

Indeed, when they express interest in partnering, they do so motivated by the increased possibilities of improvement and perfecting techniques, which they understand as some sort of professionalism consisting in trying to achieve a broadcasting quality standard akin to or above that of their competitors, the commercial radio stations. On the contrary, they believe that a possible partnership with other community radio stations carries the risk of reducing their ability to fill the content gap left by commercial radio stations because that entails negotiating with the other community radio stations, which have a different stake on programming. In other words, community radios are more preoccupied with the goal that with the process of community-building, with the image they portray to their competitors than with community participation.

Conclusions

This article aims to demonstrate the hegemonic force that, thanks to globalization, acquires the concept of journalism in Eurocentric modernity, a phenomenon that I have here called *Reporterística*. This stands as the discourse that legitimizes the predominant practice of journalism in Chile. To illustrate the influence that this legitimating discourse reaches, I have presented the way in which *Reporterística* even permeates into the perception of alternative models of communications, namely community broadcasters in the province of Valparaiso, Chile.

This is particularly relevant because the model of community radio in Chile had traditionally been associated with the notion of a liberating communication and with the struggles and demands of popular sectors (Ramírez, 2004). Despite this origin, the community radio concept of broadcasters in the province of Valparaiso is strongly influenced by *Reporterística's* legitimating discourse. This means that instead of understanding their mission as a contribution to the revitalization of community life (López-Vigil, 2004), they understand it the same way as Eurocentric modernity has understood the role of journalism: a provider of information for an acclaiming citizenship.

The points raised serve to identify three challenges for community communication in the country and, by extension, to the continent. First, the need to pluralize the understanding of journalism by removing the univocality of the idea that places this activity at the service of the expansion of the Enlightenment's ideals, ultimately, of the thought of Eurocentric modernity. As it is known, this thought defines itself as universal and, therefore, by the mere fact of failing to acknowledge its own place, acquires a colonizing drive (Escobar, 2003).

To achieve this purpose, a second challenge arises: to deconstruct the discourse that legitimizes the predominant practice of journalism, and then build one of situated character, namely, one that manages to identify the contribution that journalistic professional practice can make to the building of an inclusive public space and to the strengthening of an exercise of citizenship that successfully combines subjectivity and institutionality.

And finally, linked to the above, we need to identify the actors serving as the carriers of the discourse that supports journalism. This will lead to an understanding of the role that universities play in engendering and spreading this legitimized discourse. Moreover, we may identify in what other social spaces, beyond the traditional media, there is a journalistic practice that seeks to contribute to the construction of a pertinent social order for an empowered citizenry.

Ultimately, my call is on how to rethink the idea of journalism that envisions an active citizenship, and thereby, contributes to the strengthening of community life. In doing so, we will advance toward the inception of a different practice of journalism that sets itself apart from the predominant practice in the country, one that so far serves local elites, thus hindering the role that local and community media can play in the emergence of an active citizenship, and thus, in the democratization of the public space.

Note

1. From here two Bachelor's theses were produced: 'Radios comunitarias: una instancia para el fortalecimiento de la comunidad y su labor como reconstructores del espacio público' (Community radios: an instance for the strengthening of the community and his work as rebuilders of public space), by Magaly Fuenzalida and Daniela Hernández, and 'Hacia un estudio de la mentalidad presente en la producción de radios comunitarias posmodernas. Experiencias de la provincia de Valparaíso' (Toward a study on mentality present in the production of post-modern community radios. Experiences in the province of Valparaiso), by Pamela Contreras and Catteryn Rodríguez.

References

Aguirre, J. M. (1998) *La estructuración de la identidad profesional del comunicador social en Venezuela* (Caracas: Universidad Católica Andrés Bello).
Anderson, B. (1993) *Comunidades imaginadas: reflexiones sobre el origen y la difusión del nacionalismo* (Ciudad de México: Fondo de Cultura Económica).

Araya, R. (2006) *Bases para un periodismo intercultural*, Master Thesis in Communication [unpublished], Universidad de Chile.

Berlo, D. (1969) *El proceso de la Comunicación* (Buenos Aires: El Ateneo).

Brieger, P. (2007) 'No todo es censura,' in VV.AA. *Entre el deseo y la realidad* (Buenos Aires: UTPBA).

Chakrabarty, D. (1992) 'Provincializing Europe: postcoloniality and the critique of history,' *Cultural Studies*, 6(3): 337–357.

Chalaby, J. (1996) 'Journalism as an Anglo-American invention: A comparison of the development of French and Anglo-American journalism, 1830–1920s', *European Journal of Communication*, 11(3): 303–326.

De Marco, M. A. (2006) *Historia del periodismo argentino: desde los orígenes hasta el centenario de Mayo* (Buenos Aires: Educa).

Dérmota, K. (2002) *Chile inédito, el periodismo bajo democracia* (Santiago: Ediciones B).

Deuze, M. (2005) 'What is journalism?: professional identity and ideology of journalists reconsidered,' *Journalism*, 20(6): 442–464.

Escobar, A. (2003) 'Mundo y conocimientos de otro modo. El programa de investigación de Modernidad/Colonialidad latinoamericano,' *Revista Tabula Rasa*, 1: 51–56.

Escobar, A. (2006) 'An ecology of difference: equality and conflict in a glocalized world,' *Focaal*, 47: 120–140 (originally prepared for UNESCO's *World Culture Report*, 1999).

Fraser, N. (1997) *Iustitia Interrupta: Reflexiones críticas desde la posición postsocialista* (Bogotá: Siglo del Hombre).

García-Canclini, N. (1990) *Culturas Híbridas* (México: Grijalbo).

Gomis, L. (1991) *Teoría del Periodismo: cómo se forma el presente* (Barcelona: Paidos).

Habermas, J. (1994) *Historia y Crítica de la Opinión Pública* (Barcelona: Gustavo Gili).

Hanitzsch, T. (2007) 'Deconstructing journalism culture: toward a universal theory,' *Communication Theory*, 17(4): 367–385.

Israel, A. M. (1992) 'The Afrocentric perspective in African journalism: a case study of the Ashanti pioneer: 1939–1957,' *Journal of Black Studies*, 22: 411–428.

Kymlicka, W. (1996) *Ciudadanía multicultural* (Barcelona: Paidós).

Lander, E. (1993) 'Ciencias Sociales: saberes coloniales y eurocéntricos,' pp. 11–40 in E. Lander (comp.) *La colonialidad del saber: eurocentrismo y ciencias sociales. Perspectivas latinoamericanas* (Buenos Aires: Clacso).

Lechner, N. (1997) 'Tres formas de coordinación social,' *Revista de la Cepal*, 61: 7–17.

Lechner, N. (2002) *Las sombras del mañana* (Santiago: Lom).

López-Vigil, J. I. (2004) *Manual urgente para radialistas apasionados* (Quito: Ciespal).

Mano, W. (2007) 'Popular music as journalism in Zimbabwe,' *Journalism Studies*, 8(1): 61–78.

Marques de Melo, J. (2009) 'Journalistic thinking: Brazil's modern tradition,' *Journalism*, 10: 9–27.

Martín-Barbero, J. (1987) *De los medios a las mediaciones* (Barcelona: Gustavo Gili).

Mato, D. (coord.) (2009) *Instituciones Interculturales de Educación Superior en América Latina* (Caracas: IESALC/UNESCO).

Mignolo, W. (comp.) (2001) *Capitalismo y geopolítica del conocimiento. El Eurocentrismo y la filosofía de la liberación en el debate intelectual contemporáneo* (Buenos Aires: Duke University/Ediciones del Signo).

Mönckeberg, M. O. (2009) *Los magnates de la prensa: concentración de los medios de comunicación en Chile* (Santiago: Debate).

Ossandón, C. and Santa-Cruz, E. (2001) *Entre las alas y el plomo: la gestación de la prensa moderna en Chile* (Santiago: Lom).

Pasquali, A. (1990) *Comunicación y Cultura de Masas* (Caracas: Monte Ávila).

Ramírez, J. D. (2004) 'Creación, desarrollo y proyecciones de la radio comunitaria en el sur de Chile,' *Revista Austral de Ciencias Sociales*, 8: 109–132.

Ricoeur, P. (1989) *Ideología y Utopía* (Barcelona: Gedisa).

Rodrigo-Alsina, M. (1989) *La construcción de la Noticia* (Barcelona: Paidos).

Sandoval, P. (comp.) (2009) *Pensando la Subalternidad* (Lima: IEP-Sephis).

Schudson, M. (2001) 'The objectivity norm in American journalism', *Journalism: Theory, Practice and Criticism*, 2(2): 149–170.

Schudson, M. (2003) *The Sociology of News* (New York: Norton and Company).

Schudson, M. (2005) 'The US model of journalism: exception or exemplar?', pp. 94–106 in H. De Burgh (ed.) *Making Journalists: Diverse Models, Global Issues* (London: Routledge).

Serequeberhan, T. (2001) 'La crítica al eurocentrismo y la práctica de la filosofía africana,' pp. 253–281 in W. Mignolo (comp.) *Capitalismo y geopolítica del conocimiento. El Eurocentrismo y la filosofía de la liberación en el debate intelectual contemporáneo* (Buenos Aires: Duke University/Ediciones del Signo).

Silva-Castro, R. (1958) *Prensa y Periodismo en Chile* (Santiago: Ediciones de la Universidad de Chile).

Skjerdal, T. S. (2012) 'The three alternative journalisms of Africa,' *International Communication Gazette*, 74: 636–654.

Sojo, C. (2002) 'La noción de ciudadanía en el debate latinoamericano,' *Revista de la CEPAL*, 76: 25–38.

Valdebenito, A. (1956) *Historia del Periodismo Chileno (1812–1955)* (Santiago: Imprenta Fantasía).

Weber, M. (1992) 'Para una sociología de la prensa,' *Revista Española de Investigaciones Sociológicas*, 57: 251–259.

Zelizer, B. (1993) 'Journalists as interpretetive communities', *Critical Studies in Mass Communication*, 10: 219–237.

15

Post-authoritarian Politics in a Neoliberal Era: Revising Media and Journalism Transition in Mexico

Mireya Márquez-Ramírez

Introduction

For the past two centuries various influences have decidedly shaped the changing relations between Mexico's private news media and the equally mutable state. Local forces and actors; the inevitable impact of global stimuli such as commercialism; and the absence, obsolescence, or non-enforcement of media regulation have profoundly shaped Mexico's news media and journalism. Throughout this chapter, it is evident that a hybrid media system and a resulting post-authoritarian journalistic culture are in place. Both are better grasped through the understanding of cultural patterns, habits, changing interests, and under-the-table arrangements that have prevailed regardless of political democratization – and sometimes as result of it. Hence, the mere study of global forces, formal legal frameworks, ownership structures, discursive adoption of journalistic norms, or institutional structures can not fully account for the 'captured liberal' nature of Mexico's news media.

A country with a long-standing history of political instability, conflict, and authoritarianism has left an indelible footprint in the structural, organizational, cultural, and individual configuration of both the media system and the culture of journalism. However, with the turn of the century and the decades prior to it, a number of studies have documented the emergence of what they deem to be patterns of journalistic professionalization, media modernization, and the 'opening' of Mexico. In comparison to earlier decades of authoritarian political rule, by the

1990s a number of authors, in fact, observed a much varied range of sources, more plural, fact-based and less sycophantic reporting, investigation of corruption and exposés, a legal framework to ensure access to information, and a more robust exercise in critical reporting and press freedom (Lawson, 2002; Wallis, 2004; Hughes, 2006). For example, Lawson (2002) claims that when compared to how things had been for decades in terms of censorship, repression, or media collusion with political elites, the press began to open with a variety of themes and critical reporting due to political democratization and commercialism. For her part, Sallie Hughes (2006) argues that while different segments of the media followed three oppositional paths – either civic, inertial, or commercial – a widespread wave of 'civic journalism' has become 'the dominant form of newspaper journalism in the country' (2006: 6).

The aforementioned authors also strongly connect the patterns of what they consider to be professionalization, modernization, and opening in journalism to the adoption of US news values, formats, and press business models that slowly distanced it from the state apparatus and gradually grew closer to either civic voices or to market logics (Lawson, 2002; Hughes, 2006). Similarly, regardless of the complicated and ambiguous ways in which Mexican journalists assimilate and adapt global frameworks of professional values – such as objectivity and autonomy – or the way in which they enact passive reporting through the adaptation of 'professional' values (Márquez-Ramírez, 2012a, 2012b), this line of research argues that by the end of the 20th century, the press had become 'more assertive, investigative, politically engaged, and generally balanced' (Wallis, 2004: 118). The electoral victory of the center-right Party of National Action (PAN by its Spanish acronym) in 2000 – the oppositional party that ended the 70-year consecutive ruling of the Institutional Revolutionary Party (PRI by its Spanish acronym) – prompted an author to predict that president-to-be Vicente Fox was going to bring 'a cataclysmic break with the past that inexorably pushes the modernization of Mexico's media forward' (Rockwell, 2002: 109).

As predominant lines of thought, these narratives of media change – henceforth referred to as 'liberal' – often highlight the positive effects of commercialism in eroding authoritarian journalistic cultures and promoting democratic deliberation through investigative and watchdog journalism. In other words, the assumption is that global trends help alleviate local ailments. By global trends these studies de facto assume the standardization of features normally attributed to liberal economies: democracy, commercialism, deregulation, private property, and commercial funding for the media; likewise, a mass-oriented press; little intervention on the part of the state or political actors; and the watchdog role of journalism (Siebert, Peterson and Schramm, 1956; Hallin and Mancini, 2004; Christians, Glasser, McQuail, Nordenstreng and White, 2009). It is hence assumed that the more liberalized the media system is, the more open and plural their news media are, and thus the more professional their journalistic standards become (Hallin and Mancini, 2004). Not surprisingly, the predominance of this narrative is found in most comprehensive studies on Mexican journalism throughout the 1990s and in fact in several other studies across the region (Tironi and Sunkel, 2000; Alves, 2005; Pinto, 2009). The underlying assumption in much of this scholarship is that in emerging democracies both a hospitable commercial environment and the solidification of a multi-party political system eventually erode the traditional complicity between the state and the media, de-legitimate the use of censorship as a mechanism of control, and foster competition that in turn broadens the spectrum of choices and voices in the media.

However, there has been a contrasting approach to media transition that focuses on the growth of unaccountable media power; the perils of rampant commercialism, deregulation, and press-state complicity; and the effects of media concentration in democratic processes. These have been long-standing topics of preoccupation in Mexican media research and in fact, in Latin America as a whole. Departing from the standpoint that the political, economic, and journalistic fields continue to be fully integrated, critical political economists view journalism as the most distinguishable instrument for media proprietors and political actors to advance and accommodate their news agendas to their economic and political interests. Far from the docile or complicit role they used to play during the authoritarian era, they claim, a Mexican 'mediacracy' has fully consolidated, re-shifting the subordination role to a more protagonist one (Trejo-Delarbre, 2001, 2005). Not only have the media filled the void left by weakly supported political parties and judicial system, but also the public space is now filled by a news agenda often defined – particularly during times of crisis and political conflict – by an established elite at the service of private interests (Márquez-Ramírez, 2012b). The fear about the rising power of broadcast media in shaping media policy and avoiding regulation has prompted definitional labels in book and article titles, such as 'governing television' (Villamil, 2005), the 'Fourth Media Republic' (Esteinou, 2008), and the 'Televisa Law' (Esteinou and Alva de la Selva, 2009).

With these contrasting readings about the Mexican media landscape, have they indeed democratized and fully opened after two decades of political reforms, transitions, and commercialism? Is journalism more professional, critical, and above all, autonomous? The clear gaps that emerge from comparing the liberal and the radical approaches to media transition revive the need to comprehensively account for the structural, organizational, cultural, and individual forces impacting news media in general and journalistic practices in particular. I argue in this chapter that the hybrid nature of Mexican journalistic culture means that clashing forces: authoritarianism (tradition) and commercialism (modernity) have blended, not unlike other forms of cultural production. As cultural scholar Néstor García-Canclini claims, tradition and modernity are highly interdependent in Latin America: 'We find in the study of cultural heterogeneity one of the means to explain the oblique powers that intermingle liberal institutions and authoritarian habits, social democratic movements with paternalistic regimes, and their mutual transactions' (García-Canclini, 2005: 3).

Private media in authoritarian hands: the captured liberal model in Mexico

Depending on the global or local forces at stake in the struggle for power, various exogenous and endogenous influences have shaped the journalistic culture, the media system, and therefore the press-state relations in Mexico. This must be analyzed in the light of the impact of continuing political instability, war and conflict, extended periods of authoritarian political rule, and a 'flexibilized' approach to commercialism and democracy. These forces all have blended to produce a hybrid press model that Guerrero (See Chapter 2 in this book) calls 'captured liberal.' Such a model retains the features attributed to two contrasting models in Hallin and Mancini's (2004) three-fold categorization of media systems: the 'liberal' vis-à-vis the 'polarized-pluralist.' The strong presence, domination, and high levels of 'political parallelism' and 'political instrumentalization' in Mexico's news media are akin to the 'polarized-pluralist' model existing in Mediterranean countries. However, these characteristics have developed not in the context of formal state intervention in public broadcasting, or in the overtly partisan press as seen in Italy, Greece, and Spain. In fact, Mexico's media have been 'overwhelmingly commercial and privately owned' (Hallin, 2000: 101) since their inception and technically qualify as 'liberal' by their property type and stated mission.

Traditionally, media property has been inherited in Mexico – Televisa being the most notable case – and thus the media business tend to stay in the family for decades (Sinclair, 2002). This was the case throughout the 20th century. Under the wing and patronage of the PRI-governments and presidents, organizations like Televisa slowly grew into multimedia conglomerates of gigantic proportions (Sinclair, 1999, 2002). The trened, however, did only intensify with the arrival of democratic and neoliberal governments. More recently, pro-business newspapers like Excelsior have vastly benefited from the past three administrations of allegedly democratic credentials: Vicente Fox (2000–2006, PAN party), Felipe Calderón (2006–2012, PAN party), and Enrique Peña Nieto (2012–2018, PRI party back in power) and have now become just a link to a much wider business portfolio (Lara-Khlar, 2007).

The captured liberal model of Mexican media has meant that at the upper levels of hierarchy, private media still exchange loyalties to the president in office for benefits, as they did in pre-democracy days or the party in power as they do in post-democracy days. These may include advertisement contracts, tax exemptions, permits, and license renewals to grow business. Unlike the highly instrumentalized media systems in Mediterranean countries wherein politicians own media organizations or media proprietors run for office, in the captured liberal model in Mexico, political neutrality is not an ideological position or a tenet of professionalism but a commodity to exchange. My previous research (Márquez-Ramírez, 2012c) shows how economic interests are more conveniently served by minimizing confrontation or maintaining political allegiances with certain political actors. Therefore, I argue that political instrumentalization or state intervention in Mexico's media system does not necessarily stem from explicit partisanships, draconian laws, or legal frameworks implemented to ensure governmental control, restrict media movements, or limit freedoms, but primarily from unwritten arrangements crafted by contexts and pragmatics.

To understand how collusion and complicity between media elites and political actors came into place, it is first necessary to trace back the development of media industries in Mexico that occurred at contrasting paces. For example, akin to many European and Latin American countries (Mancini, 2000; Hallin and Papathanassopoulos, 2002; Hallin and Mancini, 2004), the Mexican print press stayed oriented toward elite readerships, developed very slowly as a commercial business, and thus had consistently small circulations throughout the 19th and 20th centuries. A sustained history of social conflict, wars, and political instability in the 19th century became the fertile terrain for the development of a very active militant and partisan press as well as for the strong influence of literary narratives and intellectual debates in the newspapers. The

19th century press in Mexico also underwent periods of freedom and censorship, partisanship and detachment – depending on the fragility or strength of whoever held power at the time (Pérez-Rayón, 2005). Conversely, the broadcast industry successfully developed its commercial position throughout the 20th century, modeling itself after the United States. A century later, Mexico has become one of the most concentrated countries in the world in the sectors of media and telecommunications. Daniel Hallin has observed that by the turn of the millennium: 'there [was] no country comparable in size to Mexico in which a single private company [Televisa] so dominate[d] the airwaves' (Hallin, 2000: 96). Up to 1993, Televisa was the sole commercial TV network in the country. It had grown from being a single TV channel in the 1950s to becoming the biggest media conglomerate of the Hispanic world by the 1980s[1]: it began its horizontal and vertical integration long before other worldwide media conglomerates did so. Only in 1993, after pressures from the competition clauses contained in the National Free Trade Agreement (NAFTA) signed by Mexico, the United states and Canada, TV Azteca came into the pitch as the second competitor in television, fuelling hopes that some plurality and content diversity would ensue. However, this much smaller corporation was one of the very few beneficiaries of the privatization of state-administered TV channels carried out by a self-proclaimed neoliberal reformer, Carlos Salinas, in 1993, a process that back in the day attracted widespread criticism and controversy.[2]

Following a short period of alternative content in the mid 1990s, soon TV Azteca became part of a growing and powerful media 'duo-poly'. Like Televisa, the new network held very clear political orientations and came into being thanks to political connections and a president's goodwill. In fact, regardless of who wielded power during PRI 70-year consecutive rule – whether nationalistic oriented presidents of the 1970s or 'modern' reformers between the 1980s and the 1990s – not only technically private media corporations but also smaller publications have enjoyed limitless benefits and financial survival in exchange for loyalty, good coverage, and publicity (Caletti-Kaplan, 1988; Cleary, 2003; Rodríguez-Munguía, 2007). Such was the media's intertwining with the country's one-party system that the country's most important media baron – Televisa's Chairman Emilio Azcárraga Milmo – famously proclaimed his utter loyalty to the system by claiming to be 'the PRI's soldier' (Fromson, 1996). The overtly clear political subordination waned with the strengthening of media markets. Nowadays, in a politically diverse context where various parties and actors hold key seats, his heir and current Chairman, Emilio Azcárraga Jean, appears to be more pragmatic and open with his political allegiances. His 'business-first whoever is in office' approach adopted during the late 1990s as part of a strategy shift, means that his main TV channel and news service has either supported or confronted through various means those political actors who represent a direct benefit or threat to his business expansion, particularly during election time (Villamil, 2005, 2012; García-Calderón, 2007).

Throughout the 20th century though, there were few incentives for media executives to shift loyalties away from the PRI system: part of the party's success to retain office despite a rotation of leadership and a façade of democratic elections was that it managed to devise mechanisms to exert control of the media without the need of harsh regulation. These mechanisms, as I have argued elsewhere (Márquez-Ramírez, 2012d, 2014), deeply impacted reporting culture, professional and ethical values, media content, and ownership structures of print and broadcast media. Such mechanisms of press-state collusion were the following:

1. *Bribery and payoffs.* A crucial aspect of the relation between the state and journalists entails the government's co-opting of salaried reporters. As Fromson (1996) notes, this operated in a myriad of ways: free meals, transportation, hotel accommodation, junkets to resorts, luxury gifts sent to newsrooms and personal addressees, and – potentially the most embarrassing but also the most common method – by direct payment, known as *chayotes* or *embutes*. Reporters received them in an envelope in return for 'planting a story, twisting a story's angle or point of view, or spiking an embarrassing piece' (Fromson, 1996: 113; Cleary, 2003).

2. *Control and handling of criticism, spin, and information flow.* Ensuring the right spin on political coverage was fundamental to the maintenance of the PRI's power as a controller of public information and was an equally crucial element in keeping control over the public agenda. In the avalanche of information that such an overarching system generated, 'newspapers reflected an overwhelming dependence on officialdom' (Lawson, 2002: 49). Apart from the sycophantic coverage of the president and his activities, monopolization of information meant that voices other than official ones were rarely met, often overlooked, and negatively portrayed in the print press.

3. *Ostensible freedom of the press.* The system claimed to be open and respectful of press autonomy, even by institutionalizing an annual reception to commemorate Press Freedom Day – an event not meant to be an opportunity for the president to acknowledge the press, but

the other way around: an opportunity for the press to show support and pay respect to the president, to express its gratitude for permitting an 'unrestrictive freedom of speech.' On its own terms, this ceremony became symbolic of the cynical display of press servitude to the system (Rodríguez-Castañeda, 1993).

4. *Control and subsidy of newsprint.* One of the most effective instruments of the state in controlling and co-opting the media was the subsidy and monopolization of newsprint production and distribution by the supplier PIPSA. This state-run company subsidized newsprint prices, so that publications could cope financially because historically low circulations in Mexico as well as insufficient private advertising made journalism outlets barely profitable. In exchange for the low-priced material, publishers were not legally obliged but certainly expected to offer support to the president and the dominant segment of the party. Each time the government wanted to review subsidies, publishers saw it as a threat to their economic interests, or as an explicit expression of reprimand (Fuentes-Beráin, 2002).

5. *Economic dependence on political advertising.* This consisted in the selective allocation and distribution of political and institutional advertising. Back in the day, state-owned or public-administered industries dominated and private advertisers were not only scarce but complicit with the government or susceptible to political manipulation. Within the vast supply of political and official advertising, the most striking form was the *gacetilla*, a paid insert typically prepared by the government to resemble a genuine newspaper article (Benavides, 2000). Moreover, the government purchased advertising space to publicize official achievements for all the state agencies. As a result, ample advertising budgets were frequently denied to independent publications as a form of reprimand and were awarded to sympathetic and loyal ones.

6. *Lax regulatory and legal framework in print and broadcast industries.* Media legislation in Mexico has been notorious for being outdated and often nonexistent in practice and for serving the economic interests of media proprietors. For example, newspapers are not licensed or regulated by any central government-related agency that oversees their functioning, content, or the public's complaints; and the only legislation concerning print media dates back to the 1917 Constitution. In practice, the press has been left to regulate itself. Likewise, there is no national association to which print media widely subscribe that might allow industry-wide adherence to voluntary codes of conduct in journalism; neither are there any institutions, public or industry-run that

verify and certify the circulation of publications or reports on media performance. There is in practice no one to channel and deal with media complaints; or a collegial, independent body or union that licenses, examines, protects, trains, or speaks on the behalf of organized journalists at a national level (Hernández-López, 1999).

7. *Discretionary awarding and renewal of broadcast licenses.* The state facilitated and promoted, rather than opposed or constrained, the consolidation of media industries by granting broadcasting licenses to key allies. The old boys' network of relationships between PRI political leaders – such as the president and his ministers – and powerful businessmen meant that in exchange for media deregulation, discretionary concessions, and extension of broadcast licenses, propagandistic plans through news and entertainment content were unbridled. The governmental protection and perpetuation of faulty (de) regulatory frameworks held the media unaccountable to the public and enabled the consolidation of radio and TV monopolies in the hands of very few individuals and families that continues to this day.

8. *Censorship, and the silencing of oppositional voices.* The aforementioned mechanisms of complicity and co-option of media elites made overt censorship and repression unnecessary. However, a few cases did stand out in recent press history when the system resorted to censorship, repression, or advertisement boycotts. The Tlatelolco student massacre in 1968 crowned a period of the worst authoritarian rule in which the press was subjugated to the state's discipline. Later, a well-documented episode known as the Excelsior-coup[3] – in which the government masterminded the deposition of a critical newspaper director – became emblematic of the conflictive relations and gradual visibility of the critical media.

As we can observe from these mechanisms implemented during the authoritarian rule, the culture of submission was not gratuitous. 'A web of subsidies, concessions, bribes, and prerequisites created a captive media establishment that faithfully reflected ruling party priorities' (Lawson, 2002: 173). From the very beginning the private media emerged as a technically 'independent' institution but in reality so deeply entrenched with the official ruling party that the system neither devised the creation of a strong state-ruled media to pursue its own propagandist aims nor an autonomous public broadcasting service as occurred with most European countries (Hallin and Mancini, 2004). The media barons and elite politicians were so in tune, that the system saw little need to encourage any public, meaningful debate – let alone advocate – for any reform proposal concerning the press and the media's public responsibility and freedom of speech. As for the working conditions of Mexican journalists, in the late 1970s and 1980s, reporters lacked skills and competence, were poorly paid, enjoyed little job security, had little training or educational background, learned on the job, and were prone to accepting and using governmental bribes and payoffs to supplement their living (Baldivia, Planet, Solís and Guerra, 1981). The aforementioned circumstances and the convulse period of key political and social events throughout three decades[4] thus prompted more debate on media reform and the need journalistic professionalization. For many, neoliberalism was the pathway for such endeavors.

Privatization and commercialism in the wave of transition

The early years of neoliberal governments evolved around the signing of NAFTA in 1992. This long negotiated treaty entailed the Mexican government's commitment to increase media competition in the broadcasting sector. As mentioned earlier, President Carlos Salinas de Gortari (1988–1994) carried out the privatization of two state-run channels called Imevision that gave rise to TV Azteca. Many analysts from that time were confident that the liberal reforms fostered by NAFTA would buttress the consolidation of the freedom and autonomy of the press that civil society and media observers had longed for. In fact, Lawson (2002) and Hughes (2006) greatly attribute the cultural conversion of authoritarian media into modern, free,civic, and democratic to the aforementioned reforms. In theory, this modernization process of the media under the new wave of neoliberal privatizations entailed a renovation of a financially autonomous media business no longer dependent on governmental assistance and therefore more prone to critical coverage; balanced reporting of oppositional political actors, particularly during election time; the end of the bribery culture and newsprint subsidies; and the overall professionalization of university educated journalists (Trejo-Delarbre, 1996; Carreño-Carlón, 2000).

The neoliberal reforms certainly affected the traditional press-state relations in a number of ways. Financially, one of the most immediate consequences of economic reforms in the media was the privatization of more than a thousand state-run enterprises that for the first time became fresh nongovernmental sources of advertising for the media (Hernández-Ramírez, 2010b). In theory, the Carlos Salinas' and Ernesto Zedillo's PRI governments (1988–1994 and 1994–2000) did establish a number of measures to modernize relations with the press: government branches refrained from financing journalists' expenses during trips; guidelines for the allocation of advertising budgets were supposedly reviewed; and the newsprint supplier PIPSA was privatized, thus ending state subvention and one of the most enduring forms of control (Carreño-Carlón, 2000). Additionally, perhaps the most iconic change occurred in 1994 when the president no longer attended or hosted Press Freedom Day, and so put an end to the customary display of flattery.

Moreover, it is also true that the newspaper industry dramatically changed with the arrival of a financially independent, commercially viable, and journalistically professional newspaper named *Reforma* in 1993 that rose editorial standards for the whole industry and addressed a captive market of middle-class, educated readers that held oppositional and alternative political views. The 1990s were thus a period of consolidation of synergies and franchises of newspapers as profitable business models that became oriented toward the market (Hernández-Ramírez, 2010b). In terms of coverage, a context of constant upheaval reflected in the media through the publication of exposes, the multiplication of political scandals, and the diversification of news sources. Not surprisingly, this period is often considered by the accounts of Lawson (2002) and Hughes (2006) as the renaissance of investigative and critical journalism in Mexico. Similarly, radio news programs whose news anchors held various political sympathies gave credence to the discourse of plurality and political diversity. As in many other countries, radio news hosts had resorted to 'discourses of integrity to consolidate the public inquisitor as a discursive figure' (Higgins, 2010) and discovered its commercial and profit-making value.

Overall, by the mid-1990s, it is fair to acknowledge that the political establishment carried out various political and economic reforms to guarantee fair and competitive elections and to foster competition and commercialization in the media landscape. As a result, they were both considerably more open, critical, and competitive than they had ever been. Many claim, however, that 'opening' in the media resulted from commercial incentives rather than from media elites' commitment to democratic values: 'Raising the game in terms of journalistic standards and political sophistication became a matter of survival in the 1990s; [since] obeisance to the regime would no longer suffice' (Wallis, 2004: 118; see also Guerrero, 2004).

So far the changes on the surface were apparent, but disguised a lot more. Despite the widespread optimism, Mexican historian Lorenzo

Meyer argues that the reforms carried out in the 1990s were as modern as they were authoritarian. He argues that President Salinas used the most traditional instruments of Mexican authoritarian politics to modernize Mexican economics (Meyer, quoted in personal interview by Thelen, 1999). The façade of neoliberal discourses of modernization at times disguised the prevalence of censorship, blackmailing, mutating allegiances and several other authoritarian inertias. For instance, in retaliation for their coverage and extensive documentation of the alleged electoral fraud that took president Salinas de Gortari to power in 1988, critical publications such as *Proceso*, *El Financiero*, and *La Jornada* struggled to obtain governmental advertising contracts or gain access to information, and many were excluded from the coverage of high profile official events (Lawson, 2002: 39).

Censorship and surveillance continued at the middle layers of the government and party, and in many news outlets the reporting of events still followed the official discourse and agenda, even if the presidential figure was more tolerant to criticism and questioning. By the late 1990s, however, a single-party beginning to lose its overarching power and the growing stake of oppositional parties seeking to advertise their candidates and platforms meant more business opportunities and less need of subordination of editorial decisions to the single-party. A devastating electoral defeat approached as both the president and the party appeared more distanced, isolated, and ideologically opposed than ever.

Change and continuity within post-authoritarianism

Despite the prevalence of the core structural conditions that have shaped the Mexican media system and its resulting journalistic culture, there are considerable differences in how journalism functions after political democratization, in regard to the authoritarian days. Without a doubt, the press is free, diverse, and competitive in a way that few could have imagined thirty years ago. A variety of changes are currently shaping journalism in Mexico: a wider and diverse range of news sources enabled by political democracy now give more balanced perspectives that were unimaginable four decades ago, when oppositional parties were illegal. News media promptly informed us, nearly without any restriction, about the multiple accusations and cases of wrongdoing committed by all political parties from 2000 to 2004. Elite journalists such as radio presenters or political columnists now interrogate presidential decisions and public policies in a way that was not possible fifty years ago. The secrecy characteristic of the authoritarian era has now given place to legislation on Transparency and Access to Information passed during Vicente Fox's term (2000–2006), which certainly propelled the opportunities to source stories and conduct investigative journalism (López-Ayllón, 2004).

However, a growing body of literature poses a contrasting view that helps to debunk the argument of media democratization and straightforward journalistic professionalization. This work points out that while journalists did gain considerably more freedom to report on critical issues, it doesn't mean investigative journalism is profitable or actively incentivated within the newsrooms, quite the opoosite in fact (Márquez-Ramírez, 2012a, 2012b). Actually, observers perceive the quality of reporting as unsatisfactory, if not low (Levario-Turcott, 2002; Riva Palacio, 2005; Hernández-Ramírez, 2010a). Instead of the liberal – and certainly global template of professionalism – argument about a Fourth Estate characterized by political neutrality, protection of the public interest, and assertive reporting, media observers like Marco Levario-Turcott (2002) find a 'media democratic drunkenness' manifested in several print reportages and news coverage. A superficial and sensationalist angle prevails, the information is based on unverified rumors or leaks, and the suppression of investigative journalism is filled with speculation and the focus is on political harangues. He claims that Mexican journalists of the post-authoritarian era display their sympathies and aversions without honesty and explicitly admitting them.

From the sum of contemporary journalists' testimonies (Márquez-Ramírez, 2005, 2012c, 2014), it is possible to observe the continuity of age-old ailments. Mexican journalistic work – much as their worldwide counterparts – is constrained by heavy workloads, low salaries, tight deadlines and pragmatic ethical values. They rely on passive reporting methods and on the (biased) agendas of a small number of elite sources and methods, or what Jay Rosen (2009) calls 'he said-she said' type of journalism and a shortage of contextualization, minimal cross-checking, and corroboration (Hernández-Ramírez, 2010a). In fact, the prevalence of on-the-spot type of news stories is also said to be the consequence of hierarchical social structures within the newsroom implemented to face increasing pressures and commercial competition (McPherson, 2012). Akin to what Silvio Waisbord (2000) found in South America, Mexican journalists "do not hold a dreamy-eyed belief in journalistic independence, but instead, show a pragmatic attitude and admission that constraints are inevitable and vary across media" (2000: 148).

The accentuation of what we find to be 'selective' and 'targeted' press freedom, censorship, and poor reporting is worse in the growing context of statelessness (Waisbord, 2007) and widespread drug-related violence across the country (Relly and González de Bustamante, 2014). Most importantly, old forms of press-state relations and reporting inertias remain. With the political and economic transformations brought about by the change of government in 2000, the media were no longer obliged to act as the organic mouthpieces of a ruling party, but instead multiplied their contacts with a diversity of available actors. Whether regional or federal, religious or corporate, the media transplanted their long-standing authoritarian business model – steady supply of advertising in exchange for coverage, and good coverage in the case of presidential elections – to new political and corporate patrons. This has impacted journalistic culture in various ways in the past decade. Many of these actors – rising-stars politicians from all parties always courting favorable publicity – also began to manifest their inexperience and vulnerability through countless gaffes, errors, and corruption cases, positioning themselves as the target of a newly gained freedom of speech manifested through scandals and overt criticism on the part of high profile radio hosts and print columnists.

For the media, political scandals and the resulting iconoclastic journalism aimed at all political parties has become both a business opportunity and a channel to appeal to audiences in an attempt to regain credibility and lay claims to critical journalism, objectivity, and impartiality (Márquez-Ramírez, 2005, 2012c). Nevertheless, frequently the target subjects of such iconoclastic journalism are chosen after consideration of the economic and political interests of the media – or market-driven partisanship (González Macías, 2013) – rather than from a genuine commitment to the public interest. As Waisbord found in his seminal study on South American newsrooms, while 'attention-grabbing exposés give temporary boosts to sales [...] the political and business costs outweigh potential market revenues' (2000: 70–71). Thus, the civic journalism approach that presupposes the exercise of a watchdog role of the press overlooks the fact that in the captured liberal model of the media and the post-authoritarian journalistic culture in Mexico, scandals may bow down to the logic of political and economic interests or to partisan diatribes, and not necessarily to democratic convictions.

Even more crucially, as state agencies continue to function like the main source of advertisement for most media, they still constitute a very important source of revenue, especially among smaller organizations across regions. Political parties, governments, and state agencies all continue to publicize their achievements through the press, often through well-known means inherited from the *Priista* era: from advertising credited and clearly identified as such, gacetillas and publicity disguised as news, or most recently, as the cynical intention of news coverage, front pages, or interviews in exchange for cash or benefits (Marquez-Ramírez, 2005, 2012c). Due to the frequent periodicity and duration of election periods in Mexico (federal, regional, municipal, and mid-term), election time has historically been the source of economic boosts for the media, particularly broadcasters, due to their high ratings among the working and middle classes. Not only political parties (up to 2007), but the government and state agencies crucially spend most of their election-time media budgets on TV and radio. Between 2000 and 2006, the state's expenditure on media increased every year (Bravo, 2009; Trejo-Delabre, 2010).

Likewise, the passing of electoral reform in 2007 that bans political parties and third parties from buying airtime on radio and TV to avoid misuse of resources and inequitable competition, fueled a media campaign to discredit congress and particularly the senators and officials who pushed through the reforms. After media expenditure became an issue of debate around fair competition after the 2006 presidential elections and post-electoral conflict (Márquez-Ramírez, 2012b), political parties are now supposedly banned from purchasing airtime in the media after the 2007 electoral reform. However, it is possible to observe such policy subverted thorugh other nonregulated forms of publicity: the old-day gacetilla spirit has resurfaced. In fact, the most recent election in Mexico, on July 1, 2012, has certainly lent plenty of credit to this practice. Analysts and commentators believe that the media had carefully helped to enable the triumphal return of the PRI and its telegenic candidate Enrique Peña Nieto to presidency: the amount of positive coverage on his political activities way before he became the official candidate arose widespread suspicions back then (Kuschick, 2009; Rúas Araujo, 2011; Villamil, 2012). Besides Televisa and TV Azteca, smaller media conglomerates like Milenio or Grupo Imagen now add to the elite of businessmen whose commercial interests across the nation are best kept when knitting alliances with strategic political actors and parties during elections.

Even in the early 2000s, when the outlook for press freedom appeared more promising, President Fox continued to control broadcast licensing. In parallel with the financial dependence on the government, a subtler, but still influential form of censorship manifest itself. The successive 'democratic' governments of center-right Presidents Vicente Fox (2000–2006) and Felipe Calderón (2006–2012) were said to have exerted constant and eventually successful pressure on certain media outlets to remove unwanted reporters due to their critical reporting. In fact, two high profile radio anchors whom at different stages hosted the morning news programs with the greatest ratings both suffered either advertising boycotts or personal pressure to quit their jobs (Márquez-Ramírez, 2012c).

The gradual polarization and over-*politization* of the media – particularly visible after the post-electoral and social conflict resulting from the 2006 presidential elections – is less connected with genuine ideological pluralism and partisan contentions and more connected with the adoption of market-driven partisanship that conveniently takes advantage of well-placed political actors, or patrons (Márquez-Ramírez, 2012c; González Macías, 2013). Instead of an assertive journalism, I observe a more distanced, cautious, passive, and detached type of reporting culture that continues to cater – with varying degrees of subtlety – to the political forces that represent better opportunities for profit, those that align with their interests, or that do not threaten media proprietors' private interests. More than ever before, radio concessionaries aim to protect the indefinite renewal of their licenses by avoiding overt confrontation with the president and other key political figures or advertisers, and so self-censorship or the 'softening' of compromising stories is still a common occurrence. The argument that connects commercialism to more editorial autonomy, assertive, and critical reporting thus loses credence in post-authoritarian politics.

Conclusion

This chapter has argued the existence of a captured liberal model of news media and the resulting post-authoritarian journalistic culture in Mexico. It is true that commercialism, competition, and political reforms have arguably paved the way for a more diverse coverage of political actors, critical voices, and disclosure of wrongdoing. But the press is now confronted by new political arrangements in a challenging social context such as emerging party-politics; social polarization; limp economic growth; poverty; economic divides; immigration; and rising concern over organized crime, violence, and the perceived 'statelessness'. At the same time, the power of democracy has failed to fundamentally change the conditions that sustained authoritarian practices of journalism, such as business models based on governmental advertising. In fact, many cornerstones of the authoritarian media-state relations still remain, although through subtler, yet still effective means that adapt to and accommodate various commercial and political interests, given the diversification of agents of power. Not surprisingly, local media scholars' accounts of the media's lack of accountability and unchallenged powers in many ways appear to clash with the positive perceptions of media change in the liberal tradition. Hughes and Lawson (2005) in fact do acknowledge the various barriers to media opening in the region, citing, among several others, weakness on the rule of law, media concentration and reliance on political advertisement. The existence of Latin American commercial media systems with authoritarian traits shows that this binary opposition is insufficient to account for hybrid media systems and journalistic cultures. There is little empirical evidence that the adoption of global journalistic norms and trends, as well as commercialism and deregulation, amounts to media modernization, democratization, and pluralism in Mexico.

Notes

1. In 1973, when Televisa acquired its current name, it was comprised of four terrestrial channels and hundreds of syndicated TV and radio stations. Throughout the late 1970s and 1980s, Televisa began its vertical and horizontal expansion. By 2013, the network consisted of 22 channels, four terrestrial and the rest on pay TV. The corporation owned 14 media-related ventures in music, film, satellite and cable services, publishing, telecommunications, internet provision, casino, football teams, and sport managements. Besides, it is a partner in 14 other ventures that include US TV channel Univision and a leader in the production of 'telenovelas,' its flagship genre.
2. State-owned TV network Imevisión was created during the early 1970s under Luis Echeverría's administration to promote national models of communications. In 1993, businessman Ricardo Salinas Pliego –a man not known in the broadcasting industry – won the bid over other more suitable bidders (see Villamil, 2005 for a summary of the process).
3. Excélsior and its director, Julio Scherer, developed a reputation for his critical stance toward the system (Rodríguez-Castañeda, 1993). The growing antipathy toward Scherer from his paper's pro-system cooperative of workers and also from advertisers and the establishment was such that the paper's headquarters was bombed, suffered of internal division and skulduggery staged by the government, and ultimately faced an 'advertisement boycott' in 1974. Nevertheless, the definitive blow came in 1976, when president Luis Echeverría masterminded the so-called '*Excélsior* coup'that involved cooperative leaders rebelling against the editorial board and taking over the paper's headquarters, ejecting Scherer and his close collaborators out the paper.
4. Among these events we can cite the student massacres of 1968 and 1971 in Mexico City, the widespread corruption and economic crisis in the early 1980s, the Mexico City earthquake in 1985, the electoral fraud in 1988, the questionable processes of privatization in 1992, the growth of drug cartels throughout

the 1980s and 1990s, the assassination of Cardinal Posadas in 1993 and of presidential Candidate Luis Donaldo Colosio in 1994, the Zapatista movement uprising in 1994, or the massacre of peasants in Aguas Blancas, Guerrero in 1995 and Acteal, Chiapas in 1997.

References

Alves, R. C. (2005) 'From lapdog to watchdog: the role of the press in Latin America's democratization,' pp.181–201 in H. de Burgh (ed.) *Making Journalists: Diverse Models, Global Issues* (London: Routledge).

Baldivia, J., Planet, M., Solís, J. and Guerra, T. (1981) *La formación de los periodistas en América Latina: México, Costa Rica y Chile* (México: Nueva Imagen).

Benavides, J. L. (2000) '*Gacetilla*: a keyword for a revisionist approach to the political economy of Mexico's print news media,' *Media, Culture and Society*, 22(1): 85–104.

Bravo, J. (2009) 'La comunicación gubernamental de Vicente Fox,' *El Cotidiano*, 24(155): 43–58.

Caletti-Kaplan, R. S. (1988) 'Communication policies in Mexico: a historical paradox of words and actions,' pp. 67–81 in E. Fox (ed.) *Media and politics in Latin America: the struggle for democracy* (London: Sage).

Carreño-Carlón, J. (2000) 'Cien años de subordinación: un modelo histórico de la relación entre prensa y poder en Mexico en el siglo XX,' *Sala de Prensa*, 2(16). Available at http://bit.ly/PaYpBB (accessed March 3, 2008).

Christians, C. G., Glasser, T. L., McQuail, D., Nordenstreng, K. and White, R. A. (2009) *Normative Theories of the Media: Journalism in Democratic Societies* (Urbana: University of Illinois Press).

Cleary, J. (2003) 'Shaping Mexican journalists: the role of university and on-the-job training,' *Journalism and Mass Communication Educator*, 58(2): 163–174.

Esteinou-Madrid, J. (2008) 'La ley Televisa y la formación de la IV república mediática,' *Revista Mexicana de Ciencias Políticas y Sociales*, L(202): 53–70.

Esteinou-Madrid, J. and Alva de la Selva, A. R. (eds) (2009) *La ley Televisa y la Lucha por el poder en México* (México: UAM/AMIC/AMEDI).

Fromson, M. (1996) 'Mexico's struggle for a free press,' pp. 115–137 in R. E. Cole (ed.) *Communication in Latin America: Journalism, Mass Media and Society* (Wilmington: Scholarly Resources).

Fuentes-Beráin, R. (2002) 'Prensa y poder político en México,' *Revista Iberoamericana de Comunicación*, 2: 61–79.

García-Calderón, C. (ed.) (2007) *El Comportamiento de los Medios de Comunicación. Elección 2006* (México: Plaza y Valdés/Universidad Nacional Autónoma de México).

García-Canclini, N. (2005) *Hybrid Cultures: Strategies for Entering and Leaving Modernity* (Minneapolis: University of Minnesota Press).

González Macías, Rubén (2013) 'Economically-Driven Partisanship – Official Advertising and Political Coverage in Mexico: The Case of Morelia,' *Journalism and Mass Communication*, 3(1): 14–33.

Guerrero, M. A. (2004) 'La apertura de la televisión privada en México,' *Política y Sociedad*, 41(1): 89–93.

Hallin, D. (2000) 'Media, political power and democratization in Mexico,' pp. 97–110 in J. Curran and M.-J. Park (eds) *De-westernizing media studies* (London: Routledge).

Hallin, D. and Mancini, P. (2004) *Comparing Media Systems: Three Models of Media and Politics* (New York: Cambridge University Press).

Hallin, D. and Papathanassopoulos, S. (2002) 'Political clientelism and the media: southern Europe and Latin America in comparative perspective,' *Media, Culture and Society*, 24(2): 175–195.

Hernández-López, R. (1999) *Sólo para periodistas: manual de supervivencia en los medios mexicanos* (México: Grijalbo).

Hernández-Ramírez, M. E. (2010a) 'El periodismo mexicano en estado de emergencia: hacia el debate necesario,' *Revista Mexicana de Comunicación*, 124: 17–21.

Hernández-Ramírez, M. E. (2010b) 'Franquicias periodísticas y sinergias productivas en la prensa mexicana: en busca de nuevos modelos de financiamiento,' pp. 55–122 in M. E. Hernández Ramírez (ed.) *Estudios sobre periodismo: marcos de interpretación para el contexto mexicano* (Guadalajara: Universidad de Guadalajara).

Higgins, M. (2010) 'The "Public Inquisitor" as media celebrity,' *Cultural Politics: An International Journal*, 6(1 March 2010): 93–109.

Hughes, S. (2006) *Newsrooms in Conflict: Journalism and the Democratization of Mexico* (Pittsburgh: University of Pittsburg Press).

Hughes, S. and C. Lawson (2005) 'The barriers to media opening in Latin America,' *Political Communication*, 22(1): 9–25.

Kuschick, M. (2009) 'Marketing y comunicación política,' *El Cotidiano*, 24(155): 31–41.

Lara-Klahr, M. (2007) 'Olegario Vázquez Raña, el amigo de todos los presidentes,' pp. 142–175 in J. Zepeda Patterson (ed.) *Los amos de México: los juegos de poder a los que sólo unos pocos son invitados* (México: Planeta).

Lara-Klahr, M. (2011) *No más 'pagadores'. Guía de periodismo sobre presunción de inocencia* (México: OSJI/Artículo 19/La Embajada Británica en México).

Lawson, C. (2002) *Building the Fourth State: Democratization and the Rise of a Free Press in Mexico* (Berkeley: University of California Press).

Levario-Turcott, M. (2002) *Primera plana. La borrachera democrática de los diarios* (México: Cal y Arena).

López-Ayllón, S. (2004) 'La creación de la ley de acceso a la información en México: una perspectiva desde el Ejecutivo Federal,' pp. 1–37 in H. A. Concha, S. López and L. Tacher (eds) *Transparentar al estado: la experiencia mexicana de acceso a la información* (México: UNAM).

Mancini, P. (2000) 'Political complexity and alternative models of journalism: the Italian case,' pp. 265–278 in J. Curran and M.-J. Park (eds) *De-westernizing Media Studies* (London: Routledge).

Márquez-Ramírez, M. (2005) *The Radio Journalist in Mexico: Practices, Notions and Attitudes to Professionalism*. MA Dissertation. Cardiff, Wales: Cardiff University.

Márquez-Ramírez, M. (2012a) 'Valores normativos y prácticas de reporteo en tensión: percepciones profesionales de periodistas en México,' *Cuadernos de Información*, (30): 97–11.

Márquez-Ramírez, M. (2012b) 'Valores, roles y prácticas en conflicto: el papel de los periodistas mexicanos en las elecciones presidenciales del 2006,'

p. 181–207 en C. Rico y A. Roveda (eds) *Comunicación y ciudadanía en las América; entre la gobernanza y la gobernabilidad* (Bogotá: Universidad Javeriana-Orbicom).

Márquez-Ramírez, M. (2012c) *Change or Continuity? The Culture and Practices of Journalism in Mexico.* PhD Thesis. Department of Media and Communications. Goldsmiths, University of London.

Márquez-Ramírez, Mireya (2012d) 'Valores noticiosos, identidades profesionales y prácticas periodísticas en el México post-autoritario', in E. Campos y S. Berrocal (eds) *La investigación en Periodismo Político en el entorno de los nuevos medios de comunicación* (Madrid: Sociedad Española de Periodística).

Márquez-Ramírez, Mireya (2014) 'Professionalism and journalism ethics in post-authoritarian Mexico: perceptions of news for cash, gifts and perks,' in W. Wyatt (ed.) *Individual, Institutional and Cultural Bases of Journalism Ethics* (New York: I.B. Tauris, Reuters Institute for the Study of Journalism, University of Oxford).

McPherson, E. (2012) 'Spot news versus reportage: newspaper models, the distribution of newsroom credibility, and implications for democratic journalism in Mexico,' *International Journal of Communication*, (6): 2301–2317.

Pérez-Rayón, N. (2005) 'La prensa liberal en la segunda mitad del siglo XIX,' pp. 145–158 in B. Clark de Lara and E. Guerra (eds) *La República de las letras: asomos a la cultura escrita del México decimonónico* [Vol. 2. Publicaciones Periódicas y Otros Impresos] (México: UNAM).

Pinto, J. (2009) 'Diffusing and translating watchdog journalism,' *Media History*, 15(1): 1–16.

Relly, J. E. and C. González de Bustamante (2014) 'Silencing Mexico: a study of influences on journalists in the Northern States,' *The International Journal of Press Politics*, 19(1): 108–131.

Riva Palacio, R. (2005) *Manual para un nuevo periodismo: vicios y virtudes de la prensa escrita en México* (México: Plaza y Janés).

Rockwell, R. (2002) 'Mexico: the Fox factor,' pp. 107–122 in E. Fox and S. Waisbord (eds) *Latin Politics, Global Media* (Austin: University of Texas Press).

Rodríguez-Castañeda, R. (1993) *Prensa vendida. Los periodistas y presidentes: 40 años de relaciones* (México: Grijalbo).

Rodríguez-Munguía, J. (2007) *La otra guerra secreta: los archivos prohibidos de la prensa y el poder* (México: Debate).

Rosen, J. (2009) 'He said, she said journalism: Lame formula in the land of the active user,' *PressThink*. Available at http://bit.ly/Pb0i1c (accessed March 27 2013).

Rúas-Araújo, J. (2011) 'Escena política y mediática en México: Las elecciones presidenciales,' *Revista de Investigaciones Políticas y Sociológicas*, 10(2): 43–58.

Siebert, F., Peterson, T. and Schramm, W. (1956) *Four Theories of the Press* (Urbana: University of Illinois Press).

Sinclair, J. (1999) 'The Autumn of the patriarch: Mexico and Televisa,' pp. 33–62 in J. Sinclair (ed.) *Latin American Television: A Global View* (New York: Oxford University Press).

Sinclair, J. (2002) 'Mexico and Brazil: the aging dynasties,' pp. 123–136 in E. Fox and S. Waisbord (eds) *Latin Politics, Global Media* (Austin: University of Texas Press).

Thelen, D. (1999) 'A conversation with Lorenzo Meyer about Mexico's political transition: from authoritarianism to what?,' *The Journal of American History*, 86(2): 601–612.

Tironi, E. and Sunkel, G. (2000) 'The modernization of communication: the media in the transition democracy in Chile,' pp. 165–194 in R. Gunther and A. Mughan (eds) *Democracy and the Media: A Comparative Perspective* (Cambridge: Cambridge University Press).

Trejo-Delarbre, R. (1996) 'Para qué alcanzar al mundo. Políticas de comunicación. Notas sobre la experiencia de México en la era del NAFTA,' pp. 27–44 in E. Villanueva (ed.) *Comunicación, derecho y sociedad. Estudios en honor al Dr. Javier Esteinou Madrid* (México: Media Comunicación).

Trejo-Delarbre, R. (2001) *Mediocracia sin mediaciones: prensa, televisión y elecciones* (México: Cal y Arena).

Trejo-Delarbre, R. (2005) *Poderes salvajes: mediocracia sin contrapesos* (México: Cal y Arena).

Trejo-Delarbre, R. (2010) *Simpatía por el Rating* (México: Cal y Arena).

Villamil, J. (2005) *La televisión que nos gobierna: modelo y estructura desde sus orígenes* (México: Grijalbo).

Villamil, J. (2012) *El sexenio de Televisa: conjuras del poder mediático* (México: Grijalbo).

Waisbord, S. (2000) *Watchdog Journalism in South America: News, Accountability, and Democracy* (New York: Columbia University Press).

Waisbord, S. (2007) 'Democratic journalism and statelesness,' *Political Communication*, 24(2): 115–119.

Wallis, D. (2004) 'The media and democratic change in Mexico,' *Parliamentary Affairs*, 57(1): 118–130.

The 'Capture' of Media Systems, Policies, and Industries in Latin America: Concluding Remarks

Manuel Alejandro Guerrero and Mireya Márquez-Ramírez

Democratization, globalization, and the 'captured liberal model'

More than two decades have passed since the start of the last wave of democratization in Latin American and though in broad terms the electoral component is now a regular and stable feature of public life, most countries are still characterized by strong disparities, income inequality, and a contested rule of law. During the 1980s and 1990s, the power clusters and groups – especially but not exclusively in the economy – that survived the transitions found better conditions for accumulation with the newly arrived political actors, who did not alter the property structures and the income distribution. Moreover, criticisms to state intervention and expansion coincided in time with democratization discourses just as privatization and liberalization policies coincided with the globalization trends.

As Waisbord notes in the first chapter of this book, the persistent emphasis on the globalization dimension in much of the existing literature on media policy has prevented the right assessment of the weight of local actors, domestic politics, and the state in shaping media systems and communications policies. These are key to understand how under the coverage of a globalization discourse – and in many cases of neoliberal politics and economics – what we can see in various Latin American cases is not only the counter tendencies to market-driven globalization but also the centrality of the state as the arena for disputes over media policy and performance. In brief, in a time when economic transactions and prophets of technological change try to convince us that globalization – herein understood as global markets, trasnational regulatory bodies and worldwide commercialism and digitalization – is an homogeneous and irresistible trend, especially in sectors like the media, cases in Latin America make us aware that local actors and politics still matter a lot. Though at first sight in the 1990s, Latin America was part of a globalized trend of political democratization and competitive market-driven deregulation and liberalization policies, local politics and actors were still shaping the rules of the game.

Throughout this book a clear pattern repeatedly emerges: politics – local politics – broadly shape the general features of the media systems and communication policies in Latin America, while some cultural industries – like publishing or entertainment content and formats – are, on the other hand, entirely left to the forces of the market. However, the nature of political influence in the media's commodity most important to politics, news and information, must be understood beyond merely regulatory frameworks. A common thread throughout this book is the predominance of common political and local environments and factors.

First, Latin American media systems share the historical development of being shaped after the U.S. commercial model, which would in theory entail a distance between state and market. However, the local private advertising markets alone were never strong enough to support a complex media structure. This situation is combined with the fact that, in the case of the printed press, the penetration and weight of readership is low in comparison to other countries and mostly directed to the upper and wealthier sectors. Thus this elite-oriented press could hardly survive from private advertising or from readership alone. As a result, Latin American private media have often been dependent or at least reliant on governmental advertising and funds that are formally and frequently informally distributed and assigned, often to the discretion of governments alone. Although the powerful private television networks are commercially successful beyond their borders, there is a considerable political and economic gain from entering into advertising deals with state agencies as well, especially during electoral periods. As in every corner of the world, Latin American politicians court eager TV channels to maximize their visibility and increase potential voting through airtime purchases. On top of formal advertising through TV spots, politicians and TV executives, or politicians and newspaper proprietors, find other ways to seal under-the-table and less formally scrutinized business deals that often imply the (good) coverage of political activities.

A second common feature shared by countries in the region is that the growth and consolidation of the large media corporations in Latin America has been dependent on the close linkages between the media owners – in most cases operating through family structures – and different political groups. Under authoritarianism, most of these corporations aligned themselves with the regimes' interests from whom they received extensive support and benefits. After the transitions spread across the region, close linkages with new political actors and groups were established, not unlike the former days of media-politics alliances and collusions.

A third feature is that, during and after the political transitions, the property structures in the media remained basically untouched. At the same time, deregulation and privatization strengthened the already established strategic and advantaged position of key media conglomerates. Moreover, corporations that grew and consolidated under authoritarianism were suddenly defending deregulation and opposing state intervention by the 1980s and 1990s with arguments of freedoms of expression and press. Mexico, Brazil, and Central American countries like Guatemala or El Salvador, are clear examples. Paradoxically, what we see across Latin America is that reforms carried out by the new democratic governments of the 1980s and 1990s aimed at market privatization and deregulation, actually enabled better conditions for media concentration and accumulation. Existing conservative media groups that grew under the patronage of authoritarian rule thus survived the political transitions without any crucial modification in their property structure or in their economic interests. In fact, media organizations became stronger with little regulated markets and favorable conditions awarded by new governments to media establishments that had not necessarily served the interests of media pluralism and democracy in the region. Some examples here are Globo in Brazil, El Tiempo in Colombia, Televisa in Mexico, Cisneros-Venevisión and RCTV in Venezuela, Grupo Clarín in Argentina, Albavisión in Central America, and many other countries in the region.

Fourth, in a context of a weak rule of law and a sustained history of clientelism, the tendency toward deregulation and the arrival of new political post-transitory actors who now compete for power all amounted to enabling the conditions for the capturing of the media systems by local (and regional) economic and political interests. The context of a weak, insufficient or inefficient rule of law that has characterized most of Latin America is crucial here. The actual existence of regulation and media policy does not automatically translate into effective performance and application, as can be seen in some of the chapters of the book. A case in point is the existence of formal legal precepts regarding freedoms of expression and press, which in different moments have not been effective or have been hindered through informal mechanisms in many Latin American countries, from Mexico to Argentina. Another example is the relatively recent developments with community media in Bolivia and Venezuela, as shown by Quintanilla and Cañizález, respectively, where new regulation in this area has served the political purposes of the government in its attempt to consolidate an alternative to the private media organizations. While the reforms on their own offer great potential for civic participation and widespread access to the media in remote communities that have long demanded self-managed spaces for expression, the actual operation still greatly depends on the overseeing and approval of governmental agencies and controlled by the executive branch. In other cases, even the work of community radio is hindered by their actual practices that still tend to mirror vertical communicational practices and professional discourses that give little empowerment to communities, as shown by Araya's chapter about Chilean community radios.

Still another example of the void left by a weak rule of law and the capture by political or private interests and discourses is the recent media law in Argentina. In spite of some of its most progressive features that on paper certainly looked promising in regard to media pluralism, access, and control of concentration, in practice the law has been mostly used by the Kirchner government as an excuse to confront one single corporation, the powerful Clarín group, and not necessarily to promote true media pluralism.

Thus, this book shows the many instances in which media policy has been a discursive practice that results from blackmailing, threats, or domination for the benefit of either media groups or political elites, often in the contentious field of partisan or highly polarized politics, like in Venezuela, Argentina, and Bolivia. Even in the best of cases or with the best of intentions, the multiple loopholes in the laws and reforms, either confusing or absent secondary legislation that sets out the actual rules and norms, or the lack of objective institutions (and sometimes even lack of existence altogether) that oversee that laws are abided are all a continuing threat to effective media regulation in the region.

As for clientelism, we can conclude that within the new democratic conditions of competition for power and support, the relevance of the media in politics increased and opened up new spaces for exchange with different political actors and groups. The cases of the media systems in Guatemala, Peru, and Argentina before Cristina Kirchner's government and to some extent, Colombia, are eloquent examples, and one could clearly add the case of Mexico as well.

All these trends favored the emergence of what we label here the 'captured liberal media system model', a common theoretical umbrella that helps explain the extent to which globalization in general, marketization and commercialism in particular, regional bodies, and the nation-state all play contesting roles in redefining the media's role in Latin American societies. The captured liberal model refers to a predominantly liberal commercial model that has been captured by economic and political interests and thus challenges much of the existing assumptions about liberal markets that are distanced from the hand of the state or threatened by it.

In an environment shaped by media conglomerates formally modeled after the commercial media corporations of the United States, the lack of open competition, pluralism, and a true representation of social groups is a continuing concern. There are cases where the economic interests (usually linked to specific political groups) have captured the media, as shown in the chapters addressing the contexts of Colombia, Brazil, Guatemala, El Salvador, and Peru. However, at the very same time, in some countries, like Venezuela, Ecuador, Bolivia, and Argentina, there has emerged an opposing trend that seeks to reposition the state vis-à-vis the power of those large corporations. In other words, the trends to capture the media system are coming in these cases not from the economy or from the combined interests of specific media and political groups, but from the state as a single actor in its institutional capacity. Thus, one can find that while some industries and markets are entirely shaped by market logics – such as the publishing industry as expressed by Puente's chapter – the past decade has also witnessed the revival of a 'neo-interventionist' type of state that has sought to counter – to varying degrees of success – the Latin American powerful media corporations through either stronger governmental control or through tighter media policy and regulation. In some cases, like Bolivia, Venezuela or Argentina, in spite of its aims, the effective application and enforcement of these rulings is capricious, selective, and directed more to exercise control over certain media groups and spaces than to promote pluralism. An outcome of such policies has been the deepening of social polarization and the emergence of an intense debate over freedoms of the press and speech and access to information. In many countries, these debates on freedom have also served as a façade to defend the affected economic interests of private corporations, like Clarín, who are used to take the lion's share of the local media markets. Thus, the picture is complex. In any case, what must be noted is that both trends – the neoliberal privatizing one and the reemergence of state intervention – move in Latin America within the same context of clientelism and of discretional and uneven application of regulation and law. At the end, the contexts in which both trends unfold contribute to the distortion of a private commercial model that does not foster pluralism and where conditions for capturing the media systems prevail. Thus, the formally liberal model remains constantly captured either by corporate or political interests, or both. As we can attest to the strong presence of media systems shaped by nation-states, there are still settings vulnerable to global trends, particularly digitalization of spaces previously occupied by distinguishable types of media platforms. Within these ongoing trends in mind, and considering the long-standing tradition of media concentration and weak rule of the law, we have yet to see successful media policies enabled in a way that such tendencies are reversed.

Mexico's new media and telecommunications policy: reasons for hope or concern?

Although we discuss the prominent features of Mexico's media system and the history of complicity between the press-state relations that underpin apparently free media, democratic institutions, and professional journalism in Márquez's chapter, we acknowledge that the book does not sufficiently address the recent media reform in this emblematic country, as key discussions occurred when this book was already in production. Host to the largest Spanish-speaking multimedia consortium, Televisa, Mexico is one of the most concentrated television and telecommunications markets in the world, the latter in the hands of one of the planet's wealthiest individuals, Carlos Slim. The recent constitutional reform in telecommunications in Mexico at the beginning was apparently responding to many of the most progressive and critical views of the existing media landscape that has concentrated property and benefits in the hands of a very few corporations for decades. In the case of broadcast TV, Televisa and TV Azteca together possess almost 90 percent of market share (regarding pay TV services, Televisa alone has 48 percent of the market); in radio, the seven largest corporations reach almost 66 percent of the market; and in telecommunication services, America Móvil alone has 74 percent of the market share (Comisión de Puntos Constitucionales, March 21, 2013).

The Mexico media market has been hyper-concentrated with strong links to the political system. It has cultivated its distortions both in terms of pluralism and professional journalistic practices and consolidated the enormous fortunes of the families and owners of the leading corporations. And, as a consequence, all attempts to restrict and limit their market privileges have been successfully blocked both politically through the capture of the legislative process and in the courts (Guerrero, 2010).

Now the constitutional reform, finally approved by the Senate House in June 2013, is apparently oriented by concepts of pluralism, market competition, quality of service, and rights to information. In a nutshell, it focuses on seven main topics where constitutional articles were amended. First, the reform added important precepts to constitutional Article 6 (the one referring to freedom of expression) and Article 7 (freedom of the press). In Article 6, the reform adds, in a spirit following Article XIX of the Universal Declaration of Human Rights, that: 'Every person has the right to free access to truthful, plural and timely information, and also the right to seek, receive and spread information and ideas by all means and platforms' (DOF, June 11, 2013). In the same article, the state becomes responsible for granting the population the right to access ICTs and broadcast services. Also, in what could be regarded as a measure difficult to operationalize, the reform adds the prohibition of publicity or propaganda disguised as genuine journalistic information, a resource widely used by incumbent politicians and candidates to promote their image. In Article 7 of the Constitution, the reform establishes the inviolability of the freedom to spread ideas and opinions by whatever means and platforms, and prohibits any law or authority act that may curtail this freedom or promote previous censorship.

Second, the reform, as originally sent out by the president to the Mexican Senate, establishes the obligation of the authority to design a national plan for digital inclusion where objectives and goals are set regarding access, connectivity, public and private investment in digital applications for health and education, and digital literacy. Third, the reform originally intended to open up the broadcast and telecommunications industries to foreign investment of up to 49 percent and 100 percent respectively in order to provide for better competition and quality services, a step that has garnered considerable debate. Fourth, the reform creates the Federal Institute of Telecommunications (IFETEL) that is in charge of applying the regulation in the broadcast and telecommunications sectors, to supervise and foster healthy economic and market competition (with the capacity to order the division or selling of market dominant companies), and to award licenses and sanction and penalize breaches and noncompliance. Secondary legislation (federal laws, specific broadcasting and telecom norms, operational rules) must be approved in congress in order for this agency to fully apply the faculties granted by the June 2013 constitutional reform. Fifth, pay TV providers are obliged to freely transmit without discrimination and edition the signals of broadcast TV channels, what is known as must-carry service. Conversely, broadcasters must allow pay TV providers to transmit their signal under the same terms, which is known as must-offer service. Sixth, the reform establishes the creation of specialized courts to hear and resolve broadcast and telecommunication cases in order to provide legal and technical certainty on the procedures. Seventh, for the first time, it recognizes the existence of socially-managed media along with private and public media (which were previously defined as "official media").

Notwithstanding all of these principles that at first sight seemed promising, there are reasons to be sceptic. As said before, in order for the constitutional reform to be fully operational it requires specific broadcasting and telecom rules, what is known as secondary legislation. In March 24th 2014 President Peña Nieto sent his Telecom Bill to Congress. This bill, whose approval is pending while we write these lines, contains several controversial aspects that not only limit what was established in the constitutional reform, but also liberties and freedoms. First, it restricts the faculties of the IFETEL and transfers the "vigilance" on broadcasting contents to the Ministry of the Interior (Secretaría de Gobernación). Second, it leaves underdeveloped the regulation regarding socially-managed and public-managed media. Third, it keeps privileges for big corporations, since its definition of predominant player does not apply, for instance, to Televisa's effective control over 60 per cent of the cable markets. Fourth, originally it included a chapter entitled "Of the obligations regarding security and justice" that contained a series of articles that severely abridge basic freedoms and liberties, like the blocking of all kind of telecom services in certain areas and the intervention on individuals' communications without properly defining legal and judicial warrants. In a country where both democracy and the rule of law have been fragile, these rulings are extremely dangerous. Thus, as can be seen there are still many worrisome aspects that indicate not only that the constitutional reform of June 2013 might be reversed with the passing of this secondary legislation, but that the capture of the media (and the communications) system might end up being more markedly captured by both the corporate and the political interests.

One must not forget that media proprietors and executives are now playing an active role in politics. In previous decades, high profile media proprietors and executives generally abstained from formally running for any public seat, or if they did, at least covered their intentions. However, the most recent election yielded at least 20 congressmen and women who were employed directly or indirectly by Televisa and TV Azteca – and in this latter case, the daughter of the main shareholder of the network is member of the senate. This group is called the 'teleban-cada' or tele-bench and it spreads throughout the legislative commissions of broadcasting, telecommunications, and communications in both chambers. As can be seen, the risk of preventing the reform from deploying its apparent benefits is latent. Thus, in the case of Mexico, as in some other countries in Latin America, a new reform has been passed in congress, but the mere approval of the legal framework only creates gray zones for discretion, clientelism, and capture.

Further discussions and future trends

There are important threads, challenges, and common terrain that underpins the discussion of Latin America's media and communications policy. In all of the countries explored in this volume there have been fields where interests and arrangements are not necessarily favorable to pluralism, market competition, and democracy. This discussion is strongly connected with the role of the state in polities where public interest has been confused with governmental interests and globalization with big corporations' privileges. As can be seen in the different chapters, regulation and legislation regarding the media in Latin America has been enacted without necessarily being effectively enforced. The reasons are attributable to factors such as clientelistic exchanges between media elites and politicians, the shallow relevance of legal precepts regarding freedom of expression and of the press during authoritarianism, the lack of proper protections for journalistic performance in many countries, the power of big corporations to block the effects of regulation both through formal (the courts) and informal (discrete political interference) mechanisms, and the blatant aims of the state to selectively advance on only certain aspects of the regulation.

In many ways, this game has involved mostly two actors, media and political groups. It is played within a historical context where the emergence and development of media have been more the result of the intermediation of political interests and groups that transforms the media into instruments to gain political leverage for elites than of a media structure based on information and debates that lead to more pluralistic, open, and accountable polities.

Without this accountability to their readers and audiences and given the context where the media has also depended for survival on governmental funds and advertising, it is easier to imagine that the roles of the media were crafted in direct relation to the state and to political groups. In the building of the public agenda, the civic claim from below has been absent, leaving only the media vis-à-vis public actors and institutions. This situation does not only help explain the uneven conditions for regulation and policy enforcement and application but explains another field for constant negotiation and exchange within a power relations structure. Of course, as has been presented in the chapters by Araya and Márquez, this context generates intrinsic obstacles to journalistic performance, since journalists become inserted into the dynamic game of power in which the structural (laws, regulations, protections, procedures) is paradoxically part of the fluid. If we consider that the readership has been low in Latin America and that the 'civic claim from below' is weak, then one may conclude that the external support for journalistic performance is also weak. Under these circumstances the capture of the media systems by economic and political interests becomes easier. Even the narratives of the media transition that normally link democracy and commercialism with quality journalism, journalistic processes of professionalization, and the paradigm of journalism are trapped in contesting forces of global vis-à-vis local discourses.

The chapters in this book provide relevant debates on these aspects that could be continued in other projects. A second discussion, only lightly outlined in some chapters here, has to do with technology and the new interactivity of audiences-citizens in these societies, which of course are already affecting not only the traditional media landscape in Latin America, but also the orientations of regulatory debates. In the last decade, governments have been promoting policies oriented to granting wider access to digital technologies. In many respects, these policies have been the outcome of the pressures from social sectors and civil society groups who are also active in exchanges and debates on the Internet and social networks. The widespread and continuing emergence of new technologies and forms of production, consumption, and distribution, as well as the blurring distinction between consumers and producers, appears to move faster than the regulatory capacities of the state, hence leaving key Latin American cultural markets solely to the dynamics of the market.

However, although things are rapidly changing due to the new interactive role that individuals, as audiences and citizens, are playing in these new digital scenarios, one cannot leave aside the disparities and sharp contrasts that characterize them. According to the Internet World Stats (2012), in 2012, only around 40 percent of the population in Latin America had some kind of access to the Internet. Nevertheless, the activity of those who are connected does seem to be high, particularly in terms of social media use: for Facebook, Brazil and Mexico are among the top five countries in the world with the most users subscribed to the network: 80 and 43 million respectively (Social Bakers 2013). For its part, in the same year, Twitter saw Brazil become the second country in the world with 33.3 million users, Mexico the seventh with 10.5 million, Colombia the twelfth with 8.2 million, and Venezuela thirteenth with 7.9 million users (Semiocast 2012). While it is true that there is plenty of room for the argument that social media users normally connect for entertainment and consumption purposes, there is also evidence that they are also doing it increasingly for work-related issues and for political discussion. As Guerrero (2014) says:

> In the past five years, most of the political campaigns and the electoral processes in the region have had a social media component. Conversely to traditional media spaces where different regulations have applied (from advertising funding to message content), digital social media are still vastly free from regulatory restrictions. This has been profited not only by parties and politicians to upload propaganda and constantly go public (like the daily tweets of Argentina's President, Cristina Fernández), but also by individuals and civil society sectors who use such spaces for civic action, discussing alternatives and watching over policies. Colombia's presidential candidate, Antanas Mokus, obtained 24.5 percent of votes through a campaign based almost solely on social media. In Chile, during the 2009 presidential elections, candidate Marco Enríquez Ominami decided to campaign outside the traditional party structures supporting his message through the Internet and the social networks. He obtained 20 percent of the vote.

Common to all these cases is both the engagement of social groups and sectors from down to top, and the fact that these are mostly composed of young, educated, and urban individuals. For example, in a recent research project, Guerrero (forthcoming) shows how the educated urban youth of Mexico are actually connected to public discussions and engage in different sorts of deliberation through their daily use of the social media. Among these sectors, one trend is beginning to emerge: despite all of its difficulties and setbacks, an incipient deliberative digital space is appearing where, for instance, networks of journalists and civic organizations are tracking and reporting on abuses against freedom of expression, threats against individual reporters, and different conditions that may inhibit journalistic performance. The digital space is also an alternative to the traditional media's strong concentration conditions: let us think of both community media and distribution of journalistic work through blogs. All in all, in today's Latin America, governments and traditional media are being compelled to respond and interact with the demands of these fast growing connected urban sectors. These are trends that require further discussion and analysis because they may be changing the actual media landscape in terms of pluralism and democracy.

References

Comisión de Puntos Constitucionales (2013, March 21) 'De la Comisión de Puntos Constitucionales, con proyecto de decreto que reforma y adiciona diversas disposiciones de los artículos 6o., 7o., 27, 28, 73, 78 y 94 de la Constitución Política de los Estados Unidos Mexicanos, en materia de telecomunicaciones,' *Gaceta Parlamentaria*, XVI (3733-III). Available at http://bit.ly/Kt6u6L (accessed December 2013).

DOF (2013, June 11) 'Decreto por el que se reforman y adicionan diversas disposiciones de los artículos 6o., 7o., 27, 28, 73, 78, 94 y 105 de la Constitución Política de los Estados Unidos Mexicanos, en materia de telecomunicaciones,' *Diario Oficial de la Federación*, DCCXVII (8). Available at http://bit.ly/Kt6B2e (accessed December 2013).

Guerrero, M. A. (2014) 'Latin American Media: the challenges to pluralism,' in Peggy Valcke, Miklos Sükösd and Robert Picard (eds) *Media Pluralism: Concepts, Risks and Global Trends* (London: Palgrave).

Guerrero, M. A. (ed.) (forthcoming). *Conexión pública. Consumo digital. ¿Mejores o peores ciudadanos?* (Mexico: NIAMH).

Internet World Stats. (2012). 'Latin America internet usage statistics.' Available at www.internetworldstats.com (accessed February 2014).

Semiocast. (2012). 'Tweeter reaches half a billion accounts.' Available at http://semiocast.com/en/publications/2012_07_30_Twitter_reaches_half_a_billion_accounts_140m_in_the_US (accessed February 2014).

Social Bakers. (2012). 'Facebook statistics by country.' Available at http://www.socialbakers.com/facebook-statistics (accessed February 2014).

Index

312 *Index*

CPSIA information can be obtained
at www.ICGtesting.com
Printed in the USA
LVHW081521191218
601068LV00011B/149/P

9 781137 409041